Forgotten Voices of
the British Empire

Forgotten Voices of the British Empire

How Knowledge Was Created and Curated in Colonial India and Burma

Carol Ann Boshier

ROWMAN & LITTLEFIELD
Lanham • Boulder • New York • London

Published by Rowman & Littlefield
An imprint of The Rowman & Littlefield Publishing Group, Inc.
4501 Forbes Boulevard, Suite 200, Lanham, Maryland 20706
www.rowman.com

86–90 Paul Street, London EC2A 4NE, United Kingdom

British Library Cataloguing in Publication Information Available

Library of Congress Cataloging-in-Publication Data
Names: Boshier, Carol Ann, author.
Title: Forgotten voices of the British empire : how knowledge was created and curated in colonial India and Burma / Carol Ann Boshier.
Other titles: How knowledge was created and curated in colonial India and Burma
Description: Lanham : Rowman & Littlefield, [2021] | Includes bibliographical references and index.
Identifiers: LCCN 2021056581 (print) | LCCN 2021056582 (ebook) | ISBN 9781538159880 (cloth) | ISBN 9781538163238 (paper) | ISBN9781538159897 (epub)
Subjects: LCSH: East India Company—Biography. | India—Civilization—1765–1947. | British—India—History. | British—Burma—History. | Scientific expeditions—India. | Scientific expeditions—Burma. | Ethnological expeditions—India. | Ethnological expeditions—Burma. | Imperialism and science.
Classification: LCC DS428. B67 2021 (print) | LCC DS428 (ebook) | DDC 954.03—dc23/eng/20211207
LC record available at https://lccn.loc.gov/2021056581
LC ebook record available at https://lccn.loc.gov/2021056582

Contents

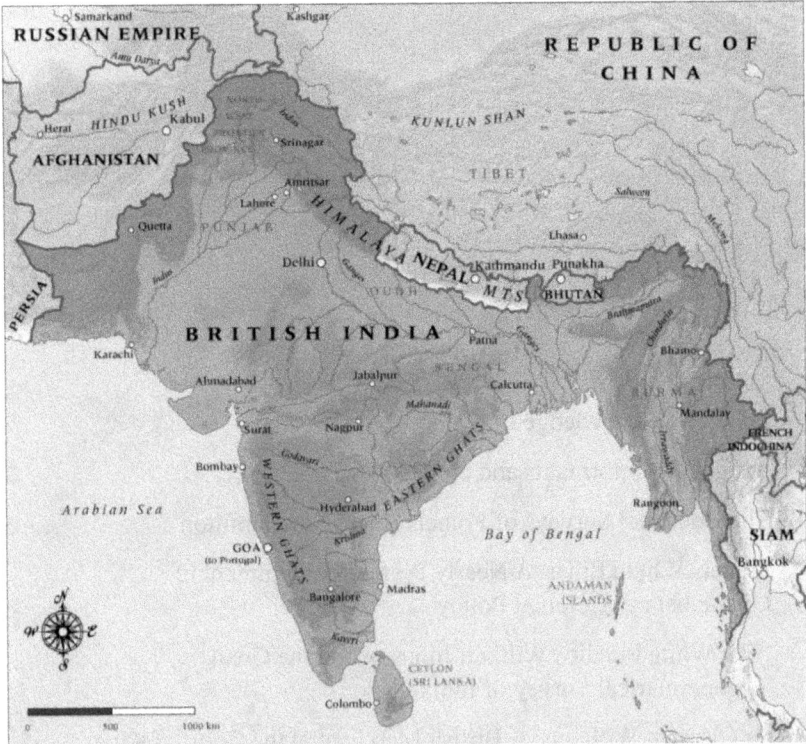

Figure 0.1. Map of British India in 1914, produced by Geographx with research assistance from Damien Fenton and Caroline Lord. URL: https://nzhistory.govt.nz/media/photo/map-british-india-1914 (Ministry for Culture and Heritage), updated 30 Nov. 2018.

List of Figures

Acknowledgements

Throughout my research into the unremembered subjects of this book, who contributed in manifold ways to our store of knowledge about India and Burma, I have been helped and encouraged by many people. Keepers of archives, institutions, libraries and independent scholars have all generously shared their expertise with me. I am grateful for their support in my quest to uncover seldom-heard voices that bear witness to the diverse connections between colonised and coloniser. Their histories contribute towards a rich tapestry of knowledge that gainsays the notion of the colonial encounter as binary or uncomplicated.

I am grateful to Dr Savithri Preetha Nair, whose extensive scholarship on Raja Serfoji II's Court at Tanjore inspired me to situate Francis Whyte Ellis within that sphere of plural cultural enlightenment. I would also like to thank Dr Isabelle Charmantier of the London Linnean Society, who generously shared her time to explain the intricacies of Carl Linnaeus's System of plant classification and to show me many of the Society's botanical drawings. The opportunity to view Francis Buchanan-Hamilton's paper index slips provided a tangible link to his great dedication to botanising. Dr Jorg A. Schendel kindly sent me his unpublished dissertation on the Mandalay economy, which gave me a valuable context when writing Chapter 6.

Despite the pandemic caused by COVID-19, all of the libraries and institutions that I approached went out of their way to help with information and high-resolution images, even when they were closed and most staff were working from home. I am grateful to the staff of the Asian and African Studies reading room at the British Library, who always do so much to assist their readers, making research such a pleasure. I would especially like to thank Asian and African Studies researcher, Aliki Anastasia Arkomani, whose skills uncovered the court case of the unfortunate Mrs De Souza and

Lieutenant Walton. Also at the British Library, I am indebted to Magdalena Peszko and her colleagues in the Map Department for arranging exceptional permission to publish the image of Dr Clement Williams's cloth map. Although its magnificent colours will only appear in the electronic version of this book, his map brings us closer to Williams's affinity with Burma and its unique culture. Ms Pam Hobbs, a nurse from Sydney, Australia, shared her family's connection with Dr Williams, whose mixed-race daughter, Marie Rose, was her great-grandmother. These personal details have helped me to bring these long-lost characters to life, allowing them to become 'real' people, rather than a forgotten voice in the archive.

My friend and Burma scholar, Patrick McCormick, kindly read and commented upon the draft manuscript, offering wise counsel and encouragement. Despite having to make the difficult decision to leave Yangon during the recent unrest after 15 years of residence, he remains one of the few Western academics who can truly claim to know the country. My thanks also go to Dr A.V.M. Horton for his impeccable index and commentary. Finally, I would like to thank my family for all their support, especially my daughter Aliette, to whom I owe a tremendous debt of gratitude. She has truly shown her mettle in her meticulous editing of my footnotes. Needless to say, all the errors and omissions in this book are my own. The joy of writing it has been not only in discovering the forgotten voices of individuals who contributed to knowledge about that behemoth known as colonial history, but also in my encounters with all those who have helped me along the way.

Introduction

*It is now clear that the colonial landscape was inhabited by a great mul-
tiplicity of groups whose constitution was neither discrete nor stable from
context to context, and each of these groups had different agendas as well
as different capacities to realize them.*[1]

Eighteenth-century European Enlightenment thinkers disseminated intellectual ideas that were informed by scientific reason, as they sought freedom
and equality for all in the application of unbounded universal knowledge.
A significant feature of this increasing knowledge was expressed in a concern for 'realism in discipline, for systematic description in collection, and
for comparative method in explanation'.[2] A new source for the production
of knowledge was provided by British expansion in India, which had been
under the governance of the East India Company[3] since its first ships had
arrived in Surat in 1608. The ways in which information was gathered and
converted into accessible forms became a vital element in the projection of
the Company's authority and in substantiating its claims to legitimacy which,
after the Revolution of 1857, were sustained by the Government of India,
and which also relied upon the acquiescence of colonisers and colonised to
carry out policies created in the metropole. From the late eighteenth century,
the Company's attention was concentrated upon commercial exploitation of
resources, with little formal thought or forward planning for how information

---

1. Norbert Peabody, 'Knowledge Formation in Colonial India', in *India and the British Empire*,
eds. Douglas M. Peers and Nandini Gooptu (Oxford: Oxford University Press, 2012), 98.
2. Derek Gregory, 'Power, Knowledge and Geography', *Geographische Zeitschrift* 86 (1998):
71. See also David Stoddart, *On Geography and Its History* (Oxford: Blackwell, 1986), 33–35; and
Charles W.J. Withers, 'Geography, Natural History and the Eighteenth-Century Enlightenment: Putting the World in Place', *History Workshop Journal* 39 (1995): 138.
3. East India Company; hereafter EIC, or the Company.

was to be acquired and political intelligence gathered. This was made possible by the endeavours of the EIC's covenanted and uncovenanted servants: soldiers, surgeons, surveyors and administrators, all aided by members of the indigenous population. Along with many others, they undertook the task of surveying new territory, collecting, cataloguing and studying languages, history and culture, as well as investigating the numerous archaeological sites and hitherto unknown species of flora and fauna.

This study endeavours to contribute to the history of ideas about colonial knowledge by showing that there was no neat division between cultural, scholarly, mercantile and political objectives, neither public nor private. Like the great Ganges-Brahmaputra Delta, whose life began from inaccessible streams high in the mountain ranges, ideas and initiatives flowed from unpredictable and improbable sources to create knowledge about an empire that was interwoven with global and local elements, and whose roots went back to the seventeenth century when the EIC established its first factories in South and Southeast Asia. By way of a series of case studies of characters, whose lives and work throw up discourses worthy of historical inquiry, this book will demonstrate that knowledge production was generated through a multiplicity of approaches and sources that transcended spatial, temporal, material and methodological limitations. Viewed through the lens of certain individuals' life experiences, it hopes to show how the ability to source new knowledge was vested predominantly in scholarship, enterprise and ingenuity, rather than in direct initiatives by the authorities who ruled India.

None of the people represented in the case studies is a 'household' name today, nor do they feature prominently in the archives; nevertheless, their collective endeavours added to the capital store of knowledge required to build and sustain an empire. Although the significance of their actions was often overlooked or misunderstood, their surveys, discoveries and collections impacted upon important modes of exchange between European and indigenous knowledge. In addition to their official duties, many individuals accomplished physical and intellectual feats of endurance in the production of knowledge that had global consequences, including collecting objects of material culture and specimens from the natural world. They explored hostile regions, mapping India's topography and studying its many languages in order to better understand the culture and customs of indigenous societies.[4] At times, the people chosen as case studies were motivated by personal gain; whilst at others, their private interests converged with those of the governing authority to produce information that was valuable for commercial and political purposes.

---

4. Tirthankar Roy, *India in the World Economy: From Antiquity to the Present* (Cambridge: Cambridge University Press, 2012), 208.

Initially, the EIC's colonisation of India was seen as a facilitator of intellectual exchange where European centres were considered to be of equal worth to those on the periphery.[5] During the early phases of its rule, collectors, scholars and other interested parties engaged with colonised subjects, allowing knowledge to pass freely between them. Many persons availed themselves of the opportunities presented by their employment, social position, education and birth to interact with networks of information that included news-writers, learned members of the local society, physicians, midwives and other informants. These pioneers acted as go-betweens, enabling those with sufficient intellectual and linguistic skills to cross boundaries, especially in fields like languages, botany and medicine, where local forms of knowledge were actively sought because they were often considered superior, or more suited to the challenges faced by Europeans unaccustomed to living in India's harsh environment.[6]

The first decades of the nineteenth century saw the abrogation of the political immunities associated with the Diwani Grant of 1765 from the Great Mughal, by which the EIC had acquired revenue rights in Bengal, Bihar and Orissa. When the Company's Charter was renewed in 1813, most of its monopolies were annulled; and by 1833, they were abolished completely.[7] Consequently, by the 1830s, the Company had transformed itself into 'an organisation that was devoted exclusively to the business of empire, representing a dramatic reversal in its fortunes and the reinvention of an institution that in the 1760s and 1770s had been widely condemned for the misrule of its business empire in India'.[8] After the EIC lost control of the sea routes to China in 1833, the ensuing decades saw its officers and other concerned persons undertaking adventurous journeys of exploration by land and river routes in search of alternative ways to access the lucrative China trade. However, the imposition of trade treaties and security policies to protect British interests adversely affected migration flows and the complex social dynamics of ethnic societies.[9]

The search for new knowledge was also focused on Burma after the annexation of much of the country's territory following the two wars fought in the first half of the nineteenth century. After the First Anglo-Burmese War

5. Ibid., 197.

6. Peabody, 'Knowledge Formation in Colonial India', 87.

7. Gunnel Cederlöf, 'Seeking China's Back Door: On English Handkerchiefs and Global Local Markets in the Early Nineteenth Century', in *Trans-Himalayan Borderlands: Livelihoods, Territorialities, Modernities*, eds. Dan Smyer Yu and Jean Michaud (Amsterdam: Amsterdam University Press, 2017), 129–130.

8. Huw V. Bowen, *The Business of Empire: The East India Company and Imperial Britain, 1756–1833* (Cambridge: Cambridge University Press, 2006), 298.

9. See Mandy Sadan, *Being and Becoming Kachin: Histories beyond the State in the Borderworlds of Burma* (Oxford: Oxford University Press, 2013).

(1824–1826), the British acquired the provinces of Arakan and Tenasserim under the terms of the Treaty of Yandabo, signed in 1826. Following further defeat in the Second Anglo-Burmese War in 1853, the province of Pegu in Lower Burma was ceded to the British, giving them control of the seaport of Rangoon and access to Burma's traditional heartland in Upper Burma via the frontier post at Thayetmyo on the Irrawaddy River. With its royal capital at Mandalay, Upper Burma remained an independent kingdom until 1886 when it, too, was annexed and the entire country became a province of the Indian Empire. Within a few years of these defeats, British explorers and surveyors were sent into newly acquired territory in Burma, and 'as European presence in the region increased, the different interests that drove mercantile commerce, colonial territorial politics and imperial ambitions coincided'.[10] As we shall see, on occasion, they also collided.

Territorial expansion brought access to new sources of knowledge and called for a more hierarchical organisation that was provided by institutions like the army and specialised government departments. Inevitably, such changes were accompanied by 'the decline of the importance of indigenous communities of embodied knowledge which had informed pre-colonial kingdoms'.[11] This gradually put an end to the pre-colonial modes of knowledge, acquired from those whom Christopher Bayly called the 'knowing people'. The old sources were derived from pundits, *munshis* (elite scribes), *dubashes* (interpreters), barbers, midwives, merchants, bazaar workers, *harkaras* (runners dating from Mughal times) and *daks* (postal runners), to name but a few. From time to time, these ancient networks of knowledge that the British aspired to master and manipulate gave way to information panics[12] that defined the limitations of their power. As Bayly has asserted, 'It was in the zone of ignorance where the knowledgeable colonial institutions met, but failed to mesh with the sentiment of the knowing people of the locality, that the stereotypes of thugs, criminal guilds, religious fanatics and well-poisoners were hatched'.[13]

After the EIC was stripped of its autonomy in 1858, following the revolution of the previous year, the bureaucratisation of imperial government, based on structured and rational systems, took many years to accomplish.[14] It involved not only fiscal and legal reforms, but also greater scrutiny,

---

10. Cederlöf, 'Seeking China's Back Door', 128.
11. Christopher A. Bayly, *Empire and Information: Intelligence Gathering and Social Communication in India, 1780–1870* (Cambridge: Cambridge University Press, 1996), 143. See also Peabody, 'Knowledge Formation in Colonial India', 89.
12. Bayly, *Empire and Information*, 143.
13. Ibid.
14. After the EIC was stripped of its autonomy in 1858, the administration of India passed to the Crown on 1 November 1858. Thereafter, fiscal and bureaucratic reforms were put in place, but the process was slow and took many years to accomplish.

aimed at tightening the imperial grip on the subcontinent, including census operations and other surveillance techniques. The task of governing India was handed over to civilian administrators, known as Indian Civil Servants,[15] many of whom were also scholars in their own right and interested in pursuing knowledge about India's culture, languages and ancient history for their personal satisfaction. Therefore, collaboration with indigenous intellectuals and networks of knowing people diminished, and attitudes hardened towards associating and co-operating with 'natives'. This restricted the reciprocal exchange of new ideas and information that had flourished since the early eighteenth century, and even before that, so that the coloniser became the active knowledge-maker and his subject, the passive informant. Now, only European centres were deemed capable of understanding the complexities of new scientific knowledge on a global scale and refashioning the world according to their own perspective.[16]

Consequently, there was 'a shift in attitude from seeking to understand and learn from India, to seeing it as a place lacking in civilised virtue needing to be properly ordered'.[17] This changed from tolerance to intolerance and introduced a rule of cultural difference that, according to Partha Chatterjee, was 'never destined to fulfil the normalising mission of the modern state', and ushered in a colonial state whose power was built on preserving the 'alienness of the ruling group'.[18] This rule of cultural difference was predicated on the assumption that cultural authority was vested in the colonisers, but at the same time, it was freighted with conditions, warnings and limitations regarding the origins, education and social status of those upon whom it was bestowed. As this study will endeavour to demonstrate, seekers of knowledge who deviated from the permitted boundaries were not recognised as having cultural authority over their research and discoveries, and their achievements were passed over or ignored.

However, beyond institutionalised sources, encounters by Europeans who existed on the margins of imperial society never really ceased, and as a result, they were more hybridised and uncontrolled. Outsiders and those who were not bound up with the social conventions of imperial society continued to collaborate with indigenous groups in ways that official organisations and public bodies could not, or would not, do. The chapters in this book will describe the multifarious ways in which some rather extraordinary individuals were able to engage with their environment and its colonised population, in order to

---

15. Indian Civil Servants; hereafter, ICS.
16. Richard Axelby, 'Calcutta Botanic Garden and the Colonial Re-ordering of the Indian Environment', *Archives of Natural History* 35, no. 1 (2008): 150–163.
17. Ibid., 160.
18. Partha Chatterjee, *The Nation and Its Fragments* (Princeton, NJ: Princeton University Press, 1993), 10.

make connections that pushed against the boundaries of recognised systems of power and known spaces of knowledge. They produced ideas generated in new places and in novel ways, obtaining information through the collection of many sentient and inanimate objects and curiosities that were to be found in the new territories of India. Even though, at times, they were unsuccessful, they participated in the struggle to create an intellectual dialogue between the West and the indigenous 'other'. As independent and determined pioneers on the periphery, they continued to cross boundaries in order to advance scientific, linguistic and cultural knowledge, thereby offering a revisionist critique of the notion that progress in modern science and other subjects was wholly Eurocentric.[19] To borrow from Céline Ronsseray's remarks concerning a modest medical doctor in eighteenth-century Cayenne, French Guiana, whose correspondence was of the first importance in providing information about France's new colony, 'if the trajectories of colonial knowledge are well known, the histories of the many *petits artisans* who helped to create them are much less so'.[20]

It is hoped, therefore, that investigating the histories of some of these now long-forgotten '*petits artisans*', active in British India from the late eighteenth to the early twentieth century, will reveal key junctures in the evolving process of comprehending the empire. A brief synopsis of the chapters which follow describes the individual case histories in order to offer a more integrated perspective on the manifold interactions that occurred between humans, objects and spaces at a time when intellectual ideas and scientific advancements united with entrepreneurship in the Indian Empire.

CHAPTER SYNOPSES

Chapter 1

From the mid-eighteenth century, the intellectual ideas and scientific developments of the European Enlightenment combined with the political and commercial ambitions of the EIC to produce a network of diverse institutions, objects and places through which knowledge was produced and circulated. Chapter 1 will consider how the elements of space and material objects interacted with human agency and practice to produce complex networks of

---

19. Gregory, 'Power, Knowledge and Geography', 79. Gregory has shown that this Eurocentric 'vision' was the product of 'absolutizing time and space, exhibiting the world, normalizing the subject and abstracting culture and nature', which had material consequences connected to systems of power and knowledge.

20. Céline Ronsseray, 'In the Shadow of Buffon: Itinerary of a Colonial Doctor in French Guiana in the 18th Century', in *L'héritage de Buffon. Textes réunis par Marie-Odile Bernez* (Dijon: Éditions Universitaires de Dijon, 2009), 22.

knowledge that circulated between India, Europe and the rest of the world.[21] This chapter also sets the scene for the case histories which follow, by offering a broad outline of how the EIC and, after 1858, the Government of India engaged with various groups that acted as sources of new knowledge. It contextualises the case histories that form the core of this study, whose intention is to illustrate the complexity and unpredictability involved in the acquisition of knowledge throughout the period under review. It calls to attention the many obstacles encountered by individuals who attempted to claim cultural authority for their research and discoveries, as well as highlighting the personal sacrifices involved in undertaking such ventures. By the mid-nineteenth century, the progressive institutionalisation of colonial government restricted the freedom of these actors to explore beyond the frontiers of empire, thereby cutting off important sources of pre-colonial knowledge embodied in indigenous communities. By the turn of the century, the establishment of more formal channels for the collection of intellectual and quantifiable knowledge, including a mechanism for centralising intelligence, which was administered by the army, allowed the state even more control over intelligence-gathering. Nevertheless, unconventional, independent-minded Europeans on the periphery of imperial society continued to penetrate regions beyond the frontier that had become inaccessible to government officials.

Chapter 2

This chapter investigates how most journeys of discovery, surveys and scholarly undertakings could not have taken place without indigenous assistance, which occurred on so many levels, from the intellectual, to the everyday business of living in an alien environment. It considers the vital aid given to adventurous Europeans by 'native' informants, go-betweens and indigenous scholars. When accompanying expeditions, their duties included attending to the daily practicalities of supplying food, setting up camps and interceding with potentially hostile groups to gain local intelligence. Their assistance was not only practical but also scholarly; as learned pundits, they provided linguistic support and interpretation of local knowledge and cultural precepts, as will be evidenced in the discussion of those who aided Sir Colin Mackenzie's (1754–1821) epic Survey. Meanwhile, the quest for knowledge about the natural world was supported by the contribution of local artists, who adapted their technique to suit British requirements, so that they produced exquisite and accurate illustrations of the many natural wonders of India's flora and

---

21. Pascal Schillings and Alexander van Wickeren, 'Towards a Material and Spatial History of Knowledge Production. An Introduction', *Historical Social Research / Historische Sozialforschung* 40, no. 1 (2015): 203.

fauna discovered by botanists. Meanwhile, in the domestic sphere, armies of indoor and outdoor servants were required to maintain the home comforts required by the colonisers; in many instances, the majority of these individuals appear as no more than a footnote in histories – a name in a report, or a brief acknowledgement by their principal.

Chapter 3

This chapter explores the work of the Scottish Orientalist Francis Buchanan-Hamilton (1762–1829), who devoted all his free time to collecting and classifying new plant species encountered in the course of his official duties conducting surveys for the EIC. Buchanan's passionate engagement with the natural world led him to create innovative methods for the retrieval and storage of botanical information, and he succeeded in harmonising divergent systems of classification that are still in use today. In retirement, Buchanan used his unique knowledge of South and Southeast Asian flora, gained during the many years that he travelled throughout the subcontinent as a surveyor for the EIC, to write commentaries in order to identify and compare them with those described in pre-Linnaean texts.[22] These provided a vital source for taxonomists for decades afterwards. Although not unknown as a botanist, his contribution to natural history has been under-appreciated, largely because, despite his close association with the President of the London Linnean Society,[23] Sir James Edward Smith (1759–1828), he lacked the patronage so necessary in the early nineteenth century to achieve publications in the metropole. Smith's own tireless efforts in seeking patronage are discussed briefly in this chapter in order to highlight its importance in bringing new knowledge to public attention and gaining recognition for its author, which largely eluded Buchanan so far away in India.

Chapter 4

Unlike his fellow Orientalist, Francis Buchanan-Hamilton, Francis Whyte Ellis (1777–1819) did not seek to publish his materials until later in life, after he had completed his research. Sadly, he died before this could be achieved and, as a result, he left little for scholars to digest and appreciate. Known chiefly for his theory of the Dravidian Proof, which argued that

---

22. The pre-Linnaean classificatory system of plants can be distinguished from Carl Linnaeus's 'modern scientific' System by the fact that it relied on implicit categories. Therefore, trees were distinguished from shrubs, then bushes and so on, as expounded by pre-Linnaean texts. See Allen J. Grieco, 'The Social Politics of Pre-Linnaean Botanical Classification', *I Tatti Studies in the Italian Renaissance* 4 (1991): 131–149.

23. Founded in 1788, The Linnean Society of London is a learned society dedicated to the study and dissemination of information concerning natural history, evolution and taxonomy.

Southern Indian languages were a family distinct from those of Northern India, Ellis's only mention of his unique discovery was in an appendix to a grammar of the Telugu language written for the students at the College at Fort St. George, Madras, which he founded in 1812. However, in the course of his duties as a magistrate, Ellis came into contact with the many European and indigenous scholars and experts who congregated at the Court of Raja Serfoji II (1777–1832) in Tanjore, which later became known as a centre of Tamil Enlightenment. Despite his relatively brief association with the Court, this period inspired Ellis in his determination to explore how pre-colonial societies functioned and the correlation between Southern India's languages. Having developed his ideas over the course of his working life, they found their expression in Ellis's treatise on Mirasi Right,[24] written in response to a questionnaire from the Government of India. As one of the few extant sources of his scholarship, Ellis's understanding of ancient Mirasi Right demonstrates his appreciation of the holistic characteristics of traditional land tenure in Southern India and its attendant cultural obligations and privileges. His theories created a pathway for later studies of language and ethnicity, known more familiarly today as anthropology.

Chapter 5

By the mid-nineteenth century, the progressive institutionalisation of government had curtailed individual freedom to explore beyond the frontier, thereby cutting off potentially important sources of pre-colonial knowledge embodied in indigenous communities. In order to compensate for the diminishing awareness of local knowledge, certain unconventional actors sought to break away from the limitations imposed by an increasingly rigid government bureaucracy. This chapter signals a departure from the traditional scholarly approaches adopted by covenanted EIC officers like Buchanan and Ellis and examines the contribution to the production of knowledge made by William Henry Johnson (1832–1883). Described in this book as 'the White Pundit', Johnson possessed considerable expertise as a mountaineer and in his work as a surveyor for the Great Trigonometrical Survey of India;[25] but as a 'white country-born' employee, his lowly social status limited his ability to succeed.

---

24. See BL/IOR/V/27/312/49/5: F. W. Ellis, Replies to Seventeen Questions proposed by the Government of Fort St. George relative to Mirasi Right with two appendices elucidatory of the subject (Madras: Government Gazette Office, 1818); BL/IOR/V/27/312/50: Charles Philip Brown (ed.), Three Treatises on Mirasi Right: By Francis W. Ellis, Lt. Col. Blackburne, Sir Thomas Munro; With the Remarks Made by the Honorable Court of Directors, 1822–24 (Madras: Christian Knowledge Society's Press, 1852); and William H. Bayley and William Hudleston (eds.), *Papers on Mirasi Right Selected from the Records of Government and Published by Permission* (Madras: Pharoah & Co, 1862).
25. The Great Trigonometrical Survey of India; hereafter, GTS.

Born to British parents and raised and educated in India, Johnson's story offers a compelling example of how the rigid definitions of racial, class and domiciliary terms came to define how only those known as 'the right sort' were considered fit to wield authority and to represent the British Raj. In 1865, Johnson used his 'indigeneity' and local knowledge of the Himalayan Mountains to make an unauthorised and dangerous visit to Khotan, a Khanate in Central Asia, in search of intelligence, with a view to reopening trade relations. The region was unsettled due to local revolts against the central authority of Peking. Despite gathering much useful intelligence from beyond the frontier, Johnson's expedition earned him the disapproval of his superiors at the GTS, chiefly because his conduct and activities manifested 'an uneasy cultural or social identification, or "role ambiguity"'.[26] In contrast to their reaction, his account of his expedition was received with great acclaim by the Royal Geographical Society in London, demonstrating the disjuncture between the objectives of those in the metropole and on the periphery. Johnson resigned his position at the GTS and continued his career in Kashmir in the service of the Maharajah, where he engaged in dubious financial activities, eventually dying there in mysterious circumstances in 1883.

Chapter 6

This chapter concerns assistant army surgeon, Dr Clement Williams (1833–1879), who was inspired by stories that he had heard about the old caravan trade routes between Burma and Western China whilst serving with the Sixty-Eighth Madras Regiment in Rangoon. Williams, therefore, decided to undertake a journey of exploration from Mandalay along the Irrawaddy River during his army furlough, travelling on his own account without permission from the Rangoon authorities. Whilst in Upper Burma, he used his professional reputation as a medical doctor to forge a close connection with the country's ruler, King Mindon (1808–1878), and members of his Court in order to obtain the royal permission in 1863 to begin his journey. His empathy and deep commitment to the country's culture and customs encouraged him to learn Burma's difficult language and to master some of its many dialects, allowing him the opportunity to gain affective knowledge, as well as political intelligence about Upper Burma, which the British were always keen to acquire. He hoped that by widely publicising his exploration findings and by discovering new routes into China that circumvented the treaty ports of its eastern seaboard, he might earn official respect for his endeavours to extend the boundaries of Britain's

---

26. Simon Schaffer, Lissa Roberts, Kapil Raj and James Delbourgo (eds.), 'Introduction', in *The Brokered World: Go-Betweens and Global Intelligence, 1770–1820* (London: Science History Publications, 2009), xviii.

commercial enterprise. However, he was mistaken, as like his contemporary, William Johnson, his discoveries were ignored by the British Burma government, who mounted their own expedition in 1868 under the leadership of his rival, Colonel Edward Sladen (1831–1890). Consequently, Williams's cultural authority over his findings, and subsequent publications, were not acknowledged or rewarded. He resigned his commission and spent the rest of his life in Mandalay involved in commercial dealings with the king, including illegally shipping arms for him, much to the displeasure of the British Administration in Rangoon. He died in Italy in 1879, on his way home to Britain.

Chapter 7

In order to maintain the illusion of its power, the empire still required its heroes, particularly after the carnage of the First World War. This need was embodied by the actions of men like Frederick Marshman Bailey (1882–1967), whose life, in true Kiplingesque fashion, perpetuated the mythology of the 'Great Game'. This chapter examines the adventurous career of Bailey, who was considered by the British establishment to be the 'right sort' of political intelligence officer. It will endeavour to understand the ways in which Bailey used his position as an officer in the Indian army, in conjunction with his passion for sports-hunting and natural history collecting, as a subterfuge for acquiring political intelligence in regions beyond the jurisdiction of British authority. Many of Bailey's natural history specimens and hunting trophies later found a home in the Horniman Museum in London, which was established in 1901. Bailey's habits as a naturalist-collector will be discussed in the context of a rather extraordinary series of adventures that befell him during his military career, when he gained a reputation as one of the army's most intrepid operatives. His enthusiasm for collecting and hunting served to legitimate his work as a political officer, especially in border regions where it acted as a 'cloak' of respectability. When he embarked on dangerous and unauthorised expeditions, he was only very mildly rebuked by the British India establishment; as, unlike William Johnson, his lineage and education made him 'the right sort' of officer, and therefore trustworthy. His adventures coincided with the awakening of national consciousness throughout South and Southeast Asia and the growth of anti-imperial sentiments in Britain.

Chapter 8

This chapter investigates James Philip Mills, ICS (1890–1960), a scholarly and adventurous colonial administrator-cum-ethnographer, whose life was dedicated to furthering the study of the peoples of the Naga Hills on the frontiers between Burma and the Indian State of Assam. Mills's devotion to the

Naga people allowed him to spend three decades of his career studying and photographing them at a time when anthropology as an academic discipline was still in an embryo state. Together with his senior colleague, John Henry Hutton (1885–1968), the pair used their ICS service as an opportunity for not only observing the lifeways and culture of the Nagas, but also collecting many objects related to the Nagas' material culture. Although untrained in anthropology and always referring to himself as an amateur, Mills demonstrated great insight into their customs and cultural practices, earning him cultural authority over his subject, as well as providing many objects for the ethnology collections at the Pitt Rivers Museum in Oxford. His linguistic fluency and years spent amongst the Nagas enabled him to meticulously gather data and take many photographs to document their lifestyle and traditions, including their practice of headhunting. Although headhunting was forbidden in the parts of the Naga Hills administered by the British, it continued on its borders, and Mills was required to lead punitive expeditions against outside headhunting villages, whose warriors had raided British-controlled areas. Despite his official role, Mills demonstrated an acute intellectual awareness and sensitivity towards this traditional practice that for generations had been the cornerstone of the Nagas' existence. He wrote many perceptive articles on its implications for the collective wellbeing of the village and its contribution to its soul force. His most well-known expedition to punish headhunting was to the villages of the Pangsha region in 1936. Accompanied by the Austrian anthropologist, Christoph von Fürer-Haimendorf (1909–1995), they were presented with a unique opportunity to make a photographic record of this expedition, much of which is archived at the School of Oriental and African Studies in London and complements the collections of material objects in the Pitt Rivers Museum.

Chapter 9

This final chapter seeks to interrogate the contribution that women made to the production of knowledge in the male-dominated sphere of intellectual histories about the Indian Empire. It was really only in the colonial domestic sphere, where the memsahib reigned supreme, that women became agents for the cultural exchange of objects, traditions and culinary practices that came to define a shared colonial experience on the periphery and at the centre. The relatively few European women in India compared to men, and the lack of primary sources, has meant that their voices are seldom heard in archival material, especially those of lone females of a lower social status. The chapter demonstrates how absence of education, literacy skills and, crucially, a husband limited a woman's ability to become an active producer of knowledge. However, whilst acknowledging that a woman's role was not ordinarily conducive to scholarly pursuits and adventurous travel, it has been possible to highlight the achievements of a number of exceptional women by reference to unpublished research on 'Women in India' carried out by Mildred Archer (1911–2005), an Oxford-educated art historian who accompanied her husband on his ICS postings throughout India during the 1930s. This chapter looks more closely at the contribution of women who have been briefly mentioned in this book and who made their views about India known, chiefly through their letters and journals. They include the early-nineteenth-century journal-writer, Lady Maria Nugent (1771–1834), and Emma Roberts (1794–1840), who became the first female journalist and writer in India to earn her own living. Her story offers a rare case of female independence. Marriage to an ICS officer enabled Roberts's contemporary, Fanny Parkes (1794–1875), to make many solo journeys throughout Northern India in search of the 'picturesque', which she published as vivid accounts on her return to England. Attention in this final chapter is also focused upon lone women of a lower social class, who, without the protection of a husband or another suitable male relative, were vulnerable to social stigmatisation. Even women who, through force of circumstance, tried to live independently and earn an honest living were viewed with disapproval, and were often labelled as prostitutes, as the account of one notorious court case describes.

Chapter 1

Spheres of Knowledge

OBJECTS, SPACES AND PRACTICE IN THE PRODUCTION AND CIRCULATION OF KNOWLEDGE

The interactions which took place during the eighteenth and nineteenth centuries between European scholars and their correspondents are indicative of the many ways in which the world was not only demystified but also analysed and reconstituted into new and different realms of knowledge, which expanded under the aegis of the abundant networks that flourished globally. Rejecting the idea of universality in science and other disciplines, Pascal Schillings and Alexander van Wickeren have argued for new connections to be made between knowledge and the place of its production and the individuals who produced it.[1] They maintain, 'It is through the practices of human actors that different objects and spatial contexts are brought into interplay in the processes of knowledge production', which has always been a matter of local circumstances.[2] Gunnel Cederlöf, meanwhile, has argued for the need for a more complex analysis of regional colonial administration and for the necessity of working with a multi-layered spatial conception without pre-set boundaries.[3] She has noted, 'The commercial logic of the EIC made them think of frontiers as expansion zones that would connect them with profitable markets and sources of wealth, so that the earliest maps often looked like trails through blank spaces'.[4]

---

1. Schillings and van Wickeren, 'Towards a Material and Spatial History', 206.
2. Ibid., 205, 208.
3. Gunnel Cederlöf, *Founding an Empire on India's North Eastern Frontiers, 1790–1840: Climate, Commerce, Polity* (Oxford: Oxford University Press, 2014), 2.
4. Ibid., 10.

1

Charles W.J. Withers has also introduced the notion of place as a primary marker of how new knowledge was ordered and promoted, not only understanding it as the geographical location where natural and man-made phenomena could be discovered, but also recognising its figurative and literal relationship with settings in Europe. It was here that objects of study were defined and ordered, and where 'the appropriate means to study was advanced as text, expedition, map or classificatory schema'.[5] As he has shown, global knowledge was increased because particular individuals worked in specific locations at certain times, where ideas took a distinctive discursive turn and interacted with social networks both in the colony and in the metropole.[6] Withers has further advocated the value of considering the mobile nature of geographical and other knowledge generated by the Enlightenment, as it moved between different sites of production. In referring to the origins of the textual descriptions and classificatory practices of botanists from the sixteenth century onwards, he has observed that 'looking at such local places has also helped to displace notions of the Enlightenment as necessarily and only European'.[7] This idea will be considered in Chapter 3 in connection with Francis Buchanan-Hamilton's role in circulating botanical specimens through different spaces and time zones, which engendered new taxonomies and methodologies of organising materials. However, place also had a negative influence upon the circulation of materials and research findings by Orientalists like Buchanan and his contemporary, Francis Whyte Ellis, the subject of Chapter 4. The length of time that it took for communications to travel between India and Europe delayed the circulation of new information, as its creators were situated far from the centres of power and patronage. Conversely, this permitted human agency the freedom to be innovative and also encouraged resourceful, independent thinkers. Therefore, by adopting an adaptable and transferable approach to notions of place, periodisation, objects and human practices, this study hopes to show that the knowledge produced in India was as much a source of enlightenment in the sub-continent as it was in Europe.

Centres or initiatives for the circulation of knowledge occurred on multiple levels, related to social and material constructions, as opportunities arose at particular times and places and were acted upon by specific individuals. There was no single centre for the circulation of knowledge, such as that which is believed to exist between the metropole and the periphery.

---

5. Charles W.J. Withers, *Geography, Natural History and the Eighteenth-Century Enlightenment* (Oxford: Oxford University Press, 1995), 139.

6. Ibid.

7. Charles W.J. Withers, 'Place and the Spatial Turn in Geography and in History', *Journal of the History of Ideas* 70, no. 4 (2009): 656. See also Charles W.J. Withers, *Placing the Enlightenment: Thinking Geographically about the Age of Reason* (Chicago: University of Chicago Press, 2007).

Enlightenment in India was about the movement of ideas and 'encounters in analytic sites such as courts, museums, laboratories, [and] botanic gardens', which this study will investigate.[8] Individuals interacted with local human agency and it responded to them, perpetually creating and recreating new knowledge networks. Institutions like the army and the colleges founded by the EIC in Calcutta, Madras and Bombay became centres of learning where European and indigenous scholars congregated, all contributing to the formation of 'analytic sites'. A further example of an 'analytic site' created by local human agency was the Court of Raja Serfoji II in Tanjore, which will be discussed in Chapter 4. Conventionally, centres for the circulation of knowledge in Europe had long been provided by learned societies, which, from the late eighteenth century, were recreated throughout South and Southeast Asia, where they provided 'safe' public spaces in which like-minded Europeans and indigenous people could meet and engage in collaborative scholarship. The next section considers the opportunities that they afforded both as independent institutions and for the individuals who frequented them, as well as highlighting other important spaces where knowledge was produced.

LEARNED SOCIETIES AND OTHER SPACES OF KNOWLEDGE PRODUCTION

The contest for cultural authority was affirmed by the foundation of learned societies and other professional organisations and associations, whose specialised journals allowed them to claim collective autonomy, both at home and on the periphery.[9] These groups emerged throughout the nineteenth century in Asia as places where Europeans with scholarly inclinations could associate with like-minded indigenous people. Ostensibly free from official interference, or bound by government rules and control, they provided spaces where papers about many topics, including the country's topography, history and culture, could be presented, discussed and later published in the society's journal. Learned societies prided themselves on their intellectual impartiality and ability to evaluate new ideas and research, as indicated by the address given in 1834 by William C. Taylor on the fiftieth anniversary of the founding of the Asiatic Society of Bengal. In his address, Taylor reflected upon the achievements of its scholars in stifling and scrutinising 'the evils of imperfect theories, half investigated truth and entirely erroneous guess that found their

---

8. Charles W.J. Withers and David Livingstone (eds.), 'Introduction on Geography and Enlightenment', in *Geography and Enlightenment* (Chicago: University of Chicago Press, 1999), 4.

9. Geoffrey R. Searle, 'Review: Public Doctrine and Cultural Authority', *The Historical Journal* 38, no. 3 (1995): 729.

way into our libraries'.[10] Even though individual initiatives were encouraged, he noted that the merits of every new discovery, and the foundations upon which it rested, were now discussed by the society.[11] Later in his address, Taylor uttered the famous aphorism that 'knowledge is power', but lamented that too few who wanted to see power increase (by which he meant primarily those engaged in commerce in the Far East), neglected 'the knowledge which is its first element'.[12] In appointing the Asiatic Society of Bengal as an arbiter of knowledge, Taylor recognised the role of learned societies in legitimating imperial power. His views also reflected the ideology of many diverse actors, who were emboldened to embark upon independent scholarly research, or journeys of exploration, and who looked to scholarly societies to affirm and uphold their authority over their mission.

Bengal was one of the first places in India to witness the flowering of an intellectual renaissance, or enlightenment, that encompassed both European and indigenous thinkers who were drawn to scholarly societies and institutes of learning. Ram Mohan Roy (1772–1833) was amongst their early supporters, and in 1828, he founded the Brahmo Samaj, a society that promoted the reform of Hinduism as a monotheistic religion.[13] Their establishment of learned societies allowed the British to 'know' India and having witnessed the foundation of the Asiatic Society by William Jones in 1784, Calcutta became the centre of intellectual pursuits. The city attracted many independent groups, like the Society for the Acquisition of General Knowledge, founded in 1838 by former students of the Hindu College in order to broadcast their ideas throughout a nascent public sphere. This led intellectuals to widen and refashion their own histories by writing their findings in antiquarian journals in their own Khari Boli Hindi language.[14] Other societies throughout Asia soon followed, from Singapore to Siam, and Rangoon to Hanoi, where membership composed primarily of indigenous and European professional elites was open, at least in theory, to anyone who could afford the annual subscription fee.

However, it was not until 1910, after the final annexation of the Kingdom of Upper Burma in 1886, which united the whole country into becoming

10. William C. Taylor, 'On the Present State and Future Prospects of Oriental Literature, Viewed in Connexion with the Royal Asiatic Society', *Journal of the Royal Asiatic Society of Bengal* 2, no. 3 (1835): 4.

11. Ibid., 5.

12. Ibid., 9.

13. For an in-depth analysis, see David Kopf, *British Orientalism and the Bengal Renaissance: The Dynamics of Indian Modernization, 1773–1835* (Berkeley and Los Angeles: University of California Press, 1969); and also, David Kopf, *The Brahmo Samaj and the Shaping of the Modern Indian Mind* (Princeton, NJ: Princeton University Press, 1979).

14. Francesca Orsini, *The Hindi Public Sphere, 1920–1940: Language and Literature in the Age of Nationalism* (Oxford: Oxford University Press, 2002), 180.

India's newest province, that Burma's own independent research society was formed. One of its doyens and founding members, J.S. Furnivall (1878–1960), famously declared that he had the idea to form a society dedicated to discovering and representing knowledge about Burma after receiving a copy of the *Journal of the Siam Society*, which had been founded in 1904. Like the Siam Society and others, the Burma Research Society[15] drew upon the traditions of Western scholarship, allowing its members to pursue projects of concern and interest to them about Burma's cultural and historical origins linked to its ancestral territory, ethnic diversity, epigraphic records and archaeology. However, unlike the Siam Society, the BRS's effective status was mediated by the colonisation of its indigenous members, which carried an implicit political statement in a way that membership of the Siam Society did not.

The origins and orientations of the École française d'Extrême-Orient (ÉFEO), founded in Hanoi in January 1900, serve to illustrate how diverse the objectives for the pursuit of scholarly knowledge could be in different colonial and political settings throughout the region. The ÉFEO, which was established under the reforming governorship (1897–1902) of Paul Doumer (1857–1932), represented a very different cultural enterprise from that of the Siam Society and the BRS, where the funds were sourced from members' subscriptions. The ÉFEO was financed from the general budget for Indochina and from revenue raised by Doumer's creation of a series of very lucrative regulations concerning import duty on salt, opium and alcohol.[16] Funded and sponsored by the French colonial government, the aim of the ÉFEO was to impose a specifically French perspective upon the acquisition of knowledge about the region under its control.

Meanwhile, in the British metropole, the Geographical Society (later, the Royal Geographical Society under the patronage of William IV) was founded in 1830, and it became one of the most important conduits for the presentation of topographical and cultural knowledge about the Indian Empire, as well as other countries around the globe.[17] With the advancement of exploration, leading to geographical and scientific discoveries, knowledge now became empirical rather than merely theoretical or conjectural, and in response to the need to promote its advancement, technical articles began to appear in the proceedings of the RGS's *Journal*. Attaining a publication in the RGS's *Journal* played an important part in confirming the findings of surveyors in the

---

15. Burma Research Society; hereafter, BRS.
16. Pierre Singaravélou, *L'École française d'Extrême-Orient ou l'institution des marges (1898–1956): Essai d'histoire sociale et politique de la science coloniale* (Paris: Harmattan, 1999), 65–67.
17. Royal Geographical Society; hereafter, RGS.

field and establishing their reputation as an authority on their discoveries. As
many of the RGS's members had formerly been employed with the Survey of
India as professional geographers and surveyors, they were able to review its
publications with the benefit of scientific knowledge and experience.[18]

Thus, throughout the nineteenth century, the RGS acted as a 'critical point
through which all relevant knowledges had to pass for legitimation and
accumulation'.[19] Detailed evaluation by learned members allowed scholarly
societies to become centres of calculation and sponsors for the circulation
of knowledge.[20] However, frequently, the knowledge presented had passed
through different sites of production and networks of exchange, thereby ren-
dering it unreliable. What seemed plausible in the lecture hall of the learned
society, 'might well become a half-truth on the ground'.[21] As Kapil Raj's
work has demonstrated, there was no single centre for the circulation of
knowledge, thereby indicating the limitations of Bruno Latour's hypothesis
that centres of calculation were exchanges that occurred primarily between
metropole and colony.[22] Raj has shown that multiple sites for the exchange
of knowledge production were part of a process of cross-cultural interaction;
and he, too, has emphasised that knowledge and science should be located
and analysed according to spatial relations. The chapter concerning the
accomplishments of Francis Whyte Ellis demonstrates this hypothesis, as the
Tanjore Court briefly became a centre for the circulation of knowledge from
local and global sources. Despite the restrictions imposed upon him by the
British in 1798, its ruler, Raja Serfoji II, wished to distinguish his reign as
one that marked Tanjore as figuratively and literally connected with scientific
advances in Europe that could be utilised for the benefit of his people. Due to
the Raja's close connections with many Europeans who frequented his Court,
it became a particular site of local enlightenment. From 1798 to 1832, the
Tanjore Court was a space for dynamic change, where, under Raja Serfoji's
benign and enlightened supervision, European and indigenous intellects collaborated to produce novel and progressive ideas for the benefit not only
of his subjects but also of the wider world. It was here that Francis Ellis's
encounters with scholars, both local and from afar, presented him with the
opportunity to develop his ideas about the origin of Dravidian languages.
Serfoji built up a cabinet of curiosities, or *wunderkammer*, modelled on those

---

18. Kapil Raj, *Relocating Modern Science: Circulation and Construction of Knowledge in South
Asia and Europe, 1650–1900* (Basingstoke: Palgrave Macmillan, 2007), 206.

19. Gregory, 'Power, Knowledge and Geography', 79.

20. Bruno Latour's definition of a Centre of Calculation was 'a learned institution which promoted
the circulation of knowledge, people and objects between metropole and colony'. See Bruno Latour,
Science in Action (Cambridge, MA: Harvard University Press, 1987).

21. Gregory, 'Power, Knowledge and Geography', 79.

22. Kapil Raj, 'Beyond Postcolonialism . . . and Postpositivism: Circulation and the Global History
of Science', *Isis* 104, no. 2 (2013): 343.

in Europe, and he encouraged indigenous and Western scholars to collaborate in scientific and medical research projects.

Meanwhile, beyond the meeting rooms and halls of learned societies, the natural environment provided a wider arena for the production of knowledge, where, from the late eighteenth century, it became an ever-expanding spatial element in geographical, botanical and scientific enquiries linked to commercial ambition and political power. As a rich theme for investigation, the environment had the capacity to link objects with diffuse spaces connected to new scientific instruments like the theodolite[23] and the plane table. As mobile objects, they promoted the circulation of knowledge and offered new insights into the processes of its production, especially in mapping.[24] Thanks to the discipline of these tools and the use of trigonometric-based mapping, which required mathematical training, borders could now be fixed, distances calculated, routes planned and military units supplied.[25] Surveying and exploration on, and sometimes beyond, India's frontiers were essential requirements for the development and promotion of new trade routes with neighbouring polities. Now, scientific findings from exploration could be categorised, recorded and archived by institutions like the GTS, whose work had begun in the late eighteenth century. However, the introduction of new scientific instruments into territories that had received little, or no contact from the modern world presented obstacles to the way that the latest technologies were able to confront and comprehend indigenous ideas about time and space and their relationship to the cosmos. The act of making maps and taking measurements with new Western equipment was regarded with suspicion by pre-colonial kingdoms and, on occasion, required the participation of 'native' pundits, disguised as holy men and other mendicants, to travel clandestinely in areas beyond the frontier, which will be discussed more fully in Chapter 5.

Pre-colonial maps as objects also represented knowledge of indigenous spatial awareness, which bore no relation to European understanding of topography, where distance could be measured mathematically through the use of tools like the theodolite. Indigenous maps discovered by colonisers were based on an understanding of the cosmology that did not conform to Western scientific concepts of empiricism and that, to a large extent, have remained indecipherable to Europeans. A set of pre-colonial maps, drawn on fabric, came into the possession of Dr Clement Williams, who spent many years living in Mandalay until his death in 1879. They were bequeathed to

---

23. Theodolite: A scientific instrument designed to accurately measure horizontal and vertical angles between designated visible points.

24. Schillings and van Wickeren, 'Towards a Material and Spatial History', 207.

25. For a discussion on surveying, the precise methods used and a description of the instruments, see also James Hevia, *The Imperial Security State: British Colonial Knowledge and Empire-Building in Asia* (Cambridge: Cambridge University Press, 2015), 98–106.

Figure 1.1.   Cloth map from Upper Burma (c. 1850) acquired by Dr Clement Williams.
Source: The British Library Board (Ref. IOR/X/12107).

his nephew, Louis Allan Goss (1846–1933), who, in 1886, was appointed Inspector of Schools in Upper Burma and eventually retired to Cambridge, where he taught Burmese language at the University. In 1910, Goss donated these precious cloth maps to Cambridge University, where they remain. Two of the maps were also donated by Goss to the British Library in London, and although they have been photographed and preserved, the knowledge that they contain has yet to be conclusively interpreted. Forming part of the chattels belonging to Williams's estate, they were possibly given to him in payment for services that he rendered to the late King Mindon or one of his ministers. They are an emblem of a pre-colonial era when spatial concepts and their relationship to the cosmos had very different meanings for the individuals who commissioned them and the Burmese artists who painted them on fabric.[26]

There were, of course, many other spatial contexts in which knowledge was produced, not all related to scholarship emanating from learned societies, but which was generated by institutions like the army. Primarily responsible for the empire's security and expansion, facilitated through the acquisition of

---

26. Map of the Maingnyaung region, located between the Chindwin and Mu Rivers in Upper Burma, in the present-day Sagaing Region: https://cudl.lib.cam.ac.uk/view/MS-MAPS-MS-PLANS-R-C-00001/1.

intelligence, the army took a close interest in any new knowledge that might help to increase its professional standing and maintain its role as defender of the empire. Increasingly throughout the nineteenth century, the army ensured that its officers were trained in the use of modern scientific instruments, allowing them to develop new techniques for mapping and other strategies for acquiring knowledge useful in the defence of the empire, which are discussed in the next section.

THE ARMY AS A SPACE WHERE HUMAN PRACTICE COMBINED WITH MODERN SCIENTIFIC OBJECTS

As the global imagination was converted into absolute space by the production of maps and other processes related to Western cartographic science, the army played a key role in the process of standardising and professionalising the acquisition of knowledge. Furthermore, changes in global demand during the nineteenth century, driven by technological advances and the impact of world markets, propelled the underlying reasons for frontier expansion and consolidation, for which the procurement of accurate intelligence was paramount.[27] The army's responsibilities advanced in conjunction with the emergence of scientific and learned professions, as it became associated with social and economic developments in Britain's overseas territories.[28] As an institution, it played an important role in the recovery and circulation of knowledge in India by responding to the need for up-to-date intelligence by utilising modern scientific instruments and, after the mid-nineteenth century, the camera. As their use proliferated, the requirement for officers trained in mathematics and other sciences became more urgent, as did the need for officers capable of understanding the new technologies associated with reconnaissance, the production of route books and the preparation of accurate maps through geographic surveys.

From 1806, the EIC established its own training college for new recruits. Initially, it was based at Hertford Castle, but in 1807, the European curriculum was transferred to its permanent base at Haileybury, where cadets were grounded in aspects of Indian life and its languages, taught by pundits brought over from India.[29] Applicants passed through Haileybury's portals until the College closed on 31 January 1858. Attempts by the EIC in 1809

---

27. Neil Fold and Philip Hirsch, 'Re-thinking Frontiers in Southeast Asia', *The Geographical Journal* 175, no. 2 (2009): 95.
28. Christopher A. Bayly, *The Birth of the Modern World, 1780–1914* (Oxford: Blackwell, 2004), 320–321.
29. Arthur Macgregor, *Company Curiosities: Nature, Culture and the East India Company, 1600–1874* (London: Reaktion Books, 2018), 18.

to offer dedicated training to its military cadets at Addiscombe in Surrey were less successful. Addiscombe's failure to deliver what appeared to be an extensive curriculum similar to Haileybury's, and adequate training to pre-pare recruits for military life in India, was judged to have been a contributing factor in the breakdown of the Company's military system, brutally exposed in the Revolution of 1857.[30] Furthermore, the failure of Addiscombe was a contributory factor in Britain lagging behind Europe until the second half of the nineteenth century in training army officers capable of competing in the contemporary world and in defending the empire. However, by the 1870s, the situation had improved after the curricula of the Royal Engineering and Artillery Schools were revised to teach the necessary mathematical skills and the basic techniques of mapping and reconnaissance.[31]

Articles on reconnaissance and mapping began to appear in military jour-nals. *The Journal of the United Services Institute*, first published in 1858, was followed in 1871 by an Indian version, *The Proceedings of the United Services Institution of India*. Both publications provided a forum for military experts to share their knowledge on important issues related to the defence of the British Empire, especially India, but which also impacted politically upon the civilian administration.[32] Knowledge was also obtained from co-operation with foreign sources, indicating how elements of cross-cultural interaction and spatial relations could coalesce. The Chief Commissioner of British Burma, Colonel Albert Fytche (1820–1892), mentioned in a letter to the Secretary to the Government of India that he had been sent a copy of an article entitled 'The Rising of the Dungens or Mussulman Population in Western China', written by a Russian Officer, O.K. Heins. The paper, which had appeared in the *Russian Military Journal* of August 1866, was translated and discussed in *The Edinburgh Review* of April 1868,[33] so that contemporary knowledge was circulated between spaces as far apart as Russia, Rangoon, Western China and Scotland. These encounters demonstrate how the admin-istration in India was not initially perceived as 'a monolithic state apparatus but as a collection of individual and unpredictable actors representing an external source of power and authority'.[34] Their scholarly exchanges pro-vided channels of communication between potentially hostile forces and, at least for a while, held out the possibility of negotiations which might even

---

30. Ibid., 19. See also John M. Bourne, 'The East India Company's Military Seminary at Addis-combe, 1809–1858', *Journal of the Society for Army Historical Research* 57 (1979): 206–222.

31. Hevia, *The Imperial Security State*, 85.

32. Ibid., 49.

33. O.K. Heins, 'Rising of the Dungens or Mussulman Population in Western China. Translated from the *Russian Military Journal* for August 1866', *The Edinburgh Review* 127 (1868): 357–396.

34. Oliver Tappe, 'A Frontier in the Frontier: Sociopolitical Dynamics and Colonial Adminis-tration in the Lao–Vietnamese Borderlands', *The Asia Pacific Journal of Anthropology* 16, no. 4 (2015): 382.

have shaped future strategic alliances.[35] But, it was not to be, as increasing tensions between the British and Russian Empires in Central Asia meant that scholarly collaboration between their respective officers became infrequent and eventually, non-existent.

As advances in cartographic knowledge, produced in places like Dehradun, the headquarters of the GTS, progressed throughout the nineteenth century, India's geographical frontiers became ever more defined, discouraging encroachment by foreigners like the French and Russians, who were perceived as threats to Britain's possessions in South and Southeast Asia and whose actions were watched warily. However, before borders were formally drawn up and mapped, attitudes towards boundary-crossing, both physical and intellectual, were more fluid, permitting greater sharing of knowledge and correspondence between colonisers and their subjects. Exploration in uncharted territory on the unsettled frontiers of India and Burma challenged imperial concepts of spatiality, introducing decisive and transformative changes to frontier dynamics, including their politics and economies.

In 1874, an article appeared in *The Proceedings of the United Services Institution of India* calling for the creation of an Indian intelligence unit that would enable military and civilian agencies to share their knowledge.[36] It was proposed that such a unit would systematically collect, digest and record the observations of political officers, missionaries, soldiers and others into a useable and easily accessible form. The Indian army's Intelligence Branch was formed in 1878 as part of the Quartermaster General's Department, allowing all intelligence operations in India to be centralised at the army headquarters in Simla. The army's Intelligence Branch now became responsible for 'producing the positive knowledge necessary for the protection of lines of communication to and from India'.[37] In particular, information previously scattered in books, journals, reports and newspapers was consolidated, so that it would provide an essential tool for the Indian army in helping to counteract the perceived threat of Russian expansion towards India.[38] Major (later Colonel) Frederick Marshman Bailey was part of this unit and, as we shall see in Chapter 7, the wide-ranging brief attached to the many assignments that he undertook on its behalf demonstrates the institution's rather esoteric nature, earning Bailey his reputation as a spy in the aftermath of the First World War.

However, there was a complex and ambiguous dividing line between the civil and military administrations in India, where the practice of producing

35. Ibid.
36. J.A.S. Colquhoun, 'Essay on the Formation of an Intelligence Dept. for India by Captain J. A. S. Colquhoun, Royal Artillery', *Journal of the United Service Institution India*, Proceedings 4, no. 18 (1874): 1–75. Colquhoun was winner of the Durand Medal for 1874.
37. Hevia, *The Imperial Security State*, 13.
38. Ibid., 68.

and circulating knowledge through articles in scholarly journals resulted in an 'integrated perspective on materiality and space in science and knowledge production' in both civil and military arenas.[39] As James Lees has observed, whilst at first sight, this may not appear to be of immediate significance, it led to a highly ambiguous dividing line[40] between civil and military officers, many of whom were employed in civil roles in the political service.[41] For instance, after conquest, Burma was classified as a non-regulation province when military officers were seconded to the civil administration.[42] Until the 1890s, colonial administrators in Burma were mainly drawn from the cadre of the military, and as more than 50 per cent of colonial officers working in the Burma Administration had begun their careers in colonial India, their thinking was dominated by the politics of that country.[43] But by 1900, after Burma had become a Province of India in its own right, their proportion declined to 23 per cent, when their number was overtaken by university-educated officials,[44] who were assigned directly to Burma from Britain without first seeing service in India.[45]

Meanwhile, David Ludden has described how, from around 1770 to 1820, the foundations of Orientalism lay in the transition in India to the rule of the EIC, manifested by the activities of its early scholar-administrators. Their thinking about India was influenced by the European Enlightenment, where knowledge was not strictly linked to the utilitarian needs of colonial rule.[46] But, as described, although many of the men who were classified as scholar-administrators in early British India were part of a group of Orientalists with disparate views and interests, their desire to accumulate knowledge about India had one thing in common – namely, that many of them started out as officers in the EIC's army. Whilst their primary motive was to 'accumulate knowledge as an instrument of government or for its own sake', their military identity was a significant factor in their views on the prominent role of the army in governing India.[47] The army was central to the security of the EIC,

---

39. Schillings and van Wickeren, 'Towards a Material and Spatial History', 204.

40. As will be noted in Chapter 5, William Johnson was employed as an uncovenanted civil assistant who, despite his undoubted talents, was considered to be much subordinate to his military superiors.

41. James Lees, 'Administrator-Scholars and the Writing of History in Early British India', *Modern Asian Studies* 48, no. 3 (2014): 839.

42. Neil A. Englehart, 'Liberal Leviathan or Imperial Outpost? J. S. Furnivall on Colonial Rule in Burma', *Modern Asian Studies* 45, no. 4 (2011): 766.

43. Ibid., 775.

44. Ibid., 767.

45. Ibid., 761.

46. David Ludden, 'Orientalist Empiricism: Transformations of Colonial Knowledge', in *Orientalism and the Postcolonial Predicament: Perspectives on South Asia*, eds. Carol A. Breckenridge and Peter van der Veer (Philadelphia: University of Pennsylvania Press, 1993), 250–78.

47. Lees, 'Administrator-Scholars', 839.

and as scholars they promoted 'the widespread belief among the indigenous population that it was futile to oppose the Company's rule'.[48] As its territories grew and centralisation became a policy imperative, the EIC's requirement for new knowledge about India became bound up with political patronage.[49] Encouraged by the EIC, surgeons attached to regiments became particularly active as botanists,[50] whilst others, like Major Colin Mackenzie, concentrated on investigating and surveying India's antiquities and studying its languages and history. Although these early scholar-administrators were driven by a sincere interest in India's antiquities and a desire to write about its history, they were army officers before they were antiquarians and historians.[51]

Donald Peers has also emphasised that the Anglo-Indian bureaucracy which dominated the operating system of British India in the first half of the nineteenth century was founded upon military ideals and attitudes. He has argued, 'Through such spokesmen as Thomas Munro, John Malcolm, Charles Metcalfe and Mountstuart Elphinstone, an increasingly militarised rule of British India was put forward, angering the EIC's Court of Directors in London and which also allowed the officers to mask their private interests under the guise of the national interest'.[52] Peers has described continuing tensions between the officers in Bengal and their superiors in Calcutta and London, who were anxious to make retrenchments in the officers' personal emoluments, known colloquially as *batta*, or field pay.[53] During his rule, Warren Hastings supported the officers, lending their cause 'immense personal and political prestige, thus sanctifying their actions and giving them the pretence of legitimacy'.[54] This position was maintained by Hastings' successor until 1828, when steps were taken to bring the army back under civil control.[55] Despite reforms, these disputes created a legacy of militarism within the civil administration that, by the mid-nineteenth century, had segued into the attitude and behaviour of army officers like Thomas Montgomerie (1830–1878) and James Walker (1826–1896), who commanded the GTS.

Furthermore, the pursuit of private pecuniary interests by army officers in the late eighteenth and early nineteenth centuries, even after reforms, left a perception amongst civilians and military alike that self-interest was compatible with military service. As previously mentioned, by 1833, the Company had lost the last of its monopolies, many of them with the Chinese,

---

48. Ibid.
49. Ludden, 'Orientalist Empiricism', 253.
50. Lees, 'Administrator-Scholars', 838.
51. Ibid., 839.
52. Douglas M. Peers, 'Between Mars and Mammon: The East India Company and Efforts to Reform Its Army, 1796–1832', *The Historical Journal* 33, no. 2 (1990): 385.
53. Ibid., 386.
54. Ibid.
55. Ibid.

especially the trade in tea, being the most profitable and expansive in relation to the global Asian markets of the time.[56] The discovery of tea plants in Assam in 1834[57] coincided with the Company's loss of control of the sea routes to China, so that the imperative of finding new overland routes into China became more urgent for both the EIC and private entrepreneurs, many of whom were former army officers. More will be said about this topic in Chapter 6, as attention was drawn towards Assam and the areas bordering Burma, India, China and Tibet in attempts to revive the tea trade, as well as other important commercial routes into Central Asia and China.

The notion that engaging in private business whilst on official duties was acceptable persisted throughout the nineteenth century and undoubtedly influenced the conduct of subordinate civil assistants at the GTS, like William Johnson. However, as he soon learnt to his cost, undertaking private commissions whilst engaged on official duties was the prerogative of the officer class and covenanted servants of the EIC. The privilege was not extended to the lower orders, who, like him, were classed as 'country-born'. A similar desire for private pecuniary advantage motivated the actions of Dr Clement Williams, who, as an assistant army surgeon, became an independent explorer. Using his army furlough to travel to Upper Burma, he was subsequently accused by the Government of India of going there to pursue private commercial ventures. Even though Johnson and Williams were sincere in their wish to serve British interests, they appeared to the Indian government to be 'chancers', who were ready to exploit any opportunities that came their way in order to make financial gains. Such perceptions had their roots in the earlier ambiguities between civil and military roles, and also in the recurring disorder in the judicial administration of India related to anxieties about European criminality that Thomas Babington Macaulay's reforms had sought to eliminate.

There were many other arenas for managing information that were generated by 'objects producing spaces'.[58] This was particularly apposite in respect of research into plants, seeds and other products of the natural world, which called for the establishment of botanic gardens throughout Europe and the world. From the mid-eighteenth century, Linnaeus's Binomial System of Classification was applied to the academic and commercial exploitation of plants contained in gardens in the Netherlands (at Leiden and Utrecht), the Chelsea Physic Garden in London, and Coimbra in Portugal, which

---

56. Cederlöf, 'Seeking China's Back Door', 130.

57. There is some doubt over this alleged discovery, which is conventionally attributed to Robert Bruce (1789–1824), a Scottish adventurer who reportedly found the plant growing 'wild' in Assam whilst trading in the region. However, the plant was well-known in China and by inference, possibly in other areas of the frontier with India, and therefore not exclusive to Assam.

58. Schillings and van Wickeren, 'Towards a Material and Spatial History', 208.

established circulatory regimes on a global scale of items generated from their flowerbeds.[59] Although less readily quantifiable, wealthy private collectors maintained professionally organised botanical spaces, which housed rare foreign plants in their flowerbeds and hothouses, some of the most famous being those at Montbard in France belonging to Georges-Louis Leclerc, Comte de Buffon (1707–1788). Renowned for their experimentation in the development and management of botanical gardens, private and public horticultural spaces participated in the circulation of knowledge between important nodes throughout Europe and the British Isles. Their activities resulted in networks of knowledge that extended eastwards to places of botanical consumption in South and Southeast Asia and westwards to the Caribbean, creating an epistemology of the natural world, which is discussed in the next section in relation to India.[60]

THE GLOBAL EPISTEMOLOGY OF PLANTS AND SEEDS IN INDIA

A prolific network of intellectual and social connections flourished between scholars in India and their overseas correspondents, which was particularly advantageous to the globalising project of natural history. India offered an abundance of exotic products – both flora and fauna – that could be preserved and sent back to England or Scotland for study and private consumption, as well as exchanged between botanists throughout Europe and other parts of the globe. Artists and scientists were able to represent the natural world according to their own vision through empirical evidence that was sent to them by their overseas correspondents. New knowledge about plants and seeds could now be promoted and ordered in locations far removed from their place of origin. Francis Buchanan-Hamilton became part of this global network of correspondents by using the opportunities presented by his surveys on behalf of the EIC to engage in collecting and classifying new botanical specimens. Together with other EIC men, like William Roxburgh (1751–1815), and Nathaniel Wallich (1786–1854), their plant-collecting expeditions not only contributed significantly towards the development of the Calcutta Botanic Garden but also helped to underwrite the work of Sir Joseph Banks (1743–1820) and other luminaries of the natural world throughout Europe and beyond. Their scholarship maintained the tradition established some decades earlier by other overseas correspondents, who had fulfilled the requirement for specimens for

59. Esther Helena Arens, 'Flowerbeds and Hothouses: Botany, Gardens and the Circulation of Knowledge in Things', *Historical Social Research / Historische Sozialforschung* 40, no. 1 (2015): 265.
60. Ibid., 268.

men like the Comte de Buffon, Carl Linnaeus (1707–1778), and the Scottish landscape artist, Alexander Buchan (d. 1769), who accompanied James Cook's first voyage to the Pacific in 1768.

Mary Louise Pratt has argued that 'the system of nature overwrote local and peasant ways of knowing within Europe, just as it did in indigenous spaces overseas',[61] as evidenced by the scientific approach adopted by the Comte de Buffon towards observing and explaining the new phenomena that exploded all around him from his laboratories and gardens based at his chateau at Montbard, in the French Burgundy. Early in his monumental career, Buffon looked towards England for scholarly support and for collaboration with his important experiments in plant physiology and other sciences. Today in France, Buffon is considered as the precursor of Darwin, especially for his work in advancing revolutionary theories concerning the age of the earth; although, he was careful not to contravene the official dogma of the Catholic Church, which limited the planet's age to 6,000 years. Thus, Montbard too became an early centre of calculation, due to the extensive scientific work that was undertaken there under Buffon's supervision and the global reach of the networks that radiated out from this small town in the French countryside. Buffon even established a magnificent forge a short distance from the town, on the Canal du Bourgogne, to experiment with new methods of smelting iron ore. As mentioned earlier, some decades later, on the other side of the globe, Raja Serfoji II also sponsored a centre of research and experimentation based at his Court in Tanjore, which regrettably only lasted for the duration of his lifetime, as he died in 1832.

In his student days, Buffon became acquainted with the Duke of Kingston and they travelled together in Europe, making many English friends through the Duke's introductions. Buffon learnt English and knew it well enough to read and use works by English scholars. In 1735, he published a French translation[62] of an important book by the scientist Stephen Hales (1677–1761), called *An Account of Some Statical Experiments on the Sap in Vegetables.*[63] Buffon was also a devotee of Sir Isaac Newton (1642–1727).[64] As his work progressed, Buffon developed close ties with Martin Folkes (1690–1754), the president of the Royal Society, with whom he maintained a long correspondence. He also collaborated with the English microscopist, John Turberville

---

61. Mary Louise Pratt, *Imperial Eyes: Travel Writing and Transculturation* (London and New York: Routledge, 1992), 35.

62. Georges Louis Leclerc, *La statique des végétaux, et L'analyse de l'air: expériences nouvelles lûes à la Société royale de Londres* (Paris: Jacques Vincent, 1735).

63. Stephen Hales, *Vegetable Staticks: Or, an Account of Some Statical Experiments on the Sap in Vegetables . . . Also, a Specimen of an Attempt to Analyse the Air* (London: W. & J. Innys, 1727).

64. For a full account of Buffon's life and work, see Jacques Roger, *Buffon: A Life in Natural History* (Ithaca, NY, and London: Cornell University Press, 1997).

Needham (1713–1781), in his research on reproduction. Needham had been recommended to Buffon by Folkes and he came to Paris to help him at the Royal Botanical Gardens from March to May 1784, where they collaborated on a series of experiments which proved controversial in the European scientific world.[65]

In 1742, soon after he was appointed *Intendant* (Director) at the Royal Botanical Gardens, later named as the Paris Museum of Natural History and known today as the Jardin des Plantes, one of Buffon's first tasks was to reorganise and enrich the king's cabinet of curiosities. In order to pursue this endeavour, he assiduously developed a network of correspondents situated throughout the world, who sent him specimens of plants, seeds, birds, insects and other natural rarities. To those correspondents whom he patronised, Buffon issued a certificate stating that they were a 'Correspondent of the Royal Botanical Gardens', an acknowledgement that the habit of collecting and association with new scientific knowledge bestowed prestige upon those who participated in this enterprise. This casts a fascinating light on a system of intellectual cooperation that, from the early eighteenth century, had occurred on a global scale before the imposition of mapped borders created physical and intellectual barriers.

One of Buffon's many overseas correspondents was the aforementioned '*petit artisan*', Jacques-François Artur (1708–1779), the French medical doctor who, following his arrival in Cayenne in 1736, began to collect botanical specimens for his former professor, Antoine de Jussieu (1686–1758). Jussieu asked Artur to concentrate his research on plants used in French Guiana, including seeds, and also to send him different types of soil samples, as well as examples of rocks and fossils. Jussieu sent him a comprehensive list which was intended to assist the Académie des Sciences in Paris with their inquiries in their new colony in Guiana.[66] Two years later, Jussieu asked Artur to send him vanilla pods and cocoa beans, and he was requested to accompany his specimens with a detailed description of the colony's trees, their fruits and the places where they grew. We will encounter Antoine de Jussieu again in the chapter concerning Francis Buchanan-Hamilton, emphasising the wide scope of the webs of knowledge about the natural world that existed for decades between European scholars and their overseas correspondents.

Meanwhile, the entomologist and writer, René Antoine Ferchault de Réaumur (1683–1757), also requested Artur to send him specimens of insects from Cayenne. In all, whilst living in French Guiana, Artur sent nineteen dispatches of cases of curiosities to scientists at the Jardin du Roi, including Buffon, through whose patronage he was later introduced to Martin Folkes

65. Ibid., 140–147.
66. Ronsseray, 'In the Shadow of Buffon', 29.

in London. In this way, the foundations of an extensive network of scholarly collaboration were created from the early eighteenth century between French academicians like Buffon, his counterparts in England and their correspondents throughout the world, who supplied them with the materials necessary for them to carry out their researches into the botany and fauna found in their respective new overseas territories. Their dispatches supported and sustained scientific endeavours throughout Europe and beyond, creating networks of influence and learning.[67] Over time, and despite the wars between the French and the English, Artur's relationship with Folkes became closer, until it was said of Artur that he was more 'English than French'.[68] Artur became a correspondent with the Royal Society in London, whose archives contain a letter of eight pages from the doctor concerning the birds at Cayenne, read to the Society on 28 June 1753 by its Secretary, Dr Maty.[69]

By the end of the eighteenth century, there is also evidence that far-reaching networks were created between scholars in Britain and their correspondents in India, as demonstrated by an interesting set of instructions composed by the Revd Dr John Walker (1731–1803), who was appointed professor of natural history at the University of Edinburgh in 1779. Walker's status provided an important opportunity for young men travelling to India to obtain his patronage, in obliging him by sending back specimens and samples of the merchandise that he mentioned in his 'Memorandum'. Published in 1793, in the now defunct *Literary Weekly Intelligencer* (known as *The Bee*), Walker prescribed a detailed list of 'dos and don'ts' in 'Memorandum to a Young Gentleman Going to India'; making in all twenty-one recommendations concerning the journey that ranged from keeping a journal, to taking on board and preserving sea animals when the ship docked at points between the Cape and Madagascar. Clearly acquainted with the merchandise on offer in Bombay, Walker urged the young gentleman to look out for articles of commerce from Surat and the Gulf of Persia; namely, 'Drugs, different gums and resins, the largest pearl oysters, or mother of pearl, and tortoise shells, or white sandalwood and ebony', to name but a few of the variety of available goods.[70]

The young voyager was also exhorted to look out for 'the fine red Persian ochre, called *Indian red* in Bombay, as well as the skins of zebras, Persian lambs, jackals, leopards, panthers and other Asiatic quadrupeds'. Whilst at

---

67. Ibid., 21.
68. Comment attributed to Jean Baptiste Christophore Fusée Aublet (1720–1778), French pharmacist and botanist.
69. Ronsseray, 'In the Shadow of Buffon', 29.
70. John Walker, 'A Memorandum Given by Dr Walker, Professor of Natural History, Edinburgh, to a Young Gentleman Going to India, with Some Additions', *The Bee, or Literary Weekly Intelligencer* 17 (1793): 331.

Bombay, he was advised to visit the shops of the lapidaries, where the finest quality products could be obtained and, when in Madras, to inquire regarding 'the new Cochineal,[71] discovered by Dr. Anderson and to preserve and send home, the species of grass on which it feeds'.[72] When in Calcutta, he was recommended to look out for the finest marine products on sale there, which were brought from all parts of India, whilst at the same time, he should be on the alert and inquire about a 'great quadruped called by the English, a buffalo, but by the "natives" the *arnee*'.[73] Realising the value of free trade, Dr Walker also admonished the young man to 'be attentive, especially, to all the productions of China which may be brought there, whether fossil, vegetable or animal'.[74]

Meanwhile, Sir James Edward Smith was a great exponent of patronage, as manifested by his copious letters to Sir Joseph Banks. Smith even resorted to supplying Banks with turkeys, which his mother purchased in the local market at Norwich, in order to solicit his patronage.[75] Having purchased the collection and library of Carl Linnaeus, some years back in 1784, Smith became the founder of the London Linnean Society and its first president in 1788. Thereafter, he became enmeshed in complicated webs of patronage, both as one who bestowed it and as one who solicited it. Seeking patronage for himself, or on behalf of others, Smith spent much of his time travelling throughout Europe, networking with eminent people who could help him to gain access to important private herbariums. He wrote to Banks from Paris in 1787, declaring that he was well in with everybody there and that Brousonnet[76] had procured him access to the herbariums of notable individuals.[77] Smith became a part of a European network of botanists dependent upon specimens dispatched to him by correspondents in India, like William Roxburgh and Francis Buchanan. As Director of the Botanic Garden in Calcutta, Roxburgh had succeeded its founder, Robert Kyd (1746–1793), in 1793.

In his capacity as President of the Linnean Society, Smith was much sought-after as a patron, particularly by young men keen to make their mark as naturalists in positions throughout the world. In a letter to Joseph Banks in 1791, Smith enclosed a letter he had received from a young man of 'independent fortune but no profession', who having studied botany and entomology,

---

71. Cochineal: A scale insect in the sub-order *Sternorrhyncha*, from which the natural dye carmine is derived.
72. Walker, 'Memorandum', 331.
73. Ibid., 332. *Arnee*: A large water buffalo found throughout South and Southeast Asia.
74. Ibid.
75. SLNSW/Banks Papers/Series 72.157: Correspondence of Sir James Edward Smith with Sir Joseph Banks (8 and 13 January 1798).
76. Pierre Marie Auguste Broussonet (1761–1807) was a French naturalist.
77. SLNSW/Banks Papers/Series 72.160–169: Correspondence of Smith with Banks (5 October 1787).

was hoping to secure Banks's patronage, as indeed was Smith himself. In the same letter, he invited Banks to attend the Linnean Society's dinner on 19 April that year at the Crown and Anchor. Banks's presence at this dinner would add an all-important endorsement to Smith's recently founded society. The Crown and Anchor was not quite so prestigious a venue as the Turk's Head, where Dr Johnson's famous 'Club' met; but rebuilt in 1790, it became associated with campaigners for political reform and featured prominently in a number of political satires of the 1790s depicted in the cartoons of James Gillray (1756–1815).[78] Some years later, Smith again sought Banks's advice in connection with an applicant in post-revolutionary France, as he was cautious about his politics and character. He suggested that they provide him merely with a 'simple certificate' stating that he was a naturalist of good character, as they did not know his circumstances. Smith flattered Banks by informing him that 'letters of recommendation from men eminent in Science have more weight than from men in power', and that 'he never grudges any pains to serve science and scientific men'.[79]

As Chapter 3 will explain, despite his erudition, Francis Buchanan-Hamilton struggled throughout his time in India to secure Smith's personal patronage in order to achieve publications in the metropole, thereby affording him cultural authority over his subject. Buchanan relied upon Smith to include his memoranda and botanical notes in the Linnean Society's publications, which he dispatched from India. Despite the men's outwardly cordial relations, Buchanan achieved limited success in publishing his work in Britain through Smith's patronage and he had to wait until his retirement in Scotland in 1815 to attain modest success. Similar dependence upon patronage and its importance in relation to social status will also become apparent in discussions concerning the careers of Clement Williams and William Johnson. However, as Chapter 7 demonstrates, Frederick Marshman Bailey's upper-class upbringing and education in England ensured that he lacked neither patronage nor the support of his superiors in the Indian army during his rather unorthodox career.

As this section has demonstrated, the relationship between botanical objects and their spatial context was of necessity mobile, but there was an increasing demand for static spaces for the display of curiosities and objects to encourage learning; this was gradually satisfied by the growth of public museums, which evolved from the private, interior spaces of individual collectors. Cabinets of curiosities, which represented early attempts at categorising objects, came into being in the sixteenth century in Renaissance Europe,

---

78. Image of the Crown and Anchor: http://www.1790salehouse.com/2009/05/crown-and-anchor-strand.html.
79. Correspondence of Smith with Banks (8 and 13 January 1798).

when wealthy private collectors began accumulating exotic and bizarre objects from overseas, often received as gifts, or purchased from returning travellers. Occasionally, *wunderkammern* were emulated by indigenous collectors like Raja Serfoji II, who acquired curiosities from the many foreign visitors to his Court at Tanjore, which he displayed in a room in his palace and, on occasion, exhibited to the local population. Valued as curiosities, these objects were intended only for the gaze of the privileged few,[80] unlike museums, which were public spaces. As the next section describes, they developed towards the end of the nineteenth century in order to satisfy communal curiosity about previously unseen objects, often acquired from far-off places, usually subject to British rule and donated by collectors who had served there.[81]

MUSEUMS AS STATIC SPACES FOR OBJECTS

From the early eighteenth century onwards, attempts were made to order knowledge more scientifically, and as the EIC's power grew, so did its influence in artistic and cultural matters. Bernard Cohn has shown how their investigations led the colonisers to view India as a vast museum that not only enabled them to remove artefacts and specimens from the natural world along with other curiosities but also gave them the power to define India's past and to recreate a history for the country in their own imagination.[82] The EIC's occupation of India offered its officers the opportunity to become collectors of the many wondrous and valuable objects that were to be found in their new abode, and also, as we shall see in the case of Major General Charles 'Hindoo' Stuart (1758–1828), the opportunity to acquire some rather alarming objects used by this 'strange' new culture. Collecting also offered its protagonists a way of crossing cultural, social and, on occasion, political boundaries, whilst at the same time, enriching themselves and enhancing their status back home. The notorious *nabobs*[83] of the 1760s and 1770s, who returned to Britain after amassing great wealth, used it to acquire land, houses, art and parliamentary influence. They did so in order to establish themselves within Britain's ruling class.[84]

---

80. Schillings and van Wickeren, 'Towards a Material and Spatial History', 213.
81. Ibid.
82. Bernard S. Cohn, *Colonialism and Its Forms of Knowledge* (Princeton, NJ: Princeton University Press, 1996), 91.
83. *Nabob*: Historically, an official under the Mughal Empire, but also, the name given to conspicuously wealthy white men who made their fortune in India.
84. Maya Jasanoff, 'Collectors of Empire: Objects, Conquests and Imperial Self-Fashioning', *Past and Present* 184 (2004): 110, 115.

Michel Foucault drew a sharp distinction between the Classical Age and the Renaissance in his book, *The Order of Things*, when he explained that strangeness and the unknown changed from being a show, or a spectacle at fairs and tournaments, to being one in the Classical Age where observation was used as the instrument of classification. It offered 'a new way of connecting things both to the eye and to discourse and a new way of making history'.[85] Foucault's observation is pertinent to the reactions of collectors like Charles Stuart when confronted with India's strangeness. The extent of Stuart's private possessions was described as a 'museum', and the inventory compiled in September 1829, a year after his death, consisted of over fifty pages of items ranging from Hindu and Burmese statuary and lingams, to jewellery, personal clothing, and even a Burmese canoe, complete with nine paddles.

Stuart's encounters with Hindu religious rituals that involved trial by painful and sometimes fatal ordeal also led him to collect a large number of instruments used for mortifying the flesh during important devotional occasions in the Hindu calendar, indicating his fascination with this unfamiliar spectacle. His inventory listed metal rods of astounding length and weight that had proved fatal to men during previous *pujas*,[86] which Stuart acquired for his collection as representations of India as a strange and exotic land.[87] One entry in the inventory was described as 'an iron rod eight feet three inches long, which was thrust through the tongue of a Hindoo in the Cherruck Pooja'.[88] Macabre fascination with these terrifying religious rituals, involving suffering which portrayed the indigenous 'other' as possessing almost superhuman qualities of endurance, propelled the European will to know and to master knowledge about the subcontinent. Yet, by acquiring such objects for his collection, which evolved into museum-like proportions, Stuart was also attempting to classify and give order to them, so that their peculiarity might be better understood by those in the home country.

By the mid-nineteenth century, collecting by cosmopolitan 'gentlemen-connoisseurs' like Charles Stuart and Claude Martin (1735–1800) gradually gave way to state-sponsored collecting in the form of surveys, the construction of archives and filling the display cabinets of public museums. Private collecting of this magnitude was replaced with 'institutionalised forms that provided the colonial state with a means of defining its boundaries, classifying cultures and trying to control them'.[89] The objects of curiosity were

---

85. Michel Foucault, *The Order of Things: An Archaeology of the Human Sciences* (London and New York: Routledge, 1989), 143.

86. *Puja*: Hindu act of worship.

87. Foucault, *The Order of Things*, 143.

88. BL/IOR/L/AG/34/27/93–760: Inventories and accounts of deceased estates (Bengal, 1780–1937).

89. Jasanoff, 'Collectors of Empire', 129, 110.

supplanted by objects intended to instruct and describe new theories, or models that had been developed from scientific discourse, and to appeal to a wider section of the public, so that knowledge was produced in museum spaces 'in the interplay between human actors, objects and places'.[90]

After more than a century of colonisation, the Indian 'other' had become more familiar, so that fascination with the seemingly macabre and exotic waned in favour of collecting enjoyed as a gentlemanly pastime that might be pursued as a diversion from the monotony of daily life in India. The earlier exclusivity of *wunderkammern*, where classification became of paramount importance, was replaced by musealised objects that inscribed knowledge in changing and mobile circumstances according to their position in relation to other exhibits.[91] As India became less isolated, improved transport networks and communications meant that people, objects and ideas circulated more freely. However, there was still a requirement for amateur collectors to supply the metropole with curiosities and specimens, although not on the scale of those amassed by Charles Stuart and the *nabobs*.

As noted in the earlier section, the agency of numerous correspondents facilitated the circulation of scientific objects like plants and seeds, and other sentient and inanimate materials that were discovered in the new territories. Their spatial movements produced complicated flows that transcended national boundaries and gave rise to new taxonomies. Even though, by the end of the nineteenth century, collecting habits had changed, overseas correspondents were still required to supply museums with objects for classification and inclusion in their displays. Whilst on official missions, Indian army political officer, Colonel Frederick Marshman Bailey, took time away from his army duties to indulge in sports-hunting for game trophies, as well as collecting rare specimens of flora and fauna, including new species of birds and butterflies, destined for museums in Britain. Chapter 7, describing Bailey's expeditions in the Himalayas, Tibet and Chinese Turkestan, will demonstrate the ways in which the habit of collecting from the natural world had devolved from that of an intellectual exercise so that the interpretation of scientific knowledge contained in the objects collected was now left to experts in the metropole. Even though Bailey was unable to bring the same intellectual rigour and innovation in classification to his discoveries as the botanist Francis Buchanan-Hamilton had done a century earlier, his collections, accumulated throughout a long career on India's frontiers, were still considered important enough to form the basis of the Horniman Museum in London. Meanwhile, by the early twentieth century, ICS officer Philip Mills's long career amongst the Naga peoples on the frontier of North-East

90. Schillings and van Wickeren, 'Towards a Material and Spatial History', 214.
91. Ibid., 213.

Burma and Assam gave him the opportunity to collect rare and wonderful objects, which found their way to Britain for classification and display in the Pitt Rivers Museum in Oxford. This will be discussed at greater length later in Chapter 8, with particular reference to how the displacement of these objects from their natural environment has altered their meaning.

Whilst attempts at ordering the objects of knowledge production thrived through circulation within different global spaces, objects of curiosity and singularity were also organised as static displays in museums, which gave the British public the opportunity to learn at first-hand about the Empire both visually and, on occasion, tactilely. Nevertheless, even though the objects displayed remained static, the knowledge they contained continued to be mobile through changes in their relationship with other exhibits, as items were periodically rearranged. Furthermore, public access maintained an evolving dialogue between the visitor's experience and curators, academics and the museum sponsors regarding the ways in which knowledge was received, understood and circulated.[92]

By the late nineteenth century, the public museum had superseded the cabinet of curiosities and great private collections, and this was due in no small part to the revolutionary ideas and work of men like the Comte de Buffon, described earlier. Buffon dedicated his life to making the world's natural wonders available to the public, thereby creating the basis upon which France's own great natural history museum was founded. His ultimate vision in cataloguing and reorganising the Cabinet du Roi in Paris, where, from 1739, he was the director, was that it should become a '*depot public*' (public repository), 'with a positive duty to rescue the contents of personal collections'.[93] Similarly, the British Museum was founded predominantly from the natural history specimens bequeathed to it from the monumental collection of Sir Hans Sloane (1660–1753). Officially known as the British Museum (Natural History) until 1922, the two were not legally separated until 1963. The final section of this chapter sums up the diverse spaces in which objects, combined with human practice, produced knowledge that was circulated and assimilated between India and the rest of the world.

CONCLUDING REMARKS

As an instrument of Western civilisation in India, the EIC's core mission on behalf of Britain was to accumulate wealth through trade and the exploitation

---

92. Ibid., 212, 214.
93. Arthur MacGregor, *Curiosity and Enlightenment: Collectors and Collections from the Sixteenth to the Nineteenth Century* (New Haven and London: Yale University Press, 2007), 122.

of primary resources. However, they required extensive knowledge of the territories under their governance in order to achieve legitimacy and con-solidate their collective cultural authority. Through their involvement with external agencies, such as learned societies and other spaces for knowledge production, like the army and botanical gardens, the EIC and the Govern-ment of India played a complex role, where knowledge itself acted as an agent, or informed agency in the struggle for domination.[94] Their association with learned societies in the metropole, like the RGS, became part of this paradigm. The colleges at Fort William and Fort St. George also played an essential part in this endeavour through their discovery, preservation and categorisation of knowledge, including the transliteration and translation of ancient manuscripts by its indigenous scholars.[95]

In their quest for new knowledge and ideas, scholar-administrators competed with one another not only to produce the information required by their employers but also to acquire intellectual prestige. From the mid-eighteenth century, they collaborated with local elites in founding learned societies, like the Asiatic Society of Bengal and the Literary Society of Madras, dedicated to researching the history, culture and language of the districts under their jurisdiction. They published their findings in scholarly journals and sought patronage from appropriate institutions and indi-viduals. They also undertook the production of volumes of official reports containing survey results, census enquiries and other information, some of it secret. Scholars' reputations were made or broken as they subjected their knowledge to public scrutiny, and rivalries were intense, particularly between foreign scholars working in the same field. It also created ten-sions between the periphery and the metropole, as there was considerable divergence between the objectives of learned societies like the RGS and those of the government, both in India and at home. Whilst the RGS was unanimous in its enthusiasm to encourage further exploration in the inter-est of enhancing geographical knowledge, government responses were more guarded.[96] As the leading public institution for the dissemination of new geographical information, the patronage and approbation of the RGS were of paramount importance to colonial institutions like the GTS. Its officers wished to publicise the results of their explorations as widely as possible in order to give cultural authority to their discoveries in the field and to gain personal recognition.

---

94. Tony Day and Craig J. Reynolds, 'Cosmologies, Truth Regimes, and the State in Southeast Asia', *Modern Asian Studies* 34, no. 1 (2000): 2.

95. Ibid., 19.

96. See Maj. Gen. Sir Henry Rawlinson's comments in William H. Johnson, 'Report on His Jour-ney to Ilchí, the Capital of Khotan, in Chinese Tartary', *Journal of the Royal Geographical Society* 37 (1868): 13.

Throughout the nineteenth century, accounts of travel to far-off locations in the empire in books, newspapers and periodicals were eagerly devoured by the British public thanks to advances in print technology, making such material cheaper and therefore more accessible to an ever-widening readership. By the end of the century, faster transport links between the metropole ensured that information was relayed to a public eager for knowledge about India. The opening of the Suez Canal in 1869 and the advent of steam ships cut the journey from Europe from months to three weeks, accelerating trade and inspiring changes in banking and commerce. News about India in newspapers and journals had an impact upon the wider population in the metropole, stimulating public debates. Equally important were advances in the imperial postal service; after new legislation was introduced in 1854, it meant that by the end of the century, an information explosion in India that cut across all classes, elites and illiterates alike had been created.[97] Whilst the Indian reforms of 1854 occurred concurrently with developments in the postal service in Britain, their success relied to a great extent upon the Indianisation of the postal service through the day-to-day use of it by its population via their pre-existing modes of transport and communication.[98] The situation, however, was less successful in the Province of Lower Burma, where reforms after conquest in 1853 were met with non-cooperation. There was reluctance to make use of the cheap postage stamps and difficulty due to the lack of postal agents who were conversant with the Burmese language.[99]

Travel for the purposes of exploration formed an important part of the 'investigative modalities' devised by public bodies in Britain and India to gather all pertinent facts related to the imperial project.[100] The encouragement of British and Asian Chambers of Commerce frequently provided the impetus for many of the journeys of exploration undertaken in South and Southeast Asia. It was important for merchants in the metropole to gain as much knowledge as possible about the commercial and political conditions in the markets that they proposed to enter; so, information was eagerly sought, particularly by those with an eye to doing business in the new markets opened up by territorial expansion, or by those on the brink of doing so. However, the contentious history of unsponsored, or unofficial journeys beyond the frontier into unknown regions and permeable areas that were still under the control of pre-colonial rulers risked undermining the prestige of the British government, should harm befall their citizens, as it so often did. Nevertheless, the

---

97. Mark Frost, 'Pandora's Post Box: Empire and Information in India, 1854–1914', *English Historical Review* 131, no. 552 (2016): 1045.
    98. Ibid., 1055.
    99. Ibid., 1059.
    100. Cohn, *Colonialism and Its Forms of Knowledge*, 5.

intelligence that resulted from these expeditions by lone adventurers proved to be valuable to a colonial state confronted with vast tracts of territory that it did not have the financial resources or manpower to explore and administer adequately.

As Felix Driver has stated, there can be 'no neat distinction between the discourses of adventurous travel and scientific exploration'.[101] And, it is not always easy to distinguish between the personal adventures of individuals and official expeditions undertaken for the purpose of knowledge-gathering and scientific observation.[102] Furthermore, he has refuted the anthropologist Claude Lévi-Strauss's (1908–2009) claim that the distinction between the adventurous explorer and the scientific traveller was a product of twentieth-century modernity. On the contrary, Driver has declared that this problem has occupied writers of anthropology and geography for the past 200 years. As Numa Broc, a specialist in the history and epistemology of geography, has observed, the journey is more than a 'cold and anonymous catalogue of scientific facts', but also one bound up with the enthusiasms and reactions of the traveller to a country, which depend in large measure on comparison with those that he has previously visited.[103]

This scenario had a powerful allure for certain unconventional individuals, who are the subjects of the case histories in the following chapters. They relished the challenge, whilst at the same time, 'it was an opportunity for an inquisitive empire, coming to terms with its newly acquired global reach to project and reaffirm its identity on canvasses new'.[104] However, before turning to the individual histories, it is important to consider how most journeys of discovery, surveys and scholarly endeavours could not have taken place without indigenous assistance, which occurred on so many levels, from the intellectual, to the more mundane daily practicalities of supplying food, setting up camps and interceding with potentially hostile groups to gain local intelligence. It is therefore to a consideration of the support and assistance given to adventurous European actors by 'native' informants, go-betweens and indigenous scholars that we turn in the next chapter. In many instances, their contribution was not recognised, nor were their names recorded. Yet, their hidden presence was a constant and vital constituent of the search for empirical knowledge, without which the long journey towards knowing India could not have been accomplished.

---

101. Felix Driver, *Geography Militant: Cultures of Exploration and Empire* (Oxford: Blackwell, 2001), 2.

102. Numa Broc, *La Géographie des philosophes. Géographes et voyageurs français au XVIIIe siècle* (Paris: Ophrys Editions, 1974), 9.

103. Ibid.

104. Martin J. Bayly, *Taming the Imperial Imagination: Colonial Knowledge, International Relations, and the Anglo-Afghan Encounter, 1808–1878* (Cambridge: Cambridge University Press, 2016), 115.

Chapter 2

Indigenous Informants
and Go-Betweens

INTRODUCTION

Even at its peak in the early twentieth century, the British presence in India never exceeded more than 100,000 civilians. Therefore, throughout the period of colonisation, they depended upon the cooperation of the indigenous population in order to maintain their hold on power. Indigenous assistance was required to perform numerous technical, administrative and domestic tasks, and equally importantly, the production of knowledge.[1] Known variously as *munshis* (writers), *gumashtas* (administrative assistants), *dubashes* (translators) and *banians* (tradesmen), they acted as go-betweens, brokers and informants, whilst legions of domestic servants were employed to maintain the comfort of the colonisers' homes. Although they supported the activities of their imperial masters, they were always subordinate, and their collaboration was rarely acknowledged. Whenever their masters travelled up-country, they undertook the mundane tasks that made the journey possible, by acting as guides, porters and interpreters, procuring and cooking food, after scouting ahead for a suitable campsite. On journeys of exploration, their role was not to take part in the discovery itself, but to enable it. They made contact with local sources to discover the location of rare flowers, plants and animals, and on expeditions in search of birds, their expertise was crucial in skinning and preserving specimens for shipment to Britain.

As key intermediaries, indigenous people were actively involved in creating new kinds of knowledge spaces, but their participation has been concealed and they have rarely been accorded the recognition due to them. As

---

1. Kapil Raj, 'Colonial Encounters and the Forging of New Knowledge and National Identities: Great Britain and India, 1760–1850', *Osiris* 15 (2000): 121.

Felix Driver and Lowri Jones have argued, there was general reluctance on the part of the British to confer the same status as themselves upon 'locals'. Occasionally, they did accord varying degrees of recognition to those who assisted them, but always emphasising their inferior role in order to reinforce their power as colonisers.[2] One popular way of according recognition in travel accounts was to describe them as a 'faithful follower' or a 'loyal servant', so that it was made clear that they did not initiate the expedition or provide agency in any of the ventures undertaken or discoveries made.[3] Their contribution in translating unfamiliar languages, facilitating encounters with other ethnic groups, sourcing artefacts and making drawings and paintings of botanical specimens has been obscured. This has presented challenges to contemporary historians, who now recognise the part played by indigenous actors in knowledge production, especially when the archives have often either omitted all mention of their presence or reduced their role to 'mere servants' or 'unnamed assistants'.[4]

Whilst there was ambivalence over acknowledging the work carried out by non-Europeans and difficulty in recovering accounts of their participation, their histories may not always be described as wholly unknown.[5] Driver and Jones have attempted to interrogate the archives in search of 'hidden histories' in order to redress the balance and write 'a more representative history of the processes and practices of mediation'.[6] But lack of evidence, particularly within cross-cultural encounters and exchanges, has hampered the detection, recovery and interpretation of 'the lives, histories and contributions of indigenous intermediaries and other "marginal" participants whose presence and contribution have been "strangely obscured"'.[7] Furthermore, there are limitations within these binary encounters, where European dependence upon locals for food, shelter, protection and sources of knowledge is representative of the polarity of colonialism itself. Driver has described this process as intrinsically flawed and called for a more nuanced approach in recognising the presence of go-betweens and other informants in unexpected areas.[8]

Recognition of indigenous achievements occurred only in rare cases, such as that bestowed upon the Indian pundit Nain Singh (1830–1882), who was

---

2. Felix Driver, 'Intermediaries and the Archives of Exploration', in *Indigenous Intermediaries: New Perspectives on Exploration Archives*, eds. Shino Konishi, Maria Nugent and Tiffany Shellam (Canberra: ANU Press, 2015), 22.

3. Ibid.

4. Ibid., 4–5.

5. See also Felix Driver and Lowri Jones, *Hidden Histories of Exploration: Researching the RGS–IBG Collections* (Egham: Royal Holloway, University of London, in association with the Royal Geographical Society with IBG, 2009).

6. Konishi et al., *Indigenous Intermediaries*, 1.

7. Ibid., 4.

8. Driver, 'Intermediaries', 15.

Figure 2.1. Nain Singh (centre), chief pundit trained by Colonel Montgomerie, with assistant pundit, Kishan Singh, and a Buddhist monk (c. 1850–1869). *Source:* Société de Géographie/BnF (Ref. SG PORTRAIT-230).

awarded the highly-prized gold medal of the RGS in 1876 on the recommendation of Sir Henry Yule (1820–1889). Nain Singh received this award for his covert exploration work in surveying and mapping Tibet, Ladakh and Central Asia, territories beyond the control of British India. As Nain Singh originated from Kumaon in the eastern Himalayas, the importance of an indigenous intermediary's ability to serve rested not upon being from the exact locality of the proposed expedition, but rather upon his qualities of intelligence and resourcefulness, which could be adapted to suit British requirements. Therefore, before venturing into the field, Nain Singh and other pundits underwent an extensive course of training lasting two years under Colonel Thomas Montgomerie's supervision at the headquarters of the GTS in Dehradun. During the 1860s, pundits travelled incognito throughout vast areas of the Himalayas and Tibet; sometimes, they were absent for years at a time and subject to many dangers and even, on occasion, death.

The role of pundits in undertaking covert survey work will be discussed more fully in Chapter 5, but their agency continued until well into the twentieth century, particularly in the context of mountaineering expeditions to the Himalayas.[9] During the first decades of the twentieth century, Frederick Marshman Bailey's[10] many expeditions in the Himalayas and Central Asia relied upon the assistance of his faithful Tibetan manservant, Putamdu, who appears to have been at Bailey's side throughout most of his army career. It is likely that Bailey first encountered Putamdu when he arrived in Tibet in 1904 with Francis Younghusband's (1863–1942) expedition and, subsequently, became the trade agent at Gyantse. More will be said about Putamdu in Chapter 7. One of the more recent cases of lack of equal recognition concerned the Sherpa, Tenzing Norgay (1914–1986), who made the first ascent of Everest alongside Sir Edmund Hillary (1919–2008) in 1953. Although lack of official acknowledgement has been blamed on the prejudice of the British establishment, particularly after controversies over which of these men was the first to step onto the summit, Tenzing Norgay's place in history is nevertheless assured.

Meanwhile, in his essay, 'Power and Production of Subjectivity in (Post) Colonial India', Mukesh Srivastava has contended that the cultural commodification of India in the late eighteenth century, through the painstaking and scholarly research of the Orientalists, was a crucial hegemonic move that made the colonial subject both docile and functional.[11] Srivastava's argument is that colonised subjects served as passive informants, who (in the words of Phillip Wagoner) merely passed information to their European masters, 'to produce new knowledge by imposing imported modes of knowing upon the raw data of local society'.[12] He has maintained that the collaboration of many indigenous informants allowed the British to create a vision of history that enabled the formation of institutional and academic innovations that articulated power via knowledge.[13] Co-opting indigenous intellects and physical

9. Driver and Jones, *Hidden Histories*, 45–46.
10. See Chapter 7.
11. Mukesh Srivastava, 'Mosaic of Narrative Manipulations: Power and Production of Subjectivity in (Post) Colonial India', *Economic and Political Weekly* 27, no. 4 (1992): 47.
12. Phillip B. Wagoner, 'Precolonial Intellectuals and the Production of Colonial Knowledge', *Comparative Studies in Society and History* 45, no. 4 (2003): 783.
13. Srivastava, 'Mosaic of Narrative Manipulations', 47.

labour as instruments of governmentality provided a means of deploying authority, as the specialised disciplines that arose allowed 'a diffuse, highly elastic, apparatus of cultural and ideological formation in India' to evolve.[14] According to Srivastava, this has had post-colonial repercussions, rooted in Orientalist frameworks that contextualised traditional sources of knowledge as 'static' and 'unchanging', and locked in perpetual subjectivity to British dominance, which increased the anxiety to associate culture with the concept of nation.[15] Such loss of agency on the part of the colonised naturally led to a position where, because indigenous forms of knowledge were displaced, there could be 'no significant continuities across the great rift generated by colonial knowledge'.[16]

Srivastava's theory has been challenged by many contemporary historians, including Phillip Wagoner, Christopher A. Bayly, Thomas Trautmann, Norbert Peabody and Eugene Irschick.[17] Their works, quoted in the context of a revisionist critique, argue that whilst new knowledge was fundamental in consolidating colonial power, the colonised were not always mere passive bystanders. They not only played an active role in producing colonial knowledge but also participated in a process of intellectual dialogue that informed the nationalist agenda of later generations.[18] This argument is particularly relevant in respect of the early period of colonial rule in India, when Orientalists relied almost entirely upon the support of local knowledge conveyed to them by learned members of the local community, notably Brahmins. Collaboration with Indian scholars provided Orientalists like Francis Whyte Ellis with an analytical framework upon which to base new knowledge about the subcontinent.[19] Ellis's discovery that the Dravidian languages of the South were distinct from the Northern family[20] was the result of European and Indian collaboration under colonial conditions. As Thomas Trautmann has explained, 'It was the product of a new way of looking at things that came about through the interaction of European and Indian mental frames under colonial conditions, creating something that went beyond the limits of each'.[21]

After the mid-nineteenth century, the active collaboration of indigenous intellectuals diminished, as markers of difference extended the colonial divide and British attitudes hardened towards fraternisation and any form of

---

14. Ibid.
15. Valerian Desousa, 'Modernizing the Colonial Labor Subject in India', *Comparative Literature and Culture* 12, no. 2 (2010), Abstract.
16. Wagoner, 'Precolonial Intellectuals', 784.
17. Ibid.
18. Ibid., 786.
19. Ibid.
20. See Chapter 4.
21. Thomas Trautmann, 'Inventing the History of South India', in *Invoking the Past: The Uses of History in South Asia*, ed. Daud Ali (Oxford: Oxford University Press, 1999), 51.

social contact with 'natives'. As the consolidation and centralisation of colonial authority gradually relegated the colonised to the status of informants, this inevitably had the effect of stifling intellectual debate and cutting off the fluid exchange of ideas and, commensurately, the loss of their active agency in researching new knowledge. Nevertheless, 'native' assistants still remained vital sources of linguistic and practical support, especially on expeditions where their ability to intercede with local groups was indispensable. It was not until the early twentieth century that colonial administrators like James Philip Mills and John Henry Hutton once again used their professional positions as ICS officers to advance knowledge in ways that were reminiscent of the challenges faced by the Orientalists.[22] Postings to remote regions in the far north-eastern corner of the Indian Empire enabled Mills and Hutton to pursue their interest in anthropology and collect many artefacts, chiefly for display in the Pitt Rivers Museum at Oxford. Engaging directly with frontier peoples in areas where few Europeans had previously ventured, they endeavoured to learn about the culture and traditions of the peoples they administered, and over whose lives they held considerable authority. However, we begin our investigation into the vital assistance and services rendered by indigenous people by considering the part they played in supporting the daily lives of their colonial masters as loyal servants both in and out of the home.

LOYAL SERVANTS AND FAITHFUL FOLLOWERS

As mentioned earlier, in comparison with the total population of India, the number of British and European colonisers was small, and stable government would not have been possible without cooperation at every level of indigenous society. The British Raj depended upon an army of servants and assistants in order to maintain its prestige domestically and, equally importantly, when performing public and professional duties. In their offices and on tour in the *mofussil*,[23] district officers relied upon their clerks to write notes, translate witnesses' evidence and provide general administrative assistance. On the domestic front *syces* were needed to care for their horses and ride out with the carriages, and *ayahs* were employed to take care of the children until they went to boarding school in England. Whilst *malis* tended the garden, many others served in the house as cooks, cleaners and bearers. At night, *chowkidars* watched over the sleeping household, and in the morning, a sweeper from the untouchable caste came to remove the night soil.

---

22. See Chapter 8.
23. *Mofussil*: 'Up-country'; regions outside the urban centres of India.

The focus in this section is with the many intermediaries, go-betweens and informants, whose participation was indispensable in preparing for and accompanying expeditions in order to discover new sources of linguistic, natural history, geographical and archaeological information. They formed an invisible army of collaborators whose identities were largely unknown and whose practical assistance in making the expedition successful often went unrecognised. Although their duties were usually far more mundane than the superior scholarly services offered to early Orientalists by Brahmin pundits, scholars and artists, they too played an essential role in gathering and converting new knowledge into accessible forms in many places. As faithful followers and loyal servants, their task was, as previously noted, not to participate in the discovery itself, but to enable it and be vigilant for their master's well-being, often in perilous circumstances, involving difficult encounters with local groups in harsh terrain. As 'knowing people' who shared the arduous journey, they applied their skills to sourcing food and locations for campsites, travelling ahead of the main party early in the day to negotiate and forewarn locals who might be hostile to European interlopers in their territory.

Felix Driver and others have interrogated what information has been made visible and what has been obscured in the standard narratives of colonial history, and why this should be so.[24] In 2009, together with Lowri Jones, he curated an exhibition at the RGS designed to reveal and celebrate the agency of indigenous intermediaries who performed duties as guides, porters and interpreters.[25] Its aim was to emphasise the collaborative role of intermediaries in the production of geographical knowledge.[26] Specifically, the exhibition was designed to challenge the dominant narrative in 'explorer biographies which privileges the actions of heroic individuals in extraordinary circumstances'.[27] By displaying the business of exploration as a collective experience, involving many different skills and relationships, they hoped to re-balance the equation.

One 'faithful follower and loyal servant' who did receive a rare acknowledgement from his master was, as previously mentioned, the manservant of Colonel Frederick Marshman Bailey. Known only as Putamdu, little else is known about his background, except that he came from Tibet. Despite the scant information known about Putamdu, his indigeneity did not belong to the areas where he accompanied Bailey on his expeditions; therefore, being from Tibet, he too was regarded as a foreigner and faced similar challenges

---

24. Maaike Derksen, 'Local Intermediaries? The Missionising and Governing of Colonial Subjects in South Dutch New Guinea, 1920–42', *The Journal of Pacific History* 51, no. 2 (2016): 111.
25. Felix Driver, 'Hidden Histories Made Visible? Reflections on a Geographical Exhibition', *Transactions of the Institute of British Geographers* 38, no. 3 (2013), Abstract.
26. Ibid.
27. Ibid., 420.

to his European masters in exploring unknown terrains. Rather exceptionally, Bailey did acknowledge Putamdu's contribution towards making his
exploration work successful in an article about his journey from Peking
through South-East Tibet and the Mishmi Hills, written in 1912. Captain
Bailey (as he then was) mentioned that having arrived at Tachienlu, an
important town in Szechaun on the tea trade route to Tibet, he sent back
a 'useless Chinese servant' who had accompanied him from Peking. He
recorded that a Tibetan took his place, who 'remained with me until I was
about to enter the Mishmi country'.[28] The replacement for the hapless Chinese assistant was Bailey's long-time manservant, Putamdu. Bailey praised
Putamdu's response to his urgent summons to join his expedition by going
to Calcutta, where he was shipped out to China by Thomas Cook.[29] Although
Bailey gave no further details, Putamdu presumably made this long journey
alone, an indication that he was a resourceful and intelligent man, of considerable status in his local community in Tibet. Bailey also remarked that
when Putamdu arrived in China, he was 'very pleased to have a friendly
face, whom he could trust'.[30]

Putamdu accompanied Bailey throughout his expedition, during which he
was able to apply his special skills in skinning birds, that he had learnt at
the Natural History Society in Bombay, where he had been sent by Bailey.[31]
Putamdu's expertise was invaluable, as skinning birds was an essential prerequisite for preservation in the field that would later allow the successful
completion of the process of taxidermy. If the task were left to untrained
hands, the delicate feathered skin and outer features risked becoming dam-
aged. The skin had to be removed intact and then stuffed with straw in order
to preserve it for shipment to England, usually to museums or private clients.
As noted in the chapter about Bailey, many of his bird specimens were sent
to William Robert Ogilvie-Grant (1863–1924), the Scottish ornithologist who
worked at the Natural History Museum in London. Here, they underwent
expert analysis and identification, and the process of taxidermy was completed, before being mounted and exhibited. Putamdu's skills in this process
were clearly of pivotal importance to Bailey, as in common with other sport-
hunters and collectors, he also sold his specimens, which, without proper
preservation, would have been worthless.

Comparable circumstances applied to another loyal servant and faithful
follower, whom Dr Clement Williams, the subject of Chapter 6, mentioned
extensively in his book, *Through Burmah to Western China*. Throughout his

---

28. Frederick M. Bailey, 'Tibet and the Mishmi Hills: Journey through a Portion of South-Eastern
Tibet and the Mishmi Hills', *The Geographical Journal* 39, no. 4 (1912): 334.
29. Ibid., 347.
30. Ibid.
31. BL/Mss Eur F157/888/21: Bailey miscellaneous (c. 1911–1940).

Irrawaddy River journey, Williams relied upon the assistance of Raj Singh to obtain information from local villagers concerning the best possible routes into Western China from Bhamo (situated in North-West Burma), after travel by river was no longer possible. Raj Singh is another example of an indigenous intermediary who was not native to the region in which he operated. However, nothing further is known about him other than his name, which signified that he was of Sikh origin, possibly someone who had served Williams during his army days in Rangoon. At all times during their journey, Raj Singh acted as a go-between for Williams, not only scouting for information in bazaars but also seeking out local ethnic groups, with whom he endeavoured to conduct intelligent conversations and acquire accurate sketch maps of the region. Even though he was apparently able to communicate in the local dialects, Raj Singh found it difficult to source reliable information. Even though the locals appeared friendly towards him, they gave evasive answers to his questions, because the majority of merchants in Bhamo were Chinese, who guarded their knowledge of the ancient trade routes into Western China jealously and did not wish foreigners, especially Europeans, to trespass upon them.[32]

Despite their best endeavours to gain useful knowledge, both Raj Singh and Clement Williams were viewed as interlopers. In conversations with the local *nikandan* (provincial governor), Raj Singh learnt that although having obtained the permission of the Burmese king, Williams's visit was not welcomed by the local authorities. They feared that he would become friendly with the Panthays, who were at that time in revolt against Peking. It was only when he approached other foreigners or outsiders, that Raj Singh had greater success in obtaining information. When he ventured beyond Bhamo to visit a Kakhyeen (Singpho/Kachin) village, they supplied him with useful information and sketch maps, which two Shan visitors whom he later encountered helped him to transpose and put into proportion.[33] The Kakhyeens even suggested that the best route was one leading from the village of Sawuddy, right across the mountains, from where there were several relatively easy passes. Their friendly advice was in marked contrast to Chinese residents of Bhamo, who, the Kakhyeens reported, had offered King Mindon a lakh of rupees to open this route and close the one leading from Bhamo, but the king had refused.[34]

The next section will examine how Orientalist ideals of intellectual collaboration between colonisers and indigenous people developed and consider just how equal they were. As noted in Chapter 1, the intellectual collaboration

32. Clement Williams, *Through Burmah to Western China, Being Notes of a Journey in 1863 to Establish the Practicability of a Trade-Route between the Irawaddi and the Yang-Tse-Kiang* (Edinburgh and London: William Blackwood & Sons, 1868), 88.
33. Ibid., 92.
34. Ibid., 89.

that occurred within learned societies, beginning with the foundation of the Asiatic Society of Bengal by Sir William Jones in 1784, engendered scholarly research that permitted boundary-crossing between Europeans and Asians. These learned societies accepted members on an 'almost equal' basis, who were primarily drawn from indigenous educated elites. Amongst the leading European members of the BRS founded in 1910, J.S. Furnivall, Gordon Luce (1889–1979) and other Europeans collaborated with Burmese intellectuals and professional men like Pe Maung Tin (1888–1973) and U May Oung (1880–1926) to produce new histories for Burma that they hoped would fit the country for the modern era. In addition to the contribution made by learned societies, from the late eighteenth century, local experts and Brahmin scholars actively participated in sourcing new knowledge by undertaking surveys and enquiries throughout areas newly occupied by the EIC. One of the most famous surveys, discussed in the next section, was conducted under the direction of Major Colin Mackenzie, where indigenous collaboration was vital in allowing Mackenzie to achieve his objective.

BRAHMINS WHO COLLABORATED
WITH COLIN MACKENZIE
AND OTHER ORIENTALISTS

Europeans relied upon indigenous peoples' expertise for their services as linguists, translators and interpreters, without which the foundations of Orientalist scholarship could not have been laid. As a result of greater indigenous input and agency, the concept of what constituted valid historical evidence and Indian historical development was more varied in Southern India than in Bengal. This gave rise to a much more 'heterogeneous archive composed of many diverse inscriptions, legends, poetry, sketches of ruins, tax and property documents, as well as little histories of Deccan villages'.[35] It allowed indigenous actors a greater voice in 'the creation of the colonial "regime of truth"', with the result that in South India it was never an exclusively British creation, but rather a product of 'indigenous input and agency', combined with European scholarship.[36] Phillip Wagoner has contended,

> Although the British undeniably held the upper hand in this relationship and set the agenda for the conversation, the colonial knowledge thus produced would not have taken the form it did, had it not been for the fact that Indian

---

35. Theodore Koditschek, '*The Origins of Modern Historiography in India: Antiquarianism and Philology* by Rama Sundari Mantena (Review)', *Victorian Studies* 57, no. 2 (2015): 297.
36. Ibid., 298.

intellectuals provided not merely the raw data but a key analytical framework that led to the formulation of the new form of knowledge.[37]

Between 1800 and 1810, Major Colin Mackenzie was commissioned by Colonel Arthur Wellesley (1769–1852), brother of the Governor General, to undertake the Survey of Mysore after the conquest of Seringapatam and the fall of Tipu Sultan in 1799. As one of the most famous surveys conducted, it comprised the whole of Southern India, for which Mackenzie depended upon the assistance of high-caste 'native' scholars, known as learned pundits. The role of Brahmin scholars in this enterprise has been well documented, and although on occasion, their dominance in this field was resented by some Europeans, they became an indispensable part of the staff at the EIC's colleges, established at Fort William in Calcutta and Fort St. George in Madras. Through their work and that of many others, the British were enabled to know India, whereby objects and images were transformed to give value and meaning to the country's past.[38] Therefore, numerous local scholars used their knowledge to decipher ancient manuscripts in order to make them intelligible to their colonial masters. Although the majority of Mackenzie's assistants identified as Brahmins, many of those who travelled on his behalf diverged from the traditional religious stereotype, belonging to a secular class of Hindu Telugu Brahmins, known as *Niyogis*, whose service at the Mughal Court at Arcot had endowed them with skills in languages, accounting and political administration.[39] The *Niyogis'* adaptability meant that they were admirably suited to the task that the Governor General had explicitly set Mackenzie in conducting the Survey, being that of providing 'a statistical account of the whole country'.[40]

As intermediaries, Brahmins began to assume an important role in allowing Europeans to appropriate knowledge and to discover India for themselves. Their interventions permitted Europeans to convert knowledge from native sources into English language forms that were 'systematic, scientific and accessible to means of truth testing'.[41] Brahmins were also employed by the Baptist missionaries at Serampore to translate the Bible into local vernaculars, even though the Scottish polymath John Leyden's (1775–1811) view of them was particularly scathing. He accused the Brahmins of mocking the missionaries' ignorance of local languages and observed that one had even written a satirical work against the New Testament. Leyden, however,

---

37. Wagoner, 'Precolonial Intellectuals', 786.
38. Cohn, *Colonialism and Its Forms of Knowledge*, 91.
39. Wagoner, 'Precolonial Intellectuals', 795–797.
40. Richard Wellesley (1760–1842), brother of the more famous Arthur Wellesley, Duke of Wellington (1769–1852), was the Governor General of Madras from 1798 to 1805.
41. Ludden, 'Orientalist Empiricism', 253.

admitted that he had not seen a copy of it himself, as the Brahmins did not wish to antagonise those who employed them.[42] In spite of his criticisms, Leyden could not function in India without their services, as he told his friend, Henry Colebrooke (1765–1837), in a letter of 1811.[43]

In order to make the land known, Mackenzie employed a combination of strategies which included detailed mapping and as many authentic local accounts as could be sourced by his 'native' informants.[44] As the first Surveyor General of India, a post he held from 1815 until his death in 1821, Mackenzie's expertise was in cartography and he made no secret of the fact that he was not a linguist. The Maratha Brahmin, Subba Rao (Row), one of the 'native' pundits who resided at Raja Serfoji II's Court in Tanjore (frequented by the Orientalist scholar, Francis Whyte Ellis), became one of Mackenzie's most important translators.[45] Between the 1790s and 1821, Mackenzie also famously depended upon the help of the Kavali brothers; firstly, Borayya Kavali and, following his death in 1803, his brothers Lakshmayya and Ramaswami.[46] The brothers' collaboration, together with other European and indigenous help, enabled Mackenzie to produce an immense archive, which to this day has not yet been fully analysed. Apart from the Kavali brothers, who are the most well-known of the early intellectual collaborationists, there were many other indigenous scholars involved in assisting the British by teaching languages in the EIC's colleges, translating manuscripts, and travelling throughout the countryside, where they collected data from the villages and made numerous facsimiles of inscriptions.

Following Mackenzie's death in 1821, Lakshmayya assisted the Orientalist scholar, H.H. Wilson (1786–1860), for a number of years with collating and analysing the products of the Mysore Survey, until Wilson returned to England to take up the position as Boden Professor of Sanskrit at Oxford University. Having been closely associated with the Survey for so many years, Lakshmayya applied to continue working on it, but he faced prejudice against indigenous scholars working on colonial projects without British supervision and his request was refused. In 1829, he went to Madras, where he followed

---

42. BL/Mss Eur F303/442: John Leyden to Henry Thomas Colebrooke (1811), in Miscellaneous papers of Dr John Leyden formerly in the possession of Col. Colin Mackenzie (c. 1800–1820).

43. BL/Mss Eur B149: John Leyden to Henry Thomas Colebrooke (1811), saying he was content to leave the personal Brahmin assistant in charge of his household working on translating manuscripts whilst he went away on tour.

44. Nicholas B. Dirks, 'Colonial Histories and Native Informants: Biography of an Archive', in *Orientalism and the Postcolonial Predicament*, 284.

45. Savithri Preetha Nair, 'Native Collecting and Natural Knowledge (1798–1832): Raja Serfoji II of Tanjore as a "Centre of Calculation"', *Journal of the Royal Asiatic Society* 15, no. 3 (2005): 281–282.

46. For a fuller discussion on the Kavali brothers, see Rama Sundari Mantena, *The Origins of Modern Historiography in India: Antiquarianism and Philology, 1780–1880* (New York: Palgrave Macmillan, 2012), 87–121.

an independent academic life and became the first Indian member of the Madras Literary Society, making his initial appearance on 1 January 1831, when he presented the Society with some gold and copper coins and two memoranda. The first concerned ancient inscriptions of copper plates in the Temple of Tripetty; and the second described the location of gold coins of ancient Hindu dynasties.[47] He later founded the Madras Hindu Literary Society in emulation of its European precursor.

Unable to accomplish such a gargantuan task without significant local assistance, Mackenzie recruited a personal staff for the collection of historical, literary and cultural materials, whom he trained with the help of Borayya Kavali.[48] Duly reporting each month to Mackenzie, Brahmins like Narrain Row, Ram Doss Brahmin and Bauboo Row Maratta criss-crossed Southern India in search of monuments, manuscripts, ancient inscriptions, books, artefacts and any information about family lineages and their households that they could glean from the elders in the villages they visited. As Mackenzie did not understand the Telugu, Tamil and Marathi languages, their frequent correspondence was translated into English by Lakshmayya Kavali and his helpers. It can be found in the India Office Records at the British Library, under the classification 'Mackenzie Translations', of which selected examples are discussed here.

On 3 January 1811, Narrain Row, one of the most prolific of Mackenzie's correspondents, recorded that he sent 'a packet to Lakshmayya Kavelli [*sic*] for translation', containing four '*keyfeyeats* in Gentoo language'.[49] Throughout his correspondence in the 'Mackenzie Translations', Narrain Row made frequent references to the term *keyfeyeat*, in connection with his enquiries at the many villages he visited. Translated as meaning 'village records', *keyfeyeats* were heterogeneous histories that covered the genealogy of important families, their landholdings, origin stories and other local histories. They also included details of land usage and revenue yields, as well as important monuments and books held by the village, together with inscriptions on temples and other edifices.[50] Mackenzie placed great emphasis upon the

---

47. Nallathagudi Srinivasa Ramaswami, *Madras Literary Society: A History, 1812–1984* (Madras: Madras Literary Society, 1985), 55.

48. David M. Blake, 'Colin Mackenzie: Collector Extraordinary', *British Library Journal* 17, no. 2 (1991): 130.

49. BL/Mss Eur Mack Trans XII.26: Three reports of Narain Rao and his journal, while employed in the Ceded* district for 1811–12 and 13. *Ceded district refers to the present-day Cuddapah district in Southern Andhra.

50. Mantena, *The Origins of Modern Historiography*, 141–142. Narrain Row's spelling of *Keyfeyeats* is understood to be the term described by Mantena as follows: '*Kaifiyats* were central to the tradition of historical narrative in South India and its textual traditions. The *Kaifiyat* collections that Narrain Row and other informants put together contained information about land records, agricultural and sociological information on caste groups prevalent in a particular village which demonstrated that that *Kaifiyats* in genealogical and historical mode were treated as historical records'.

collection of inscriptions, recognising their historical value in describing family lineages and in reconstructing 'the history of the succession of the Rajahs,
Naigs, Poligars,[51] or Chief families'.[52] He therefore instructed his assistants
to make facsimiles of them whenever possible, and also to make sketches of
interesting landmarks. In the packet that Narrain Row sent to Mackenzie in
January 1811, he also referred to enclosing 'accounts for the year 1810'. As
Niyogi Brahmins were trained in financial accounting, Narrain Row may
have been referring to the village's financial status, having procured details
of its annual revenues.

In the same correspondence, Narrain Row reported that he had a fever and that
he was obliged to employ a man to finish some of the accounts.[53] This was not
unusual, as the principal often sub-contracted the work to suitable acquaintances
because in common with many at that time, they were frequently laid low by
illness. In his *keyfeyeat* by the same dispatch of January 1811 (sent after an
unexplained absence of nearly a year), Narrain Row also referred to writing
'vouchers' for Raumachendrapoor, a village in Sauducotta, which appeared
to be an early form of census, detailing who was absent from the village on
the day that he visited. On 12 January, still afflicted by illness, he recorded
'I was writing vouchers from [*sic*] the absence of the inhabitants thereof as
they got leave from Cutchery for the Suncarantree festival, the same day I got
the itch full of my body'.[54] For the rest of that month, despite his illness, Narrain Row continued to write *keyfeyeats* for the villages he visited, mentioning
also that he had made facsimiles of stone inscriptions. However, by the end
of the month he became so unwell that he was unable to leave his bed, so he
delegated his assistant, Letchmen Row, to finish his work.[55]

A dispatch to Mackenzie by another Brahmin assistant, named Ram Doss
Brahmin,[56] in December 1816, concerned an indigenous group named the
Roddacuttoo Sourahs (or Surahs). It presented in fascinating detail an early
ethnographic account of these people, describing them as 'having broad ugly
faces, small eyes and crooked noses'. Their short hair grew undivided all
over their heads, because they lacked oil, only combing their plait, which was

51. *Rajahs, Naigs, Poligars*: Chief or leader under the Madras Presidency. *Poligar*, specifically in
Southern India, was a territorial administrative and military governor appointed by the Nayaka rulers
during the sixteenth to eighteenth centuries.

52. Wagoner, 'Precolonial Intellectuals', 790. See also BL/Mss Eur F128/213/3–6: Notes made
for Strachey by Colin Mackenzie on the Southern Deccan and on the history of the Marathas, their
sovereigns and government (1804).

53. BL/Mss Eur Mack Trans XII: Report of Narain Rao (1811).

54. Ibid.

55. Ibid.

56. BL/Mss Eur Mack Trans XII.37/4/182: Report of Ramadas, Brahmin, Telegu writer (10–25
May 1818). This account comes from a report of the journey of Ram Doss Brahmin, a Tellunga
(Telugu) writer employed in the Kalinga country by Colin Mackenzie from 10 November 1816 to
25 May 1818.

bound with large ropes of a kind of grass.[57] Ram Doss described how they tied another rope around their waists, from which they hung small branches bound with leaves. He also observed that they used bows and arrows with iron heads to hunt wild animals, which they cut into pieces and dried to be sold in the markets in exchange for pots and salt. They wore a piece of cloth of considerable value to market, which was discarded when they returned home. Ram Doss's account was accompanied by a small, perfectly executed ink drawing of one of their houses,[58] which, he explained, were always situated on rivulets. The reason is that their construction afforded protection from reprisals by the *zemindars* (landowners), whose cattle they raided at night in bands of between twenty and fifty men, when they habitually stole upwards of 100 cattle. If *zemindars* tried to attack them, they escaped into the rivulet by descending from poles situated in the deepest part of their houses, which prevented them being followed. Afterwards, they built themselves new houses, as the *zemindars* burnt their homes in reprisal.[59]

Further evidence of the extensive enquiries undertaken by Mackenzie's assistants throughout Southern India can be found in the responses submitted by another Brahmin, Bauboo Row Maratta, who described himself as a writer to Colonel Mackenzie.[60] His correspondence contained information about his journey along the coast to Pondicherry between 24 December 1816 and 27 May 1817 for the purposes of gathering information, particularly about ancient coins, which might have been washed up from shipwrecks or found in trading posts. Bauboo Row Maratta reported that on his journey, he had encountered a party of Europeans, who wanted to know where he had found the coins and other curiosities that he had shown them. Instead of returning the coins, they tried to keep them and offered him payment, but Bauboo Row Maratta declined their money, 'for fear of losing my character with my master Mackenzie'.[61] Working for Mackenzie was considered a prestigious occupation, not to be jeopardised by taking bribes or other emoluments from passing European collectors or treasure hunters.

In this same account, the Maratta reported that he visited the village of Vedoor, where he met learned men whom he requested 'to give him the particular amount of their Rajah's casts of old Busttes [*sic*]'. They also gave him a book, which he got a learned Brahmin to copy.[62] He noted that although he enquired in the villages for ancient books, the people said that they had lost all the books and documents in the wars of Hyder Ali (c. 1720–1782).

---

57. Ibid.
58. Ibid.
59. Ibid.
60. BL/Mss Eur Mack Trans XII.55/23/18: Report of Narain Rao for January 1817.
61. Ibid.
62. Ibid.

Nevertheless, Bauboo Row Maratta persisted and succeeded in gathering together about twenty old men, from whom he procured oral histories and also collected coins.[63] His account supports the heterogeneous nature of Mackenzie's Brahmin travellers' records, whose frequent correspondence with their master demonstrates that their peregrinations throughout Southern India gave them access to rich sources of information contained in the *key-feyeats* of the places that they visited, which were duly sent to Lakshmayya Kavali and his assistants for translation into English.

It is clear, therefore, that Mackenzie could not have fulfilled Wellesley's orders without the extensive support of his numerous Brahmin assistants, who bore the burden of unremitting travel to unfamiliar villages throughout the South Indian countryside, even in poor health. However, there are no known records for the number who succumbed to their illness due to the hardships of a life on the road. Although they collected valuable information about the histories of their country, they were always treated as subordinates by the British, who were steadfast in not permitting knowledge supplied by 'native' informants to surpass their authority. As mentioned earlier, the authorities refused to allow Lakshmayya Kavali to continue to work alone on Mackenzie's project after the departure of H.H. Wilson in 1829, whose return to England meant that he was no longer available to supervise him. Despite his extensive knowledge of Mackenzie's survey, which was arguably greater than Wilson's, Lakshmayya Kavali was unable to overcome his inferior status, nor indeed were his fellow Brahmins, whose services were indispensable to Mackenzie.

Surgeon-botanists were another important group who depended upon 'native' expertise by commissioning drawings and paintings of flora and fauna from talented indigenous artists. Their illustrations were highly prized by British botanists and private collectors alike, and the skills that they developed allowed them to participate in a unique collaboration between science and art by replicating empirical evidence of the natural world in peerless detail. The next section examines their involvement as artists in producing knowledge about the wealth of India's natural resources, thereby becoming an intrinsic part of networks of scientific exchange, locally and globally, that at that time were unique.

SURGEON-BOTANISTS AND THEIR RELATIONSHIP WITH INDIGENOUS ARTISTS

In the quest for new knowledge about the natural world, the EIC's directors explicitly made it known that medical officers who travelled widely with the troops in their service should use their scientific skills continuously to

63. Ibid., 6.

advance the Company's interests in medicine and commerce. In March 1777, one of the EIC's packets[64] carried a memorandum from them to the Governor General in Bengal to that effect. It stated,

> It is our wish at all times to consider the merits of such an act in any capacity under our services or protection not only in the immediate branch of their stated duties or employment but in every application that may enlarge the minds of our servants in general to liberal and useful enquiries.[65]

Having travelled up the Hooghly River in 1772 towards Calcutta to take up a position as a physician with the EIC's troops, Edinburgh surgeon, James Kerr (1738–1782), proved to be more than adequate to undertake this task. During his time travelling with the troops, Kerr made 'many able and diligent researches of natural history and into the arts and manufactures of Indestan [*sic*]'.[66] Furthermore, he was responsible for making one of the earliest significant post-Linnaean uses of indigenous painters by commissioning them to reproduce the flora that would help the Company to attain its goals.[67] One of the first drawings that Kerr commissioned by an Indian artist is now in the Hope Collection in Edinburgh, being that of the *Burrum chundalli*, 'the moving plant of Bengal' (now known as *Codariocalyx motorius*), which he gifted to his mentor, the Scottish physician and botanist, John Hope (1725–1786), complete with a written description.[68]

Inspired by earlier works like the *Hortus Indicus Malabaricus*,[69] Kerr succeeded, with the help of indigenous botanic artists, in producing over 660 drawings of plants fish, birds, quadrupeds, water insects and amphibious animals, which sadly have all now been lost.[70] However, that they once existed attests to the fact that by the last decades of the eighteenth century, the boundaries between fine art and the documentation of empirical scientific evidence had become blurred by 'a unique collaboration between the artist and the scientist'. This allowed for 'meticulous accuracy and the elaboration and number of the analytical floral details on the drawings'.[71]

The use of art in the service of science,

> reconciled two differing views of the natural world – one that aestheticises nature relying on the idea of the plant as motif or pattern, the other seeking to

64. Packet: A ship employed to carry mail to the colonies.
65. BL/IOR/E/4/622/315: Despatches to Bengal (1774–1775).
66. BL/IOR/E/4/623/393–394: Recommendations coming via ships' packets from the Board of Directors.
67. Henry J. Noltie, 'John Bradby Blake and James Kerr: Hybrid Botanical Art, Canton and Bengal, c. 1770', *Curtis's Botanical Magazine* 34, no. 4 (2017): 431.
68. Ibid., 437.
69. Hendrik van Rheede, *Hortus Indicus Malabaricus* (Amsterdam: Johannis van Somersen & Joannis van Dyck, 1678–1703), 12 vols.
70. Noltie, 'John Bradby Blake', 440.
71. Ibid., 431.

understand and document it, warts and all, relying on empirical observation in
its natural habitat.[72]

Therefore, the most significant aspect of the work made by these artists was
produced by combining India's artistic heritage with the legacy of Western
scientific practice, thereby uniting traditional indigenous arts and crafts with
the European requirement for empiricist portrayals of scientific knowledge.
Whatever the spatial and conceptual variations and provenance of the work
that they made, which cannot be fully known, the artists who collaborated to
produce the magnificent drawings and paintings of subjects from India's natural world were drawn from a variety of traditional Indian crafts. As makers,
they adapted their skills to suit the genre demanded by their patrons, whether
foreigners or locals, as their forbears had done for centuries.

In their discussion of the localities of science, David Wade Chambers and
Richard Gillespie have suggested that, since the sixteenth century, science
has been characterised by polycentric communication networks, where different localities developed scientific centres and 'peripheries rose and fell
within and without Europe'.[73] They have emphasised that the demands of
articulating 'the *place* of knowledge or the *locality* of science' have transcended the tangibles of topography, legalities and technologies, so that the
intellectual roles played by traditional knowledge can also define a locality.[74]
Therefore, they argue, the use of the terms 'local' or 'locality' in this context is flexible and may incorporate social, cultural, political and economic
factors and relationships in both centres and peripheries.[75] Thus, the close
relationship established between surgeon-botanists and the indigenous artists
whom they commissioned may also be considered as constituting a 'locality'
or relationship, which functioned as a vital element in advancing colonial
botanical science. This relationship represents an exceptional collaboration
between colonised and coloniser, as indigenous artists provided empirical
evidence of botanical discoveries. Without their accuracy and minute attention to detail, scientific investigation about the natural world in India could
not have advanced to the state that it did by the early nineteenth century. Even
today, their drawings and paintings are prized as a vital resource for botanical
scholars, despite their intellectual property rights having been subsumed into
the lexicon of European natural science, due to the lack of information about
those who made them.

---

72. Sita Reddy, 'Ars Botanica: Refiguring the Botanical Art Archive', *Marg* 70, no. 2 (2018–2019): 16.
73. David Wade Chambers and Richard Gillespie, 'Locality in the History of Science: Colonial Science, Technoscience and Indigenous Knowledge', *Osiris* 15 (2000): 223.
74. Ibid., 228–229.
75. Ibid., 222.

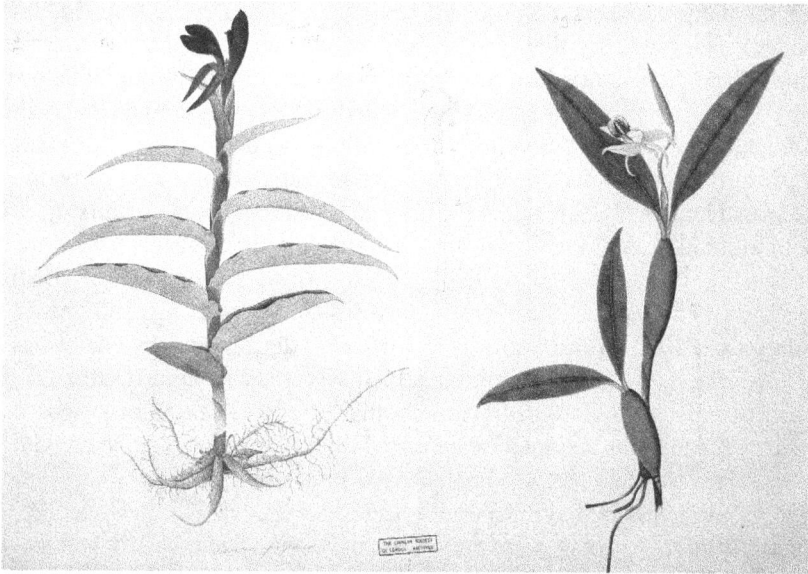

Figure 2.2.   Watercolour drawing by an unknown Indian artist depicting the *Hatucona purpurea* plant from Nepal (1802). *Source:* The Linnean Society (Ref. MS/401D/1/20/1).

Surgeon-botanists were not the only group who prevailed upon the services of indigenous artists, as many private well-to-do Europeans were avid collectors of Indian art. Amongst the usual traffic of packets, cargo vessels and local craft making their way up the Hooghly River towards Calcutta in January 1812 was the three-decker East Indiaman, Baring. One of the passengers on board was General Sir George Nugent (1757–1849), the new Commander-in-Chief of India, who was accompanied by his wife Maria. Lady Nugent had already seen service in the colonies, having resided in Jamaica, where her husband was the Governor General. From her arrival there in October 1801, for four years until her departure, Lady Nugent had made it her mission to bring Christian salvation to the souls of those whom she called 'the blackies'.[76] However, she had an altogether more diverting goal in mind when she set foot in India, as she wrote in her journal[77] that she intended to get drawings of everything and make a collection of curiosities for her dear children, whom she greatly missed.

<hr>

76. Kayli McCullough, 'Lady Maria Nugent: A Woman's Approach to the British Empire', unpublished M.A. Thesis (Oxford, Ohio: Miami University, 2012).

77. Maria Nugent, *A Journal from the Year 1811 till the Year 1815, Including a Voyage to and Residence in India, with a Tour to the North-Western Parts of the British Possessions in That Country, under the Bengal Government* (London: T. and W. Boone, 1839), vol. 1.

Like many of the men and women who came out to India from England, she was fascinated by this strange land, whose architecture, richly carved temples and picturesque festivals they saw as they moved through the towns and villages. A visit to the great bazaar in Calcutta amused and astonished Maria Nugent and she marvelled at the variety of goods on sale, exclaiming at 'all sorts of coloured turbans and dresses, and all sorts of coloured people – the crowd immense – the sacred Brahmin bull walking about and mixing with the multitude'.[78] The merchandise and the exotic appearance of the crowds made a vivid impression upon Lady Nugent, which, like many other British visitors, she was eager to capture by commissioning paintings and drawings from local artists.[79] Lord Moira (1754–1826),[80] the Governor General under whom Francis Buchanan-Hamilton served, was also an enthusiastic collector of botanical drawings. So much so, that he coveted the illustrations that Buchanan had commissioned on behalf of the EIC and eventually succeeded in appropriating them, as will be discussed in the next chapter.

Many contemporary scholars have endeavoured, with limited success, to identify who these artists were and where they came from. Nearly half a century ago, Mildred Archer, the doyenne of the genre, wrote her book, *Company Drawings in the India Office Library*,[81] in which she argued that after their services were no longer required by the Mughal rulers, indigenous artists modified their traditional techniques and adapted their subjects and media to appeal to British and European tastes. Archer also suggested that because of its association with traditional Indian painting, the style that developed, known as 'Company painting' (*Kampani Kallam*), was first centred upon Tanjore in the second half of the eighteenth century, whose artists, called *moochies*, gradually adjusted their style and subject matter to conform to British tastes.

However, apart from determining attribution where, in a few cases, works were signed, or in some instances through diligent research of secondary sources, there has been only modest progress in uncovering information about the names and backgrounds of these artists. Whilst their histories were not exactly hidden, their contribution through art to colonial science has, for the most part, been concealed. Notwithstanding the difficulty in identifying individual artists, as a group their interpretative skills were indispensable, not only to botanists like Kerr and his fellow surgeon,

---

78. Ibid., 111.

79. Mildred Archer and Graham Parlett, *Company Drawings: Indian Paintings of the British Period* (London: Victoria & Albert Museum, 1992), 3.

80. Lord Moira: Francis Edward Rawdon-Hastings, first Marquess of Hastings and Governor General of India from 1813 to 1823.

81. Mildred Archer, *Company Drawings in the India Office Library* (London: Her Majesty's Stationary Office, 1972).

Buchanan, but also to private collectors like Maria Nugent and patrons of art, like the Impeys. As the first Chief Justice of the new Supreme Court in Calcutta, Sir Elijah Impey (1732–1809) and his wife Mary were leading patrons of local artists, whom they commissioned to make drawings of the rare animals that they collected. One of the most famous was that of a pangolin, or Chinese anteater, made by a Patna artist in 1779, who unusually was named as Shaikh Zain al-Di.[82]

Archer, and others who followed her, interpreted Company painting primarily as an attempt by Indian artists to adjust their styles to British requirements and to paint subjects that would appeal to them.[83] However, Archer's definition of Company painting was much more simplistic than that of later scholars like Sita Reddy, who has argued that it is a broad term that covers a wide variety of styles of painting developed by Indian artists.[84] Reddy has suggested that there was more to the process of artistic transition than discovering Western ideas on perspective and changing to watercolours or sepia wash instead of the heavy layers of gouache in bright colours used in Mughal paintings.[85] She has concurred with the Edinburgh scholar, Henry Noltie, that a school of painting should not be named for its corporate sponsor, but primarily for its Indian artists.[86]

In evaluating Archer's work, contemporary scholars like Henry Noltie, Kapil Raj, Sita Reddy and Savithri Preetha Nair have adopted a much more nuanced approach to the question of where these artists came from, the range of their skills and how they adapted them to produce such exquisite work for scientific purposes. Although Mughal power had waned and Indian rulers had surrendered their political authority to the British, they maintain that they still retained their cultural authority. One of the *moochies*' most important patrons was Raja Serfoji II, whose Court at Tanjore became an extraordinary centre of enlightened collaboration between indigenous and European scholars. As Nair has shown in her work on the Tanjore Court (discussed in Chapter 4), Serfoji presided over a unique collaboration that attained a flowering of scientific and artistic knowledge. In particular, she has recently identified the provenance of thirteen miniature watercolour paintings of grain crops from the Tanjore region as the work of one of the most famous of the *moochy* artists, Coopan Sithar.[87]

---

82. BL/Add Or 4667: A pangolin or scaly anteater, from Lady Impey's collection, Zain al-Din, Shaikh (fl. c. 1780). See also T.H. Bowyer, 'Impey, Sir Elijah (1732–1809)', *Oxford Dictionary of National Biography* (Oxford: Oxford University Press, 2004).
83. Archer, *Company Drawings*, 1.
84. Reddy, 'Ars Botanica', 15.
85. Ibid.
86. Ibid., 16, referring to Noltie's work on the Cleghorn Collection.
87. Savithri Preetha Nair, 'Illustrating Plants at the Tanjore Court' *Marg* 70, no. 2 (2018–2019): 46, 50.

As an early example of the genre of botanical illustration made for a European patron, the paintings by Coopan Sithar were sent to London, where Richard Molesworth (1737–1799) annotated and bound them into a manuscript.[88] As Nair has also pointed out, 'Many paintings by Serfoji's *moochies* were sent to the former Resident, Benjamin Torin (1762–1839), in London, who then presented them to the EIC's Directors on behalf of Serfoji. Under the collective title of *The Natural Products of Hindustan*, they represented a further example of the collaboration between colonial science and art in a metropolitan setting'.[89] Thus, Mildred Archer's theory that the Company School was made up of redundant Mughal artists really only holds true in North India, where their art flourished in centres like Calcutta and Patna.[90] Not only did some artists adjust their style to appeal to different patrons – and not necessarily just the British – their styles differed according to the regions in which they worked.

Meanwhile, in Southern India, different theories abounded regarding the origins of these artists, leading Nair to suggest that the Tanjore *moochies* were a group of Telugu-speaking artists who migrated there in the early eighteenth century. Attracted by the Royal Court at Tanjore, which was frequented by European travellers and colonial officials, they adapted their style to secure their patronage, leading to a hybrid genre known as 'Company paintings'.[91] N.S. Ramaswami has contributed another layer to the mystery of their origins by offering an alternative version of the story, where the *moochies* migrated to Tanjore from Hyderabad much later, in around 1775; although, he was doubtful about this version, because political conditions were still too unsettled in 1776 to allow hybrid versions of art to flower.[92] As an Indian art historian, Ramaswami based much of his authority on information that he gleaned during a journey through Southern India that he made in 1976 with the artist Koduru Ramamurthi, visiting Tanjore, Tiruchirapalli and Madurai.[93] During their travels, they met artists from many different backgrounds, some of whose ancestors had worked during the early nineteenth century, when the genre still flourished. He noted that none of them mentioned the Tanjore *moochies'* connection with Hyderabad, as they explained to Ramaswami that their forefathers had arrived in Tamil Nadu with the Nayaks in the sixteenth

88. Ibid.

89. Ibid. See also BL/IOR/NHD7/1001–1116: One hundred and seventeen drawings in watercolour and gouache, Raja Serfojee of Tanjore Collection.

90. Henry Noltie, *The Cleghorn Collection: South Indian Botanical Drawings, 1845–1860* (Edinburgh: Royal Botanic Garden, 2016), 6.

91. Nair, 'Illustrating Plants', 46.

92. Nallathagudi S. Ramaswami, *Tanjore Paintings: A Chapter in Indian Art History* (Madras: Kora's Indigenous Arts and Crafts Centre, 1976), 23.

93. Koduru Ramamurthi: An artist who promoted the revival of indigenous arts and crafts that were in danger of disappearing.

century.[94] Whatever the true explanation for the origins of the *moochies* and the reason for their presence in Tanjore, after the arrival of the British, the 'Tanjore idiom developed quickly'.[95] The British presence there encouraged many local artists to make work that featured its subjects in naturalistic settings, painted in subdued watercolours, rather than the customary media used in Mughal paintings.

The names given to artisans varied depending upon the locality in which they worked, and also their caste, as some groups worked in paint and others in wood. As well as *moochies* in Tanjore (also known as *muchies* in Madras), two other groups whose services were used as painters were *banagars*,[96] and *jingars*, as they were called in Madras.[97] Meanwhile, Henry Noltie has gone even further by identifying a wide variety of artisans allied to the arts, who adapted their skills to meet the demand for paintings and drawings of natural history subjects by surgeon-botanists and others. In particular, he has discovered a group of renowned artists, Mahrathas from the Shimoga District of Mysore, who were known as *gudigars*, or sandalwood carvers, and who also executed temple paintings.[98] Another theory as to the antecedents of these artists and the ways in which they adapted their skills to reproduce botanical specimens may be found in centres manufacturing painted cloth or chintzes, for which India is famous.

One of the earliest examples of this occurred in connection with the work of the Frenchman, Nicolas L'Empereur (c. 1660–1742), whose decision to develop a herbal[99] of constituent medical knowledge for India arose in response to the problem of maintaining Europeans' health in the Far East.[100] In 1706, it led him to take up residence in the French settlement of Chandernagore in Bengal, where he produced a manuscript entitled, 'Botanical Elements of the Plants of the Flora of Orixa, Their Virtues and Qualities, both Known and Unknown, with Their Flowers Fruits and Seeds'.[101] As a major trading port, Chandernagore attracted painters who earned their living

---

94. Ramaswami, *Tanjore Paintings*, 23.
95. Ibid., 23–24.
96. *Banagars*: A community of painters and a subsect of Lingayats, a religious sect dating from the twelfth century.
97. Noltie, *The Cleghorn Collection*, 7–8.
98. Ibid.
99. Herbal: A term used to describe a compendium of products and medicines made from herbs.
100. Kapil Raj, 'Surgeons, Fakirs, Merchants and Craftspeople: Making L'Empereur's *Jardin* in Early Modern South Asia', in Londa Schiebinger and Claudia Swan (eds.), *Colonial Botany: Science, Commerce and Politics in the Early Modern World* (Philadelphia, PA: University of Pennsylvania Press, 2005), 256. Born in Normandy around 1660, Nicolas L'Empereur enrolled as a surgeon's apprentice on a French East Indiaman. After ten years, he finally earned the title of Surgeon-Major, but instead of returning to his homeland, he decided to make his living in India.
101. MNHN/Mss/1915–1926: Nicolas L'Empereur, 'Ellémans botanique des plante du Jardin de Lorixa, leur vertu et quallité, tans conus que celle qui ne le sont pas, avec leur fleur, fruis et grainne, traduit de louria an francés, contenans sept thome'.

making floral designs on calico fabrics (chintzes), which were some of the main Indian exports to Europe.[102] L'Empereur recorded that he had no trouble in getting 'natives' to draw the plants for his monumental work that described 722 medicinal plant species, accompanied by 725 drawings by anonymous Indian artists, compiled in Orissa and Bengal between 1698 and 1725.[103] Kapil Raj has conjectured that the artists that L'Empereur commissioned may have acquired the necessary skills required to carry out this work from earlier precedents set by the Portuguese and Dutch, thereby providing a template for later European botanical conventions. This invites the intriguing possibility that amongst some of the many caste groups employed as botanical artists throughout India, their forebears were painters of chintzes.

Should this be the case, then networks of exchange between Portuguese and Dutch artistic traditions and local Indian cloth-painters blurred the knowledge boundaries between the centre and periphery, and introduced multiple spatial concepts. By producing botanical paintings and drawings in localities where their hereditary trade flourished, they 'opened up cross-cultural spaces for new research directions within the history of science in local contexts'.[104] To add another fascinating thread to the web of indigenous artists throughout India, in the mid-eighteenth century, when James Kerr was practising as a surgeon-botanist in Bengal, he also maintained a profitable side-line as a cloth merchant.[105] He would no doubt have come into contact with artists who painted on cloth and whom he might also have employed to illustrate his botanical specimens, which as mentioned earlier are now sadly lost.

CONCLUDING REMARKS

In his introduction to *The Brokered World*, Simon Schaffer has recognised that local intermediaries have always played a crucial role in 'making sustained encounter and interaction across different cultures possible'; but questions still remain.[106] Within the colonial world, close relationships and bonds established between Europeans and 'natives' always appear to be in some measure contrived and unequal, because of the binary nature of colonialism itself. Furthermore, the nomenclature 'local knowledge' is ambiguous, as many intermediaries, like Putamdu, Raj Singh and the pundits, did not originate from the areas where they operated. Local villagers were as suspicious of the motives of indigenous strangers as they were of Europeans, which is why

102. Raj, 'Surgeons', 259.
103. Kapil Raj, 'Le Jardin de Lorixa', *Marg* 70, no. 2 (2018–2019): 52–53.
104. Wade Chambers and Gillespie, 'Locality in the History of Science', 237.
105. Noltie, 'John Bradby Blake', 437.
106. Schaffer et al., *The Brokered World*, xiv.

the pundits travelled incognito, disguised as holy men or other mendicants. Loyal servants and faithful followers they may have been, but these terms insinuate condescension on the part of those who employed their services. Except in rare cases, concealment of their contribution and skills is indicative of the colonisers' need to retain their superiority in any relationship at all times. This results in the term 'collaboration' becoming problematic when describing their relationship and it cannot be truly justified, except in the case of the botanical artists whose unique skills created a symbiotic relationship between art and science, where cultural authority was shared.

A corollary of this consequence is that it is very difficult to ascertain or to explore the true opinions and feelings of indigenous intermediaries who assisted colonisers at any level of participation, however elevated their status. It may be recalled that in 1811, John Leyden made adverse comments in a letter to his friend Henry Colebrooke about the Brahmins at the Danish mission at Serampore.[107] Leyden could not truly know what these learned gentlemen thought of the British, only that they apparently mocked the missionaries' ignorance. This raises the perpetual difficulty, if not the impossibility, in such an unequal relationship of understanding the 'native's' point of view, or perspective.[108] All those who assisted the British from the Brahmins and botanical artists, whose skills and knowledge were respected, to servants and faithful followers like Putamdu and Raj Singh would not, or could not, disclose their true thoughts and feelings, because of their subordinate status as colonial subjects.

This subject was discussed by Clifford Geertz in his book, *Local Knowledge*, in relation to the ways in which anthropologists could analyse and interpret local sensibilities.[109] Geertz tackled the issue by relating the furore that arose when Bronisław Malinowski's widow posthumously published his *Diary in the Strict Sense of the Term*,[110] in which Malinowski demolished the myth that anthropologists were perfectly attuned to their exotic surroundings and the sensibilities of the locals, including the ability to interpret what the 'natives' really thought and how they felt.[111] According to Geertz, the most profound question that Malinowski's revelation raised was, 'How is anthropological knowledge of the way natives think, feel and perceive possible?'[112] Geertz explained that Malinowski's methodology of how to interpret 'the

---

107. John Leyden to Henry Thomas Colebrooke (1811).
108. Clifford Geertz, *Local Knowledge: Further Essays in Interpretive Anthropology* (London: Fontana Press, 1993), 55–70.
109. Ibid., 56.
110. Bronisław Malinowski, *A Diary in the Strict Sense of the Term* (London: Routledge & Kegan Paul, 1967).
111. Geertz, *Local Knowledge*, 56.
112. Ibid.

native's point of view', without becoming part of it oneself, was to employ the concepts of 'experience-near' and 'experience-distant'.[113] Malinowski maintained that you don't have to be a 'native to know one', and that it was possible to deploy the concepts of 'experience-near' and 'experience-distant' in order to allow a balanced interpretation of indigenous peoples' existence without actually becoming part of it oneself.[114] All of which helps to explain the shock felt when the publication of Malinowski's diary revealed that the legendary anthropologist did not particularly enjoy fieldwork and living with indigenous people. His frank comments were interpreted as impugning his moral character and wrecking the sentimentality that surrounded exploratory missions.[115]

The binary nature of colonialism placed an ineradicable obstacle in the path of ever achieving a relationship that was truly empathetic from the perspective of both the colonised and the coloniser. Maintaining prestige was the guiding principle behind the majority of interactions between Europeans and 'native' intermediaries. Therefore, from the comments made by John Leyden, long before the study of human societies became a subject for formal inquiry, to Malinowski's revelations, Europeans experienced no genuine compulsion to empathise with the indigenous population of the country that they occupied. Their prime objective was to maintain dignity in order to assert authority, despite a desire by some colonisers to cross boundaries and to get to know 'the other' in his environment.

We turn now to the case histories that form the foundational ethos of this study, which endeavour through close investigation of the individual subjects and their histories to demonstrate how knowledge at the periphery was acquired and in what value it was held by the metropole and other global arenas. We begin with studies of two important, but less well-known Orientalists, Francis Buchanan-Hamilton and Francis Whyte Ellis, who advanced the understanding of natural history and languages by working closely with 'native' scholars and artists.

---

113. Ibid., 57.
114. Ibid.
115. Ibid., 56.

Chapter 3

The Botanical Surveys of Francis Buchanan-Hamilton

INTRODUCTION

During the late eighteenth and early nineteenth centuries, botany was the first and most basic of the sciences;[1] and in the quest to master the natural world, strong links were established between colonisation and botanical research. The development of this branch of colonial science owed much to the activities and enthusiasms of the surgeons who accompanied the fleets from Europe on their voyages to South and Southeast Asia, and who remained there to practise medicine as covenanted servants of the EIC. As well as caring for the sick, they were among the first to report on the flora and fauna of the Company's newly acquired territories, and also their cultural and religious practices.[2] Consequently, surgeons emerged as powerful interlocutors in the debates surrounding the classification of new specimens of plants and living organisms, including the methodology by which this should be achieved. The information and specimens that they sent back to leading scientists in the metropole formed the bedrock of important European collections, including those of the Herbarium of the London Linnean Society and that of Sir Joseph Banks, who held the Presidency of the Royal Society for over forty-one years from 1778 to 1820.[3]

---

1. Marika Vicziany, 'Imperialism, Botany and Statistics in Early Nineteenth-Century India: The Surveys of Francis Buchanan (1762–1829)', *Modern Asian Studies* 20, no. 4 (1986): 647.
2. Deepak Kumar, 'Science and Society in Colonial India: Exploring an Agenda', *Social Scientist* 28, nos. 5–6 (2000): 32.
3. Joseph Banks's home in Soho Square, London, housed an important collection of botanical materials and became a noted centre of botanical research. It was bequeathed to the British Museum in 1827 by his librarian, the botanist Robert Brown (1773–1858). See MacGregor, *Curiosity and Enlightenment*, 129–132. Refer also to earlier collectors, like Sir Hans Sloane.

The Court of Directors of the EIC[4] was as interested as any of Europe's leading scientists in learning about the natural resources of their newly acquired possessions in India, as their profits depended upon their exploitation and associated manufactures. Accordingly, they appointed suitably qualified individuals, especially those with medical training, to conduct surveys and enquiries to support their mercantilist activities. This chapter focuses on the work of Scottish surgeon, Francis Buchanan-Hamilton's (1762–1829)[5] position at the interstice between botanical observation and classification as a scholarly pursuit, in accordance with European Enlightenment and Orientalist precepts and the entrepreneurial objectives of the EIC, for whom surveys functioned primarily as pragmatic exercises in gathering data for commercial purposes. In order to do so, it will investigate Buchanan's career and the related output of his surveys, reports and official missions. It will interrogate why, despite his erudite contribution to the discipline of botany, Buchanan's scholarship has remained largely unacknowledged, and why so little of his work has been published. To understand why this should be so, it will consider his original working notes, methods of record-keeping and survey reports, together with his important correspondence with Sir James Edward Smith, who founded the London Linnean Society in 1788.[6]

In the late eighteenth century, Scotland was the focus of a great deal of attention associated with the study of the natural world, chiefly because the subject was considered by its universities to be part of a liberal education.[7] Buchanan was one of a number of medical students who were also enthusiastic private plant collectors. Born at Branziet, near Bardowie, Stirlingshire, Francis Buchanan studied at the University of Edinburgh, where he attended the lectures of the physician and botanist, John Hope, a follower of the Swedish botanist, Carl Linnaeus, famed for his work on plant classification. Consequently, Buchanan became familiar with this branch of science even before he left his native Scotland for India, where his eyes were opened to the vast number of new species of flora and fauna waiting there to be discovered and classified. After qualifying as a doctor in 1783, Buchanan worked at the city's general hospital, spending all his free time botanising, but he found the 'rude mountains' and the perpetual mists of his home in the Scottish Highlands

---

4. The Court of Directors was the body that controlled the activities and interests in the Indian subcontinent.

5. Francis Buchanan-Hamilton took the surname Hamilton after he returned from India in 1815 in order to comply with the terms of an inheritance that required him to adopt the name of the female line of his family. For simplicity, this chapter will refer to him by his birth name, Buchanan, which he was known by throughout the period that he worked in India.

6. Sir James Edward Smith founded the London Linnean Society in 1788, having purchased Carl Linnaeus's collections from his son after his death in 1778.

7. Mildred Archer, *Natural History Drawings in the British Library* (London: Her Majesty's Stationary Office, 1962), 2.

unfavourable to his calling.[8] As an Edinburgh-trained surgeon, he decided to join the EIC, a move which would not only increase his personal finances, but also satisfy his passion for botanising in an unexplored region of the world.

Accordingly, 'place' for Buchanan became an important component in the production of knowledge, and after arriving in India in 1784, he served the Company for over twenty years until his retirement in 1815. Initially, he began working as a doctor, accompanying the ships chartered by the EIC's marine service; but from 1795 until 1814, he was employed throughout the subcontinent in carrying out surveys on behalf of the EIC. The Company regarded these surveys as vital instruments in planning future political, social and economic policies, but they presented Buchanan with an exciting opportunity of occupying a pioneering role in the discovery and classification of new species of plants and animals. Throughout his working life in India, Buchanan strived to serve two masters, one as a covenanted servant of the EIC who was required to submit the products of his surveys for the Court of Directors to do with them as they saw fit, the other as a scientist dedicated to botany. Through his untiring efforts in collecting and researching the natural world, Buchanan built up a large collection of new plant specimens and drawings, with which he aspired to become one of Europe's leading botanists. One way in which Buchanan hoped to gain admittance to this learned fraternity was through regular correspondence with its leading protagonists, particularly Sir James Edward Smith, whom he looked upon as a mentor and a friend. Even before he left Scotland, Buchanan began a correspondence with Smith which continued throughout the many years that he lived in India. Both men had studied medicine together at Edinburgh University and Smith too had attended John Hope's lectures. William Roxburgh, the Scottish surgeon and botanist, who was appointed Superintendent of the Calcutta Botanic Garden in 1793, was also a member of Buchanan's circle of botanical enthusiasts with whom he corresponded regularly, sending him many of the specimens that he had discovered.[9]

For most of his botanical enquiries Buchanan adopted the system of modern taxonomy, or binary nomenclature, begun by Carl Linnaeus in the mid-eighteenth century.[10] The Linnaean hierarchical system is known in botanical circles as an artificial scheme, being based on the sexual reproductive parts of plants, which separates all organisms into successively smaller groups. It assumes that organisms within a specific group resemble one another more

---

8. LC/GB–110/JES/COR/2/118: Correspondence with Sir James Edward Smith (16 November 1783).

9. Dr William Roxburgh became Superintendent of the Calcutta Botanic Garden in 1793 after the death of its founder, Robert Kyd (1746–1793).

10. Carl Linnaeus: Swedish scientist known as the 'father of modern taxonomy' for introducing a formal two-part system in Latin for naming living organisms.

than organisms in a different group. Hence, the Linnaean System groups plants in order, from largest to smallest, which are known respectively as kingdom, phylum or division, class, order, genus and species.[11] Linnaeus's basic classification method is still in use today, but since the late eighteenth century, it has been rivalled by the Natural System, invented by the French botanists, Antoine de Jussieu, his brother Bernard, and his uncle. The cause of much debate in the botanical world over which is the most effective system, the Jussieus's Natural System of classification offers greater versatility in classifying nature's vast resources, but its flexibility lacks the straightforward characteristics of Linnaeus's System. Although Linnaeus was familiar with the Natural System, he maintained that nature was best represented through classifications based on the variations in a single character or structure of a plant, namely its reproductive parts.[12]

A meticulous collector and record-keeper, Buchanan's absorption in his subject allowed him to evaluate methods of classification from different perspectives, which evolved during the course of his working life in India and through his scholarship after he retired to Scotland in 1815. As will be discussed, his correspondence with Smith demonstrates that in pursuit of his objective of mastering the natural world Buchanan applied his considerable scientific expertise to the development of new methodologies, concepts and classifications. Although adhering largely to the Linnaean System in classifying his specimens, this chapter will examine how Buchanan experimented with the Jussieus's Natural System, particularly in his classification of Nepal's plants. His experimentation with the Jussieus's methodology led him to recognise biogeographic links between Nepal, Japan and Siberia that placed his scholarship in the vanguard of early developments in natural science, whilst also distinguishing him as being possessed of a powerful intellect.[13]

Through a steady flow of specimens and commentaries from foreign locales, 'natural history, both as a discourse and material practice, provided the primary discursive and material sites where Europeans learned about, interpreted and appropriated the colonial world'.[14] Mary Louise Pratt has described how, as a colonising science, natural history played a vital part in a 'European knowledge-building project that created a new kind of Euro-centred planetary

11. Anne M. Streich and Kim A. Todd, *Classification and Naming of Plants* (Lincoln: University of Nebraska-Lincoln Extension, 2014), 3.

12. Phillip R. Sloan, 'John Locke, John Ray and the Problem of the Natural System', *Journal of the History of Biology* 5, no. 1 (1972): 4.

13. Mark F. Watson and Henry J. Noltie, 'Career, Collections, Reports and Publications of Dr Francis Buchanan (Later Hamilton), 1762–1829', *Annals of Science* 73, no. 4 (2016): 1.

14. Alan Bewell, 'Romanticism and Colonial Natural History', *Studies in Romanticism* 43, no. 1 (2004): 11–12.

consciousness'.[15] But natural history also shaped the societies of the colonisers as much as it did the colonised and Francis Buchanan played an integral part by helping to identify and define that world.[16] As an academic purist, who presented his immaculately handwritten catalogues of plants to the Court of Directors written in Latin, Buchanan sought to reverse 'the hierarchy of knowledge in which indigenous plant lore and illustrative skill were subordinated to Western science and in which colonial science frequently lagged behind that of the metropolis'.[17] During retirement in Scotland, his synthesising of pre-Linnaean classical botanical studies of South and Southeast Asia with contemporary Asian discoveries produced commentaries that were still of scientific importance decades later.

However, difficulties in publishing his scholarly materials amassed whilst in India placed constraints upon Buchanan's scholarship becoming more widely acknowledged, so that his achievements remained largely unknown in the metropole and hence, not fully appreciated by the wider scientific community of his day. As an employee of the EIC and unable to afford to conduct his own botanical surveys, or pay botanical artists privately to reproduce specimens, Buchanan's surveys were, first and foremost, governed by the wishes of the EIC's Court of Directors, whose primary focus was on the commercial and political opportunities that they presented. Although the founding of learned societies from the mid-eighteenth century did much to encourage the spread of information to a broader social demographic, they were still contained within a class of well-to-do elites, the majority of whom were gentlemen with the leisure to pursue scholarly interests. It was not until the late nineteenth century that improved communications networks and the growth of a low-cost print culture allowed new ideas to become more mainstream and to circulate within an expanding public sphere.

The circumstances under which scholars could publish their work has much to say about how colonial knowledge was disseminated, debated and contested and by whom, particularly in the early days of empire. As expressions of cultural authority, publications in the eighteenth century usually necessitated patronage, either through membership of a learned society (the recourse of many scholars) or through the support of a powerful individual or organisation, like the EIC, or Royal Society. As President of the London Linnean Society, Sir James Edward Smith was not only the main arbitrator in Britain of how specimens of new plants from the subcontinent should be classified, but he was also the gatekeeper to achieving publications, thereby

---

15. Pratt, *Imperial Eyes*, 38.
16. Ibid.
17. David Arnold, 'Plant Capitalism and Company Science: The Indian Career of Nathaniel Wallich', *Modern Asian Studies* 42, no. 5 (2008): 899.

gaining recognition and prestige for their author. Cordial though his relationship with Smith was, without his wholehearted endorsement and powerful
patronage, Buchanan's ability to publish his work was limited, not least by the
tyranny of distance between India and the metropole. It was further restricted
because his collections officially belonged to the EIC, for whose benefit he
conducted surveys. As an employee of the EIC, dependent upon them for his
livelihood, Buchanan was a very small cog in a vast wheel, where the spread
of knowledge was controlled by vested interests and the social, political and
economic expediencies of governing India that are beyond the scope of this
study to interrogate. However, in drawing attention to Buchanan's significant
scientific achievements as a botanist, this chapter hopes to contribute to the
mounting body of work by post-colonial scholars in establishing his place
amongst the pathfinders of knowledge about India's natural world.[18]

One of the first surveys that Buchanan undertook was to Ava, in Upper
Burma, when he accompanied Major Michael Symes's (1761–1809) expedition in 1795. Returning from his mission with Symes in October 1796,
Buchanan reported to Smith from his base at Luckipore, Bengal, that he
had collected many specimens of plants for Sir Joseph Banks, together with
duplicates, which he hoped Banks would pass on to Smith. Buchanan was so
inspired by his discoveries in Upper Burma, which were not solely confined
to botany, that he told Smith he had collected sufficient materials during his
stay 'to be able to give a satisfactory account of the religion and cosmogony
of the Burmans, Siamese and other Eastern nations', and that he expected
soon to receive a copy of the *Great History of the Burman Empire* with a
Latin translation.[19] His essay 'On the Religion and Literature of the Burmas'
published in the *Journal of the Asiatic Research Society*[20] contains one of
the earliest descriptions of daily life in Hinayana Buddhist society. In his
article, Buchanan praised the egalitarian society of Buddhism, in contrast to
the hierarchical nature of Brahminism.[21] He also told Smith that he had given
'a very considerable collection of manuscripts, Burma, Siamese, Shan and
Palli' to Sir John Murray, who was returning to England, and whom Smith
might approach, presumably in order to study them. According to Buchanan,
Murray was very accessible and happy to 'indulge laudable curiosity' and he
begged Smith 'to correspond with him on a regular basis'.[22]

---

18. See Watson and Noltie, 'Career, Collections, Reports'; Arnold, 'Plant Capitalism'; Isabelle
Charmantier and Staffan Müller-Wille, 'Carl Linnaeus's Botanical Paper Slips (1767–1773)', *Intel-
lectual History Review* 24, no. 2 (2014): 215–238.
    19. LC/GB–110/JES/COR/1/122/2: Francis Buchanan to James Edward Smith (2 October 1796).
    20. Francis Buchanan, 'On the Religion and Literature of the Burmas', *Journal of Asiatic
Researches* 6 (1807: London reprint): 163–308.
    21. Vicziany, 'Imperialism, Botany and Statistics', 632 (quoting Buchanan's essay).
    22. Buchanan to Smith (2 October 1796).

His remarks to Smith reinforce the notion that, over and above the demands of his official role of conducting surveys for the EIC, Buchanan sought to achieve intellectual recognition, becoming part of a global network of natural history scholars who shared and exchanged manuscripts and other materials with the aim of furthering scientific enquiry. But he complained to Smith that in India, he lacked the financial resources or library facilities to publish his own materials, and that he would need the help of a geographer like Major James Rennell (1742–1830) to arrange his maps.[23] From such comments, it may be perceived that it was exceedingly difficult for an individual like Buchanan, especially someone living far from the centre without sufficient financial means or patronage, to achieve publications. Instead, Buchanan sent Smith a description and drawings of an animal and three plants from his Ava collection, hoping that he might correct them for inclusion in the *Transactions of the Linnean Society*.[24] Also in the hope that the Court of Directors might publish his 'Enumeratio Plantarum of Burma', Buchanan asked Smith if he would have 'the friendship to look it over and correct errors'.[25]

Amongst post-colonial scholars, Francis Buchanan has become part of a polemic surrounding the ways in which scientific colonial knowledge was acquired and used. It is clear from his remarks to Smith that Buchanan viewed the Company's surveys less as exercises in gathering commercial knowledge, and more as valuable opportunities to explore India's natural resources, in order to further the advancement of botanical knowledge about India. Insightful articles by David Arnold and Marika Vicziany have contributed to the debate about Buchanan's involvement in the conflicted relationship between science and empire in the late eighteenth and early nineteenth centuries. Vicziany has focused on the objectivity of the socio-economic data arising from his surveys, notably those of Mysore and Bengal. She has suggested that the statistics that they produced were not statistics in the way that they are understood today and consequently, they have led contemporary historians to distort the view of Indian society in the early days of British rule.[26] Meanwhile, David Arnold has argued that the career of the Danish-born botanist, Nathaniel Wallich,[27] who succeeded Buchanan as Superintendent of the Calcutta Botanic Garden in 1815, better illustrates the way in which the EIC was able to capitalise upon talent like Wallich's in order to make plants a capital resource to further its economic interests. It was also the case that Wallich was more adept in seeking patronage, as his introductory letter to

---

23. Ibid.
24. Published by the Society in London from 1791–1875.
25. Buchanan to Smith (2 October 1796).
26. Vicziany, 'Imperialism, Botany and Statistics', 649.
27. Nathaniel Wallich was one of the Calcutta Botanic Garden's longest-serving Directors from 1815–1846.

James Edward Smith in 1818 demonstrates. Addressing Smith in the most effusive manner, he wrote,

> In venturing to address these lines to one of the first and most meretricious bota-
> nists of the age, soliciting the honor of his notice and requesting the privilege
> of being indulged with permission to offer my humble services to the utmost
> extent of the means of this garden and of my most anxious and sincerest wishes,
> I should feel the greatest embarrassment imaginable had I not the good fortune
> of being supported by the enclosed two letters.[28]

As Arnold has observed, the Company harnessed Wallich's 'multiple identities: as an itinerant plant collector and enthusiastic "improver", as a botanical entrepreneur, who made the "riches" of Indian plant life known and accessible to Europe'.[29] Buchanan apparently lacked the necessary sycophancy and entrepreneurial skills to adopt similar multiple identities and therefore, was unable to persuade his superiors that he was capable of engaging with the commodification of botany in the ways that Wallich and his predecessor, William Roxburgh, were able to do.

As noted earlier, over the course of his working life, Buchanan accumu-lated a large collection of specimens, drawings and related materials that he intended to work on after he retired to his native Scotland, with a view to achieving publications. His comments in his letters to Smith reveal his con-stant frustration that he did not possess the necessary freedom and financial means to make his botanical discoveries more widely known by publishing them under his own name, and therefore, he looked principally to Smith for support. Buchanan's concerns presage the conflict that would arise some years later between him and the Court of Directors regarding the ownership of specimens and other materials, such as drawings that he had commis-sioned. Meanwhile, his botanical expertise was a valuable component of the Company's political agenda, which was progressively motivated by the need to profit from new plant discoveries and exploit them for agricultural and medicinal purposes. Unsurprisingly, this eventually resulted in a conflict of interest, as Buchanan became increasingly frustrated by the Company's demands upon him. In 1815, when he retired to Scotland a disappointed man and in poor health, a large portion of his collection was confiscated by the Governor General of India, Lord Moira. Thereafter, Buchanan became locked in a bitter dispute with the Court of Directors over the rightful ownership of the botanical drawings and materials in his possession.

---

28. LC/GB–110/JES/COR10/65: Nathaniel Wallich to Sir James Edward Smith (12 Janu-ary 1818). Wallich had obtained letters of introduction from Colonel Thomas Hardwicke and the Archdeacon of Calcutta.

29. Arnold, 'Plant Capitalism', 928.

The next section discusses the many surveys undertaken by Buchanan on behalf of the EIC and their products, which, alongside the official reports, also included more than a decade's accumulation of drawings that he had commissioned from local indigenous artists, as well as plans and specimens that he had collected. It will examine how Buchanan's career as a Company man conflicted with his personal goals as a botanist, so that his surveys, rather than being viewed as a valuable resource to enhance knowledge about the natural world, were directed towards their validation as a capital resource. Instead of being harnessed towards the general wellbeing of the empire and its subjects, colonial science became a commodity to be appropriated by the EIC's future colonial governments to further their respective mercantile interests.

THE INDIAN SURVEYS OF FRANCIS BUCHANAN-HAMILTON AND HIS PASSION FOR BOTANISING

By the early nineteenth century, the EIC was developing new managerial structures that involved a complex relationship with outcomes in Indian political and economic life that were increasingly bound up with the capitalisation of new plants. David Arnold has argued, 'Plants became a versatile resource, situated within the "volatile nexus" of science, commerce, state politics and personal ambition; a process in which India itself was commodified and marketed'.[30] By making use of Buchanan's skills in conducting surveys, to which he brought a professionalism that previous haphazard accounts by other travellers could not, the Company demonstrated its commitment to gathering systematic and accurate information on social and economic conditions in rural areas.[31] The detailed reports that he produced, full of statistics,[32] differed fundamentally from travellers' reports, which although judged as important in contributing towards the advancement of Britain's enquiries about India, were subjective and often inaccurate. Buchanan even attempted to unravel the mysteries of the various castes, which led him to comment that he found that the chronology of Hindu dynasties was 'horribly distorted'.[33]

After spending his first decade in India serving on the Company's ships as an assistant surgeon in the Bengal Service, Buchanan was assigned to

---

30. Arnold, 'Plant Capitalism', 902. Also quoted in Schiebinger and Swan (eds.), *Colonial Botany*, 2.
31. BL/Mss Eur C289/34: Robert C. Emmett, 'The Gazetteers of India: Their Origins and Development during the Nineteenth Century', M.A. thesis (University of Chicago, 1976).
32. For a detailed discussion of the meaning of 'statistics' at the time of Buchanan's surveys and how they differed from our understanding today, see Vicziany, 'Imperialism, Botany and Statistics', 648–650.
33. See Buchanan, 'On the Religion and Literature of the Burmas', 166.

surveying missions on the mainland; the first, as noted, being to Ava in Upper Burma with Captain Michael Symes. Two years after his return to Luckipore in 1796, where he worked on his 'Burmah Journal', Buchanan was sent on another surveying mission to Chittagong in 1798. His increasing skills as an accomplished botanist led to his next commission in 1800 to conduct a survey of Mysore after the defeat of Tipu Sultan at Seringapatam in 1799. This was in addition to the main topographical survey undertaken under the command of Major Colin Mackenzie, as discussed in the previous chapter. This commission occurred because the Governor General, Lord Wellesley (1760–1842),[34] needed a short investigative survey that would detract from the bad publicity in England that his recent conquest in Southern India had occasioned. On 24 February 1800, Buchanan's expertise was once again called into service, and during the next two years, he travelled widely throughout Southern India to Mysore, Canara and Malabar, in order to quickly produce a document that would silence Wellesley's detractors in England. This is an indication of the political agenda that lay behind many of Buchanan's roving commissions and surveys.[35]

By now, Buchanan had gained sufficient experience to be in charge of this investigation into the opportunities that might be available in the newly conquered territories of Mysore and its adjacent provinces. As Head of Mission, he was specially instructed by the Governor General to report on the state of agriculture, the machinery used and the cash crops that might be commercially viable. Buchanan was further ordered by Lord Wellesley to pay attention to 'the condition of the inhabitants in general', for which he required his skills as a medical doctor in order to do justice to this wide-ranging brief.[36] Even though his true vocation was botanising, Buchanan's investigations were always conducted in a thorough and professional manner that demonstrated his keen observational powers as a scientist. A handwritten document in the British Library entitled, 'Observations on the Southern Provinces',[37] describes how Buchanan produced a detailed commentary on his Mysore Survey, ranging from observations on the usages of the many oils extracted from trees and bushes, to descriptions of the ravaged state of the countryside after it had been destroyed by Hyder Ali's wars.[38]

Buchanan's frustration at the constraints that Company service imposed upon him in general, and the EIC's political agenda that lay behind his many surveys in particular, illustrate the disjuncture between government scientific

---

34. Richard Colley Wellesley, 1st Marquess Wellesley, was Governor General of Bengal from 1798–1805.
35. Vicziany, 'Imperialism, Botany and Statistics', 628.
36. Ibid.
37. BL/Mss Eur D639: Additional Francis Buchanan-Hamilton papers (1800–1802).
38. Ibid., 6.

enquiries for political and economic purposes and the private passions and intellectual ambitions of scholar-officials like Buchanan whose job it was to carry them out.[39] This conflict became apparent during Michael Symes's second mission to Ava, which also was undertaken for political motives because the EIC was anxious to maintain cordial relations with the Burmese Kingdom. An extract from a political letter to Bengal in March 1800 emphasised 'the political importance of a friendly intercourse and connection with the Court of Ava', to which the situation regarding the fugitives from Arakan had lately become an impediment to possible commercial ventures.[40]

As a result, Symes was sent on a second mission in 1802, ostensibly to protest about the treatment of emigrants from Arakan, who had sought refuge from Burmese cruelty and oppression in the British territory of Chittagong. But based on the results of Buchanan's earlier survey, made in 1798, Symes was also interested in investigating the feasibility of introducing spice cultivation to Chittagong for commercial purposes.

Even as early as the beginning of the nineteenth century, the British were concerned about French ambitions towards their territories, as the writer of the political letter also observed, 'it was not impossible that the French may entertain views, however distant, or at present impracticable of forming an establishment within the Burma dominions, either by force or insidious negotiation'.[41] Anticipation of possible French expansion into Burma and the use of diplomacy to maintain cordial relations with Ava through commerce indicates early British pre-occupation with French ambitions in this region, which continued throughout the nineteenth century. It suggests an increasingly sophisticated use of the surveys, generated by experienced officers like Buchanan for the purpose of retrieval and assessment of information beneficial in the political arena. Although he did not accompany Symes's second mission and Buchanan's original assessment of the province's suitability for spice cultivation was unfavourable, his report was once again used as political propaganda with a view to limiting French ambitions in the area.

It points to the development of a more nuanced political engagement between the Company and the metropole with regard to relations with India and specifically, towards the manner in which information collected on its behalf was employed.[42] Some years after his return from Southern India in 1801, the Company's Court of Directors ordered that Buchanan's record of his Mysore tour be published in Britain. Despite its comprehensiveness, this

---

39. Arnold, 'Plant Capitalism', 899.
40. BL/IOR/F/4/162/2805/209: Papers regarding Lieut. Colonel Michael Symes's embassy to the Court of Ava (March 1800–September 1803).
41. Ibid.
42. Tony Ballantyne, 'The Changing Shape of the Modern British Empire and Its Historiography', *The Historical Journal* 53, no. 2 (2010): 431–432.

did not accord with its author's views, as Buchanan felt that publication had been rushed through, allowing him no time for revisions. Before he was able to abridge, or otherwise alter and check his work, a subscription was got up by 'respectable booksellers' and in 1807, his *Mysore Survey* was quickly published in three lavishly illustrated volumes.[43] Buchanan's attempts to gain cultural authority from this publication were frustrated by the speed at which the EIC published his Mysore tour, denying him the opportunity to present his results in a more scholarly and considered manner. As Buchanan stated in his 'Foreword' to Volume One, printing had already begun by the time he returned to England on leave. Consequently, he had not been able to make improvements or to edit the text. Furthermore, he had been obliged to obtain help in producing the maps; but even so, 'the very imperfect nature of the materials rendered many errors unavoidable'.[44]

The early publication of Buchanan's *Mysore Survey* was used as part of a public relations exercise to counteract growing concerns about the Company's indebtedness and the arrears in its accounts.[45] The EIC's manipulation of its contents for political motives demonstrates how colonial science was to become an even more complex and contested political instrument. Notwithstanding Buchanan's personal dedication to botanising, commerce and politics were the overriding concerns of the EIC, as well as subsequent colonial governments, and they took precedence over scholarly considerations. The speed demanded by the EIC's directors for this publication to be placed in the public domain cannot readily admit the publication of Buchanan's *Mysore Survey* as representative of an exercise in intellectual creativity, nor an example of his devotion to botanising. Its hurried publication was motivated by political interest on the part of the Court of Directors, who were anxious to broadcast the extent of the Company's recent acquisitions in Southern India. They were in financial difficulties at the time, which threatened to jeopardise their organisation, and questions were being asked in the British Parliament.

This was also evident from Buchanan's Survey of Nepal, which he undertook between 1802 and 1803, where his discoveries not only yielded information on dynastic relations and religious sites but also produced rich material on new species of flora for medicinal purposes. Keenly aware of the EIC's interest in discovering new medicinal plants for commercial exploitation, Buchanan was able to employ his medical training in evaluating previously unknown plants that could be manufactured as drugs destined for the

---

43. Francis Buchanan, *A Journey from Madras through the Countries of Mysore, Canara and Malabar* (London: T. Cadell & W. Davies and Black, Parry & Kingsbury, 1807), 3 vols.
44. Ibid., vol. 1, Introduction.
45. See HC Deb/9/833–836: *East India Company's Bonds Bill* (16 July 1807), which states that 'the last accounts of the India Company, to which the house could resort for information, shewed the affairs of the company to be in a ruinous state'.

European market. As Buchanan reported to Smith in 1811, he found specimens in Nepal that were in high demand,

> I procured however specimens of one genus that is much in request, two spe-
> cies are used in medicine and one is the most violent poison known in India,
> being equally deleterious when taken internally or applied to wounds. The
> natives always poison their arrows with it. The genus approaches very near
> to Caltha [. . .] the plants very much resemble the *Ranunculus arvensis* or
> *Ranunculus acris*.[46]

Despite the dangerous side effects that many of these plants would cause if
ingested, topical remedies for aches and pains and the common cold were
eagerly sought-after for sale in Europe. *Ranunculus acris*, the meadow buttercup, was used for the relief of colds and chest pains and the treatment of
rheumatism, but it was highly poisonous if taken internally, or entered the
body via wounds, hence its use by indigenous people to poison their arrows.
In Nepal, Buchanan also identified the drug '*Gunja* [*sic*]', or *Cannabis
sativa*, reporting that although it was a common weed and not cultivated, 'it
was much used for the purposes of intoxication'.[47] Undoubtedly, the commercial possibilities of promoting the cultivation of this potent drug would
have been of considerable interest to the EIC's directors, but difficulties of
gaining access to Nepal and the general political instability of the frontier
regions at that time precluded them from capitalising upon this particular
asset. Buchanan also noted that Tibet produced the best variety of the drug
known locally as *cirrus*, and he described the methods for extracting it, stating that its effects were similar to opium. He also mentioned that one of the
shopkeepers who visited their camp in Nepal had smoked so much *cirrus* that
it had proved fatal to him.[48]

Between 1807 and 1814, Buchanan was once again engaged in making a
large survey on behalf of the EIC, this time in Bengal; but his appetite for
botanising was constantly directed towards realising scholarly achievements,
where recognition would allow him to fulfil his ambition to preside over
the collections at Calcutta's important Botanic Garden. However, as he told
Smith in 1796, he had to be content with sending anything that came his way
to its Superintendent, William Roxburgh; nor did he have the financial means
to afford an Indian painter or to publish his work privately.[49] It was not until

---

46. LC/GB–110/JES/COR/2/133: Francis Buchanan to Sir James Edward Smith (Norwich, 1
February 1811).
47. Additional Francis Buchanan-Hamilton papers (1800–1802), 24.
48. Ibid.
49. LC/GB–110/JES/COR/2/122/2: Francis Buchanan to Sir James Edward Smith (Luckipore, 2
October 1796).

1814 that Buchanan finally achieved his long-held ambition to be appointed its Superintendent, but he held the post only for a very short time, before poor health compelled him to retire to his native Scotland and he left India for the last time in 1815. However, retirement to his ancestral home, Leny House, near Callander, did bring some comforts; in the same year as he returned to Scotland, he married Anne Brock and in 1822, a son, John, was born to them.

It has been suggested that, in the course of surveying and mapping India, Francis Buchanan, in common with contemporaries like Colin Mackenzie and the geographer, James Rennell, was merely a collector of data rather than analysing or making empirical use of it.[50] Therefore, despite their activities, they could not be considered active agents of imperialism but rather, fact-finders and gatherers of qualitative and quantitative data, presented in the form of reports and specimens for more learned minds at the centre to reflect upon and interpret. In his essay on the changing political contexts of Orientalist studies, David Ludden has defined active agents of imperialism as those whose 'path-breaking discoveries' became authoritative wisdom and who originated new methods or systems.[51] He has cited the contributions of men like Sir William Jones (1746–1794) for Indology and Sir Thomas Munro (1761–1827) for his innovations in systems of revenue administration, both of whom pioneered a discipline. Jones created a systematic code of Hindu law; and Munro's conception of rural India as primarily village-based influenced British fiscal policy for decades.[52] By creating new intellectual concepts in order to understand and govern India, Munro and Jones could claim agency and cultural authority, as their work helped to construct an empire.

Conversely, Matthew Edney has argued that surveyors and geographers have now entered the literature as 'active agents of imperialism' rather than as 'passive data collectors'.[53] He has contended that increasing sensitivity to epistemological issues has rendered everyone involved in defining the empire of equal importance, including those who facilitated the process by collecting and providing data.[54] This argument deserves further consideration in light of Buchanan's intellectual engagement with colonial science to consider whether he is entitled to be known as an 'active agent of imperialism',[55] rather than a passive collector and dispatcher of specimens and statistics. In order to evaluate the claim that he was a pathfinder in the field of colonial science, by originating new scientific methods or systems, the next section examines

---

50. Matthew Edney, *Mapping an Empire: The Geographical Construction of British India, 1765–1843* (London and Chicago: University of Chicago Press, 1997), 31.
51. Ludden, 'Oriental Empiricism', 257–258.
52. Ibid.
53. Edney, *Mapping an Empire*, 31.
54. Ibid.
55. Ludden, 'Oriental Empiricism', 257–258.

Buchanan's personal botanical records and the methods by which he arranged his materials.

THE FORGOTTEN PATHFINDER IN THE CLASSIFICATION OF INDIA'S NATURAL HISTORY

Despite Buchanan's prolific output as a natural scientist, his divergent roles as a Company surveyor and a botanist meant that 'his multitudinous botanical discoveries are particularly poorly known, with the vast majority of his material on this subject languishing unpublished in archival collections'.[56] These include his original records and working notes showing his methodology for dealing with 'information overload',[57] and for arranging his syntheses ready for publication.[58] As a result, he has not received widespread recognition for his pioneering experiments with classification, particularly concerning the products of his Survey of Nepal, when, as described, he accompanied Captain Knox's mission from 1802 to 1803. This is indicative of the lacuna that existed between new techniques in classification and the ability to popularise them through appropriate publications in order to advance colonial science. This section discusses the innovative methods by which Buchanan retrieved and stored his information using paper index slips that could be employed at will to compare, contrast and re-arrange his classifications. It also investigates how the EIC's rights of ownership over the knowledge produced from surveys and collections conflicted with Buchanan's personal goals as a botanist, leading him into direct confrontation in 1815 with India's Governor General, Lord Moira. The products of his surveys were considered by the EIC to be their intellectual property; a problem perhaps that Buchanan might have hoped would have been avoided had he been able to attain the appointment of Superintendent of Calcutta's Botanic Garden sooner.

Early in his career, Buchanan recognised the potential of paper index slips as a tool for bridging the divide between Linnaeus's simpler artificial method of classification and the greater versatility offered by the Jussieus's Natural System. Buchanan's active use of them signposts his participation during a transitional period in the late eighteenth century, when the interests of promoting colonial science came to the fore.[59] While systems of arranging and storing botanical information using individual paper index slips were not

56. Watson and Noltie, 'Career, Collections, Reports', 1.

57. 'Information overload' is the term used to describe the increasing amounts of knowledge presented in print and manuscript forms that needed to be analysed and understood. See Charmantier and Müller-Wille, 'Carl Linnaeus's Botanical Paper Slips', 215–238.

58. Watson and Noltie, 'Career, Collections, Reports', 1.

59. Edney, *Mapping an Empire*, 31.

novel, Buchanan applied them to the task of attaining colonial mastery over India's natural world by creating a scheme that combined Linnaeus and the Jussieus's methods of classification, so that they complemented, rather than competed with one another.[60] Buchanan believed that paper slips were the best option for dealing with a very large number of plants and reducing them to order, which he put to effective use during his Survey of Nepal, in which he described and classified between 1,100 and 1,200 plants, of which around 800–900 were new specimens. This herculean task was made easier by paper index slips, which provided a flexible system of classification that could be altered and adjusted as new plants were introduced into the order.

Paper index slips provided a means of resolving the divergence between Linnaeus's simpler Artificial Classification Method and the Jussieus's more versatile Natural Method; and they were the precursor of filing cards used by libraries and other institutions for decades.[61] They could be employed for recording, storing and retrieving botanical data, and their order shuffled like playing cards, juxtaposed and compared with other entries.[62] Information stored in this manner could be moved around at will. They offered a much more flexible way of dealing with 'information overload' than the common-place book, which had been in use as a popular way of storing information in one fixed place since the Middle Ages. The commonplace book took the form of a bound manuscript, subdivided into headings for individual topics, and was used by many famous, as well as more humble people to record anything from new ideas and philosophical musings, to recipes, medicinal cures, prose snippets, drawings and even well-loved poems and songs.[63] Commonplace books were also the choice of early naturalists, like John Covell (1638–1722), Master of Christ's College, Cambridge, who, from 1688, filled his book with sketches of flowers and other plants, noting their distinguishing characteristics.[64] As the subject grew in popularity and the empire expanded, scholars 'collected observations from specimens, annotated and excerpted new publications, and engaged with far-flung correspondence networks, all along developing their own common-placing techniques to process the information thus gained'.[65]

Isabelle Charmantier and Staffan Müller-Wille have described how, towards the end of his academic career, Carl Linnaeus used loose paper slips

---

60. LC/MS 403/1/2/3: Images from the collection of plant and animal paintings of Dr Francis Buchanan-Hamilton (1762–1829) drawn in the Kathmandu Valley, Nepal.
61. Charmantier and Müller-Wille, 'Carl Linnaeus's Botanical Paper Slips', 216.
62. Ibid.
63. For a discussion on the uses of commonplace books, see David Allan, *Commonplace Books and Reading in Georgian England* (Cambridge: Cambridge University Press, 2010).
64. Ibid., 30.
65. Charmantier and Müller-Wille, 'Carl Linnaeus's Botanical Paper Slips', 215.

as a means of dealing with 'information overload', when his many correspondents throughout the world inundated him with specimens.[66] But as they
have also explained, Linnaeus's adoption of this method late in his working
life was more for the purposes of expediency, rather than with any intention
of pioneering new methods of classification and storing material.[67] The use
of small pieces of hand-cut paper, about the size of a playing card, allowed
Linnaeus and his helpers to note down a plant's characteristics, to compare
species and to allocate names. As information was transferred into printed
form, some paper index slips were discarded, whilst others were retained
and reused. Although Linnaeus used them for practical purposes, without
thoughts of breaking new ground in taxonomy, Charmantier and Müller-
Wille have nevertheless viewed this innovation in 'paper-technology' in the
late eighteenth century as a revolutionary way of storing large quantities of
botanical data in an accessible form that could be continually updated and
re-ordered into any desired new classification.

The London Linnean Society holds examples of the actual paper index
slips and field notes that Buchanan produced during his stay in Nepal, which
have miraculously survived the ravages of time and climate to demonstrate
his ingenuity in evolving new techniques in classification suited to the conditions and environment there. Explaining in a letter to Smith how he set
about classifying his extensive collection of Nepalese plants, he wrote, 'an
index of the whole has been formed according to the Jussieus' arrangement,
but as each plant has a separate piece of paper any other arrangement may
be adopted'.[68] His modest statement set out in simple terms how, by using
this form of information management, he created a way of harmonising the
potentially divisive elements of the 'Artificial' and 'Natural' systems of classification. Whilst conveying the effectiveness of using the Jussieus's Natural
System for classifying a very large number of specimens, Buchanan had also
found the means of introducing more flexibility into taxonomy by incorporating other arrangements like Linnaeus's method.

Buchanan's advocacy of the technique of using paper index slips reveals
that despite being isolated in India from books and other research tools, he
was able to draw upon a web of global taxonomic knowledge propounded by
some of the greatest intellects in his discipline, including his contemporary,
the Swedish naturalist, Carl Peter Thunberg (1743–1828). As an 'apostle'
of Linnaeus, Thunberg spent many years collecting specimens for the great
man; his travels took him from South Africa to as far away as Japan, a
country where access for foreigners was restricted until 1868. Inspired by

---

66. Ibid., 216.
67. Ibid.
68. LC/GB–110/JES/COR/2/126: Francis Buchanan to Sir James Edward Smith (17 March 1806).

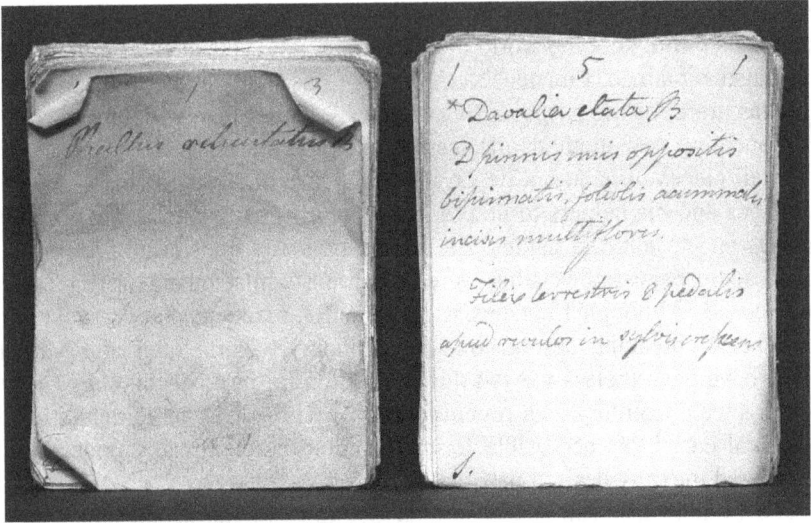

Figure 3.1. Paper index slips created by Francis Buchanan-Hamilton to arrange his Nepalese species according to Jussieu's Natural System of classification in preparation for his unpublished manuscript, 'Flora Nepalensis' (1802–1803). *Source:* **The Linnean Society (Ref. MS/399).**

Thunberg's botanical observations in his *Flora Japonica*,[69] Buchanan was able to make biogeographic links between the new plants that he discovered in Nepal and other sites throughout the world, which he noted were 'a mixture of European, Siberian, Japanese and Indian Genera'.[70] His ability to make biogeographic links signals the range of Buchanan's intellectual curiosity. Furthermore, it allowed him to consider emulating Thunberg's example in his *Flora Japonica* of publishing a separate *prodromus*[71] for his Nepalese collection. He thought that this might be an inexpensive way of avoiding the frustrating delays that he encountered in trying to obtain publications from the Court of Directors.[72]

Further evidence that Buchanan was part of a global network of natural history scholars may be found in a volume containing Buchanan's descriptions of fifty-nine animals and birds at the Barrackpore Menagerie, where he was placed in charge from 1803 to 1805.[73] It was the brainchild

---

69. Carl Peter Thunberg, *Flora Japonica: sistens plantas insularum Japonicarum* (Leipzig: I. G. Mulleriano, 1784).

70. LC/GB–110/JES/COR/2/127: Francis Buchanan to Sir James Edward Smith (20 March 1806).

71. In botanical terms, a *prodromus* describes a preliminary publication intended as the basis for a later, more comprehensive work.

72. Buchanan to Smith (20 March 1806).

73. BL/Mss Eur D94: Untitled volume of descriptions of animals and birds compiled between 1803–1805.

of the Governor General, Lord Wellesley, to whom he was also surgeon. Unfortunately, Buchanan and Wellesley's enthusiasm for the Barrackpore Menagerie was not shared by the EIC's directors, who refused to sanction a scheme to enlarge research into natural history.[74] Although Buchanan's descriptions of the animals at Barrackpore were the work of a copyist, on this occasion, his own voice can be heard as he disputed a discovery of a species of monkey by contemporary observers in India. It appeared that in their attempts to prove that their description of a species of male monkey, *Simia ferox*, was the same as that of the Comte de Buffon's, a Dr Shaw and a Mr Pennant suggested that Buffon had used a mutilated specimen, as some features of their discovery differed from Buffon's. Because Buffon's specimen lacked a tuft on its tail, Shaw and Pennant claimed that it did not give a true idea of the animal. As a respectful follower of the great French naturalist, Buchanan was quick to dismiss any suggestion that Buffon as 'an observer of this accuracy could be deceived on this point'.[75] The voice that commanded respect for Buffon in rejecting the possibility that the French naturalist could have erred resonated with a passionate involvement for his subject that was not reflected in his survey reports for the EIC. Yet, it can be detected on every occasion that Buchanan was engaged in botanising for his own personal satisfaction.

A large portion of Buchanan's correspondence with Smith was directed towards trying to persuade him to publish information that he had collected whilst he was travelling during his surveys. For example, his Mysore Survey had produced 131 drawings of plants, many previously unknown or badly described. He wrote to Smith, 'If you will take the trouble and think that any part of them will answer for your publications, it will give me great pleasure to send you the whole materials knowing that I can depend on your care and judgement'.[76] A similar situation pertained with his innovative classifications of the Nepal materials, as in the hope of persuading Smith to publish them, Buchanan offered him the whole of his collection, including the drawings, on the understanding that he returned the original manuscripts, which he needed for his future researches.[77] He also lobbied the Court of Directors, whose dilatoriness had caused him so much frustration over their lack of commitment towards bringing his discoveries to wider attention in publications. But being unable to acquire permanent recognition and a reputation for cultural authority within influential bodies in the metropole, like the London Linnean Society, or on the periphery at Calcutta's Botanic Garden, meant that much of

74. Ibid.
75. Ibid., 66.
76. Buchanan to Smith (17 March 1806).
77. Ibid., 3.

Figure 3.2. Watercolour drawing depicting a Gangetic fish, made by an unknown Indian artist under the supervision of Francis Buchanan-Hamilton (c. 1798–1800). *Source:* The British Library Board (Ref. Mss Eur E72 f47).

Buchanan's work remained unpublished, at least until after he retired in 1815, when he published solely for the benefit of the global scientific community.

Buchanan ended his long career with the EIC in dispute with Lord Moira, whom he sarcastically referred to as 'that generous protector of Science'.[78] Prior to Buchanan's final departure from India, Lord Moira had confiscated all the natural history drawings that had been made by the artists attached to the statistical survey, which Buchanan had applied to take with him, intending

---

78. LC/GB–110/JES/COR/2/136: Francis Buchanan to Sir James Edward Smith (Callander, 27 October 1815).

to present them to the EIC's directors. Even though the directors ordered the drawings to be dispatched to England immediately, Buchanan feared that they would come to harm in the interim, as he remarked, 'there was no knowing what that animal [Lord Moira] may do to them'.[79] His strong denunciation of India's Governor General demonstrates the depth of his frustration that had steadily built up over the years of his employment with the EIC.

Writing to Sir James Edward Smith in October 1815, after his return from India, he again referred to the Governor General in derogatory tones, describing him as a 'vain empty creature'.[80] By seizing all the natural history drawings, work commissioned by indigenous artists during his surveys of India, Lord Moira had disrupted Buchanan's retirement plans. He had intended to use some of them to help him publish a study of Gangetic fish, leading him to consider abandoning this important project entirely. He did eventually manage to obtain a sufficient quantity of drawings to continue with this work, which he later published.[81] In November 1816, a year after his retirement, Buchanan was still locked in dispute with the Court of Directors of the EIC, and he therefore resolved never to ask them again for any drawing, manuscript or specimens.[82] He wrote once again to Smith telling him that he was disgusted with the EIC's treatment of him and that he was unable to even obtain temporary use of the natural history materials that he had given to them, so that he could work on his publication.[83]

The next section concludes this chapter by considering how the EIC's treatment of Buchanan's survey reports and other materials resulted in the knowledge that they contained becoming fragmented. This created a lack of coherence and continuity within Buchanan's archive that was ultimately limiting to his ambition to participate in the advancement of colonial science and diminished his opportunities of becoming more widely known as an authority on his subject.

THE FRAGMENTED ARCHIVE OF BUCHANAN'S SURVEYS AND ASSORTED *MATERIA BOTANICA*

Although Buchanan produced a large body of work as a surveyor for the EIC, which offered detailed observations and many statistics, it rarely contained

---

79. Ibid.
80. Ibid.
81. Ibid.
82. LC/GB–110/JES/COR/2/137: Francis Buchanan to Sir James Edward Smith (23 April 1816).
83. LC/GB–110/JES/COR/2/138: Francis Buchanan to Sir James Edward Smith (24 November 1816).

any new intellectual insights.[84] Therefore, his surveys alone cannot be classified as containing 'pathbreaking discoveries', or intellectually defining a new
discipline, as Sir William Jones's and Thomas Munro's work had done. They
cannot claim cultural authority, nor, based on David Ludden's definition, do
they qualify him to be named as an active agent of imperialism. As previously
noted, his official duties as a government surveyor did not allow him the time
for revision of reports, let alone the leisure to generate intellectual concepts
that might influence new methodologies for plant collections.

The British Library holds a considerable volume of survey reports and
other material gathered by Buchanan throughout the twenty years of his
working life in India, but much of it is in the form of copies and sole author-
ship cannot be definitively attributed to Buchanan. Information contained in
survey reports was often broken up and copies distributed amongst various
interested parties, like the Home Office and the Surveyor General's Department, making it problematic to identify Buchanan's authentic voice as their
author. Furthermore, as the information in survey reports was often shared
between various government departments, the importance that the recipients
attributed to the contents of their copies varied in accordance with each
department's particular concerns and responsibilities.

Officers like Buchanan were accustomed to writing their field notes at the
end of each day's exploration, on the understanding that clean, neat copies
would be made after they returned to base; but by whom, and how long after
the field work occurred, cannot be known with any certainty. This raises
questions regarding the accuracy and integrity of these sources, especially
as it cannot be established definitively that the copies were always edited or
checked by Buchanan. In addition, variations in the quality of handwriting, as
well as difficulties in deciphering notes made in the field, do not readily permit the survey reports to be authenticated as accurate copies of Buchanan's
original documents. Therefore, because it cannot be ascertained beyond all
reasonable doubt that copies were exact replicas of Buchanan's work, his
cultural authority over their content was unavoidably compromised.

Sir David Prain (1857–1944), Superintendent of the Calcutta Botanic
Garden from 1898 to 1905, and subsequently Director of the Royal Botanic
Gardens at Kew, was one of the earliest modern historians to comment on
Buchanan's work. His paper of 1905 claimed that Buchanan's original 'Burmah
Journal' was never published in full; consequently, information from it has
been scattered in numerous sources, copied from the original to fulfil the
requirements of various departments within the EIC.[85] A journal comprising

---

84. See additional Francis Buchanan-Hamilton papers, 1800–1802.
85. David Prain, 'A Sketch of the Life of Francis Hamilton (Once Buchanan)', *Annals of the Royal Botanic Garden, Calcutta* 10 (1905): 1–75.

over 250 immaculately handwritten pages may also be found in the British Library, entitled Buchanan's 'Burmah Journal'.[86] It describes in detail his journey to Amarapura between April and November 1795, reaching the royal capital in July. The 'Journal' lists information on such diverse subjects as the extraction of saltpetre for the king's gunpowder, to descriptions of the differences between the many racial groups that he encountered on his journey through Burma.[87] Like the aforementioned works, this too is a copy.

George R. Kaye and Edward H. Johnston have also suggested in their *Catalogue of Manuscripts in European Languages: Minor Collections and Miscellaneous Manuscripts* in the India Office Library that provenance was difficult to establish.[88] Despite the uncertainties concerning attribution, at least two copies of Buchanan's 'Burmah Journal' were made (now held in the British Library), which fit the description given in Kaye and Johnston's compendium. Although their content is identical, they are clearly by different copyists, which Kaye and Johnston suggest may be the same copies that disappeared before 1857 and were later rediscovered. Although apparently alike page-for-page, the first copy appears older than the second and by a different hand. There is a note on page 106 of the first copy instructing the copyist not to write across the margin of the page, indicating that it has been copied under supervision. Therefore, it can be safely concluded that this item is not Buchanan's original journal.[89]

Kaye and Johnston's catalogue also describes a manuscript created by an unknown author between 1824 and 1829 entitled, 'Extracts and Observations Respecting the Dominions of Ava'.[90] Created more than twenty years after Buchanan undertook his mission to Ava, this document's opening remarks, allegedly written by Buchanan in his 'Burmah Journal', note:

> The policy of the barbarous nations who inhabit the Peninsula to the east of the Ganges, where the only [*sic*] chapman of foreign merchandize is a despotic sovereign almost precludes the possibility of a European traveller obtaining an authentic information much less any intimate knowledge of the statistics or even geographical features of these realms.[91]

---

86. BL/IOR/H/687: Extracts relating to geographical subjects from Dr Francis Buchanan's 'Burmah Journal' (20 March 1795–23 November 1795).

87. Ibid.

88. George R. Kaye and Edward H. Johnston, *Catalogue of Manuscripts in European Languages, Vol. II, Part II: Minor Collections and Miscellaneous Manuscripts* (London: His Majesty's Stationary Office, 1937), 389. See, BL/Mss Eur D106/1–47: Extracts, compiled c. 1824–1829, from various papers and maps relating to Burma and Assam, including extracts from a journal kept by Dr Francis Buchanan-Hamilton.

89. BL/Mss Eur C12–13: Papers of Francis Buchanan-Hamilton. See Kaye and Johnston, *Catalogue of Manuscripts*, 585.

90. Extracts, compiled c. 1824–1829, 2.

91. Ibid.

As Kaye and Johnston have emphasised, these 'extracts and observations contain no direct quotations from Buchanan and only meagre information'.[92] Consisting of forty-seven handwritten pages, sketchily arranged, the manuscript contains no insightful comments and purports to use Buchanan's 'Journal' of his 1795 mission to Ava with Colonel Symes as its source, concurrently with other journeys and surveys to Burma. They also make clear that this entry has little connection with their main catalogue entry for Buchanan.[93] Its anonymous author's assessment of fragments from Buchanan's 'Journal' represents a very poor evaluation of his intellectual capabilities, and must therefore be viewed as a deliberate misinterpretation of his work for political, rather than scholarly purposes.

The author appears to have used Buchanan's 'Burmah Journal' to rail against the damage caused to foreign trade by a 'despotic sovereign' in Burma, noting that although Buchanan supposedly questioned intelligent persons of all ranks during his journey up the Irrawaddy River, his observations did not possess the accuracy of science. However, the writer conceded that they were sufficient for the purposes of native travellers and, in the absence of anything better, must be considered extremely valuable.[94] Such comments do not appear to be compatible with Buchanan's meticulous and detailed scholarship and working practices. As one of the pioneers of natural history exploration and botanical classification in the early nineteenth century, it is difficult to attribute these off-hand remarks to Buchanan, who had demonstrated empathy towards the egalitarian Hinayana Buddhist society that he had encountered on his mission to Ava.[95]

CONCLUDING REMARKS

In summary, an unknowable number of copies of Buchanan's survey reports were circulated for the benefit of various government departments and interested bodies, thus signifying their use for commercial and political purposes. As the brief discussion of archival materials attributed to Buchanan has shown, it is not within these fragmented and widely dispersed accounts of his survey work that we must look in order to detect the true breadth of his authority as a leading botanist. It is instead to his personal correspondence, principally with Sir James Edward Smith, and also his Asian commentaries, that we must turn in order to hear his authentic voice, which identifies

---

92. Kaye and Johnston, *Catalogue of Manuscripts*, 389.
93. Ibid., 156, 585.
94. Extracts, compiled c. 1824–1829, 2.
95. Buchanan, 'On the Religion and Literature of the Burmas', 163–308.

Buchanan as a pathfinder in the exploration and classification of India's natural history.

Forced by ill health to leave India in 1815, Buchanan was no longer able to hold down the influential position of Superintendent of the Calcutta Botanic Garden, which he had so long desired. His tenure lasted barely six months. It is therefore difficult not to surmise that the restrictions of his arduous survey-ing duties on behalf of the Company, over the course of twenty years, had embittered Buchanan and prevented him from realising his true vocation as a botanist and scientist. His dependence upon the goodwill of his mentor James Edward Smith, and disputes over the rights of ownership by the EIC of the drawings and specimens that he had collected, meant that he could not devote his time to securing scholarly publications. Instead, his energies had gone into producing survey reports that, as government property, were broken up and distributed according to the requirements of various government departments. As previously noted, before his departure from India, he became embroiled in a dispute with the Governor General, Lord Moira, and the directors of the EIC regarding the ownership of the large quantity of natural history materials that he had acquired during his years working for the Company. Although disappointment and disillusionment afflicted the early years of Buchanan's retirement in Scotland, he nevertheless devoted all his leisure time to classi-fying his specimens and becoming an active member of the Linnean Society, which he joined on his return from India.

For the remainder of his life in Scotland, Buchanan dedicated himself to the task of analysing all the material he had collected and managed to retain during his tours of Northern and Southern India, resolving to work and pub-lish solely for the scientific world.[96] His time-consuming labour and dedica-tion to the practice and understanding of colonial flora has provided a vital source for taxonomists working on the plants of South Asia.[97] During his retirement, he set about using his unique knowledge and the experience that he had gained as a botanist in India to write a commentary based on all the plants he had observed there, and which he could also identify and compare with the pre-Linnaean works by the botanist, George Eberhard Rumphius (c. 1627–1702).[98] Only a botanist with the breadth and depth of Buchanan's knowledge and experience could have produced these commentaries, which made close comparisons between specimens of the living plants that he had seen in India and the pre-Linnaean texts described by Rumphius and his fellow

---

96. Vicziany, 'Imperialism, Botany and Statistics', 657.
97. Ibid.
98. George Eberhard Rumphius was the Resident and Chief Merchant of the Dutch EIC at Ambon; Buchanan used his study and that of his contemporary, Hendrik van Rheede, to make important com-parisons between Asia's flora.

botanist, Hendrik van Rheede (1636–1691).[99] His commentary on the first
volume of the *Herbarium Amboinense* was published by the Edinburgh Wernerian Society in 1823.[100] This volume is a tribute to the scale of Buchanan's
scholarly ambition and the scientific importance of the commentaries that he
produced, with the result that they have earned him the reputation of a distinguished botanist. His commentaries have been appreciated by botanists for
decades since they were first published in the 1820s and they are still useful
even today.

Through the science of botany, Buchanan aspired to become an heir to the
extensive network of collaborators that was created in the mid-eighteenth
century between Europeans like the French academician, Georges-Louis
Buffon, and his English counterparts at the Royal Society. With the help of
many correspondents throughout the world, these European scientists began
the great task of understanding a vast cornucopia of wonders in the natural
world of their respective countries' newly acquired colonial possessions. As
an Orientalist, Francis Buchanan-Hamilton was the beneficiary of their contributions to colonial science and deserving of greater recognition than simply
as a correspondent, or '*petit artisan*', who carried out surveys and collected
data to be remitted to the EIC's Court of Directors in London.

Therefore, it is through his skills as a botanist that Buchanan's intellectual
capabilities and his contribution to colonial science are truly evident, as his
passion for his subject propelled his desire to become part of a global web of
great naturalists and botanical scientists. It is his achievements in this sphere
that confirm his cultural authority and his status as an active agent of imperialism. Their value to the history of colonial science may be considered of
greater significance than his activities as a surveyor and collector of data for
the EIC.

In the next chapter, we turn to the work of another Orientalist, Francis
Whyte Ellis, whose affinity with place also allowed him to claim cultural
authority through his discovery of the derivation of Southern India's languages and its attendant links with the ancient social structure of indigenous
land tenure. His contribution towards extending knowledge through collaboration with Indian scholars deserves to be far better known. Ellis's early
death and his decision not to publish his scholarly findings, possibly due to
the burden of his official duties as a magistrate with the EIC, have deprived
the academic world of the output of a rare intellect, whose appreciation of the
history of indigenous societies helped him to produce specialised knowledge
about pre-colonial India.

---

99. Vicziany, 'Imperialism, Botany and Statistics', 658.
100. Francis Buchanan-Hamilton, 'Commentary on the *Herbarium Amboinense*', *Memoirs of the Wernerian Natural Society* 5, no. 2 (1824–1825): 307–384.

Chapter 4

Francis Whyte Ellis: 'A Nearly Perfect Embodiment of Orientalism as Colonial Policy'[1]

INTRODUCTION

Like Francis Buchanan-Hamilton, the subject of the previous chapter, Francis Whyte Ellis devoted all of his spare time to scholarly pursuits, whilst also maintaining a prolific output as a covenanted servant of the EIC. Buchanan's passion was for botanising, whereas Ellis immersed himself in the study of Southern India's languages, history and antiquities, a subject which he pursued for over twenty years, following his arrival in India in 1796. Ellis entered the Madras Civil Service, initially filling the offices of Assistant and Deputy Secretary, until he was appointed Secretary to the Board of Revenue in 1802. He was selected for the position of judge and magistrate at Komba-konum in 1806 and thereafter, transferred to the *zillah* (district) of Masulipa-tam in 1808. By 1809, he had risen to become the Collector of Land Customs, a post which he held until his appointment as the Collector of Madras in 1810. He continued to occupy this important office until his untimely death in 1819 at the age of forty-two,[2] which occurred after he had allegedly taken poison by mistake, instead of medicine.[3]

---

1. Thomas R. Trautmann, *Languages and Nations: The Dravidian Proof in Colonial Madras* (Berkeley, CA: University of California Press, 2006), 79.
2. BL/Mss Eur F370/1544: James T. Rutnam to Professor R.E. Asher regarding Francis Ellis (16 May 1977).
3. Transcript of the Register of the Supreme Court of Judicature Madras (July 1819), British Library. Francis Ellis communicated his last wishes from his death bed at Ramnad to Rungiah Naik, one of his *dubashes*. See Ellis's note to his servant Rungiah Naik (Ramnad, 9 March 1819), written the day before his death and copied into the Registry of the Supreme Court of Judicature, Madras, which will be discussed more fully in this chapter. The court transcript recorded that Ellis had bor-rowed money in November 1818 at 6 per cent interest from a man named James Scriven, in order to buy land, and the loan was due for repayment from March 1819 in four monthly instalments. Rungiah Naik was instructed to repay the whole of the debt owing on the Bond, although the transcript stated

At the time of his death, Ellis was staying at Ramnad with Rous Peter, the Collector of Madurai, while visiting the district in search of ancient manuscripts.[4] By all accounts, Rous Peter was negligent in discharging his duties as the local collector and the subject of many complaints, which Ellis may also have been investigating.[5] Shortly after his death, in July 1819, all of Ellis's personal property in India was auctioned at Madurai and Madras, under the orders of the Administrator General. Unfortunately, the majority of his private papers, save for a few fragments, were either lost or destroyed (some were even burned as kindling by Rous Peter's cook).[6] Ellis's failure to appoint a literary editor, as his friend John Leyden had done in nominating William Erskine (1773–1852),[7] meant that there was no one with sufficient scholarly authority to retrieve and edit his research materials after his death. This might have resulted in more of his work being published posthumously, allowing his scholarship to be saved and appreciated.[8]

Nevertheless, these sad events have not tarnished Ellis's reputation as one of the most accomplished and sensitive of the early Orientalist scholars.[9] Over half a century after Ellis's death, Walter Elliot (1803–1887),[10] the Scottish naturalist and Orientalist, was still lamenting his loss to the learned world.[11] Quoting the Madras Literary Society's opinion of their distinguished founder, Elliot wrote in a letter to the *Journal of the Indian Antiquary* in 1875 that Ellis was 'pre-eminent for indefatigable and successful work into the languages, history and learning of Southern India, for extensive knowledge, ancient and modern, Oriental and European, for accurate judgement and elegant taste'.[12] But as Ellis had resolved to dedicate his life up to the age of forty to research and investigation and to not write up any of his findings, 'he carried to his early tomb the stores he [had] accumulated and before that time prepared nothing for communication to the world'.[13]

This chapter endeavours to situate Francis Whyte Ellis within a period of plural cultural enlightenment centred upon Tanjore and the districts of the

---

that Scriven had died insolvent for the principal sum of 30,000 star pagodas. Insolvency was not uncommon amongst the European population of the Presidency, and from the information in the Court Transcript, it would appear that Ellis's indebtedness would be resolved after his death. See also comment in a 'Letter from Walter Elliot', *Journal of the Indian Antiquary* 4 (1875): 220.

4. Ramnad: A permanently settled Zamindari estate that had been under British influence since the 1790s.

5. For further details about Rous Peter, see BL/IOR/E/4/937/317–345: Despatches to Madras (Original Drafts, May 1829–September 1829).

6. Trautmann, *Languages and Nations*, 79.

7. William Erskine: Scottish Orientalist and historian.

8. Trautmann, *Languages and Nations*, 81.

9. Cohn, *Colonialism and Its Forms of Knowledge*, 52.

10. Walter Elliot served in the Madras Presidency from 1820–1860.

11. 'Letter from Walter Elliot', 220.

12. Ibid.

13. Ibid.

Madras Presidency during the first decades of the nineteenth century. It was characterised by an intense desire on Ellis's part to advance local knowledge, not only to consolidate the power of Orientalism through dedicated institutions like the College at Fort St. George but also to define the importance of the periphery as a sphere of knowledge in its own right. During his relatively brief but significant time in India, Ellis interacted within a social and intellectual world that included not only his colleagues at the EIC – learned scholars like John Leyden and Colin Mackenzie – but also with wider knowledge spaces and particularly, one important contact zone,[14] which emanated chiefly from the Court of Raja Serfoji II at Tanjore. Spanning more than three decades from 1798, this progressive environment attracted both European and indigenous actors, and was a place where Ellis made connections with intellectual and cultural developments on a global and local level.[15] As a centre of learning and enlightenment, the Tanjore Court exposed Ellis to new ideas that informed his concept of Southern Indian Orientalism and its place in the colonial order. His other notable contacts, often through indigenous intermediaries, were with local monasteries, known also as *mathas*, which were the repositories of ancient Tamil manuscripts, and also with the Halle Lutheran Mission. Operated from the Danish settlement of Tranquebar, near Tanjore, the missionaries there included Christopher Samuel John (1747–1813), who was dedicated to initiating radical reforms in the education system of the local population.[16]

In writing this chapter, I am indebted to Dr Savithri Preetha Nair, whose book on the Tanjore Enlightenment[17] inspired me to situate Francis Ellis within that milieu, if only for a short period between 1806 and 1808, whilst he was working as a magistrate at nearby Kombakonum. Although Francis Ellis is only mentioned briefly in Nair's book, in connection with the installation of a printing press, her scholarship, together with that of Thomas R. Trautmann, has allowed me to contextualise Ellis in this rare moment of plural enlightenment in South India's history, when the Tanjore Court facilitated rewarding encounters between diverse actors from both sides of the colonial divide. As this chapter will endeavour to show, Ellis's encounters at Tanjore influenced his later scholarship on the Tamil language and literature, and also inspired him to found the College at Fort St. George in 1812, where the staff was composed of European and indigenous teachers.

---

14. See Pratt, *Imperial Eyes*, 6–7.
15. Savithri Preetha Nair, '". . . Of Real Use to the People": The Tanjore Printing Press and the Spread of Useful Knowledge', *The Indian Economic and Social History Review* 48, no. 4 (2011): 499.
16. Ibid., 508.
17. Savithri Preetha Nair, *Raja Serfoji II: Science, Medicine and Enlightenment in Tanjore* (New Delhi: Routledge, 2014).

As a result of his encounters at Raja Serfoji's Court and other experiences, Ellis's contribution to our understanding of how pre-colonial societies functioned and their relationship to language was far greater than his short lifespan allowed. Ellis's official position with the EIC, as Collector of Land Customs, permitted him to gain intimate knowledge of ancient systems of land tenure, known as Mirasi Right. He supported the retention of this tradition, where landowners were obliged to maintain privileges and obligations that respected local customs, and he opposed Thomas Munro's attempts to introduce a new system of Ryotwari land tenure, which favoured the colonial state.

Despite the scarcity of his published output, Ellis was especially celebrated for his scholarship on the languages of Southern India and his reading of its texts, which led him to propose the theory that the major Dravidian languages were a family distinct from those of Northern India, as discovered by Sir William Jones (1746–1794) and his circle in Calcutta.[18] Although the argument for the Dravidian Proof was formally published in 1856 by Robert Caldwell (1814–1891), its theory was first articulated by Ellis in a dissertation contained in the 'Appendix' of Alexander Duncan Campbell's *Grammar of the Teloogoo Language*,[19] first published by the College at Fort St. George in 1816.[20] Composed in conjunction with his colleagues for the benefit of the College's junior students, this was Francis Whyte Ellis's major linguistic discovery.

Despite the tragic loss of the archive of one of early colonial India's most distinguished Oriental scholars, and the limited material available as sources for study about his life and work, there has been a revival of interest by contemporary scholars to trace fragments of his studies that exist among the papers of his contemporaries and others. Through the publication of his magisterial work, *Languages and Nations: The Dravidian Proof in Colonial Madras*, Thomas R. Trautmann has placed Francis Ellis in the pantheon of the great Orientalists, alongside men like Sir William Jones and Henry Thomas Colebrooke (1765–1837). In his book, Trautmann pays homage to Ellis's great scholarship, according him recognition not only for his extensive knowledge of the Tamil language but most importantly, for being among the first to study the comparative philology of the Dravidian languages. Although this chapter cannot hope to add anything to Thomas Trautmann's superb study, it will endeavour to evaluate the ways that the cultural, political and social spaces in which Ellis and his colleagues operated created conjunctures that eventually saw the demise of Orientalism as colonial policy.

---

18. Trautmann, *Languages and Nations*, 79.
19. Alexander D. Campbell, *A Grammar of the Teloogoo Language, Commonly Termed the Gentoo, Peculiar to the Hindoos Inhabiting the North Eastern Provinces of the Indian Peninsula* (Madras: College Press, 1816).
20. Trautmann, *Languages and Nations*, 136.

In eighteenth-century European thought, languages and nations were held to be analogous, as both their histories were believed to be governed by genealogical relations. Thus, the genealogical relations that were established within language families could be used to increase understanding of the relationships between Southern India's native populations. Principally comprising Tamils, being the earliest inhabitants of Dravid'am, the South-West division of India, they also included the Cannadiya and Telugu people, who at an early period were more intermixed with strangers from North and Central India.[21] At the College at Fort St. George, Ellis and his fellow intellectuals pioneered an understanding of the diversity of Southern India's languages by arguing that they were distinct from the Northern Indo-European language family, which was based on Sanskrit. Through their study of the region's comparative philology and its ancient roots, they established kinship links between the languages which presaged a comparable understanding of kinship links in ethnology, thereby providing a pathway for the study of ethnic origins and their history.[22] In due course, kinship relationships became an object of comparative study that developed into the independent discipline that we know today as anthropology.

The achievements of Ellis and his colleagues' investigations of these instruments of colonial power placed them at the frontier of the EIC's mission to consolidate Orientalism as government policy in Southern India, in which learned societies and institutions like the College at Fort St. George were vital elements. An important feature of that policy was its aspiration to conserve as many pre-existing customs and institutions as possible, for which a knowledge of Indian languages and their learned texts was deemed necessary. As a practical example of how Orientalism influenced colonial policy, the Madras Presidency continued to maintain native courts, where civil matters like marriage, property and inheritance were still governed by Hindu and Muhammadan laws.[23] In order to meet the demand for knowledge about how these religious laws functioned, Ellis prepared a list of what he considered were the most important Sanskrit works of Dharmashastric literature for use by Brahmins for the administration of Hindu law in the Madras Presidency. He recommended that they should be translated into Tamil verse, so that Hindu students in the College at Fort St. George could learn them by rote in the traditional manner.[24]

---

21. William H. Bayley and William Hudleston (eds.), *Papers on Mirasi Right Selected from the Records of Government and Published by Permission* (Madras: Pharoah & Co, 1862), 229–286; containing Ellis's replies in 'Appendix 1 to the Question of Mirasi Right', 252.

22. See Trautmann, *Languages and Nations*, 1–41.

23. Ibid., 79.

24. Cohn, *Colonialism and Its Forms of Knowledge*, 52.

However, beyond the walls of the College another language prevailed, namely 'the language of legal chaos and confusion', that the British maintained they had found upon their arrival in India, 'being the result of Oriental despotism and the infirm Mughal Empire'.[25] Throughout the early decades of the nineteenth century, 'discussions about the mismanaged administration of justice in India repeatedly turned to this image of pre-colonial turmoil, in order to justify new forms of colonial intervention and to disguise the Company's own failures in administering justice'.[26] While Ellis and his fellow scholars were undertaking pioneering scholarship on the comparative philology of Southern India, the moral and legal climate within indigenous and European society became increasingly disordered. This frequently led the EIC's Court of Directors to censure misconduct and judicial mismanagement amongst its officials and their 'native' assistants. In the end, this contributed towards undermining the power of an Orientalist colonial policy, which 'aspired to rule India in accord with Indian culture', whose entrenched power Thomas Babington Macaulay's (1800–1859) reforms were designed to eradicate.[27]

Nevertheless, working at the frontiers of colonial knowledge, Ellis and his fellow scholars at Fort St. George successfully fulfilled colonial policy requirements at that time by supplying Oriental knowledge intended to consolidate the EIC's authority. In fact, throughout his short life Ellis proved to be the exemplar of 'a nearly perfect embodiment of Orientalism as colonial policy'.[28] It is therefore in this context that this chapter seeks to investigate the work of a man whose scholarship distinguished him as a pioneer, profoundly versed in knowledge about Dravidian languages and their culture, before Macaulay's attempts to institute uniform legal equality through codification of the law. Initially driven by anxieties about European criminality and the lack of jurisdiction over Englishmen in the interior of the country, Macaulay's reforms inevitably introduced a colonial rule of difference, which withstood all attempts throughout the nineteenth century to implement an impartial and uniform rule of law.[29] But instead they opened up a chasm between Europeans and the 'native' population, so that the motivation to accommodate Indian customs and culture within the boundaries of colonial rule was gradually destroyed.

As one of the most gifted of the early Orientalists, Ellis demonstrated his acuity regarding Indian scholarly practice through his understanding of the way that Indian reasoning was based on the habit of their education, which

---

25. Elizabeth Kolsky, 'Codification and the Rule of Colonial Difference: Criminal Procedure in British India', *Law and History Review* 23, no. 3 (2005): 652.

26. Ibid.

27. Trautmann, *Languages and Nations*, 80.

28. Ibid.

29. Kolsky, 'Codification and the Rule', 649, 653.

'rested on the memorisation of concentrated not diffuse knowledge'.[30] In this way, indigenous methods of rote learning functioned as a tap root that allowed the scholar or the pundit to draw upon their store of knowledge to explain or illustrate his pronouncements.[31] Rote learning is still extant today in some South and Southeast Asian schools, particularly in Myanmar. Knowledge was far easier to comprehend in verse form in the Tamil language and Ellis commented that 'all knowledge and science in India from the lowest to the highest form of logic and theology were acquired by committing to memory technical verses'.[32] In pioneering an understanding of the relationship between languages and a coherent social organisation and the philosophy upon which it was founded, Ellis's scholarship in turn became a taproot upon which subsequent lineages of colonial knowledge could draw. However, as mentioned, before this could occur Francis Ellis was to become deeply influenced by a formative cultural encounter at Tanjore's Royal Court that linked people, practices and places in a unique knowledge space, which is discussed in the next section.[33]

FORMATIVE CULTURAL ENCOUNTERS AT THE TANJORE COURT

Francis Ellis's seminal experiences occurred early in his career, when he came into contact with 'a Tamil centre of enlightenment' at the Court of Raja Serfoji II in Tanjore, frequented by members of European society, who interacted with the Raja's trained experts and scholars and many other visitors.[34] Serfoji's Court became a centre of unprecedented intellectual ferment in early nineteenth-century Southern India, where he presided over 'a rich flow of "late-Enlightenment" ideas, objects and natural knowledge'.[35] These local and global connections allowed the Raja to be considered, even when only in his twenties, as a 'man of knowledge' and his Court at Tanjore to be 'recognised as a "centre" by European society of the period'.[36] These ideas flowed principally from four important networks; one was derived from the metropole/EIC after the fall of Tipu Sultan in 1799 had obliged Serfoji to cede Tanjore to the British. The next two were created through links with

30. BL/IOR/F/4/556/51: Francis W. Ellis to the Governor of Madras (12 May 1814). See also Cohn, *Colonialism and Its Forms of Knowledge*, 52.
31. Ibid.
32. Ellis to the Governor of Madras (12 May 1814).
33. Nair, *Raja Serfoji II*, 15.
34. Ibid., 15–16. See also 'Introduction', xx.
35. Nair, 'Native Collecting and Natural Knowledge', 281–282.
36. Ibid., 284.

Protestant missionary networks at the Danish Mission settlement at Tranquebar, and also with the Baptist Mission at Serampore near Calcutta. Lastly,
private European and indigenous collecting networks and educational and
scientific institutions became major contributors to Raja Serfoji's quest to
acquire useful knowledge through discovery, personal interactions, pilgrim-
age and collecting.

Serfoji was educated in Madras by German Pietist missionaries, where he
was tutored by Christian Frederick Schwartz and Wilhelm Gericke of the
London-based Society for the Propagation of Christian Knowledge.[37] As a
result of his education, Serfoji was motivated by 'a particular configuration
of ideas and practices relating to European science in the eighteenth century'
that inspired him to build a collection of remarkable objects, which reflected
contemporary knowledge on both a global platform and a local platform.[38]
Modelled on the *Kunstkammer* that were popular in Europe in the seventeenth and eighteenth centuries, Serfoji received many visitors to his cabinet
of curiosities, who were fascinated to view the collection that he had built up
of specimens from art and nature, as well as scientific objects from Europe
and elsewhere.[39]

By drawing together global and local networks in response to the Western encounter during the first three decades of the nineteenth century, the
Tanjore Court became an intellectual powerhouse, where Serfoji assembled
a wide range of people from the locality and from overseas. Their skills,
practices and theories, both severally and collectively, incorporated 'elements of process and accumulation'.[40] In her description of this phenom-
enon, Savithri Preetha Nair has turned the conventional idea of Bruno
Latour's centre of calculation[41] on its head, where Tanjore acted as the
centre and the metropole as the periphery.[42] The cross-pollination of ideas
that occurred at the Raja's Court fostered an interchange of knowledge
between protagonists from diverse cultures and social backgrounds. For
example, one of the native pundits who resided at Serfoji's Court was the
Maratha Brahmin, Subba Row, who, as noted in Chapter 2, became one of
Major Colin Mackenzie's most important translators.[43] These encounters

---

37. Ibid., 283.
38. Indira V. Peterson, 'The Cabinet of King Serfoji of Tanjore: A European Collection in Early
Nineteenth-Century India', *Journal of the History of Collections* 11, no. 1 (1999): 72.
39. Ibid., 71.
40. Wade Chambers and Gillespie, *Locality in the History of Science*, 221–240.
41. Bruno Latour's influential model defined a 'Centre of Calculation' as a learned institution
which promoted the circulation of knowledge, people and objects between metropole and colony.
Nair has reversed the conventional Latourian framework so that Tanjore became the centre. See also
Latour, *Science in Action*.
42. Nair, 'Native Collecting and Natural Knowledge', 281–282.
43. Ibid.

Figure 4.1. Portrait of Raja Serfoji II gifted to King Frederik VI of Denmark. *Source:* John Lee, National Museum of Denmark (Ref. Dc.197).

resulted in mutual enrichment, which formed the basis of Ellis's philosophy of Orientalism as a strategy compatible with colonial governance. It also suggested to Ellis the possibilities for a similar future engagement of ideas centred upon the College at Fort St. George, which he founded in 1812 under the auspices of the colonial government in Madras, establishing a printing press there the following year. In due course, several teachers from Tanjore found their way to the College.[44] Even after Ellis's death in 1819, advice was still being sought from the Tanjore Court when, in 1829, it was

---

44. Stuart H. Blackburn, *Print, Folklore and Nationalism in Colonial Southern India* (Delhi: Permanent Black, 2003), 96.

approached to suggest a suitable candidate to fill the post of Deputy Tamil Headmaster at the College.[45]

Ellis was introduced to Raja Serfoji around 1806 by the current Resident, William Blackburne (1764–1839), who described him as someone 'whose meritorious & extraordinary acquisition of Native Languages & progress in Indian Literature was highly commendable'.[46] He encountered a hybrid expression of Enlightenment ideas of progress far from the metropole that circulated amongst the diverse actors whom Serfoji received at his Court. EIC officials, notably the Resident, Benjamin Torin (1762–1839), were among the Europeans who frequented the Court, as well as surgeons, medical men (Serfoji had a particular interest in medical matters), missionaries and indigenous scholars. Serfoji accumulated an extensive library which Company scholars were invited to use, many books having been acquired through his friend Torin following his return to England. Consequently, all of the individuals who congregated at the Tanjore Court assisted Serfoji in one way or another to acquire 'useful knowledge', by obtaining objects, providing technical know-how and labour, or debating new ideas.

At a time when there were few printing presses in Southern India, apart from the ones later established by Ellis at Fort St. George and the missionaries at Tranquebar, Serfoji commissioned the typographer and Orientalist Sanskrit scholar in England, Charles Wilkins, to design Devanagari types[47] for the press that he wished to establish. By 1802, his objective was achieved when a printing press was installed at the palace in order to print traditional literature in the Marathi and Sanskrit languages.[48] However, as it was Serfoji's mission to unite Tamil and European intellectual thinkers in order to circulate 'useful knowledge' which articulated enlightened modernity to his people, there was soon a requirement for the installation of a second printing press.[49] In late 1806, it became expedient to source the appropriate fonts for the languages most commonly used in Tanjore, namely Tamil or Telugu.[50] Ellis was involved with the missionaries and the Madras Agent, John Hunter, in assisting Serfoji to obtain the necessary Devanagari types for his scheme to

45. Nair, 'Raja Serfoji II', 11.

46. Nair, '". . . Of Real Use to the People"', 519.

47. Devanagari: The script written from left to right used for over 120 spoken Indo-Aryan languages, including Hindi, Nepali, Marathi, Maithili, Awadhi, Newari and Bhojpuri, and also for writing classical Sanskrit texts.

48. Nair, 'The Tanjore Printing Press', 501.

49. Ibid., 526.

50. Blackburn, *Print, Folklore and Nationalism*: 'Because there was a limited supply of good types for printing in Tamil and Telugu and those were of inferior quality, Ellis suggested that local goldsmiths should be employed by the Government until artisans could be trained to cut proper types and be trained to operate the presses' (79). 'By 1862, sufficient improvements had been made to the fonts, as well as standardisation of spelling, punctuation and orthography had been made for them to be used in Winslow's dictionary' (126).

publish printed materials in the Tamil and Telugu languages.[51] It was an experience that he put to good use some years later when, as mentioned earlier, he set up his own press at the College at Fort St. George in 1813.

Unfortunately, in his professional capacity as District Magistrate, Ellis incurred the anger of Raja Serfoji for his overzealous application of the law. Although the Raja was greatly disturbed by Ellis's interference in an internal judicial matter, he bore him no ill-will on an intellectual level, and they maintained their contact through correspondence after Ellis was transferred to another post in 1808. Their quarrel arose because a dependant of the Raja had ordered the use of torture against the wrong man in order to collect taxes. Ellis summoned the Raja's employee to Court, who failed to appear; meanwhile, the torturer was seized under Ellis's warrant while he was in the Tanjore palace.[52] Ellis's actions threatened to destabilise the treaty with the British that had been ratified in 1799, which granted the Raja, his family and dependants immunities and privileges.[53]

The Judicial Department's correspondent was willing to give Ellis the benefit of the doubt in light of his youth and inexperience; however, he criticised him because he considered that by the time of the incident, Ellis had been living in India long enough to know how Hindus of rank dreaded any public insult to their personal dignity.[54] Accordingly, Ellis and his colleague, Daniel Crawford, were removed from their posts at Kombakonum and from causing further political trouble at Tanjore. It was hoped that their transfer would serve as an example to all officers in the Madras Judicial Department of the need for moderation in dispensing justice.[55] Ellis was transferred to the Telugu-speaking region of Masulipatam and his transfer had a fortunate outcome for his linguistic studies, as he was required to learn the Telugu language, which later assisted him in formulating the Dravidian Proof. Notwithstanding his judicial dispute with Serfoji, Ellis corresponded with him frequently on scholarly matters, often borrowing and exchanging books.[56] However, for a few years prior to this incident, Ellis was able to take advantage of the opportunity to frequent Serfoji's Court, to use his extensive library and to interact with its many visitors.

Throughout the early decades of the nineteenth century, the trajectories assembled by Raja Serfoji in his quest for useful knowledge brought together

---

51. Nair, '"... Of Real Use to the People"', 517.
52. Trautmann, *Languages and Nations*, 99.
53. BL/IOR/E/4/904/556: Judicial Department answers to letters (6 March 1807).
54. Ibid., 570.
55. Ibid., 578.
56. BL/IOR/V/27/36/80/3/129: Request to his Excellency to lend certain books to Mr Ellis for his perusal, in *Guide to the Records of the Tanjore District, 1749–1835.*

'an array of differing practices, instrumentation, theories and people'.[57] In 1819, they culminated in Serfoji's desire to publish a bilingual 'national gazette'[58] in Tamil and English on the Tanjore palace's own printing press.[59] The idea for the publication of such a paper reputedly came from Ellis's former assistant *Sheristadar*,[60] Bomaconta Sancaraya Brahmin.[61] As a tangible method of establishing a 'direct' relationship between English and Tamil, the national gazette articulated a biopolitical concept of colonial governmentality.[62] The idea for such a publication was really the synthesis of the 'language and nations' project that Francis Ellis had initiated in 1812 at the College of Fort St. George, which embraced ideals of colonial governance rooted in social 'improvement'.[63] Indeed, the inception of this concept is apparent in the few of Ellis's writings that have survived, notably his treatises on Mirasi Right and the legend of the cow pox vaccination.[64] Ellis wrote his original version of the 'Legend of the Cow Pox'[65] in the Tamil language and translated it into English, a copy of which was later discovered amongst the papers of Ellis's friend, William Erskine.[66]

Thus, his association with Serfoji's Court at Tanjore was a period which, for Ellis, was filled with creative encounters that laid the groundwork for his appreciation of the holistic characteristics of traditional land tenure, with its attendant cultural obligations and privileges that he so ably expressed in his treatise on Mirasi Right. His sojourn at Tanjore, together with his professional duties as a Revenue Collector in posts around Southern India, combined with his language skills, allowed him to frame an Orientalist discourse that not only asserted EIC power but also established him as a pioneer in the field of early colonial knowledge. His scholarship was based on a deep understanding of 'a polity in which the villagers and villages were permanent fixtures in the

---

57. Nair, 'Native Collecting', 284.

58. See Satyajit Das (ed.), *Selections from the Indian Journals, 1933* (Calcutta: Firma, K. L. Mukhopadhyay, 1963), vol. 1, 152–155.

59. David Turnbull, 'Local Knowledge and Comparative Scientific Traditions', *Knowledge and Policy* 6, nos. 3–4 (1993): 30.

60. *Sheristadar*: Tamil word meaning chief officer in an Indian Court.

61. Bomaconta Sancaraya Brahmin (aka Sankaraiah) was Ellis's assistant while he was the collector at Madras, and later became the English Headmaster of the College at Fort St. George. He served for more than thirty years in various situations in the Revenue and Judicial Departments, both in the northern and southern provinces of the Madras Presidency. See Ellis, Replies to Seventeen Questions.

62. After Foucault's theory of controlling indigenous populations through dispersed networks of authority via social control and knowledge.

63. Nair, 'The Tanjore Printing Press', 525.

64. Ibid., 523.

65. Ellis's version of the 'Legend of the Cow Pox' is discussed in the section entitled 'Medical Matters'.

66. BL/Mss Eur C9–10: Francis W. Ellis, Legend of the Cow Pox, found in the Erskine Collection, papers collected by William Erskine (1773–1852).

cultural landscape whose constituent elements could be counted'.[67] A large part of this may be discerned in one of Ellis's rare publications, which appeared in 1818 entitled, 'Replies to Seventeen Questions Proposed by the Government of Fort St. George Relative to Mirasi Right', to be discussed in the next section.

MIRASI RIGHT

In Northern India, Sir William Jones had discovered the historical relationship of the Sanskrit language to Greek and Latin, which he proposed had occurred 'via an ancestral language now perhaps lost', and also with Celtic, Gothic and Old Persian; in short, what we call the Indo-European language family.[68] But in his investigations of the Southern Indian concept of Mirasi Right, Ellis went a stage further by demonstrating that the ancient laws concerning hereditary rights governed genealogical relations that were intrinsic to the relationship between languages and nations. Connected with the possession or usufruct of land, they were an indication of the construction of an ancient agrarian society, whose history was rooted in the soil, allowing it to function as a coherent social unit.

In his treatise, Ellis demonstrated that the term *Mirasidar*, which was applied to an individual who enjoyed Mirasi Right, meant more than simply someone possessing land. It endowed its owner with social influence and privileges which ensured that they formed the core of the village community and were its leaders.[69] Ellis's concept of the rights and privileges of possession enjoyed by *Mirasidars* since the time of the Chola dynasty and the rights to cultivation claimed by two groups, namely, Ulkudis and Parakudis, was that they were indicative of a social and cultural hierarchy that had formed the bedrock of historical knowledge about India for centuries. In this way, by reference to Mirasi Right, Ellis was able to contest the view that India had no history, until it could be made known by accounts of foreigners gathered from translations of ancient poems, literature and other documents.[70]

In 1816, Francis Ellis, together with all the other collectors in South India, was asked by the Government of Fort St. George to supply the answers to seventeen questions relating to Mirasi Right.[71] Prompted by his deep interest

---

67. Thomas R. Trautmann, 'Does India Have History? Does History Have India?' *Comparative Studies in Society and History* 54, no. 1 (2012): 181.
68. Ibid. See also Thomas R. Trautmann, *Aryans and British India* (Berkeley, CA: University of California Press, 1997), 37–52; and Trautmann, *Languages and Nations*, 13–21.
69. https://www.indianetzone.com/51/mirasi_rights.htm.
70. Trautmann, 'Does India Have History?', 174–175.
71. Ellis, Replies to Seventeen Questions.

in the history of groups such as the Tamil Pariahs, Ellis's responses to the questions were by far the most comprehensive of any that may have been submitted by other Collectors. It is, however, pertinent to mention that although, in 1818, the government expected to receive a number of responses to their questionnaire on Mirasi Right, Ellis's was apparently the only completed response received from the various collectors around the district. The only other response recorded was from Ellis's assistant, Bomaconta Sancaraya Brahmin, the late *Sheristadar* of Cutcherry, who was at that time the English Headmaster of the College at Fort St. George, and whose views concurred with Ellis's.[72] It may be recalled that it was Sancaraya who proposed to Serfoij the publication of a 'national gazette'. It is not known what happened to the replies of other Collectors, nor indeed, if any were actually received, but it seems that in their absence, Ellis was the only one to have embraced the task with such dedication.

In his examination of the complex question of Mirasi Right in rural Southern India, Ellis observed that this group considered themselves to be 'the real proprietors of the soil'; that is, the aborigines or, according to the Brahmins, the *adi-kulam*.[73] He identified common aspects of India's ancient past through his contemporary observations. As noted, he was in a unique position, through his work as a Revenue Officer, to gain an insight into how ancient land rights functioned. Due to Mirasi's intimate connection with the social structure of the South Indian countryside, Ellis was afforded a unique opportunity to develop an understanding of its history. Historical records dating from the seventeenth and eighteenth centuries have shown the complicated ways in which land tenure and its rights in respect of its transfer and usage were not just restricted to people of the same village. In fact, many transfers took place between the people of different villages. There were also many transactions between people of different castes, such as Mudalis and Brahmins, or Mudalis and Gramanis.[74] This suggests that the interactions created by such territorial flexibility over land rights and ownership in pre-colonial Southern India were autochthonous. In other words, social and cultural mobility occurred naturally, and movement of people did not depend upon migration or colonisation, as it did throughout British colonial rule.

In Appendix 1 of his treatise on the subject, Ellis noted that his replies on Mirasi Right were chiefly drawn from the district known to the indigenous population as Tondaimandalam. This district was originally settled prior to the Christian era by a group of agriculturists known as the *Vellala*

---

72. Ibid.
73. Ibid.
74. https://www.indianetzone.com/51/mirasi_rights.htm

Tondaimandalam, who still held Mirasi; *Vellala* being understood to denote the high-ranking peasant class.[75] As Ellis stated in his treatise,

> The extent and boundaries of the country thus settled, the number of settlers and its variation in population and prosperity in after times are to be traced not by vague tradition only, as is too commonly conceived to be the case with respect to the remains of Indian history, but in writings of different periods as substantially authentic, probably though intermixed with undisguised fable.[76]

Ellis then cited a series of Tamil verses describing the landscape, which 'contain much of what may be considered as the real history of the country, though still obscured occasionally by allegory and distorted by extravagance'.[77]

As Eugene Irschick has argued, Ellis regarded the government's enquiries concerning Mirasi Right as an attempt to impose European ideas and institutions upon ancient traditions, in order to define the ethnic boundaries and set the terms of their interaction with the 'natives'.[78] Also according to Irschick, ' "Seventeen Questions proposed by the Government of Fort St. George Relative to Mirasi Right" was a way to gain power in an uncertain colonial context'.[79] Ellis was therefore anxious that his replies should emphasise the superior authority of the periphery and its indigenous population over every aspect of this subject. In the 'Preface' to his responses, he stated unequivocally that should there be any differences or disputes concerning the replies received, 'native' views should take precedence. He reasoned that 'the facts respecting Mirasi and its privileges are not a matter of speculation, they are known to every inhabitant of the country where they exist, who are brought up in the habitual exercise or observation of them – the terms which express them they have received from the lips of their mothers'.[80] As an Orientalist, Ellis believed that by representing Mirasi Right as a timeless tradition known and accepted by all, 'he could define the terms of the interaction to reinforce British constructions about the local society, while at the same time incorporating and invoking a perceived indigenous code'.[81] His categorical assertion that Mirasi Right was a matter of indisputable fact, and not speculation, appeared to be a warning to the government that as Collector of Madras, he would not countenance interference in hereditary rights and customs handed down for generations.

75. Bayley and Hudleston, *Papers on Mirasi Right*, 229–286.
76. Ibid., 230–231.
77. Ibid., 233.
78. Eugene F. Irschick, 'Order and Disorder in Colonial South India', *Modern Asian Studies* 23, no. 3 (1989): 479.
79. Ibid.
80. Ellis, Replies to Seventeen Questions.
81. Irschick, 'Order and Disorder', 489.

As previously mentioned, Ellis's work on land tenure, undertaken in his capacity as revenue collector for Madras, led him to oppose the Governor of Madras, Thomas Munro's, attempts to introduce the Ryotwari system, which pioneered a new mode of land tenure and revenue collection to the South Indian countryside. He clashed with Munro over the disruption that the Ryotwari system brought to ancient forms of land tenure and its accompanying rights and privileges, whereby, according to Munro's system, ownership was handed over to the peasants, who paid their taxes directly to the government. Although Ellis did not express his opposition directly to Thomas Munro's Ryotwari system of land tenure, he revealed his disagreement in his responses to the government's questionnaire on Mirasi Right. Using as his authoritative sources digests of Hindu law, Ellis suggested that under Mirasi, land was possessed jointly by the ruler and the landholders, with each having their share of the rent, with the king or ruler having the right to transfer his royal rights to land tax to the religious institutions.[82]

Under the Ryotwari system, peasants were treated as tenants of the king (in this instance, the British king), where they paid their revenue dues directly to the government in cash, foregoing customary privileges. In the 'Appendix' to his questionnaire, Ellis again expressed his opposition to the Ryotwari system with the statement that although neighbouring principalities differed, 'in the Tamil country the power was vested [. . .] in one man as the head of a Nadu, a Cottam or of a Viceroyalty, the administration of the Township was uniformly conducted conjointly by the whole of the Sharers'.[83] Historically, joint ownership at the level of the township or village was the driving force behind Ellis's belief that ancient texts advocated that kinship and family connections had prior claim in matters of land tenure, so that private ownership was embedded in kinship relations and locally acknowledged social and moral structures, as opposed to the capitalist values dictated by the free market, of which the Ryotwari system was an integral part.[84]

In 1822, in a letter written to Fort St. George, the current members of the EIC Court posthumously censured Ellis's conduct in this matter. The Court's letter concluded that because they had only received Ellis's questionnaire, the government in Madras at that time had been deprived of the means of forming a balanced judgement on Mirasi Right. They commented, 'We disapprove of this printing and circulating of Mr Ellis's opinions alone, upon the ground that it must, to a great degree, have the effect of imposing

---

82. Thomas R. Trautmann (ed.), 'Riot over Ryotwari', in *The Madras School of Orientalism: Producing Knowledge in Colonial South India* (New Delhi: Oxford University Press, 2009), 318.
83. Bayley and Hudleston, *Papers on Mirasi Right*, 252
84. Trautmann, 'Riot over Ryotwari', 328.

upon the service the opinions of Mr Ellis as the authoritative conclusions of the Government'.[85] Retrospectively, it seemed to them that the 'opinions of Mr Ellis happened to coincide with the preconceived opinions of the Board of Revenue at that time'.[86] As Ellis was the Collector of Madras, their conclusions were undoubtedly correct; therefore, in the absence of any other opinions on Mirasi Right, Ellis's views had prevailed and at least for a few years, they also became those of the government of the Madras Presidency. Meanwhile, Ellis's main objective during his relatively brief lifetime spent in Southern India was in making the Tamil language and literature an integral part of Orientalism as government policy. His founding of the College at Fort St. George was his most lasting legacy to this ambition and a fitting memorial to his profound scholarship, which is considered in the next section.

THE COLLEGE AT FORT ST. GEORGE

The College at Fort St. George was founded in 1812, where, under the leadership of Francis Whyte Ellis, British Orientalists who were mostly covenanted servants of the EIC, together with indigenous scholars, actively promoted the teaching of languages and the publication of grammatical and literary works.[87] Enjoying the patronage of the EIC, the College was concerned not only with the education of its civil servants, but also with ensuring that 'native' students were educated to become Hindu and Muslim law officers and pleaders in the Courts of Justice. In May 1814, Ellis and his associates sent a very long letter to the Governor of Madras requesting funds to train up 'a sufficient number of respectable natives' to fill the places in courts and, over the course of many pages, they submitted details of how these arrangements should be put in place.[88] However, because of the scarcity of suitable candidates resident in the Presidency, they proposed to extend their selection to the provinces by communicating with collectors and judges to help them recruit the best informed talent throughout the country to train for the roles.[89] Their proposition was accepted on the understanding that the government would not agree to any permanent expenditure until the experiment had proved successful and a report had been submitted to the Governor. It was not, however, agreed that only individuals who had qualified with a certificate

---

85. Ellis et al., Three Treatises on Mirasi Right.
86. Ibid.
87. Rajesh Venkatasubramanian, 'Patrons and Networks of Patronage in the Publication of Tamil Classics, c. 1800–1920, *Social Scientist* 39, no. 3–4 (2011): 67.
88. Ellis to the Governor of Madras (12 May 1814).
89. Ibid., 51.

from the College should be allowed to plead in court, as the government felt that 'it would prevent others, besides the inhabitants of Madras and its neighbourhood, from entering upon the necessary course of study'.[90]

As a government-funded institution, another of the College's primary functions was to produce and print grammars and dictionaries in the Tamil language for the education of the EIC's young civil servants. It was also necessary to produce textbooks for the use of classes in law, and this necessitated resolving questions of copyright. It was fundamental to the success of the Southern Indian Government's Orientalist mission to promote a sense of common purpose between British and indigenous interests. Therefore, following a request from the College, the Governor authorised them to negotiate for the ownership of the copyright of the translation of a work on Hindu law, because it would be of great use to classes in their studies of Hindu law in the Tamil language.[91] Presently being revised by the head Tamil master at the College, the copyright was the property of his brother's widow, and the College's concern to comply with copyright law showed due regard and respect for the work of an erudite indigenous scholar. In pursuit of its aims to educate the EIC's civil servants, Tamil pundits ('native' scholars), also known as headmasters, were appointed by the College to teach indigenous languages to junior government officials. The pundits were encouraged to write books (which the College printed in order to equip a library) that heralded the beginning of their vital role throughout the rest of the nineteenth century in publishing traditional Tamil works, editing texts and promoting the work of other pundits by writing prefaces either in prose or in verse.[92]

As previously mentioned, in order to further these aims, the College had installed a printing press in 1813 with English and Tamil fonts, which Ellis was instrumental in setting up.[93] Apart from Raja Serfoji's and the missionaries' presses, it was one of the first to be established in Southern India. The College published important works, which included the Italian Jesuit priest, Constantine Joseph Beschi's (1680–1742), *Latin Grammar of the Low Tamil*, as well as his dictionaries in Low and High Tamil.[94] Francis Ellis made good use of Beschi's works in his own scholarship; as he told John Leyden in their mutual correspondence, he modelled his version of the cow pox legend on Beschi's work, which is discussed further in the next section.[95] It was not until

---

90. Ibid., 90.
91. Ibid., 50.
92. Blackburn, *Print, Folklore and Nationalism*, 73–75.
93. Venkatasubramanian, 'Patrons and Networks', 67.
94. Ibid., 68.
95. BL/Mss Eur D30/130: Francis Ellis to John Leyden (20 August 1808), papers on Francis Ellis found in the Erskine Collection.

Charles Metcalfe (1785–1846)[96] passed the Act in 1835, which allowed 'natives' to own printing presses, that there was a proliferation of Tamil literary works that were printed and published independently of government patronage.[97] The pundits' active engagement with the College at Fort St. George, helping to promote Tamil works of classical literature through the medium of print, signalled a transformation in Tamil philology that was to last throughout the nineteenth century. It began in 1812 with the publication of a clean, edited copy of the Tamil classic, *Tirukkuṟaḷ*, undertaken by a consortium of scholars situated throughout the region, who sent their texts back and forth in a process of correcting and revising until a final version was agreed.[98]

In his article on changing social conditions in the history of publishing in Southern India in the nineteenth and early twentieth centuries, Rajesh Venkatasubramanian has cited three main phases in the rapid increase of Tamil literary works by the end of the nineteenth century. The first phase of this ambitious project was instigated by Francis Whyte Ellis at the College of Fort St. George, where the installation of one of Southern India's first printing presses saw the early publication of major Tamil literary works. Meanwhile, the second phase was associated with the Saiva[99] revival movement set up in opposition to the Christian missionaries in Jaffna, which was notable for the dual role played by the Tamil scholar-pundits as printers and editor-publishers. During the third and most prolific phase, which began in the 1870s, three major Tamil epics, namely, *Cilappatikāram*, *Cīvaka Cintāmaṇi* and *Maṇimēkalai*, were published for the first time under the leadership of C.W. Damodaram Pillai, U.V. Swaminatha Aiya, and others.[100] As Venkatasubramanian has emphasised, this important third phase needs to be understood in relation to the first two, especially for its inception at the College in Fort St. George. The pundits' involvement with printing at the College also indicated a major shift from their customary duties of oral recitation and memorisation of Tamil literary classical works and the copying of palm leaf manuscripts. It was the precursor to a wider engagement with reading that, by the end of the century, had become a public activity rather than a private one confined to scholarly elites and their wealthy patrons.[101]

---

96. Charles Theophilus Metcalfe, first Baron Metcalfe, was acting Governor General of India from 1828 to 1835. He was credited with significant social and educational reforms.
97. Ellis to the Governor of Madras (12 May 1814), 69.
98. Sasha Ebeling, 'The College of Fort St. George and the Transformation of Tamil Philology during the Nineteenth Century', in *The Madras School of Orientalism*, 239.
99. *Saiva*: Sanskrit word relating to the God Shiva.
100. Venkatasubramanian, 'Patrons and Networks', 66.
101. Ebeling, 'The College of Fort St. George', 238.

Francis Ellis and his fellow scholar-administrators' involvement with this early phase of publication of Tamil texts was made possible through their collaboration with learned pundits, who had close connections with religious institutions. The class background of the native pundits appointed by the College was important and it is significant that most of them belonged to the landholding, non-Brahmin upper castes, and many had links with the traditional dominant landholding monasteries.[102] Known as *mutts* or *mathas*,[103] many of the ancient Tamil manuscripts were in the possession of this particularly Southern Indian form of religious institution that approximately conformed to monasteries. As a result, *mathas* exerted a powerful influence throughout the nineteenth century on the editing and publishing of Tamil classics, chiefly through their association with pundits who, as noted, acted as editors and publishers. Their patronage and that of other landowners in funding printing presses endowed this period of Tamil literary history with prestige, so that it has been dubbed 'The Age of the Mutts'.[104]

Ellis's links beyond the College both personally and through its scholar pundits, who were connected with the traditional landholding upper castes, put him in touch with wider scholarly networks, of which the *mathas* were an integral part. Unlike European monasteries, these institutions were not enclosed orders. Elaine Fisher has described them as places where not only scriptural learning occurred but also as institutions which could 'act as local power-broker, landlord, bank, or even as a self-contained fiefdom with a standing army – all defying Eurocentric pre-suppositions about what the word "monastery" may purport to translate'.[105] Consequently, they retained a fundamental position in administering the welfare and education of the local population and were held in high esteem, wielding considerable power and influence. The managers of the *mathas* were often very wealthy landowners, who enjoyed the patronage of others of their kind. As Venkatasubramanian has also noted, 'Apart from controlling vast tracts of wet and dry lands in and

---

102. Venkatasubramanian, 'Patrons and Networks', 69, 85.

103. Many of the Tamil Saiva *mathas* were confined to the Tamil lands, but some had wider links with northern monasteries. Besides their secular interests, *mathas* often assisted pilgrims in their progress between shrines with food, medical help and other services as required, and there were specific endowments earmarked for this. The *mathas*, like the temple, had a strong multipurpose social side to their work and their inhabitants often devoted themselves to the needs of the local people in matters of education, medical help and nourishment. As well as being active agents for the promotion of spiritual learning, they were agencies of social welfare. See Kallidaikurichi A. Nilakanta Sastri, *Development of Religion in South India* (Bombay: Orient Longmans, 1963), 116–19.

104. Richard W. Weiss, 'Print, Religion and Canon in Colonial India: The Publication of Ramalinga Adigal's *Tiruvarutpa*', *Modern Asian Studies* 49, no. 3 (2015): 667.

105. Elaine Fisher, 'Translating Vīraśaivism: The Early Modern Monastery as Transregional Religious Network', draft submitted to Oxford University Press in June 2016 for publication in an edited volume on the South Indian Maṭha, 35.

around their location, *mathas* were also patronised by lay followers, especially the landowning class from whom they derived a large share of their wealth'.[106]

However, the establishment of the College at Fort St. George under the patronage of the EIC, as the occupying governing power, may have been regarded with disfavour by the *mathas*, whose entrenched control had been bound up with the structure and function of the local society since the sixteenth century. Even before the arrival of the British, those in charge of *mathas* managed large endowments of land and had done so from at least the time of their founding in the 1500s, when these religious institutions were brought under the patronage of the Vijayanagara rulers. Although these monasteries housed many ascetics and scholars, their complex roles in Southern Indian society meant that their leaders came to wield much local political and economic power.[107] Both because of their potential royal connections and their self-perpetuating authority, *mathas* proliferated as a form of religious institution even among those communities, such as the Vīraśaivas, who did not receive royal support, until their power was curtailed by the EIC in 1803.[108] As Christopher Baker has stated, some of the wealthiest temples had flourished under their patronage, allowing them to have a wide-ranging impact on Southern Indian society.[109] Although not all *mathas* functioned in the same way, their diverse roles within society allowed them to perform many functions on behalf of the Vijayanagara Empire in far-flung rural areas.[110] Even the Muslim invasions, which had cut them down to size, had barely penetrated districts such as Madurai, Ramnad, Trichinopoly, Tanjore and Tinnevelly. Baker has also stated in relation to the temples and *mathas*, that 'there was embezzlement pure and simple, although it is difficult to gauge the extent to which temple funds were siphoned off and difficult to prove, there are clues which suggest that misappropriation was carried out on a grand scale'.[111]

The *mathas* adjacent to the temples were the repositories of many of the ancient manuscripts that, spearheaded by Francis Ellis, the College at Fort St. George attempted to recover. The pundits' links with these institutions provided scholars like Ellis with the contacts they needed in order to acquire palm leaf manuscripts, upon which classical Tamil literary works were inscribed. It was therefore a crucial factor in the success of such endeavours

106. Venkatasubramanian, 'Patrons and Networks', 74.
107. Ibid.
108. Ibid.
109. Christopher J. Baker, 'Temples and Political Development', in Christopher J. Baker and David A. Washbrook, *South India: Political Institutions and Political Change, 1880–1940* (Delhi: Macmillan Company of India, 1975), 77.
110. Valerie Stoker, *Polemics and Patronage in the City of Victory: Vyasatirtha, Hindu Sectarianism, and the Sixteenth-Century Vijayanagara* (Berkeley, CA: University of California Press, 2016), 130–131.
111. Baker, 'Temples and Political Development', 77.

that pundits employed by the College were drawn from the ranks of these learned, upper-class non-Brahmins, with close links to important religious institutions. One of the leading pundits, who published a book in 1840, was A. Muttuswamy Pillai, a Tamil scholar who had been sent by Ellis on a mission to the *mathas* in search of manuscripts.[112] Acquisitions like these enabled Ellis to begin his own (unfinished) version of the *Tirukkuṟaḷ*, complete with commentary, whose author, Valluvar (c. AD 500), was probably Jain and a member of the Paraiyar, the lowest caste in Tamil society.[113] As an 'untouchable', Valluvar's ancient verses personified a pre-Sanskrit folk culture that expressed a Dravidian moral system that was pure Tamil and wholly free of the idolatry associated with Brahminical Hinduism.[114]

Although the pundits' close links with *mathas* made a wider network of scholarly institutions accessible to Ellis, he also travelled frequently in the course of his duties for the EIC and explained to John Leyden in his letter of 7 August 1808, 'I have been continually in motion – I have scarcely been out of tents for three months together – I have rolled through the Company's territories from Jaggenath to Canara now still am rolling on'.[115] These journeys enabled him to acquire a unique insight into the cultural landscape of Southern India and its Tamil population, where the village-based proprietary system of Mirasi Right had remained relatively unchanged for thousands of years.[116] He also made many private excursions and it is possible that, prior to his untimely death in 1819, Ellis visited the famous *matha* at Ramnad in search of manuscripts.

The next section will investigate the circumstances surrounding Ellis's death in light of the proliferation of medical experiments and untried medicines that were produced at Tanjore, one of which may even indirectly have been responsible for his demise. As previously mentioned, Raja Serfoji was especially interested in medical matters and he acquired many medical texts, written not only in the vernacular, but also in English. In this section, we will return to the symbiotic relationships that were established at the Raja's Court at Tanjore and their influence on scientific matters, specifically medical, that

112. Blackburn, *Print, Folklore and Nationalism*, 99–100. In 1817, Ellis sent the pundit Muttusami Pillai south to collect palm leaf manuscripts.

113. Ibid., 162.

114. Ibid., 163.

115. BL/Mss Eur D30/127: Francis Ellis to John Leyden (7 August 1808), papers on Francis Ellis found in the Erskine Collection. Ellis wrote: 'I am still rolling on'. He also wrote that during this time, he had received 'a check or two in my progress – but two only have been of sufficient consequence to give me a shock of any violence. One of these was my removal from Tanjore and consequent banishment from the southern provinces and the other a damnable fit of Dyspepsia which has tormented me for the last five months and I fear will ultimately drive me to England or out of the world'. It seems that over ten years later, Ellis was still suffering from problems with his stomach that were ultimately responsible for his death.

116. Irschick, 'Order and Disorder', 472.

ironically, may have inflicted unintended but fatal consequences upon Ellis. It also describes Ellis's response to the controversy regarding the introduction of the new smallpox vaccination from Britain by his adaptation of an old Tamil legend, in order to present the new vaccine in a way that would respect local cultural and religious sensibilities.

MEDICAL MATTERS

As a 'Centre of Enlightenment', the Tanjore Court not only promoted an exchange of scientific, literary and cultural ideas, but under Raja Serfoji II's patronage, became an important centre for the practice of medical plural-ism where Western and indigenous doctors shared expertise in health care, notably in developing medicines and methods of prophylaxis. At the Palace *Arogyasala*,[117] patients were offered a range of therapeutic options that encompassed traditional country medicine, as well as accommodating treat-ments based on Western medicine.[118] Eclectic methods of diagnosing disease and administering medications were investigated and experiments conducted, in order to discover useful knowledge that would enhance the health and wellbeing of the Raja's subjects. On occasion, they proved efficacious, as indicated further by Serfoji's support for the use of the 'modern' smallpox vaccination, to which he and his family submitted themselves in order to encourage others to follow suit.

This was not novel, as since the sixteenth century, 'country medicine' in Southern India had been a reflection of a syncretic history based on trading networks between Europeans and Indians. By the late seventeenth century, the systematic collection of Oriental botanical specimens by English and Dutch surgeons and naturalists had developed through these trading net-works.[119] Together with spices and other ingredients, these botanical products were incorporated into an English pharmacopoeia at Madras comprising both 'country' medicines and English remedies.[120] In this way, Indian mate-rials became part of Orientalist studies and also scientific investigations in Europe. John Fleming (1747–1829), a surgeon with the Indian Medical Ser-vice in Bengal, studied local Tamil texts to identify the medical preparations used by the Tamil physicians to produce a catalogue of the Indian medicinal

---

117. *Arogyasala*: Word derived from Pali meaning 'hospital' where sick pilgrims and local resi-dents were cared for.

118. Savithri Preetha Nair, 'Diseases of the Eye: Medical Pluralism at the Tanjore Court in the Early Nineteenth Century', *Social History of Medicine* 25, no. 3 (2012): 574.

119. Pratik Chakrabarti, *Materials and Medicine: Trade, Conquest and Therapeutics in the Eigh-teenth Century* (Manchester and New York: Manchester University Press, 2010), 41.

120. Ibid.

plants and drugs.[121] As an amateur botanist, he befriended Francis Buchanan-Hamilton and also conducted a long correspondence with Sir Joseph Banks, sending him specimens of plants.

Meanwhile, Raja Serfoji had always welcomed medical men and surgeons to his Court, where under his leadership, medical science 'was conceived as a practice shaped by globally situated inter-cultural exchanges'.[122] His interest was encouraged by EIC surgeons, James Anderson (1739–1809), William Somervell Mitchell (1785–1844), Sir Thomas Sevestre (1786–1843) and Bannatyne William Macleod (1790–1856), as well as the physician at the Danish Mission at Tranquebar, who helped him to acquire surgical instruments and medical textbooks, written not only in the vernacular but also in English.[123] Serfoji was especially interested in anatomical matters and even commissioned a skeleton, which, in 1805, was sent from England by Benjamin Torin, who lived in Harley Street. Although a model in ivory was preferred, it proved to be prohibitively expensive, so it was made from durable wood from the holly tree.[124] Through the enlightened interest of Raja Serfoji, medical pluralism flourished at Tanjore, where 'there was a growing recognition that categories such as "Western medicine" and "indigenous medicine" were fluid ones'.[125] However, the divergence between European and indigenous medical practice became paradoxical when the British attempted to introduce Edward Jenner's smallpox vaccine, instead of the ancient practice of variolation, used for centuries by Indians as a prophylactic against the disease.

In May 1805, Serfoji employed Dr William Somervell Mitchell on a salary of one hundred pagodas[126] to teach him the principles of the European system of medicine, but this arrangement proved to be short-lived, as the government at Fort St. George decided to preclude Dr Mitchell from continuing to provide his medical services to the Tanjore Court. The decision to withdraw Dr Mitchell's services may have been a response from the Madras government, who were keen to retain the initiative in promoting the widespread use of the West's new smallpox vaccine. However, the Resident, William Blackburne, had always welcomed Serfoji's interest in medical matters, as he thought that it would help remove the prejudices against the introduction of Jenner's vaccine in Tanjore. Therefore, in 1806, after an appeal by Serfoji

121. Ibid., 42.
122. Nair, 'Raja Serfoji II', xix.
123. Nair, 'Diseases of the Eye', 577.
124. Nair, 'Native Collecting', 290.
125. Nair, 'Diseases of the Eye', 574.
126. Pagoda: A unit of currency; a coin made of gold or half-gold minted by Indian dynasties, as well as the British, the French and the Dutch. The most valuable was the star pagoda, issued by the EIC at Madras; 100 of them were worth 350 rupees. See Peter R. Thompson, *The East India Company and Its Coins* (Honiton: Token Publishing, 2010).

and encouragement from the Resident, Dr Mitchell was reinstated.[127] Having supported British efforts to introduce the new smallpox vaccine, Serfoji duly submitted himself and members of his family to be inoculated. Not only was he one of the first people to be protected against the disease, but he also promoted the EIC's vaccination scheme by making his palace available for members of the public to be immunised there.[128]

As a dedicated Orientalist, sensitive to the importance of maintaining local customs and religious traditions, Francis Ellis also became involved in the fight to control 'the ravages of that disease which causes terror and anguish to all on whom it seizes, the cruel smallpox',[129] and to shift centuries of cultural conditioning by adapting the legend of the cow pox.[130] In doing so, his poem made new connections between knowledge and the place of its production, and fostered a sense of common purpose between British and indigenous interests.[131] His adaptation of the ancient legend about smallpox connected with Serfoji's goal of promoting a plural medical practice that aligned indigenous medicine with Western approaches,[132] as his version not only took account of European medical advances, but also acknowledged local tradition and its attendant religious and cultural sensibilities.

His objective was to present a narrative that would appeal to a heterogeneous audience, whilst simultaneously respecting the hereditary practice of variolation, which Ellis viewed as intrinsic to the local culture. Therefore, his version of the Tamil legend was created in the belief that the promotion of modern methods of vaccination from the West should be adapted to suit this ancient practice whenever possible, rather than the other way round. Traditionally, the method used by Indians to protect their population against smallpox was known as 'variolation'. It was a practice carried out in a religious ceremony by a hereditary *tikadar* (variolator), where, as well as special dietary precautions and the administration of material 'harvested' from previous eruptions on smallpox victims, the protective power of the goddess Sitala was invoked against the dreaded disease.[133] Ellis wrote his poem firstly in Tamil, then in English, describing how a crystal liquid flowed from the udders of the cow. After being inoculated into the body of a man, it ensured that the disease would take a mild form, from which no one would suffer death or pain.[134] He recounted how the gods took refuge from the demons and

127. Nair, 'Diseases of the Eye', 577.
128. Nair, 'Native Collecting', 287–289.
129. Ellis, Legend of the Cow Pox.
130. Ibid., 54.
131. Schillings and van Wickeren, 'Towards a Material and Spatial History', 206.
132. Nair, 'Raja Serfoji II', 42.
133. David Arnold, *Colonizing the Body: State Medicine and Epidemic Disease in Nineteenth-Century India* (Berkeley, CA: University of California Press, 1993), 120–157.
134. Ibid., 59–62.

were instructed to take the sacred mountain Mandharam as a churn and the serpent Vasuki as a rope. They should churn the ocean of milk until a black poison arose which terrified the whole universe and which Sivah swallowed at the request of the gods: 'These holy gifts, sent to protect the gods came forth from the ocean and amongst them were the sacred productions of the cow by which all diseases were cured'.[135]

Whilst there are no known primary sources to support the theory that Ellis composed his poem in order to collaborate with William Blackburne's desire to encourage the local population to accept the new vaccine, it undoubtedly served as useful propaganda for the EIC. In August 1808, he wrote to his friend John Leyden that he was so far advanced in writing the poem that all that was needed was to arrange and revise it, 'You may remember before you quitted this side of India that I wrote in Tamil a treatise on the cow pox in which I endeavoured to imitate, as Beschi had done before me, the familiar style and arrangements of the Tamil authors, this work was in the low dialect but I have since mastered the high'.[136] He concluded by asking Leyden's advice on its eligibility for publication in *The Asiatic Journal* because the Madras Literary Society and its journal had yet to be founded.[137]

Conversely, the EIC's surgeons, like those mentioned earlier, also relied upon knowledgeable indigenous medical practitioners to help them treat diseases that were particular to India. They turned to local doctors to help them identify and classify diseases that, as Western-trained physicians, were beyond the scope of their European-based knowledge at that time.[138] It is therefore not surprising that indigenous remedies became part of the lexicon of medical treatments used in the Madras Presidency to cure illnesses that arose principally from local climatic conditions and other hazards. One such medicine, widely available on the Coromandel Coast, was known amongst the British community as the 'Tanjore Pills'. The Danish missionaries at Travancore were in touch with local practitioners and it was through them that the British surgeons were introduced to the 'Tanjore Pills', illustrating once again the conjunctures that occurred when indigenous and European actors attempted to bestride two divergent worlds. The 'Tanjore Pills' were renowned for their efficacy in treating venomous snake bites, despite reservations over their use because, after analysis, the pills were found to contain arsenic and were not sanctioned by the British government.[139]

135. Ibid., 51–54.
136. Ellis to Leyden (20 August 1808).
137. Ibid.
138. Nair, 'Diseases of the Eye', 576.
139. For a full explanation of the Tanjore Pills, see Chakrabarti, *Materials and Medicine*, 182–187.

However, there was also controversy when the local surgeons' fascination with exotic medicines and indigenous medical practices confronted the British medical establishment, whose cultural choices were predicated on Western scientific reason and analysis.[140] Whilst European medicine stressed the importance of clinical observation, particularly through anatomical dissections of cadavers, many being carried out in medical schools and open to the public, Indian medical tradition ignored this practice. In place of rationalism and scientific objectivity, the Siddha practitioner relied on his pills, many of which were rejected by the British medical establishment because, like the 'Tanjore Pills', they contained arsenic and other noxious substances, despite the fact that arsenic continued to be used in Western medicine for the treatment of syphilis.[141]

Furthermore, the effects of the climate on European medicines proved to be problematic and as there were few, if any, effective methods of ensuring their preservation, decay was rapid. The Residency surgeon, Thomas Sevestre, had occasion to throw out many medicines found in such a state of decay at the Black Town Dispensary in Madras.[142] Thus, the use of indigenous preparations and medicines became an attractive alternative, but the prescription of local treatments and medications was unreliable and side effects were often unknown. On occasion, they proved to be positively dangerous, and may even have contributed to Francis Ellis's sudden and untimely death whilst he was on tour at Ramnad.

Although sensitive to the prejudices of the local population against any alteration in traditional prophylaxis against smallpox, and lending his support by adapting a traditional Tamil legend on the subject, Ellis himself may not have been so fortunate in embracing the practice of medical pluralism. For many years, he had suffered from a stomach complaint and in another letter to his friend, John Leyden, in 1808, he told him that he had experienced 'a damnable fit of Dyspepsia[143] which has tormented me for the last five months and I fear will ultimately drive me to England or out of the world'.[144] As it was not uncommon for Europeans to use local medicine like the 'Tanjore Pills', throughout his years in India, Ellis also may have had recourse to various indigenous remedies in order to alleviate his suffering, including syncretic treatments prescribed by the physicians at Tanjore. However, he may have had cause to regret his decision, because, as he lay dying on 9 March 1819, Ellis placed on record the words, 'I take poison instead of

---

140. Ibid.
141. Ibid., 187.
142. Nair, 'Raja Serfoji II', 42.
143. Dyspepsia: Caused by a stomach ulcer, or acid reflux disease.
144. Ellis to Leyden (7 August 1808).

medicine at Ramnad and am at the point of death'.[145] His use of the phrase 'instead of' indicates that he was aware that he had erroneously ingested a fatal substance and unless he had wished to take his own life (for which there is no evidence), it may be assumed that he did not deliberately take poison. As there are no records of a post-mortem, we shall never know exactly how or why at Ramnad, Ellis came to take 'poison instead of medicine', a substance which finally proved fatal to him on 10 March 1819. However, it would be a sad irony if the fatal dose had been an amalgam of Western and native medicine, and perhaps a bleak metaphor for the ultimate failure of Orientalism as colonial policy in Southern India.

CONCLUDING REMARKS

Through his conceptualisation of the Dravidian language family, Francis Whyte Ellis became a pathfinder in 'generating an array of new understandings of South Indian history and culture concerning such matters as law, land, literature, religion, and caste'.[146] His work as a revenue collector for the EIC brought him into contact with many diverse ethnic groups within Southern India's population. This allowed him to observe the similarities and variations between their cultural characteristics and social mores, leading him to an understanding, not only of their languages but also of the origins and affinities of the various 'tribal' groups and their relationship with the land. The influence of Ellis's work on Mirasi Right and his recognition of the underlying social practices, obligations and privileges with which these rights endowed their owner may be discerned in the ways in which subsequent colonial scholar-officials have observed indigenous societies and the local customs of the people amongst whom they served. A century after Ellis's work, scholar-officials in Burma like J.S. Furnivall and S. Grantham, whose own work was also concerned with revenue and land tenure, made use of their 'Settlement Reports' to express their disquiet regarding the changes that colonialism had brought to their districts. In particular, they complained about the impact that these changes had in disrupting the hereditary fabric of society and its ancient traditions. In his 'Settlement Report, 1909–1913', J.S. Furnivall wrote, 'Until within recent times when men became mad and cast aside their hereditary dignities, the Burman population was not homogenous.

---

145. From the Register of the Supreme Court of Judicature (Madras, 9 March 1819). As he left no will, Francis Ellis communicated his last wishes from his deathbed at Ramnad to Rungiah Naik, one of his *dubashes*, which were subsequently recorded in an official transcript from the Register of the Supreme Court of Madras.
146. Trautmann, *Languages and Nations*, 186–211.

Formerly, there were at least two major castes, an aristocracy of officials with the duty and privilege of serving the government (meaning the monarchy) and the debased or non-official classes of quasi servile status'.[147] J.S. Furnivall's scholarship on questions of indigenous land tenure and revenue and its relationship with hereditary practices was an early indication of his support for Burmese nationalism, views which he shared with fellow colonial officers who, like him, were members of the British Fabian Society.[148] A century earlier, Ellis had observed similar characteristics in South India's heterogeneous rural society, which were soon to be obliterated by the new structures imposed by Macaulay and Munro's reforms. His work on Mirasi Right may therefore be understood in the context of later expressions of raising national consciousness, which invoked the inherent right of indigenous people to claim their independence by reference to their cultural heritage and ancient traditions rooted in the land.

As Thomas Trautmann has stated, 'Orientalist policy which aspired to rule India in accord with Indian culture, required investigation of that culture through the study of Indian languages and the reading of Indian texts that were its repositories'.[149] Yet, despite the scholarly objectives of Francis Whyte Ellis and other Orientalists to fulfil these requirements and assert colonial authority based on the synergy of enlightened European ideas with hereditary constructions of Southern India's ancient social order, disorder and misconduct prevailed throughout the first half of the nineteenth century. This occurred, in part, because the boundary-crossing exchanges, which were necessary to support the EIC's attempts to integrate its policies with the existing indigenous infrastructure, allowed corruption to flourish on both sides of the colonial divide.

Whilst boundary-crossing exchanges proved to be mutually beneficial to the intellectual projects that emanated from the College at Fort St. George and other arenas of intellectual collaboration like Colin Mackenzie's survey, they could not be translated successfully into the necessary social and political policies required to govern India, particularly in judicial matters. Much of the opportunity for misconduct was presented by the essential need to employ 'native' intermediaries, acting jointly within the long-established cultural and religious structure of the social order in the Madras Presidency, but the

---

147. BL/W1241/27/8: J.S. Furnivall, Report on the First Regular Settlement Operation in the Myingyan District (1909–1913).

148. J.S. Furnivall became a lifelong member of the British Fabian Society whilst on furlough in England in 1908 and he was still a member in 1958, two years before his death, when he received an invitation to the celebrations to mark its seventy-fifth anniversary. Furnivall and his colleagues' left-wing political ideas, whilst not overtly anti-imperialist, applied socialist values to the rights and freedom of colonial people.

149. Trautmann, *Languages and Nations*, 79.

negative aspects of collaboration in the day-to-day administration of India made reforms inevitable.

However, reforms, including those instituted by Macaulay, introduced a rule of difference into the social order, particularly in Southern India, that abrogated the long-term possibility of Orientalism as a viable colonial policy, with its facility to accommodate the others' history, culture and traditions for the betterment of both imperial governance and indigenous social and economic welfare. As the nineteenth century progressed, new structures of government that were more financially advantageous to the British were put in place, including, as noted, the introduction of Thomas Munro's Ryotwari system of land tenure. By creating a system where peasants were treated as tenants, paying their revenue dues directly to the government in cash, a fundamental rule of difference was imposed between colonised and coloniser that would never be eradicated. The outcome was that customary privileges, as well as the communal responsibilities, like those inherent in Mirasi Right, disappeared.

Over the course of the nineteenth century, the bureaucratisation of the colonial service distanced its officials from these information networks, particularly as expatriate society became more racially conscious. The heterogeneous knowledge networks that developed in the Madras Presidency from the late eighteenth century, in common with those centred upon Bengal, were compromised by the lack of a strong framework of formalised institutions necessary for the EIC's governance to endure, ultimately resulting in the catastrophe of the great Rebellion in 1857.[150] Post-1857, when the British Crown assumed control of the subcontinent from the EIC, a much more rigid system of governance was put in place, which detached colonial officers from the traditional sources of knowledge as the ability to communicate easily with 'the knowing people' of the locality ensured a supply of 'useful knowledge', even if it could not always be relied upon.[151]

By the mid-nineteenth century, collaboration and cooperation between European and indigenous actors now became exceptional rather than commonplace. It was left to those on the margins of imperial society and other unconventional outsiders to fill in the knowledge gaps. Such individuals attempted, sometimes unsuccessfully, to fill the void left by the collapse of the old order and the rupture of formerly fluid networks. It was dependent upon the initiatives of lone adventurers like William Johnson and Dr Clement Williams, whose stories are told in the following two chapters. Using their own initiative and local knowledge, they ventured beyond the imperial frontier, exceeding the limits of their official orders to visit the Courts of foreign

150. Raj, 'Colonial Encounters', 133.
151. Bayly, *Empire and Information*, 140.

rulers in search of intelligence that might be of use, not only to the Indian government but also to themselves. Independent expeditions were fraught with danger, and lacking official authorisation, those who undertook them were vulnerable to accusations of misconduct and social exclusion from the colonial hierarchy. Such considerations had not constrained the adventurous spirit and pioneering intellectual initiatives of Orientalists like Francis Buchanan-Hamilton and Francis Whyte Ellis. But by the mid-nineteenth century, the changing political landscape of colonial India and Burma was detrimental to the efforts of Johnson and Williams, as the following chapters recount.

Chapter 5

'The White Pundit': William Johnson and the Great Trigonometrical Survey of India

INTRODUCTION

As the preceding chapters have shown, the EIC made good use of the scholarly abilities of its covenanted officers – men like Francis Buchanan-Hamilton and Francis Whyte Ellis, whose dedication to researching India's natural world, languages and classical texts endowed them with the cultural authority to determine the value of the knowledge they produced, whilst also legitimising the EIC's power.[1] Assisted by patronage, their interests were served by a burgeoning publication system of books and journals 'set up to filter and classify [knowledge] into hierarchies'.[2] The EIC's requirement for new knowledge about India was bound up with political patronage,[3] a pattern which survived after 1858 when its governing powers were transferred to the British Crown. Therefore, a close connection developed between the production of colonial knowledge and the maintenance of order and discipline in the Empire.[4] Nevertheless, until the formalisation of organisations dedicated to the acquisition of intelligence, the Government of India continued to rely upon information supplied by indigenous intermediaries and go-betweens, as it had since the eighteenth century. Knowledge provided by 'native' informants was an indispensable part of allowing the British to know the country, although only Colin Mackenzie appears to have trusted his 'native' informants implicitly.[5]

---

1. Wayne A. Wiegand, 'The Politics of Cultural Authority', *American Libraries* 29, no. 1 (1998): 80.
2. Ibid., 81.
3. Ludden, 'Orientalist Empiricism', 253.
4. See also Edward Said, *Culture and Imperialism* (London: Chatto & Windus, 1993); and Cohn, *Colonialism and Its Forms of Knowledge*.
5. Dirks, 'Colonial Histories', 292.

Regardless of the cultural and social ambiguities that surrounded the activities of informants and, at times, distrust of their motives, by the mid-nineteenth century, the necessity of advancing exploration and surveying on the frontiers became more urgent, due to increasing anxiety about Russian advances. In order to satisfy this requirement, since 1862, the training and use of indigenous surveyors had been enthusiastically promoted by Colonel Thomas Montgomerie, the officer in charge of the 'Trans Himalayan exploring parties'.[6] He made the first public mention of the scheme in an address to the Asiatic Society of Bengal, where he spoke of 'the advisability of employing "native" agency'.[7] In 1863, because of the danger to European officers travelling in inhospitable regions, the government permitted Montgomerie to recruit and train suitable 'native pundits' to carry out undercover reconnaissance missions in hostile terrains adjacent to the frontier, by secretly taking readings with a theodolite from fixed triangulation points.[8]

Known as pundits, and disguised as mendicants and pilgrims, these men were trained to move at a measured pace[9] in order to time their movements and calculate distances using instruments hidden in their robes, staff and prayer wheels.[10] The material that they brought back was then checked and compiled into maps at the GTS of India's headquarters in Dehradun. Between 1863 and 1885, fifteen 'native' pundits, usually minor employees of the GTS, were trained as covert surveyors to accomplish missions forbidden to European surveyors. As they criss-crossed Central Asia, they experienced many hardships – two were murdered, one was sold into slavery and another was imprisoned on suspicion of spying.[11] Pundits were often away from their base at Dehradun for months, sometimes years, at a time, and were required to behave clandestinely and, occasionally, to take steps that contravened local laws.

Intelligence-gathering beyond the frontier therefore required its 'native' protagonists to be resourceful, ever on the alert and ready to react when challenged, in order to avert suspicion. Kapil Raj has argued that pundits acted as complicit collaborators, who were trusted to provide accurate topographical readings and other information, thereby acknowledging the legitimacy of the intelligence that they provided on behalf of their superiors.[12] The colonial paradigm of disciplining 'native' bodies to serve imperial needs might

---

6. Derek J. Waller, *The Pundits: British Exploration of Tibet and Central Asia* (Lexington: University Press of Kentucky, 1988), 59.

7. Raj, *Relocating Modern Science*, 187.

8. Waller, *The Pundits*, 29.

9. The pundits were trained to count their paces, which remained at a constant 31.5 inches in length.

10. Hevia, *The Imperial Security State*, 85.

11. Raj, *Relocating Modern Science*, 185.

12. Ibid., 216–222.

apply to Montgomerie's use of trained pundits, their bodies were considered expendable and as they posed little risk to imperial prestige, no retaliation would be required in the event of their death. However, 'native' pundits, who allegedly enjoyed peer status[13] at the GTS, were well rewarded for their clandestine missions because, as indigenous informants, they did not compromise the cultural authority of their superiors. But when William Henry Johnson (1832–1883), one of the GTS's uncovenanted 'country-born'[14] civil assistants, behaved in a similar manner to them, he received neither recognition nor remuneration. In fact, he was roundly condemned for his actions by his superior officers at the GTS.

This chapter will investigate William Johnson's conduct and activities during the course of his working life on the frontiers of India. Being 'country-born', he was considered an outsider in colonial circles even though he was white. Although Johnson cannot be categorised as an indigenous intermediary, he manifested 'an uneasy cultural or social identification or "role ambiguity"', described by Simon Schaffer in *Brokered Worlds* as crucial to the mobility and innovative behaviour associated with the go-between.[15] He exhibited cultural and social ambiguities that placed him on the margins of British society in India, which brought him into disrepute with the government and his colleagues at the GTS. In their 'Introduction', Schaffer and his co-authors have identified the go-between as not just a passer-by, or a simple agent of cross-cultural diffusion, but as 'someone who articulated relationships between disparate worlds or cultures by being able to translate between them'.[16] Often individuals who fitted this classification were members of the colonising community who, like Johnson, had close ties with the local milieu, through birth, marriage or occupation, especially trade.

As Felix Driver has argued, frequently the people most relied upon for local knowledge were 'strictly speaking neither local nor indigenous'.[17] In addition to 'native' pundits, extempore intelligence was also provided by country-born British, or other long-term European residents of India, who were familiar with its languages, culture and environment. Such was the position of William Johnson, whose life story offers a compelling example of how the rigid definitions of racial, class and domiciliary terms came to define

---

13. Ibid., 221.
14. The term 'country-born' describes someone born in India to parents of pure British or European blood, who remained in the country and was not sent home to school in Britain. For a fuller discussion of the meaning of the term, see Harald Fischer-Tine, *Low and Licentious Europeans: Race, Class and 'White Subalternity' in Colonial India* (New Delhi: Orient Swan, 2009), 73–74; and also Satoshi Mizutani, *The Meaning of White: Race, Class and the 'Domiciled Community' in British India, 1858–1930* (Oxford: Oxford University Press, 2012).
15. Schaffer et al., *The Brokered World*, xviii.
16. Ibid., xiv.
17. Driver, *Intermediaries and the Archives of Exploration*, 15.

those who, being 'the right sort', were considered fit to wield authority and represent the British Raj,[18] whilst those who did not conform to this model were always constrained by their outsider status. Relegated to the bottom of the social scale, the country-born were grouped with those known as 'poor whites', the 'domiciled community', and Eurasians.[19] Regarded as being physically 'contaminated' by Indian blood, they were set apart from respectable white middle classes, who retained strong links with Britain.

William Henry Johnson was born in India in March 1832, the son of Thomas and Hannah Johnson, both originally from England. As white British parents who could not afford to send their son back to Britain to be educated, as was customary, Johnson was educated in India. Having spent all their lives in India, the 'country-born' had no first-hand knowledge of Britain and were deemed to be in danger of becoming 'nativised' and degenerate, thus jeopardising British prestige.[20] William Johnson's father, Thomas Johnson, worked as a sub-conductor in the Ordnance Department of the EIC army, where, as a covenanted officer, he held the rank of Sergeant Overseer, entitling him to a pension. His son William was educated in the frontier town of Mussoorie, in the foothills of the Himalayas, near to the headquarters of the GTS at Dehradun, where, on leaving school aged fifteen, he obtained employment in 1848 as a civil assistant. In the minds of men aspiring to make a good living in India in the early decades of the nineteenth century, 'the "Trigonom Survey" was regarded as a good government situation, superior to any other, and 'for which possession of a watch was considered indispensable'.[21] But unlike his father, Johnson's position was not secure; as an uncovenanted civil assistant, he was not entitled to a pension or other allowances normally allocated to the Company's indentured employees recruited in Britain. Johnson, whose remarkable talent as a mountaineer was soon spotted, was trained by Sir Andrew Scott Waugh, and later he worked under Colonel James Walker, who became the GTS's Superintendent in 1861. When Colonel Thomas Montgomerie was in command of the Kashmir Survey between 1855 and 1865, Johnson served as his deputy; hence, he was aware of Johnson's social background, mountaineering skills and adventurous, if at times, unreliable character.[22]

Meanwhile, life on the Indian frontier in the mid-nineteenth century, where William Johnson was brought up, was truly an existence 'at Empire's edge'.

18. Satoshi, *The Meaning of White*, 76.
19. Fischer-Tine, *Low and Licentious Europeans*, 74.
20. Satoshi Mizutani, 'Constitutions of the Colonising Self in Late British India: Race, Class and Environment', *Zinbun* 38 (2005): 38.
21. Mauger Fitzhugh Monk, Ganesh Sailli (ed.), *Letters of a Mussoorie Merchant: Mauger Fitzhugh Monk, 1828–1849* (New Delhi: Niyogi Books, 2006), 1, 23.
22. Waller, *The Pundits*, 18.

Whatever their origins or class, its inhabitants were obliged to live by their wits in a harsh environment, where few amenities of civilised society existed. Consequently, they had to display chutzpah, enterprise, resilience and even, at times, deceit, in order to survive. Johnson's up-bringing and education in the foothills of the Himalayas gave him the ability to move between the regulated environment of surveying at the GTS and the local society, allowing him to interact with indigenous people in the forbidden lands beyond the frontier, where lawlessness prevailed. Such ambiguities are consistent with the characteristics that defined an informant as someone who could not be wholly trusted and who was tainted by the suspicion of disloyalty and lack of moral probity. Consequently, by adopting a role similar to that of a 'native' pundit and engaging in questionable activities beyond the frontier, Johnson's behaviour contravened the bourgeois norms and sensibilities of British Indian society that, by the mid-nineteenth century, had become much more rigid. As this chapter will describe, Johnson's private business operations were dubious, and so too were the circumstances surrounding his death, which occurred in Kashmir in 1883.

In 1865, whilst surveying on India's unstable frontier, William Johnson made an unauthorised visit to Khotan, one of the Khanates of Central Asia, at a sensitive time when they were in revolt against the central authority of Peking.[23] His epic journey to Khotan and his subsequent life in Kashmir exemplify the conflicting standards which applied within the carefully controlled social hierarchy of the British Empire. His experiences with the GTS reveal that without the correct education and appropriate patronage, it was virtually impossible for the country-born to cross social, educational and professional barriers. Johnson's actions caused embarrassment to his superiors at the GTS and to the Government of India, even though there was tacit interest and agreement amongst senior personnel of the desirability of obtaining information about establishing future trade links with Central Asia. Johnson's extraordinary feats of surveying at the highest altitudes, which no one else had previously attempted, were ignored, and unlike 'native' pundits, they went unrewarded. Furthermore, in order to maintain control over the knowledge that Johnson produced on his expedition, senior staff in Dehradun made it clear to the Government of India that his survey results were unsatisfactory and required correction. Therefore, his allegedly 'incomplete' report was rewritten and his maps redrafted so that they would carry the stamp of the GTS's authority, rather than that of a maverick employee who had disobeyed orders. [24]

---

23. For further information, see Yuan Tsing, 'Yakub Beg (1820–1877) and the Moslem Rebellion in Chinese Turkestan', *Central Asiatic Journal* 6, no. 2 (1961): 134–167.

24. BL/IOR/L/PS/6/522, Coll. 178/2, 1125: India Office London to Governor General of India (May 1867).

Surveying and mapping played a crucial role in establishing colonial authority and in order to legitimise their maps, the British required the 'cultural authority' of the surveyor in the field.[25] But growing up in India embedded within the local society, Johnson lacked the necessary 'cultural authority' to produce survey results and maps that could validate and uphold colonial rule. In the early years of his career, his intrepid feats as a mountaineer were praised by his mentors, Sir Andrew Scott Waugh and Colonel James Walker. Despite his prodigious talent as a mountaineer and familiarity with local customs and languages, being country-born meant that Johnson could not advance in his career at the GTS, unlike covenanted military officers.[26] Notwithstanding, his desire to make his mark led him to take risks in the course of his duties and to behave in a manner that threatened to disrupt the established order of colonial authority. The next section will investigate how the GTS's surveys played a vital role in establishing a link between knowledge and power, and the imperative of ensuring that those who undertook that responsibility possessed the desired character and social status in order to exercise the requisite authority over the knowledge they produced.

SURVEYS AS AN EXERCISE IN IMPERIAL POWER AND THE VIEW FROM THE METROPOLE

The harshness of the topography, much of it at high altitudes, as well as the hostility of its inhabitants, made the frontier of North and North-West India an inherently unstable location in which to gather new knowledge.[27] Although the government welcomed new intelligence, they were not prepared to condone outrages against British subjects in areas over which they had no power to defend or avenge.[28] Without a military presence, it was very difficult for surveying to proceed on the frontiers of empire and if the GTS's surveyors strayed beyond it into hostile territory, they took a great risk where outcomes were unpredictable. Therefore, whenever possible, surveying operations in these areas were performed under the protection of the Indian army and conducted openly without the need for subterfuge.[29] But when conditions were considered too dangerous even with the protection of the army, 'native' pundits were

---

25. Edney, *Mapping an Empire*, 25–30.

26. BL/IOR/L/PS/6/550, Coll. 93, 47–51: Extracts from Correspondence between Johnson's superior officers at the GTS, regarding his service between 1854 and 1859.

27. Edney, *Mapping an Empire*, 25–30.

28. Waller, *The Pundits*, 21.

29. The British-Indian Army was officially raised in April 1895; but after the Revolution of 1857, the term was used informally as a collective description of the presidency armies; namely, Bengal, Madras and Bombay.

pressed into service, because should harm befall them, they posed no risk to British prestige and authority. Johnson's ambivalent position presented a challenge, as although country-born and categorised socially among Eurasians and 'poor whites', he was nevertheless part of the colonising community.

As a significant analytic site, the GTS set limitations to the spaces and contexts in which Johnson could operate, curtailing his freedom to be resourceful and innovative in his interactions beyond the bounds of British jurisdiction. In so doing, the Survey's actions compromised the idea of an adaptable and transferable approach to notions of place, as described in the first chapter. However, as Matthew Edney has argued, the GTS's surveys were 'exercises in negotiation, contestation and mediation between the surveyors and their native contacts, so that the knowledge which they generated was representative more of the power relations between the conquerors and the conquered, than of some topographical representation'.[30] In fact, 'What the British implemented was not the ideal, but only the *image* of the ideal and that image, which was transcribed into the archive, was the bounded world of colonial authority'.[31] That order did not derive directly from the surveys themselves and 'whatever order was imposed on the detailed surveys came *after* the fact, when they were incorporated into the general archive'.[32] As representations of power relations, it was the task of those in the GTS's senior hierarchy, who were invariably members of the military, to impose order on the information generated by the surveys carried out its behalf.[33] Despite being indirectly encouraged by his superior officers at the GTS to proceed beyond the frontier, Johnson's unfettered conduct in this uncontrolled space interrupted the precepts of that order and emphasised the ambiguity of his position. Hence the GTS's need to redraft and rewrite Johnson's materials after he returned from Khotan in order to reassert their authority and ownership of them.

Before imperial governance became more structured, there was far greater divergence of opinion between professional and amateur bodies about the ways in which colonial knowledge should be understood and employed, and especially between those in the metropole and the periphery. As the leading public institution in the metropole for the dissemination of new geographical knowledge, the authorisation and approbation of the RGS was of paramount importance to the GTS and its officers, who were eager to obtain the RGS's patronage, because they wished not only to publicise the results of their explorations as widely as possible but also to acquire personal prestige for their discoveries. But as noted in the introductory chapter, there was

---

30. Edney, *Mapping an Empire*, 25.
31. Ibid., 30.
32. Ibid.
33. See Chapter 1.

considerable divergence between the objectives of learned societies and other concerned groups in the metropole and those involved on the periphery, particularly regarding the importance of exploration and its impact on commercial and political outcomes. Meanwhile, in a parallel development, the gradual introduction of greater bureaucracy in the management of colonial affairs throughout the nineteenth century led to more formal approaches to the ways in which intelligence was obtained, thus allowing the Indian government to exert greater control over its acquisition and management.

However, a different perspective prevailed in the metropole within the institutions involved in the production of knowledge from that bounded by the social and political hierarchy in India. As Derek Gregory has observed, 'What seemed plausible in the lecture hall of the RGS might well become a half-truth on the ground'.[34] Although Johnson's report on his journey to Khotan's capital at Ilchí was deemed unsatisfactory by the GTS, it was acclaimed by the RGS, who later rewarded him with a fellowship. Johnson's account of his tribulations and extraordinary feats of physical endurance in unknown regions of Central Asia was received with the utmost respect and earned fulsome praise from the learned and distinguished members of the RGS. The new knowledge that his report conveyed to the Society in 1866 not only informed its own work and status as a learned society but also accorded it a role in negotiating the complex questions of authority and its relationship between political power and knowledge in Central Asia.[35]

His report was read to the RGS's members in London on 12 November 1866 by Major General Sir Henry Rawlinson (1810–1895), Orientalist and former EIC army officer and veteran of wars in Afghanistan, and published in the Society's journal in 1868.[36] After his death in 1883, the RGS's obituary praised Johnson's great achievements and criticised the Government of India for not encouraging and promoting those officers of the Survey who were able and willing to penetrate beyond the frontier. His obituary writer observed that in failing to recognise and reward the success of Johnson's unofficial adventurous expedition, so far beyond the Kashmir frontier, 'much valuable knowledge of the countries beyond the Himalayan chain had not been acquired'.[37] Unsurprisingly, the RGS was unanimous in its enthusiasm to encourage further exploration in the interests of enhancing geographical knowledge in that region.[38] Rewarding Johnson with the customary gold

---

34. Gregory, 'Power Knowledge and Geography', 79.

35. Dirks, *Colonial Histories*, 296.

36. William H. Johnson, 'Report on His Journey to Ilchí, the Capital of Khotan, in Chinese Tartary', *Journal of the Royal Geographical Society* 37 (1867): 1–47. See also Henry C. Rawlinson, 'On the Recent Journey of Mr W. H. Johnson from Leh, in Ladakh to Ilchí in Chinese Turkistan', *Proceedings of the JRGS* 11, nos. 1–6 (1866–1867): 6–14.

37. 'Obituary: Mr. W. H. Johnson', *Proceedings of the Royal Geographical Society and Monthly Record of Geography* 5, no. 5 (1883): 291.

38. Rawlinson, 'On the Recent Journey', 13.

watch, they considered that he 'had achieved an extraordinary geographical feat, one of the greatest of value',[39] and they regretted the government's condemnation of him. The president of the RGS said that he had never heard a paper which 'more completely developed the character of a true bold, and scientific manner of an expedition' than Johnson's, without which most of those present would have been lost in an 'unknown world'.[40] Lord Stangford said that Johnson's paper was one of the most important that had ever been read before the Society. The RGS's unanimous conclusion was that the government should be encouraging, not discouraging, 'its subordinates to visit those countries, where there was now no difficulty in Englishmen going'.[41]

The RGS's intervention into the politics of Central Asia complicated an already unstable situation regarding intelligence in unknown lands, as their interpretation of the political situation there and British relations with Russia diverged considerably from the government's point of view, particularly regarding opportunities for trade within the region. Whilst the ignorance of local climatic and topographic conditions, not to mention the danger of attack from hostile 'natives', may have predisposed members in the metropole to this view, it is difficult to understand why members like Sir Henry Rawlinson, who had previously served in these dangerous regions, appeared to be oblivious to the risks posed by lone exploration in such hostile terrain. Rawlinson declared that 'there could be no risk of war between Russia and ourselves in consequence of our exploring and trading with these countries', so that 'both nations might trade with perfect safety with the cities of Chinese Turkestan'.[42] For his part, Lord Strangford emphasised the significance of Johnson's intelligence regarding the political and commercial importance of the break-up of the external dominions of the Chinese Empire and the Khan of Khotan's desire to enter into commercial relations with British India, and to end the monopoly of the Maharajah of Kashmir.[43] Their comments following Rawlinson's reading of Johnson's paper illustrate the wide divergence of opinion between the Indian government and interested bodies like learned societies and other public institutions at the centre, who were keen to promote new trading links, but who took no account of the difficulties at the periphery of managing conditions and the grave political consequences of errors. In 1877, the Chinese authorities in Peking regained control of the rebellious Central Asian provinces, so that Derek Gregory's statement seems particularly apposite.[44]

The RGS adopted a different perspective towards Johnson's adventurous conduct from that of the hierarchy of the GTS, who were concerned not only

39. Ibid., 12.
40. Ibid., 11.
41. Ibid., 12.
42. Ibid., 14.
43. Ibid., 11.
44. Gregory, 'Power, Knowledge and Geography', 79.

to establish their cultural authority in a harsh environment but also to uphold British prestige and ensure the security of their personnel. After his death in 1883, the RGS praised Johnson as 'one of the few men living, who had greater experience of mountain work', and hailed his achievements as being of 'considerable value and magnitude'.[45] Such conflicting opinions are not only indicative of the tensions that existed amongst different social classes in India but also highlight inconsistencies between the metropole and the periphery about how new knowledge should be acquired and managed. Newspapers in the metropole fuelled the public debate, but they too could not fully appreciate political conditions on the ground. Meanwhile, Municipal Chambers of Commerce viewed expeditions such as Johnson's as important elements in advancing knowledge and forging mercantile connections with territories beyond the frontier, as the next section, describing the details of Johnson's journey to Khotan, reveals.

WILLIAM JOHNSON'S 1865 JOURNEY TO KHOTAN AND ITS CONSEQUENCES

William Johnson's journey to Khotan was remarkable for its audacious attempt to penetrate a previously unknown frontier and courageous because it involved ascending to higher altitudes that supposedly had only been achieved previously by men in balloons.[46] By exploring hitherto unknown territory, Johnson was able to acquire secret intelligence, useful not only to the GTS but also to the government and the mercantile community in India and Britain. Therefore, in 1865, whilst surveying on behalf of the GTS in North-West India, near Kashmir, Johnson exceeded his official orders to survey within the territory controlled by the Indian government and crossed the mountainous regions beyond the frontier to explore the neighbouring kingdom of Khotan, allegedly at the invitation of the country's ruler, the Khan Badsha. Johnson was the first European traveller in recent years to have penetrated so far beyond the frontier of India and returned safely. Until his visit, Khotan's only European visitors since Marco Polo's arrival in the thirteenth century had been the Portuguese missionary Benedict Goez in the sixteenth century, and a few Jesuits in the past century, whose work had not contained any geographical information.[47] The only other explorer, Adolphe, one of the Schlagintweit brothers, had been murdered in 1857.[48]

Whilst the use of 'native' pundits proved expedient in exploring and mapping difficult regions beyond the frontier, there were occasions which required an

---

45. 'Obituary: Mr. W. H. Johnson', 291.
46. BL/IOR/L/PS/6/550, Coll. 93: Letter from Col. James Walker to E. C. Bayley, Sec. to the Govt. of India, giving his explanation of Johnson's conduct (3 January 1867).
47. Rawlinson, 'On the Recent Journey', 12.
48. 'Obituary: Mr W. H. Johnson', 291.

experienced surveyor, familiar with British commercial and political ambitions, who was also able to identify the most favourable routes. In order to validate his belief in 'the continuing vitality of trade' in the provinces of Central Asia beyond the Himalayas,[49] Colonel Thomas Montgomerie considered William Johnson to be the surveyor most suited to this task. Before going on leave to England in January 1865, Montgomerie left instructions in a memo to Colonel Walker suggesting that, 'a large tract of country might be sketched and, if judiciously taken up, the whole of the ground up to the range *above* Khotan might be sketched in a general way'. He continued, 'If Mr Johnson thinks he could get on the range south of Khotan, and if so, no doubt a great many more points ought to be fixed in that vast *terra incognita*, east of the Pangong Lake'.[50]

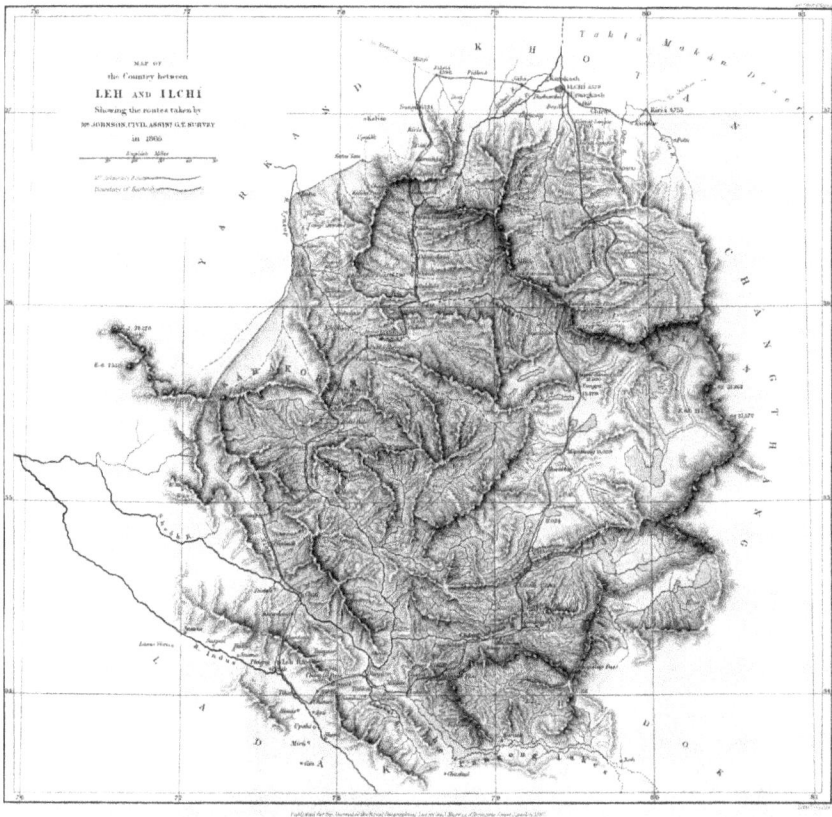

Figure 5.1.   William H. Johnson's map of North-East Ladakh and route to Khotan from 'Report on his Journey to Ilchí, the Capital of Khotan, in Chinese Tartary,' *Journal of the Royal Geographical Society of London* 37 (1867), 1–47.

49. BL/IOR/L/PS/6/552/873: Reports by Her Majesty's Secretaries of Embassy and Legation on the Manufactures, Commerce etc. of the Countries in which they reside (London: Harrison and Sons, 1867).

50. BL/IOR/L/PS/6/550, Coll. 93: Memorandum from Col. Thomas Montgomerie to Col. James Walker (January 1865).

Therefore, during the course of his surveying operations over the extreme northern limits of the Maharajah of Kashmir's territory, Johnson did as Montgomerie had suggested. Commencing his expedition at Leh in Ladakh in July 1865, his route took him via the Changchenmo Valley, over mountain passes of nearly 20,000 feet. He crossed the border into Khotan near the G.T. Station at E 57 (21,767 feet), on the K'un-lun Mountain Range, reaching Khotan's capital, Ilchí, in mid-September of the same year. Johnson spent some time in Ilchí gathering geographical, cultural and political information, and also exploring its environs. After a stay of sixteen days spent exploring Ilchí and the buried cities of the surrounding desert, he departed on 4 October 1865,[51] reaching Leh on 1 December via the Karakorum route.[52]

Johnson returned to the GTS's headquarters at Dehradun on 28 February 1866, having been attacked on the way by 'Kherghiz' shepherds. However, he was swiftly reprimanded by his superiors,[53] principally because his conduct had purportedly breached racial and class hierarchies, imposed to maintain European moral superiority and cultural boundaries.[54] Rather than being rewarded for his journey to Khotan, as was customary for pundits who accomplished similarly hazardous expeditions, Johnson was admonished for submitting an allegedly incorrect and incomplete report that had to be rewritten by a senior member of his Department.[55] Furthermore, whilst preparing for his journey to Khotan, he was accused of using his country-born status and local knowledge of banking procedures to obtain secret loans from the bank at Mussoorie. He did so again, prior to his departure from Ilchí, when he allegedly obtained money by deception from the country's ruler and engaged in other irregular financial activities. To make matters worse, on his return to Dehradun, Johnson offered contradictory explanations for discrepancies in his financial transactions and conflicting reasons why, without official orders, he had embarked on such a dangerous journey. Consequently, in 1867, he resigned from the GTS and took up a post as *Wazir* (minister)[56] to the Dogra Maharaja of Kashmir, Gulab Singh, who in 1846 had become the ruler of Ladakh after the region was transferred to him by the British under the terms of the Treaty of Amritsar.[57]

51. Johnson, 'Report', 16.

52. Rawlinson, 'On the Recent Journey', 10.

53. India Office London to Governor General of India (May 1867).

54. Helen Callaway, 'Review: Frederick Cooper and Ann Laura Stoler (eds.), *Tensions of Empire: Colonial Cultures in a Bourgeois World* (Berkeley, CA: University of California Press, 1997)', *Journal of the Royal Anthropological Institute* 4, no. 2 (1998): 368.

55. India Office London to Governor General of India (May 1867).

56. It was not unusual for those who remained in India after their contract with the EIC had ended to be employed by 'native rulers', often serving as officers in their armies or, like Johnson, becoming a minister at their courts, known as a *Wazir*.

57. In 1870, the Maharaja of Kashmir signed a commercial treaty with the British which allowed them to establish a post of Joint Commissioner at Ladakh. William Johnson became one of two commissioners appointed to oversee trade from the capital at Leh. He held this post until his alleged death

Johnson's survey was based on three previously determined trigonometrical stations on the K'un-lun Range and executed on a plane table, which he carried with him as part of his equipment. His starting station was Ilchí, then Sanju, and sixty miles as the crow flies to the Karakoram Pass.[58] Although the Khan had raised no objection to the use of the plane table, Johnson was obliged to carry out astronomical observations to determine latitude in secret because the Khan and his courtiers viewed them with suspicion.[59] Even though the Khan Badsha was anxious to cultivate trading relationships with Britain, having been impressed by their rule during a visit to India,[60] Khotan had been devoid of sustained and meaningful European contact for centuries and therefore could not hope to attain a similar epistemological collaboration with Western knowledge as a country like Siam had achieved. When confronted with the pressures of Western knowledge at this time, Siam's elite had already adopted accommodating policies that allowed older concepts to coexist alongside the new world order.[61] As a result, 'By the 1880s Western "geography" and the concept of the "map" had become powerful agents in this transformation of the old Siamese *phraratcha-anachak* (royal kingdom) into a modern *prathet* (nation)'.[62] Meanwhile, in Khotan, centuries of lack of contact with the world beyond its borders had not allowed its rulers to become familiar with new Western innovations in technology and science.

Johnson's official report stated that his reason for venturing beyond the frontier into Khotan was to enable him to provide the British government with valuable information regarding those provinces of Central Asia, which at that time were largely unknown to Europeans. He also asserted that he wished to obtain information on the movements of Russian forces in those parts of the world.[63] In his report, Johnson also provided secret intelligence, which was not made available to the RGS, that the Khan of Khotan had been the first to raise a successful rebellion against the Chinese in 1863. The Khan told Johnson in an audience that he now wanted the British government to send troops to help, not only against the advance of Russian forces but also against those from nearby states in Chinese Turkestan, which were then in a situation of anarchy. Whilst he was in Ilchí, the inhabitants of neighbouring Yarkand had allegedly asked Johnson to take possession of their city on

from poisoning in 1883. Lieutenant-Colonel Sir Oliver St. John, the officer sent to Jammu, the capital of Kashmir, to investigate Johnson's death, described the circumstances as 'embarrassing'. His comment highlights the problems faced by the Government of India when confronted with a European death in unexplained circumstances beyond its borders.

58. Rawlinson, 'On the Recent Journey', 10; and Johnson, 'Report', 20.
59. Johnson, 'Report', 14.
60. Rawlinson, 'On the Recent Journey', 8.
61. Day and Reynolds, 'Cosmologies', 10.
62. Ibid.
63. Johnson, 'Report', 3.

behalf of the British.[64] As noted earlier, apart from the loss to Khotan of trade
with the Chinese, the Maharajah of Kashmir had also paralysed trade in the
region by levying very high transit duties on goods passing through his territories, which adjoined the mountain passes into Turkestan.[65]

As the first European to enter Khotan for many years, Johnson's presence
was regarded by the Khan and his retinue as that of an external agent, or
representative, sent by the British government; hence, it was their expectation that he would pass on their requests for help, which were accompanied
by generous gifts for government officials. In reality, Johnson possessed
no power to intervene in Khotan's political affairs on behalf of either the
British or Indian government, nor to grant aid and support them against
their enemies. Nevertheless, the knowledge acquired by Johnson contained
potentially valuable political intelligence useful to the Indian government
in exercising control on its frontier with Central Asia. However, it could
not be authenticated, as the circumstances surrounding Johnson's journey
to Khotan were far from straightforward. From the outset, they revealed the
existence of a number of 'different truths' involving various agencies and
networks of exchange, as tensions surrounding professional status, education and lack of cultural authority were brought to bear on the situation.

Johnson lacked any formal mandate to gather intelligence, either as an
envoy of the Indian government or the GTS. He appeared rather to have been
motivated by the opportunity of the visit to pursue personal business interests,
which was not uncommon according to earlier precedents set by the EIC's
officers. Due to the uncertainties of life in India, the EIC had tacitly allowed
its covenanted servants to engage in private commercial ventures, as long as
they did not interfere with Company business. This practice had continued,
particularly amongst members of the army, many of whom were employed by
the GTS. Government officials looked to make personal financial gains to aug-
ment their income by negotiating bills of exchange and reinvesting funds sent
to them by relatives in England in local banks at a higher rate of interest. They
often engaged in risky commercial ventures and speculative financial schemes,
taking out unsecured mortgages on land and property; even the scholar, Francis
Ellis, had lived on the 'financial edge', incurring debts and borrowing money to
buy land, all of which came to light after his untimely death.[66]

On his return from Khotan, Johnson offered conflicting accounts of why
he had crossed the frontier, declaring that, whilst surveying, he had received
an invitation from the Khan Badsha of Khotan, which, in accordance with
Montgomerie's orders, had incited him to visit the Khan in his capital at

64. Ibid., 14.
65. Rawlinson, 'On the Recent Journey', 9.
66. See Chapter 4.

Ilchí.[67] In another version, he alleged that he had been kidnapped en route by the Khan's envoys and forced to accompany them to Ilchí.[68] Colonel Walker had asked Johnson to include a separate 'secret' section in his Report to the GTS, dealing with 'matters of special nature', which, as noted, did not appear in the article that Rawlinson read to the RGS.[69] This was a clear indication that Walker and Montgomerie were complicit in Johnson's disobedience of official government orders not to stray beyond the Indian frontier. His secret report contained information concerning the Commandant of the Khan of Khotan's infantry, a man named Mahomed Ali, whom Johnson believed was the 'treacherous and dangerous' fugitive formerly known as the Nana of Bithoor, wanted after the massacre at Cawnpore in 1857.

The Nana of Bithoor was infamous in the recent history of the Indian Revolution because, having by deception obtained the surrender of the British garrison at Cawnpore, he had then led his rebel Sepoys in a notorious massacre, during which many British women and children were murdered.[70] After the British recaptured Cawnpore and the Nana's forces were defeated, he disappeared. It was rumoured that the Nana of Bithoor had fled firstly to Nepal, which at that time was off-limits to the British. However, Johnson discovered that although Mahomed Ali said that he had come to Khotan via Kabul two years earlier, others told him that he had in fact been there for four years, arriving not long after the Revolution.[71] But as the Khan Badsha was surrounded by adventurers at his Court, Mahomed Ali had, until Johnson's arrival, aroused no particular suspicion. As possibly the most wanted man in British India at that time, Johnson observed that Mahomed, who commanded the Khan's 6,000-strong infantry, was educated and spoke English and Hindustani, and that his weapons included a cavalry percussion pistol marked No. 3 EIC.[72]

According to Johnson, whilst assuming the appearance of a Mahomedan, aspects of Mahomed Ali's dress, conduct and manner of speech betrayed him to be a Maratha. Johnson noted that he was also sufficiently affluent 'to feed different batches of about three hundred of his Sepoys in Khotan daily'.[73] The GTS ignored the information in Johnson's secret report that the wealthy Maratha, masquerading as the Mahomedan Commandant of the Khotan

---

67. Johnson, 'Report', 3.
68. BL/IOR/L/PS/6/550, Coll. 93, 103: Colonel Walker to Sec. to the Govt. of India (Dehradun, 22 April 1866).
69. Ibid. See also BL/IOR/L/PS/6/456, 1318–19: Copies of Political Letters and Despatches to India, vol. 2 (14 September 1861–31 December 1867); BL/IOR/L/PS/6/548, Coll. 38/1: Letter no. 650 from Sec. to the Govt. India (Simla, 22 June 1866).
70. For further information, see Anand Swarup Misra, *Nana Saheb Peshwa and the Fight for Freedom* (Lucknow: Information Department, Uttar Pradesh, 1961).
71. Letter no. 650, 35.
72. Ibid.
73. Ibid., 34.

Infantry, was formerly the infamous Nana of Bithoor.[74] The problem was that Johnson's intelligence could not be validated and it had been obtained without official authorisation. Furthermore, there could be no possibility of redress against the Nana's previous outrages whilst he resided in a remote Khanate of Central Asia. Failure of a mission to recapture him would undermine prestige and compromise the already fragile political situation on Britain's Indian frontiers. Whilst acknowledging that 'no doubt his conduct was enterprising and public spirited and the information he has been enabled to gather may prove useful', the GTS's Superintendent Colonel James Walker reiterated his condemnation of Johnson's conduct. He concluded his Report to the Governor General at Simla by stating, 'On the other hand, had Mr Johnson and his party been detained at Khotan or murdered on the way, he would have involved the Government in all the odium arising out of an un-redressed injury to one of its British born servants'.[75] There was worse to come, as after Johnson returned to Dehradun, accusations of his misconduct whilst at Khotan surfaced, which are considered in the next section.

ACCUSATIONS AGAINST JOHNSON RELATING TO HIS CONDUCT IN KHOTAN

The prospect of re-establishing lucrative trading links with markets in Central Asia no doubt tempted Johnson to extend his surveying operations and visit Khotan in order to make contacts with its merchants and investigate the prospects for the possible collection and distribution of their goods in India. In the subsequent enquiry into Johnson's alleged misdeeds, evidence came to light that he was already involved with the Indian Carrying Company and, whilst in Khotan, he may have been attempting to open negotiations for future commercial contracts.[76] The evidence was supplied by Mr Edwin Collard Smith, the Carrying Company's superintendent, who stated that early one morning in January 1867, whilst in Delhi, he had witnessed Johnson paying money to recipients who were not Europeans.[77]

---

74. Ibid.
75. Ibid.
76. BL/IOR/L/PJ/3/1091, No. 45, 2: Papers regarding the abolition of the Government Bullock Train Establishments, and the transfer to the Indian Carrying Company of the whole business hitherto performed by those Establishments. In 1864, the Indian Carrying Company had taken over the Government's Bullock Train Establishments with the objective of transporting goods from the rail terminal and intermediate stations along the lines of the Indian Railways. After the expansion of the railway network, a large number of its wagons and carts had become surplus to requirements, allowing them to be bought by a private company who, similar to Messrs Pickford and Company, England, would collect goods for dispatch by rail and distribute them on arrival at their destination.
77. BL/IOR/L/PS/6/552, Coll. 182: Index to newsletters submitted by newswriters at Ladakh (11 August 1866).

In addition to Collard Smith's revelations, numerous indigenous local networks and agencies throughout India, known collectively as news-writers, were involved in supplying the government with information. In due course, news-writers from Ladakh submitted accounts of Johnson's behaviour during his visit to Khotan, which traduced his character and motives for the visit. As a result, official enquiries were instigated by the Indian government regarding these allegations, especially after Johnson had submitted two conflicting accounts of the reasons for his journey to Ilchí.[78] However, the accuracy of news-writers' accounts could not always be relied upon; it was alleged that some were illiterate and that 'native underlings placed at so great a distance from control, cannot resist the temptation to commit petty oppression'.[79]

Having received information from the Khan's envoys, Zuman Khan and Jooma Khan (who were also his sons), the news-writers accused Johnson of theft.[80] In their letter of 11 August 1866, they stated that Johnson was received with great hospitality by the Khan when he arrived in Khotan, who gave him presents, including four horses and *khilluts* (carpets), as well as money for the Governor of the Punjab. Reaching Lahore on his way back to Dehradun, Johnson was accused of only giving the horses and carpets to the Governor and keeping the money for himself without informing the government. Zuman Khan also complained that he had only received 150 rupees from the Khotan authorities for accompanying Johnson on his journey to the capital at Ilchí. Therefore, it would appear that Johnson's statement that he had been escorted to Ilchí by the Khan's followers was true and that his visit was anticipated. Zuman Khan was dissuaded by his brother from pursuing the matter further, pointing out to him that if a complaint were made against Mr Johnson, the good name of their own sovereign would be compromised. As the Khan was anxious to secure trade deals with the British, he did not wish to indict the first European intermediary to visit his country for a long time with fraud.[81]

It was further alleged that before his departure from Ilchí, Johnson had attempted to borrow twenty-five silver koors (4,150 rupees) from the merchants of Khotan, on the promise of repaying the same, with interest, at Ladakh. When the Khan heard that Johnson was only able to obtain a loan of five koors, he ordered that the twenty-five silver koors be paid to Johnson from his own treasury.[82] Meanwhile, aware that Colonel Montgomerie had left it to his discretion whether to attempt to get on the range south of

---

78. BL/IOR/L/PS/6/550, Coll. 93: Colonel Walker to E.C. Bayley, Sec. to the Govt. of India (3 January 1867).
79. Index to newsletters (11 August 1866), 15.
80. Ibid.
81. Ibid.
82. Ibid., 3–4.

Khotan,[83] Johnson had considered himself free to make his own arrangements for his journey there. This included privately securing bank loans, which he later stated he needed in order to bribe the Khan's officials when he got to Ilchí. The irregularities surrounding Johnson's financial dealings whilst in Khotan suggest that he may have obtained these loans not only to bribe the Khan's chief officers to secure his safe passage out of the Khanate but also to transport commercial goods out of Khotan, or to purchase goods in India on behalf of merchants whom he had met there.[84]

In his submission, Johnson stated that on his return, he had borrowed some money from the Mussoorie Savings Bank and 'part from the firm of which I am the Manager' in order to repay 'notes in hand',[85] which had been made over to him by merchants in Khotan. Much to the annoyance of the local government, Johnson claimed that he had repaid these 'notes in hand' with his own money, even though he was aware that the government was willing to discharge them on his behalf. In doing so, he had prevented the government from making enquiries as to their authenticity, prior to authorising repayment to him. Therefore, the government was unable to ascertain whether the 'notes in hand' that Johnson alleged he had given to the merchants as security were genuine, inviting the possibility that he had forged the notes in order to obtain money by deception.[86]

As mentioned in the earlier section, in his report to the Governor General, the GTS's Superintendent, Colonel James Walker, made it clear that Johnson had exceeded his official orders by visiting Khotan. Whilst conceding that Johnson's 'unofficial' journey had been the means of the GTS acquiring a considerable amount of information regarding regions which had previously been almost unknown, he emphasised Johnson's subordinate status at the GTS and lack of authority to act on behalf of the Government of India. Furthermore, Walker stated that 'until he went to Khotan he had done nothing to distinguish himself, more than the majority of the other Surveyors'.[87] Walker traduced Johnson's character, education and lack of professional status, observing that 'his shortcomings are excusable enough in a man of his position, who has not had the advantages of a good education, but it is evident that however meritorious his services as a subordinate may be, as a

---

83. BL/IOR/L/PS/6/552/873: From Colonel Thomas Montgomerie in Reports by Her Majesty's Secretaries of Embassy and Legation on the Manufactures, Commerce etc. of the Countries in Which They Reside (London: Harrison and Sons, 1867).

84. BL/IOR/L/PS/6/552, Coll. 178, 1125: Lord Northcote, Sec. of State for India, to Governor General of India (May 1867).

85. Note in hand: A promise to pay a specified amount on demand or a written promise to repay a debt by a certain date.

86. BL/IOR/L/PS/6/552, Coll. 178: Revenue Dept. to Lord Northcote (22 April 1867).

87. Walker to Bayley (3 January 1867).

superior Officer their value would be questionable'.[88] He continued by noting that, unlike the Engineer officers who joined the GTS, Johnson lacked
an education in Britain and had not gone to military college to study for his
profession, but had instead joined the GTS merely as a copyist carrying out
simple calculations.

Emphasising the GTS's authority over its materials and sources of knowledge, Walker reiterated to the Governor General that Johnson's report had
to be entirely rewritten, his map recast, and that reductions of astronomical
observations had to be recalculated because all three were judged unfit for
publication in their original state.[89] Walker concluded his report by referring
once again to the shortcomings in Johnson's education, observing that 'he
has not had the benefit of a liberal education, nor are his natural abilities such
as to enable him to rise above the disadvantages of his position. Military
Officers could not be expected to serve under his orders, and, if directed to
do so, would certainly resign their appointments in the Survey'.[90] Not only
do Walker's comments highlight the divisions between the military and
civilians, but they also confirm that by the mid-nineteenth century, the
disadvantages of being country-born and belonging to the domiciled community were embedded within the imperial class hierarchy. Johnson vigor-
ously contested these accusations by stating that instead of being rewarded
financially like the 'native pundits', he had been unfairly reprimanded and,
unlike officers who were his juniors and had superseded him at the GTS, he
would not receive a pension.[91]

By acting as an unofficial go-between to secure intelligence and using
his undoubted talents as a surveyor to conceal private trading schemes and
dubious financial arrangements, Johnson complicated the inherently unstable
process of knowledge production on India's frontier. It was an arena where
space and the objects that it produced were debased by conflicting motives
of human agency. Despite being encouraged to do so by Colonel Thomas
Montgomerie in his memorandum to Colonel Walker, Johnson took a risk,
whereby he crossed professional, racial and class boundaries by undertaking
his journey to Khotan without receiving official orders. He further compounded his error by making private business arrangements whilst there
that involved dubious financial dealings. When these came to light through
news-writers' and others' reports, Montgomerie and Walker (now the GTS's
Superintendent) distanced themselves from their earlier comments. Instead,

88. Ibid.
89. Ibid.
90. Ibid.
91. BL/IOR/L/MIL/10/65/597–5: Bengal Army Service Lists (1857), 1, 448:712. See the Army
Service Lists for Bengal in 1857 as an example of pension rights. They record that Thomas Montgomerie was entitled 'to reckon 1 year, 10 months and 7 days with a view of retirement on full pay'.

as Johnson's superintendent, Walker made acerbic remarks about his lack of education and country-born status and discredited his earlier work as a surveyor.

After his departure from the GTS in 1867, Johnson took up the position as *Wazir* (chief minister) with the Maharaja of Kashmir, a position which he held until his death in 1883. He was also appointed joint British commissioner at Leh in Ladakh, so that despite dissatisfaction arising from his last mission, his abilities as a go-between were still recognised in this strategic trade entrepôt, where he continued his rather dubious commercial and financial dealings, as the account of his death in the next section explains. Its occurrence in 1883, in Jammu, was an event that stirred up a great deal of controversy in the region, occasioning adverse reports in local newspapers.[92] This resulted in a thorough investigation being conducted by the Government of India, which although inconclusive, pointed once again to Johnson's duplicity in trying to clear his debts by making his death appear to be caused by poisoning.

THE EXTRAORDINARY CIRCUMSTANCES RELATING TO JOHNSON'S DEATH IN JAMMU

William Johnson had no difficulty in making enemies, as indicated by the financial irregularities, not to say improprieties, surrounding his expedition to Khotan, which continued whilst he was *Wazir* in Kashmir. These circumstances were not lost on his obituary-writer, a fellow surveyor on the Kashmir mountains' survey from 1857 to 1863.[93] Whilst noting that Johnson had been 'a valued and trusted servant of the Maharaja', he observed, 'his position must have been one most difficult to fill without creating great jealousy, and no doubt, many enemies'.[94] He continued, 'His services have been of no ordinary kind, and I am now glad to be able to bring them to public notice as they deserve'.[95] Reports that Johnson had allegedly been poisoned initially appeared credible and remain on public record to this day. Having relinquished his post as commissioner at Ladakh in December 1882, Johnson was appointed to the lucrative position of superintendent of timber exports to the Punjab. As reports in the *Times of India* stated, 'This position had been previously held by "natives", giving rise to extensive peculations in the department'. *The Times* rather egregiously stated that although the

92. BL/IOR/P/2110: Circumstances attending the death of Mr W.H. Johnson in Kashmir (June 1883), No. 40.
93. 'Obituary: Mr W. H. Johnson', 291–293.
94. Ibid.
95. Ibid., 293.

appointment of an Englishman might secure the profits for the state rather than in the pockets of persons, it was an appointment that would make him enemies.[96] From this time onwards, Johnson made repeated assertions that he was being poisoned.[97]

William Johnson's death occurred at his home in Jammu on the morning of 3 February 1883, after the poisonous drugs, ether and chloroform, were found in the whiskey bottle from which he and his friends had drunk the previous night. As the local Indian doctors could not make up their minds about the cause of death, Lt. Colonel Sir Oliver St. John was sent to Jammu from his camp at Sialkot to investigate matters. He thought it advisable to be accompanied by a medical man, who could assist him with enquiries into the symptoms and circumstances of Johnson's last illness, and with questioning witnesses and arranging for post-mortem examinations to be carried out in Lahore.[98] As no doctor was available, he was accompanied by Mr H.W. Bellew, the sanitary commissioner for the Punjab, who happened to be in the camp. St. John considered that this would be important if no traces of poison were found in the body, despite their presence in the whiskey bottle. He made these observations in a demi-official letter to the Foreign Secretary of the Government of India, whilst at the same time informing him that 'the organs, as it would present, appear having been in such a state as to render it possible that the deceased did not die from natural causes'.[99] With regard to poisoning by ether and chloroform, St. John expressed the opinion to the Foreign Secretary that, even if Johnson had drunk the drugs, either knowingly or unknowingly, 'it is very doubtful that this would have killed him, and that it would have killed him after three and a half days seems quite incredible'.[100]

Nevertheless, the sudden and unexplained death of a British subject, albeit one who was country-born and of the subaltern class, was a serious matter requiring investigation. Of particular concern to the Government of India was the fact that the Maharajah of Kashmir was angered by the case and that, whatever the cause, the publicity surrounding the death of this prominent British resident of Jammu would make it very difficult to prove to the 'ordinary public' that Johnson had not been poisoned by some unknown person, or persons. The only chance of doing so appeared to depend upon establishing that Johnson had purchased the poison himself.[101] Therefore, enquiries were

---

96. Report in the *Times of India* (10 February 1883).
97. Ibid.
98. BL/IOR/P/2110: Nos. 39–63, 33–45; quoting BL/IOR/P/2110: Letter to the Foreign Secretary for India (6 February 1883).
99. Ibid.
100. Ibid.
101. Circumstances attending the death of Johnson (June 1883).

made in Lahore and Calcutta to discover whether a man fitting Johnson's description had bought the drugs, but they proved fruitless.

It took Johnson three and a half days to die, during which time his condition fluctuated between periods when he was in severe pain, delirious and suffering from sporadic fits and periods of lucidity. At times, he was even well enough to rise from his bed, drink coffee, take light nourishment and smoke a cigarette. But on the morning of 3 February 1883, he did not recover from his coma and died. In the hours leading up to his death, Johnson left a series of handwritten notes in which he alleged that he must have ingested the poisonous drugs when he drank 'a small peg' of whiskey after returning from spending the evening with friends. At around midnight on 30 January, Johnson wrote in a legible hand that he believed that he had been poisoned but, following a restless night, his writing became increasingly indecipherable. It was not until his friend, Mr P.E. Browne, called upon him the next morning at around 7 o'clock, that anyone knew that Johnson had been unwell during the night; even his servant Ramzan was unaware of this. Later that morning, Johnson asked his friend to seal his whiskey bottle and take charge of the keys to his dispatch box.

Statements were taken by St. John from everyone who attended Johnson in his last illness, including three Indian doctors and his friends, Mr P.E. Browne and Mr A.E. Jenkins, who had both drunk whiskey from Johnson's bottle on the last evening that they spent together. Colonel St. John's enquiries revealed that there was no possibility of repeated doses of ether and chloroform, or any other poison having been administered to Johnson by anyone other than himself. St. John was also anxious to obtain a concise medical opinion, as it would raise a second question: namely, were Johnson's symptoms compatible with the possibility that he had, over time, taken repeated doses of ether or chloroform, or a similar drug such as hydrate of chloral, a large bottle of which had been found among Johnson's personal effects.[102] Meanwhile, in the opinion of Sanitary Commissioner Bellew, Johnson's mind was disturbed by troubles in his private affairs and so he concluded that his death was due to 'natural causes' and consequently, it was certified as 'apoplexy'. Bellew declared that 'beyond the first idea in the mind of Mr Johnson (an idea it appears that had disturbed his thoughts for many months preceding) that his enemies were bent upon his death by poison, I have not been able to discover any grounds for believing that his death was caused by the felonious administration of poison'.[103]

However, the post-mortem in Lahore revealed that no drugs were found in Johnson's body, only in the whiskey bottle from which he had drunk during his last evening in the company of his friends, Browne and Jenkins. On breaking open the bottle's seal, the chemical examiner detected a strong smell of chloroform and when the liquid in the bottle was separated, it totalled ten drams, of

---

102. Ibid.
103. Ibid., 48, 43.

which three were whiskey and the rest chloroform and ether. No other poisons were detected.[104] It would appear that Johnson had adulterated his whiskey bottle himself, in order to make his death appear to have been caused by criminal poisoning. His motive seems, yet again, to have been debt, as immediately following his death, his executors submitted a claim against the State of Kashmir and Jammu for over three lakh (300,000) rupees, which he had deposited for safe keeping with the Kashmir Treasury. Johnson believed that this sum was owed to him after its disappearance following an alleged robbery, for which Johnson accused Kashmir's treasury officials of being responsible. Johnson's executors also laid a claim against the State of Kashmir for another alleged robbery that had supposedly occurred at Johnson's house some time earlier, for which the same treasury officials were also blamed. However, Colonel St. John dismissed all of these allegations and claims as wholly fictitious.[105]

Meanwhile, it was revealed that Johnson himself owed large sums of money to the Maharajah, leading St. John to conclude that these bogus claims were the key to the whole mystery. As he wrote to the Foreign Secretary of the Government of India, 'Being unable to meet this deficit in the ordinary way by cooking his accounts, he imagined these methods of balancing them and at the same time providing a comfortable provision for his widow and children and either poisoned himself, or took measures, feeling himself to be dying, to make out that he had been poisoned'.[106] It would seem that in order to absolve himself from debt and to make provision for his wife and five children by possibly obtaining compensation from the Maharajah of Kashmir, Johnson had faked the cause of his death to make it appear that he had been poisoned. Having ingested neither chloroform nor ether, how then had he died after spending a convivial evening with friends and retiring in apparent good health around midnight on 30 January 1883?

One answer may lie in the discovery by the investigators of a large bottle of hydrate of chloral in Johnson's house, and also from medical evidence provided by the Indian doctors who attended Johnson during his last illness. The habitual use of chloral hydrate became common in the Punjab in the late nineteenth century, when the price of alcohol rose after increases in excise duty. Adding a gram or so of hydrate of chloral to alcoholic drinks increased their intoxicating effects, so that less alcohol was consumed in order to reach a state of inebriation. Poor people especially started using chloral hydrate because of its cheapness and easy availability and the substance became responsible for much addiction in India.[107] As the consumption of chloral hydrate is habit-

---

104. Ibid., 47.
105. Ibid.
106. Ibid., 48.
107. R.N. Chopra and I.C. Chopra, *Notes from Drug Addiction with Special Reference to India* (New Delhi: The Council for Scientific and Industrial Research, 1965), 7, 77.

forming and Johnson was in financial difficulties, the presence of a large bottle of the substance in his house points to its role in his death. During the course of their treatment, the Indian doctors administered an enema of castor oil and turpentine to him, extracting what they termed was a large 'seyballa' or 'scyhalla', a condition that was associated with the chronic use of opiates.[108] They also noted that Johnson was over fifty years old and addicted to alcohol. There is little doubt that on the night of 30 January 1883, William Johnson, suffering from the effects of long-term addiction to alcohol and chronic substance abuse, decided to fake the cause of his death by adulterating his whisky bottle and leaving notes that he had been poisoned by his enemies.

A colourful character, who in some reports was described as a rogue, William Johnson's life on the frontier was a precarious existence that ended in his early death at the age of fifty-one years. He left a widow, by whom he had several children. They had wed at Mussoorie when Johnson was nineteen and his mixed-race bride was herself a young widow of only sixteen years of age, having previously been married to another 'chancer' called Mauger Fitzhugh Monk.[109]

CONCLUDING REMARKS

Lack of well-defined and professional structures allowed a number of vested interests, both private and official, to contest their right of cultural authority over colonial knowledge and to jostle for position in claiming responsibility for its acquisition. Despite his undoubted talent and mountaineering achievements, Johnson was never able to attain the position to which he aspired, that of a respected senior officer with the GTS. As a white country-born resident of India, he was forever condemned to subaltern status, able only to obtain uncovenanted employment with the GTS and, unlike his father, without a pension. This imposed insurmountable barriers to his ability to succeed in the uncertain and harsh conditions of life on India's frontiers. The precarious nature of his financial and social status, coupled with his own propensity for dishonesty, led him to take risks financially and incur debt, a not uncommon situation for those whose lives were lived on empire's edge. It was a sad ending for an individual of such obvious talent, showing that the inequalities of empire could be as devastating for Europeans as they were for the colonised. William Johnson's story demonstrates that the quest for colonial knowledge,

---

108. This occurs when faeces sometimes accumulate in distinct indurated 'scybala', or enormous masses, that are solid and compact. It is often associated with the chronic use of opiates.

109. See G. Sailli, 'Letters of a Mussoorie Merchant'. Note also that although descended from the rather unprepossessing origins of a country-born citizen, Johnson's daughter, Teresa, married into the minor ranks of the British aristocracy in 1899, when she became the wife of the Seventh Baron Headley. See Chapter 9, pp. 222–224.

Figure 5.2. Peak in the Kuen Lun [K'un-lun] range, in Robert B. Shaw's book, *Visits to High Tartary, Yârkand, and Kâshghar* (London, 1871). *Source:* **Public Domain.**

especially on the frontier, was not only physically dangerous but also fraught with uncertainties and mental pressures.

Controversy existed for many decades amongst the mountaineering community over Johnson's claim in his report of 1866 to Colonel James Walker of the GTS of India that he had climbed three peaks in the high K'un-lun range on his way to Khotan. Articles by Major Kenneth Mason and Sir Aurel Stein in the *Alpine Journal* of 1921 attempted to address what Stein considered to be a 'historical puzzle'.[110] After a lengthy investigation, Mason concluded that Johnson had not ascended the highest of the three peaks, namely E61, on his way to Khotan, as he had claimed in his report to Walker. Unable

---

110. Kenneth Mason, 'Johnson's Suppressed Ascent of E 61', *Alpine Journal* 34 (1921): 54–62.

to find the original plane table sketches responsible for the introduction of errors into Johnson's maps, Mason determined that Walker's suppression of these errors, due to a faulty plane table and attempted correction, had led to the confusion.[111] Mason conceded that Johnson was not wholly to blame for starting out with a faulty plane table, but he also maintained that the Government of India had acted very leniently towards Johnson's breach of discipline in straying beyond the British boundary.[112] Meanwhile, based on his experiences during his second expedition in 1906, Sir Aurel Stein agreed with Mason that Johnson had not climbed E61 but, as the only European traveller to have visited that mountain region since Johnson, he himself had been unable to determine where the third peak actually lay.[113] In light of his own experience in these difficult terrains, where he lost the toes of his right foot through frostbite, Stein paid 'a tribute of respect to the feat of pluck and perseverance which Johnson performed in making his way to Khotan across ground of such exceptional difficulty as the K'un-lun'.[114]

As Johnson's story has indicated, beyond the hierarchies of the colonial state a fluid society existed, populated by chancers, rogues, risk-takers and eccentrics. Its existence on the imperial margins helped to sustain the networks of intelligence required to keep the empire afloat, just as the knowing people had done over a century earlier. The next chapter will investigate how army Surgeon, Dr Clement Williams, although more of a risk-taker than a rogue, also aspired to make commercial gains from trading beyond the frontier. Although possessed of a good education in Britain and trained as a surgeon, Williams too lacked cultural authority by virtue of his close association with the Burmese king and his people. He endeavoured to promote British interests by seeking to open new trade routes into Western China through the independent Kingdom of Upper Burma. Like William Johnson, the knowledge that Clement Williams acquired on his journey was not given the recognition or reward that it deserved by the Government of India. The next chapter will discuss Williams's transformation from an adventurous army surgeon, who became the first British Political Agent in Upper Burma, to an independent entrepreneur closely involved with the Burmese king. This relationship created suspicion and dislike of him in Rangoon, the capital of British Burma, causing Williams to lose his commercial enterprises and ending with his early death at the age of forty-six.

---

111. Ibid., 59.
112. Ibid., 60.
113. Aurel Stein, 'Johnson's Map and the Topography of the K'un-Lun, South of Khotan', *Alpine Journal* 34 (1921): 63.
114. Ibid., 67.

Chapter 6

Dr Clement Williams: A British Merchant at the Court of King Mindon

INTRODUCTION

Inspired by stories that he had heard about the old caravan routes between Burma and Western China, Dr Clement Williams (1833–1879) decided to undertake a journey of exploration from Mandalay, during the dry season of January 1863, to explore these ancient pathways. They formed a corridor across Northern Burma with many connecting points, crossroads and openings that had created complex networks of overland trade from Bengal to the China Sea.[1] For centuries, negotiations and transactions had taken place between the Chinese and the diverse interests of the local Burmese, Kakhyeen (nowadays known as Singpho/Jinghpaw), and Shan populations.[2] This chapter investigates how Williams used his medical skills to gain access to royal favours, which, in 1863, included receiving King Mindon's personal permission to make a journey along the Irrawaddy River towards this main commercial vein. Immersing himself in Burmese society and interacting with its people and their objects allowed him to acquire affective knowledge about the country, which stimulated his imagination to produce new intellectual constructs.[3] Affective knowledge in the context of this chapter is understood to mean an emotional understanding of the ways in which indigenous communities functioned, which was useful not only to the Governments of India and British Burma but also to political and commercial interests in the metropole.[4]

---

1. Cederloff, 'Seeking China's Back Door', 127.
2. Ibid.
3. Clement Williams's deep commitment to understanding Upper Burma's culture and customs encouraged him to learn Burma's difficult language and to master some of its many dialects.
4. See Athena Athanasiou, Pothiti Hantzaroula and Kostas Yannakopoulos, 'Towards a New Epistemology: The "Affective Turn"', *Historein* 8 (2008): 5–16: 'Since the mid-1990s, theoretical engagement

Taking leave from his post as an Assistant Army Surgeon with the Sixty-Eighth Madras Regiment in Rangoon, Williams set out with the intention of following the course of the Irrawaddy River as far as the frontier with Western China, and further if possible. He undertook his solo journey at his own expense and, like William Johnson, he had neither official approval nor sponsorship. However, during the 1860s he did enjoy the patronage of Burma's Chief Commissioner, Sir Arthur Phayre (1812–1885).[5] Although not the first European to venture past Mandalay, Williams was the first Englishman to sail beyond the Defiles of the Irrawaddy River. Accompanied only by his Indian servant, Raj Singh, Williams aimed not only to make his mark as an explorer but also to seek out opportunities to open up new trade routes that would allow British merchants to gain access to China's lucrative markets through its western frontier with Burma.[6] He hoped that by widely publicising his discoveries, he might gain public recognition for his attempts and earn a permanent role in the British Burma Administration, which had been established in Rangoon since 1853 following the end of the Second Burmese War.

After his return from his voyage of discovery, Williams contributed to the public presentation of knowledge by publishing an account of his travels in the *Journal of the Asiatic Society*, followed in 1868 by a book titled, *Through Burmah to Western China, Being Notes of a Journey in 1863 to Establish the Practicability of a Trade-Route between the Irawaddi and the Yang-Tse-Kiang*. He believed that showing empathy towards Burma's many peoples and sharing his knowledge of Western medicine would help to create the conditions that would enable colonial regimes to expand their territories peacefully and productively. In his book, he observed that 'Looking at the low state of the healing art in Burmah, I have often thought over the influence which a few skilled medical missionaries could readily command'.[7] But at the same time, the affective knowledge that he acquired through his affinity with the country and its people perversely contributed to the colonial state's epistemic anxieties about the dangers posed beyond its frontiers by potential enemies and their collaborators.[8] In Williams's case, his close relationship

---

by historians, anthropologists and literary critics with emotions and affectivity has altered the analytical perspective of the relationship between empire and metropole. Scholars have analysed the way in which "the languages of class, gender and race have overlapped with the politics of emotions in the social fabric of both the empire and the metropolis"' (9).

5. Arthur Purves Phayre was at that time Commissioner of Pegu (Lower Burma), and in 1862, he became Commissioner for the whole of British Burma, which included the provinces of Tenasserim and Arakan, a position which he held until his retirement in 1867.

6. Williams, *Through Burmah to Western China*, Introduction, vi.

7. Ibid.

8. See Ann Laura Stoler, *Along the Archival Grain: Epistemic Anxieties and Colonial Common Sense* (Princeton, NJ: Princeton University Press, 2010).

with the Burmese king brought him into conflict with other hierarchies concerned in the governance of the colonial state, whose integrity and authority had to be maintained, even though they did not possess privileged knowledge as Williams did.

The early years of Britain's engagement with India and Burma, particularly after the Rebellion of 1857, were fraught with difficulties as ruptures occurred within the government and wider society between actors of the same rank, class or professional status. As noted in the preceding chapter, they were an indication of the unease felt at the absence of reliable sources of knowledge, creating tensions amongst the members of the imperial establishment beyond any that were felt towards its colonised subjects. But as Christopher Bayly has observed, the colonial government's concern to gain mastery over affective knowledge did not diminish until the latter part of the nineteenth century, when imperial governance became more hierarchical and a matter of routine.[9] This coincided with greater independent initiatives to further knowledge by outsiders like William Johnson and Clement Williams, as increasingly institutionalised mechanisms of government distanced colonial officials from their subjects. However, this alteration produced its own tensions within the empire, as it became imperative for institutions to stamp their authority on any claims to new knowledge, not the least being recognition that the periphery was a sphere of knowledge in its own right, firmly under their control.

Publication by approved academic sites like learned societies went some way towards resolving these tensions, but, as we have seen in the case of William Johnson, there were clear differences between the reception of his findings by the RGS and the GTS of India. Furthermore, ruptures that occurred over competing claims to authority could not always be resolved by reworking results, as the GTS had done in Johnson's case. As this chapter will demonstrate, private publication of his book by the Edinburgh house of W. Blackwood and Son, arranged by Clement Williams's friends in Britain, was beyond the control of the government at the Burmese periphery. Therefore, the Rangoon government resorted to other means of disassociating themselves from his discoveries concerning the important political question of trade with China, by issuing Williams with an ultimatum requiring him to choose between his role as a Political Agent in Upper Burma and his army commission.

When individuals like Johnson and Williams developed their own modes of mastering affective knowledge, they carried the potential to create conflict within official and unofficial circles. Questions related to an individual's

---

9. Christopher A. Bayly, 'Knowing the Country: Empire and Information in India', *Modern Asian Studies* 27, no. 1 (1993): 37.

motives, personal loyalty and ambition intruded upon how the initiatives of private adventurers should be received and how any knowledge acquired by them might be interpreted. As will be discussed in this chapter, these complexities were especially related to insecurities about nascent political hierarchies in the new province of Lower Burma. Personal loyalty to the imperial project also came under scrutiny when individuals sought to further their own private mercantile interests, whilst at the same time serving in the government or holding an official position, as both Williams and Johnson endeavoured to do. Nevertheless, as has been previously mentioned, the British relied upon informal or unofficial contacts with polities beyond their frontiers to keep them abreast of developments in the political arena and to alert them to opportunities to establish new trade links.

Williams first travelled to the independent Kingdom of Upper Burma in 1861, whilst on furlough from his army post in Rangoon, when he was received by King Mindon at his Court. Throughout the rest of his life, until his death in 1879, he acquired great influence at the Burmese Court, developing a close and cordial relationship with the king.[10] He assumed the role of go-between or informant, becoming one of Arthur Phayre's correspondents, when, in 1862, he was appointed British Burma's first Political Agent. However, his relationship with King Mindon and his interactions as a go-between, eventually aroused suspicion and jealousy amongst the mercantile classes in Rangoon and Mandalay, chiefly because of his ability to connect with the indigenous population at the highest levels of Burmese society. Unlike Johnson, who only spent a brief time in Khotan's capital, Ilchí, Williams resided in Burma's capital for many years, so that his value as an informant became ever more significant. But as his knowledge about the political situation in Upper Burma increased, so too distrust intensified towards his commercial ventures with Britain's potential enemies, who lived in close proximity to its boundaries. In 1867, Arthur Phayre was succeeded as chief commissioner by Albert Fytche (1820–1892), and Williams lost his patronage and consequently, his position as Political Agent, which ever after placed him at loggerheads with the Rangoon government.

Without the continuing patronage and support of Arthur Phayre, Williams's hopes of forging a career in the British Burma Administration foundered. In 1864, he was replaced as Political Agent by Captain Edward Sladen, a man whom he despised,[11] and who was a close confidant of

---

10. Williams, *Through Burmah to Western China*, vi.

11. Sladen and Williams's dispute became public in 1866 after both men were present at the royal palace during the rebellion, when the king's brother and heir apparent was killed alongside other courtiers by his son, the Myingun Prince, who subsequently sought refuge in British Burma. Sladen commandeered an Irrawaddy Flotilla Company steamer to evacuate Europeans from Mandalay to Rangoon, which Williams considered unnecessary. Although willing to lease a steamer to King

Fytche, whose patronage Sladen now enjoyed. Williams returned to his home in the county of Somerset, in South-West England, on extended leave, where he considered what new exploration prospects might be open to him. Ever the adventurer, he made enquiries in a personal letter to Sir Austen Layard (1817–1894) about opportunities in Abyssinia.[12] However, as nothing came of this contact, he resigned his army commission and returned to Mandalay as a private citizen at the end of 1866, where he was soon joined by his brother, Howard Williams. The brothers' subsequent commercial activities provoked considerable animosity amongst the mercantile community in Mandalay and Rangoon. Much of it was orchestrated by Edward Sladen, with whom Williams became embroiled in a bitter feud over business deals, to which the Chief Commissioner was also party. Disapproval of Williams's activities on both sides of the British-Burma frontier, including smuggling arms to the king, prompted Fytche to remark in a private letter to Sladen that, 'Dr Williams is detested at Mandalay by all classes'.[13]

Nevertheless, Williams became a key figure amongst the Europeans who frequented the Royal Court, and also one of the capital's most prominent entrepreneurs. He was involved in commercial arms dealings not only with the king but also on his own account, as well as acting as an agent for many Rangoon firms, including the Irrawaddy Flotilla Company, established in 1865. As an 'outsider', Williams's close connections with the Burmese, placing him in the role of an intermediary, demonstrates how Europeans came to be implicated in nuanced ways with the political and economic outcomes that influenced the governance of British Burma until the final

---

Mindon for defensive purposes against the rebels, when the king summarily seized the vessel with the IFC's Captain Bacon on board, Williams was highly critical of Sladen's conduct in not protecting British interests. He expressed his 'horror and surprise' when Sladen declined to support his request to the Burmese *woongyees* to guarantee the safety of the IFC's vessel and its cargo. See BL/Mss Eur E290/2/48: Controversy with Williams (1866–1868); extracts from Dr Williams's statement.

The dispute over Sladen's conduct after the 1866 Mandalay Palace rebellion against King Mindon widened when Williams went public with his disapproval in an anonymous letter in *The Friend of India* magazine, signed 'a trader'. Sladen complained to the Governor General he received no satisfaction, as he considered that 'there was no necessity for his [Sladen] noticing an anonymous letter in a newspaper'; adding that without proof (for which he had no desire to call), he could not accept Captain Sladen's theory that it had been written by Dr Williams. See BL/Mss Eur E290/2138: Letter No. 1443 from GG of India to CC of Burma (26 August 1867).

12. Sir Austen Layard was an English traveller, archaeologist, cuneiformist, art historian, draughtsman, collector, politician and diplomat. He was well-known for his account of his exploration of the ruins of Nimrud on the Tigris River in modern-day Iraq; he was author of *Nineveh and Its Remains: With an Account of a Visit to the Chaldaean Christians of Kurdistan, and the Yezidis, or Devilworshippers; and an Inquiry into the Painters and Arts of the Ancient Assyrians* (London: John Murray, 1849). At the time Williams wrote to him, he had become a politician in London. Layard had visited India in 1857 to investigate the causes of the Rebellion and had therefore formed some understanding of the country, hence Williams's interest in seeking out his patronage.

13. BL/Mss Eur E290/32: Letter from Albert Fytche to Edward Sladen (2 August 1867).

annexation of the Kingdom of Upper Burma in 1886. Williams's engagement with the Court at Ava and his interactions with the people whom he encountered on his journey upriver are an example of the important knowledge that 'Burmaphiles'[14] could bring to imperial governance, particularly in sensitive interactions beyond the frontier. Williams's contacts with King Mindon and influential members of his Court demonstrate how informal and friendly overtures often had greater influence than official communications and diplomatic missions. Nevertheless, the affective knowledge that he gained risked compromising future political relations between Upper and Lower Burma.

Following Britain's acquisition of Assam after the First Burmese War, ratified by the Treaty of Yandabo in 1826, the pace of exploration increased as British explorers and surveyors were sent into newly acquired territories on Burma's frontier. In 1835, another medical doctor, George Thomas Bayfield, also an army surgeon from a Madras regiment, preceded Williams in making one of the first expeditions to the far North-West of Burma, where the Hukawng Valley met Upper Assam. The Surveyor General's office did not permit publication of original reports, but in 1873, Bayfield's account was republished in selections of government papers. His mission was to determine the exact boundary between Burma and Assam, and also to ascertain what new trading opportunities might become available in the areas that he visited. He particularly observed the proliferation of cotton handkerchiefs and English piece goods offered for sale, which became more costly the further the distance from the seaports.[15]

Although not in the public sphere, Bayfield's account, together with those of earlier expeditions discussed in the next section, may have inspired Clement Williams to travel to Upper Burma some decades later to investigate the ancient trade routes into Western China. Following the British acquisition of Lower Burma in 1853, a series of official missions to Ava began with a view to concluding a trade agreement with King Mindon. They were led by General Sir Arthur Phayre and Williams accompanied his 1862 mission. In order to contextualise the political landscape in which Williams undertook his Irrawaddy journey, the next section briefly examines earlier expeditions and Phayre's famous mission of 1855, paying attention to the degree of affective knowledge that participants were able to gain about the Burmese kingdom throughout the first half of the nineteenth century.

---

14. Burmaphiles: Expression used by Stephen L. Keck in his book, *British Burma in the New Century, 1895–1918* (London: Palgrave Macmillan, 2015), to describe individuals like Williams who took an interest in the history and culture of Burma and engaged with its people.

15. Cederloff, 'Seeking China's Back Door', 128.

AFFECTIVE KNOWLEDGE ABOUT THE BURMESE KINGDOM AND THE QUEST FOR TRADE TREATIES

Since the early nineteenth century, military officers like Major Henry Burney, Captains Simon Fraser Hannay, Francis Jenkins and Robert Boileau Pemberton; Lieutenant Richard Wilcox; and Assistant Surgeon George Bayfield had published extracts from their exploration journals in several places, including articles in the *Journal of the Asiatic Society of Bengal*. However, their accounts never mentioned that they were written whilst they were on active military service, so that they gave the impression of being reports of the discovery of important natural resources of commercial significance, such as the tea plant. Some decades later, Dr Clement Williams's exploration narrative emulated these officers' accounts by perpetuating the myth of imperial expansion as being founded upon the acquisition of intellectual and physical knowledge of places and their objects, rather than military action. However, the vexed question of how to reconcile the myth with the reality that most journeys of discovery were undertaken by military officers in the course of their official duties is manifested in the conflicting standards that were subsequently applied to Williams's conduct.

When he undertook his Irrawaddy journey in 1863, Williams was on official leave from his regiment, whilst, since 1862, also holding the appointment of Britain's first Political Agent in Upper Burma. But soon after his return, questions arose regarding his suitability to continue to hold this appointment at the same time as serving as an Assistant Army Surgeon. Because he had been granted permission to undertake his journey by the King of Burma, it was considered a private venture and whilst he remained a commissioned officer, it compromised the army's status as a provider of knowledge acquired 'in the field'. Specifically, it threatened to undermine the key role played by the periphery in the recovery and circulation of knowledge. Therefore, in 1864, Williams was advised by the Government of India that if he wished to remain as Political Agent, he was required to resign his army commission, which would involve him in considerable financial loss, including his pension rights. As mentioned earlier, the army had a tradition, since the days of the EIC, of allowing its officers to engage in private business provided it did not compromise their official duties. But Williams's close relationship with the Burmese, and especially his commercial dealings with King Mindon, created irreconcilable conflicts within the fragile political landscape of mid-nineteenth century Burma.

Meanwhile, since the early nineteenth century, attempts by the EIC to push the boundaries of their territories had resulted in several missions to Burma's capital at Ava.[16] It may be recalled that in 1795, the botanist Francis Buchanan-Hamilton accompanied Major Michael Symes on one of the first surveys to Ava.[17] Buchanan's account of their mission, published in the *Journal of the Asiatic Research Society* in 1807,[18] contained one of the earliest descriptions of daily life in Ava and provided affective knowledge about this egalitarian Hinayana Buddhist society, which he contrasted favourably to the hierarchical nature of Brahminism.[19] In 1826, the Scottish physician, John Crawfurd (1783–1868), undertook another mission, followed soon afterwards by Henry Burney (1792–1845), who was appointed Ava's first Resident in 1829, having successfully negotiated the border between Siam and Burma with King Rama III at the conclusion of the First Burmese War. In August 1830, the surveyor, Captain Robert Boileau Pemberton (1798–1840), reported in his journal that Burney had noticed 'numerous packages of English broad cloths, principally red and green, of coloured cotton handkerchief and a good deal of China ware', displayed along the front of each of the houses that he passed on his route to visit the king.[20] During the 1830s, such observations, together with the discovery of the tea plant in Assam, had added greatly to the urgency to explore new trading opportunities in the territories adjoining Assam. It had generated a drive to discover new markets and map the natural resources beyond the Irrawaddy, especially after 1833, when the EIC lost the last of its monopolies and also control of the sea routes to China.

On 13 December 1836, accompanied by the new Governor of Mogoung, Dr George Thomas Bayfield left Ava to attend a conference with officers in Assam; convened by the Governor General's Agent, its purpose was to determine the boundary between Assam and Burma. Bayfield's orders also included reporting on the extent and nature of the trade that was being carried on 'between China and the Burmese dominions, and between them and our territories in Assam'.[21] As the British wished to establish a safe passage between their settlements in Assam and the Burmese dominions, Bayfield was instructed to advise the Governor of Mogoung that 'the Burmese were

---

16. Located on the left bank of the Irrawaddy River, Ava (or Inwa), in the Mandalay Region, is the site of the ancient capital of successive Burmese kingdoms from the fourteenth to nineteenth centuries. In 1861, King Mindon, the penultimate monarch of the Konbaung Dynasty, occupied the new capital that he built at Mandalay until his death in 1878.

17. See Chapter 3.

18. Buchanan, 'On the Religion and Literature of the Burmas'.

19. Vicziany, 'Imperialism, Botany and Statistics', 632.

20. BL/IOR/L/PS/19/36/75: R. Boileau Pemberton's Journal from Ava to Arracan (1830).

21. BL/IOR/V/23/104/3/134: Narrative of a Journey from Ava to the frontiers of Assam by Mr G.T. Bayfield of the Madras Medical Establishment of Fort St. George.

expected to adopt measures to prevent the Singfos and other tribes [*sic*] subject to Ava committing incursions into their territories'.[22]

However, Bayfield was unsuccessful in persuading the Governor of Mogoung to prevent enmity between various local factions, who were intent on disrupting trade carried through territory in Assam newly acquired by the British. Long before their arrival, various warring groups had come to an accommodation with particular traders who passed through their areas. Some thirty years later, when Williams made his journey, there had still been no containment of hostilities. As he discovered when his journey was interrupted at Bhamo and he was prevented from continuing on to Yunnan, there were concerns that his presence on the frontier would disrupt the fragile stability of long disputed routes through Kakhyeen frontier communities, jealously overseen by local Chinese officials in Bhamo.

In his journal, Bayfield commented on the poor state of the countryside and its people and considered that the prospects for trade were limited, chiefly because the Chinese, whom he called 'those antidotes to morality and improvement', occupied the upper part of the bazaar.[23] The few English piece goods and common cotton handkerchiefs that he saw for sale were beyond the means of the local people to purchase. Although Bayfield and his companion, the botanist Dr William Griffith, did their best to help the impoverished villagers and persuade them to try English medicine instead of the local cures, their efforts met with little success.[24] However, the villagers were fascinated by their medical equipment and pocket watch, which provided a talking point that allowed them to interact with the people and gain affective knowledge about an unknown region. They also reported on the local ecology: Griffith discovered a peach tree and Bayfield reported the presence of the tea plant in the plains and nearby hills.

Some decades later, following successful cultivation of the tea plant in Assam (with Chinese assistance), the region presented new challenges for those intent on pursuing trade in these turbulent frontier regions. Bayfield's mission into the borderlands of Assam and Burma returned safely to Ava on 15 May 1837, after an absence of just over five months, but it did not produce any substantive gains in trade initiatives in these impoverished and disputed areas. It was many years before Clement Williams made his own singular attempt to forge an alternative river route to Yunnan in the hopes of establishing a backdoor trade route into Western China. Meanwhile, having

---

22. Ibid.
23. Ibid., 144, 157.
24. BL/IOR/V/23/104, No.3, 200: Selection of papers regarding the hill tracts between Assam and Burmah and on the Upper Brahmaputra (Calcutta: Bengal Secretariat Press, 1873). William Griffith described one of the villagers whom they tried to treat as 'an emaciated, dirty smoke-dried little man', who had sacrificed no fewer than ten buffaloes to the 'nats' and failed to find a cure.

reached an accommodation with the local population of North-East Burma, the caravans from China, that for centuries had plied the ancient trade routes, rumbled on. However, on India's north-western frontier, the hoped-for revival of the tea trade with Central Asia by retired army-officers-turned-tea-planters in Assam failed to progress; and neither did it help to bring any significant gains to British trading initiatives in a region that had long been subject to the control of Peking.

Following their conquest of the Province of Pegu in Lower Burma in 1853, the British tried a new approach by staging set-piece official missions to the king and his Court at Ava. They hoped that displays of British imperial power and scientific knowledge might encourage the Burmese to take more active measures to prevent disruption on their frontier with China, which remained too dangerous for British merchants to venture near. In 1855, prior to his appointment as Chief Commissioner, Major Arthur Phayre undertook an important diplomatic mission to Ava on behalf of the Governor General of India. Its purpose was to persuade King Mindon to put his name to a treaty that would formalise trading relations between Britain and Upper Burma; however, it was unsuccessful. The main reason why the king refused to agree to a treaty at this time was because he was sensitive about how his reign would be portrayed in the chronicles, fearing that it might be dishonoured, if they described him as a monarch who yielded territory and concessions to a foreign enemy.[25] Despite the failure of Phayre's first mission to Ava, informal exchanges of information between the British and correspondents like Clement Williams and the merchant, Thomas Spears,[26] resulted in two trade treaties being signed with the Burmese in 1862 and 1867. These treaties extended commercial opportunities to entrepreneurs on both sides of the frontier, which previously had only been available to the small band of foreigners who resided in Upper Burma.

King Mindon's official reception of foreigners, like those who accompanied Phayre's mission, usually took place under the most formal of circumstances with protocol strictly observed. However, in the course of his day-to-day meetings with resident foreigners who frequently attended Court, Mindon's dealings were more informal, especially if they were able

---

25. Henry Yule, *Narrative of the Mission Sent by the Governor General of India to the Court at Ava in 1855* (London: Smith, Elder & Co., 1858), 194.

26. Thomas Spears was one of the earliest foreigners to reside at the Burmese capital, having been a merchant there since the 1830s, and he regularly supplied the British with information. Spears was present when the Second Burmese War broke out in 1852, which led to his imprisonment and the confiscation of his goods. After the war, Spears resumed trading and acting as the unofficial 'eyes and ears' at the Royal Court for the Commissioner of Pegu, Arthur Phayre, transmitting confidential information to him in Rangoon. In the wake of the internal palace revolution in 1866 and ongoing concerns about the stability of the Burmese kingdom, the British Administration in Lower Burma placed even greater reliance on gathering intelligence from its correspondents within the kingdom.

to provide him with information and assistance. Despite being closely chaperoned by Burmese ministers, the members of Phayre's 1855 mission were able to gain some insight into the region's topography, architecture and customs. But being unable to interact with ordinary people, they acquired little first-hand affective knowledge, which previous expeditions like Bayfield's had been able to. The observations of the members of Phayre's mission were recorded by its Secretary, Henry Yule (1820–1889), who published an official account titled, *A Narrative of the Mission Sent by the Governor General of India to the Court at Ava in 1855*.[27] Yule's narrative contained information concerning their encounters with the Court, its daily life and rituals, as well as descriptions of the surrounding countryside and the towns and villages that they passed on their voyage upriver. Descriptions of elaborately carved buildings, especially monasteries, were illustrated with fine drawings and sketches by the mission's official artist, Mr Colesworthey Grant (1813–1880).

Although King Mindon and his ministers were interested in new scientific knowledge, the Burmese did not possess sufficient practical and technological expertise at that time to make meaningful use of the scientific wonders that the visitors brought from the West. However, by their presence at Court, the British were enabled to exhibit epistemological authority through their mastery of advances in science, thereby demonstrating the changing structures of power emanating from Europe. In a demonstration of 'Orientalist empiricism', Henry Yule noted in his narrative that the Burmese king was particularly interested in Western medicine.[28] As noted earlier, it was through his professional abilities as a doctor that Clement Williams was able to establish a personal relationship with the king and members of the royal family, providing him with a pathway towards gaining affective knowledge about the kingdom.

Yule recounted in his narrative how Arthur Phayre had attempted to explain the Western concept of the solar system to the *woondouk*,[29] which allowed him, as the possessor of a universal truth, to display his superior knowledge about the cosmology. Phayre told the minister about Northern Europe, where, during a part of the summer, the sun remained above the horizon without setting. The minister had never heard of this before from any foreigner and remained unconvinced by the envoy's explanation.[30] However, the Court displayed a lively interest in photography and were fascinated by Captain Linnaeus Tripe's demonstrations, which produced what they termed

---

27. Yule's account was published in 1858, some years after the mission returned.
28. Henry Yule related how the king was interested in medical matters and had requested Dr Forsyth, the Phayre mission's medical man, to obtain a model of a human skeleton for him, of natural size in white wood with pliable joints. Yule, *Narrative of the Mission*, 196.
29. *Woondouk*: Burmese minister.
30. Yule, *Narrative of the Mission*, 67.

'sun pictures'.[31] But as there was no one with sufficient technical ability at Court to operate the photographic equipment that the mission had brought as a gift for the king, it could not be put to good use. Although Yule's narrative contained few of Tripe's photographs, those that were included provided an insight into the technological proficiency of early photography in Europe.[32]

Some years later, in 1862, when Williams accompanied Arthur Phayre on his second mission to Ava, British Burma was successful in negotiating a treaty with the king, which stipulated that neither side would interfere with migration across their common frontier at Thayetmyo.[33] This allowed the British free access to Upper Burma and opened up opportunities for trade with the Burmese kingdom and beyond. Yet, despite two official missions, nearly a decade after the conclusion of the Second Burmese War, the British had yet to gain any truly affective knowledge about its near neighbour, nor to develop any clear understanding about the possible political outcomes of its relations with this independent polity, now isolated within its Indian possessions. Nevertheless, in 1867, another treaty was successfully negotiated with the Burmese, whereby King Mindon was obliged to make significant concessions in exchange for the right to purchase a limited supply of arms from the British, which will be discussed further in a later section.

Prior to the ratification of this treaty, Clement Williams sought adventures beyond the frontier with Lower Burma. As a young assistant army surgeon, deeply interested in the culture and traditions of the indigenous other, he imagined that exploring unknown regions and generating new knowledge might open a pathway to success for him in Britain's newest province of its Indian empire. Unfortunately, this did not prove to be the case, but before considering the controversies surrounding Williams's subsequent mercantile

31. Roger Taylor, 'The Pioneering Photographic Expeditions of Linnaeus Tripe', in *Captain Linnaeus Tripe: Photographer of India and Burma, 1852–1860*, eds. Roger Taylor and Crispin Branfoot (Munich: DelMonico, 2014), 24. Born in into a large family of twelve children, Linnaeus Tripe was the ninth child of Mary and Cornelius Tripe, who had settled in Devonport, where his father was a surgeon, having trained at the Royal Naval Hospital in nearby Plymouth. Tripe was educated at Devonport's Classical and Mathematical School, which, with its naval background and culture, prepared students for cadetships with the EIC, which Tripe duly joined in 1839, where he was attached to the Twelfth Madras Native Infantry. Tripe sailed for India in August 1839, where he was to spend the next ten years as a lieutenant in the EIC's army. Viewed initially as an absorbing pastime for the leisured classes of Victorian England keen to try out modern ideas, Tripe recognised photography's enormous potential for conveying accurate information about the empire's hitherto unknown cultures and regions. Tripe's submission to an earlier exhibition showcasing products of Southern India had won him the First-Class Medal for Photography, Architectural Antiquities and Landscapes. His rigorously aesthetic approach to his subjects attracted the attention of the Governor General of India when considering who should be included in Phayre's mission to Upper Burma.

32. Ibid., 4–47.

33. Thayetmyo: Border town on the River Irrawaddy, which represented the divide between the independent Kingdom of Upper Burma and the newly acquired province of Pegu in Lower Burma, ceded by the kingdom following the conclusion of the Second Burmese War in 1853.

activities in Mandalay, we turn now to his original purpose in going to Upper Burma in 1860. The next section describes his Irrawaddy journey and discusses the contents of his book on the subject, in which he provided detailed descriptions of the countryside and his impressions of the people that he met there.

CLEMENT WILLIAMS'S JOURNEY TO
THE BURMA FRONTIER

Colonial officials like John Crawfurd (1783–1868), Arthur Phayre, Henry Yule and Albert Fytche wrote extensively about their experiences during diplomatic missions to the Burmese Royal Court and in the process of evaluating them they made formative judgements about the country and its people. Meanwhile, on his lone mission, undertaken without the protocol associated with official expeditions, Clement Williams was able to bring a new historical perspective to writing about Burma, which saw beyond their judgements about the backward state of the country and its lack of modern governance and social institutions. Travelling independently, without official sponsorship, and assisting the people that he met along the way with medical advice enabled Williams to set aside British preconceptions concerning social hierarchies, as exemplified by the British experience of official missions to the Court at Ava.

By investigating ancient caravan routes into Yunnan during the early months of 1863, Williams endeavoured to unravel the complicated relationships that King Mindon and his Court officials had brokered with local indigenous powers in their trading activities with Western China during the height of the Panthay Rebellion.[34] But the impenetrable ways in which the Burmese managed the various frontier communities, like the Kakhyeen, Shan and Chinese, proved in the end to be one of the major impediments to the British in their desire to open up a successful trade route through Upper Burma into Western China. Whilst at Bhamo, Williams regularly came up against the intractability of local Chinese officials, who were supported by their allies at the Royal Court in Mandalay.

---

34. The Panthay Rebellion (1856–1873) was a long-running rebellion of the Muslim Hui people and other ethnic groups against the Manchu rulers of the Qing Dynasty in south-western Yunnan Province. It disrupted trading and communications in the region for nearly two decades until the Imperial Court sent more troops and a new Governor General, Cen Yuying, who ended the siege of Kunming, the last stronghold of the rebels. He pursued the fleeing troops to Dali, where the rebel leader, Du Wenxiu, handed himself over to avoid major bloodshed among his followers. For further information, see David G. Atwill, *The Chinese Sultanate: Islam, Ethnicity, and the Panthay Rebellion in Southwest China, 1856–1873* (Stanford, CA: Stanford University Press, 2005).

Williams embarked on his journey at a time when China was attempting reform in an effort to meet the demands of the military and political challenge from the West, and when blockades of Chinese ports were seriously hampering the British opium trade with China from India. Even though there had been much discussion in British newspapers of discovering a backdoor route into China in order to solve this difficulty, Williams's initiative was ignored by the Burma Administration. In its intention to gather geographical and cultural knowledge, it held a scientific and commercial purpose, as demonstrated by the account of his travels that he first published in the *Journal of the Asiatic Society* in 1864, in which he outlined the practicality of using this route for the purposes of trade. As previously mentioned, his journal article was followed in 1868 by the publication of his book, which offered a detailed scientific account of the physical and human geography of an unknown area on Burma's north-western frontier. As he wrote in the preface, 'He resolved to test personally the practicability of establishing a modern route via the Irrawaddy River, as far as navigable and then across the narrowest part of Yunnan or other available points on the Chinese frontier'.[35]

Towards the end of 1862, after several years spent negotiating the jealousies and obstructions of Burmese officials in Mandalay, Williams finally earned sufficient trust through his personal contact with the king to secure the royal commission to set out on his journey of research and exploration. Departing from Mandalay in January 1863, he ascended the Irrawaddy River as far as the Upper Defile beyond Bhamo, and made a sketch survey of the river during the voyage. Whilst at Bhamo, Williams made excursions to the Taping River and other tributaries of the Irrawaddy and he reported that, as he travelled, 'he conversed freely with Shans, Kakhyeens and Chinese, obtaining all that could be learned from them, both orally and by sketch maps of the routes that lay between Bhamo and the Chinese frontier and of the nature of the trade that was carried on by their caravans'.[36] On reaching Bhamo in March 1863, Williams paid his respects to the *woon*,[37] who received him very civilly and placed a house at his disposal, but he warned him that the routes beyond Bhamo were impracticable on account of the Kakhyeens, who had recently murdered a man armed with a musket very near to the town.[38] The *woon* also refused Williams permission to visit the silver mines at Bodwin, in the Kakhyeen Mountains, which the king wished Williams to inspect with a view to having them worked.[39]

---

35. Williams, *Through Burmah to Western China*, vi.
36. Ibid.
37. *Woon*: local governor.
38. Williams, *Through Burmah to Western China*, 76.
39. Ibid., 124–125.

Figure 6.1. The Woon, or Governor, of Bhamo with three attendants, taken by Dr Clement Williams (c. 1863). *Source:* Courtesy of the Royal Ontario Museum, © ROM (Ref. ROM2018_16742_18).

Despite many conversations with various members of the local community, Williams was unable to obtain a consistent account of the current state of affairs on the frontier, as each person he consulted expressed his own conflicting opinion on how he might find the most reliable road to the Chinese border. Even though Williams did not entirely believe these stories, he nevertheless decided to continue his journey northwards towards the Taping River.[40] As he became more accustomed to the local community, and they to him, Williams became friendly with the *nikandan* (a second ranking local governor), who was a knowledgeable man with whom he could hold an intelligent conversation. The *nikandan* suggested that as some of the Panthays were in town to buy muskets, Williams might be able to gain safe passage

---

40. Ibid., 100.

with them to the Chinese frontier when they returned after a caravan came from Momien, a town recently captured by them. Whilst at Bhamo, Williams was able to glean the most reliable information through the mediation with local indigenous groups by his trusted servant, Raj Singh, as he was able to enter the Kakhyeen and Shan villages and communicate freely with them.

However, there was considerable resentment towards Williams's presence in the town of Bhamo and he was unable to continue his journey to the Chinese frontier. He was detained there by a jealous local official who purported to doubt the real meaning of the king's mandate because he feared that Williams's presence might endanger the lucrative trading channels that they had set up in this turbulent frontier region. Therefore, he prevented Williams from progressing further on his journey towards China until a new order could be obtained from the king. But before the new permission arrived, an insurrection broke out in Mandalay and the king demanded that Williams return to the capital during this crisis.[41] Having been appointed as the first Political Agent the previous year, Williams's presence was now urgently required to act as representative of the foreign community and protect their interests.[42]

Upon his return, Williams's discoveries received no recognition from either the British Burma government in Rangoon, or officials at the metropole. As we have seen, Johnson's decision to visit Khotan on his own account risked undermining the GTS's ability to retain control over the information that it generated. Similarly, Williams's enterprise conflicted with the desire of the periphery to maintain control of any new knowledge produced in its sphere of influence; and where it could not be effectively managed or repossessed, it was ignored by the authorities. As a riposte to both administrations, his friends in Bristol assisted him in publishing his book in order to draw attention to the efforts of a 'medical man, who became the first Political Agent, whose long residence in Burma long entitled him to recognition'.[43] They intended it as 'a vindication of his suggestion for a simple trade route in the face of what Williams perceived as the misrepresentations of those who confounded it by declaring it impractical, proposing instead railway routes and other schemes of transit through Burma to China'.[44] His friends declared that its publication would ensure that Williams's name would be permanently associated with a subject of immense importance to the British mercantile community, as well as to the Indian empire.[45] They commended Williams 'for his long residence in Burma, his position as Political Agent and above all, that family intimacy which none but a medical man can secure'.[46]

---

41. Ibid., vi–vii.
42. Ibid., vii.
43. Ibid., x.
44. Ibid., viii
45. Ibid.
46. Ibid.

Although disappointed that he could not progress beyond Bhamo, Williams believed that he had nevertheless gained sufficient intelligence to be convinced of the practicability of opening a trade route into Western China via the Irrawaddy River. On his return to Mandalay, he forwarded a memorandum to the government in India advocating the advance of British commercial and political interests with Upper Burma, which, having won the trust of the king and his ministers, together with his knowledge of the area around Bhamo, he felt well-equipped to take forward.[47] The government ignored Williams's Memorandum and instead, in 1868, they supported a major expedition to the same area that Williams had visited five years earlier. It was financed by members of the Rangoon commercial community and led by Major (later Colonel) Edward Sladen, who had replaced Williams in 1864 as the Political Agent in Mandalay. Although making greater geographical progress than Williams by crossing into Western China and reaching Momien in the province of Yunnan, Sladen's party was also forced to turn back due to continuing disturbances arising from the Panthay Rebellion and obstructions by local groups of Kakhyeens.

Although today a forgotten study by an explorer-adventurer and disregarded by the British and Indian governments, Williams's work may be considered as a credible attempt at an early anthropological study. Lone adventurers like Williams and Johnson were able to produce original accounts that foreshadowed the way that the discipline of anthropology was understood. As a subject worthy of serious scientific attention, anthropology remained very much on the margins of colonial knowledge in Burma until well into the twentieth century, much to the detriment of its frontier peoples. The acquisition of reliable and informed knowledge about Burma's diverse population was not managed effectively by the colonial government and was a contributory factor in the political instability of the post-Independence years. Through detailed scientific observation, Williams's book recorded the customs and lifeways of a section of Burma's frontier peoples, where communities of Shans, Kakhyeens and Burmans lived together in various states of harmony and disharmony alongside Chinese insurgents during the long-running Panthay Rebellion. Such was the fluid and unpredictable nature of the alliances which took place along Burma's northwestern frontier at that time, Williams was able to report that the Panthays had armies of between 200,000 and 300,000 people formed from a mixture of Shans, Kakhyeens and Chinese, all fighting alongside one another.[48]

Whilst detained at Bhamo for two months, Williams made productive use of his time by observing the customs and manners of the Northern Burmans

47. Ibid.
48. Ibid., 8.

and adjacent hill peoples and their working practices.[49] Although Williams made no attempt in his book to analyse or explain the reasons or circumstances for the social practices, customs and traditions of groups that he encountered, as a prototype of an early anthropological study, it was replete with illustrations, maps and descriptions of the geographical and geological features of the landscape. He described the behaviours and cultural activities of the diverse inhabitants whom he encountered during his ascent of the Irrawaddy. His book contained many drawings of the people illustrating their customs, the implements that they used in their daily life, their dwellings and social habits. Whilst at Bhamo, he managed successfully to take a few photographs of the old *woon*, some Chinese people and various groups and buildings around the town.[50] But unfortunately, his attempts to make further use of the new technology of photography were frustrated when several of his boxes of prepared plates and his chemicals were destroyed by the ingress of water into the boat in which he was travelling.[51]

Williams also participated in the social life of the community by paying for a *pwe*[52] to entertain the local population, thereby gaining affective knowledge about its multi-ethnic population. Being a major entrepôt on the route into Western China, Bhamo attracted many traders, workers and entertainers, including a troupe, who arrived during Williams's stay to stage the *Susseenah pwe*, which Williams attended and paid for some of the performances. *Pwes*, especially important ones like the *Susseenah pwe*, drew large crowds from faraway and were occasions for sharing and gathering intelligence between locals and travellers. Williams was able to take advantage of this opportunity not only to gain possible political intelligence about the state of the frontier but also to gain affective knowledge that allowed him to make observations in his book about the lifestyle of the people in this region. He affectionately described the *Susseenah pwe*, with its 'gay theatres, the varied costume and features of Burmese, Shans, Kakhyeens, and Pansees [Panthays], the friendly Tsiké and his lively chat, the hospitable Nikandan, the pompous old Woon on his elephant, his wife in her palanquin, and all the motley throng and abandon of the place' as 'a sight seldom seen, and ever to be remembered'.[53]

As the *pwes* were events that went on for many hours, Williams came and went at will, and on one occasion, he noticed that the agent and interpreter of the commander-in-chief of the Panthay forces, together with his son, was

---

49. He watched blacksmiths at work in their forge making iron and steel *dahs* (sword/knife) in the styles of the various ethnic groups, for which he provided illustrations in his book.
50. Williams, *Through Burmah to Western China*, 93, 97.
51. Ibid., 48–49.
52. *Pwe*: Traditional Burmese dramatic performance including dance, singing and clowning.
53. Williams, *Through Burmah to Western China*, 118.

among the audience at the *Susseenah pwe*. As a result of the intelligence brought by the interpreter, Williams was later informed by the *nikandan* that, apart from the dangerous Kakhyeens, the road was safe as far as Tali and that the Panthays had no intention of going beyond the boundaries of China.[54]

Williams also used his time to treat various medical cases that were brought to him, which he described in his book as mostly common complaints of the ear and eye, the former usually being caused by accidents when inserting the traditional ring or tube into the ear lobes. Most eye patients sought help for cataracts, which Williams considered to be 'one of the most frequent and distressing complaints in the country, especially in the lower provinces'.[55] He reported that 'the restoring of the eye sight is a miracle and my fame has gone before me from Mandalay even to the Kakhyeen hills!'[56] Although he provided no details as to how and under what conditions he performed this procedure, including what precautions he took to avoid infection, and how successful its outcomes were, his surgical skills must have been sufficiently advanced to enable him to proceed with confidence. He also observed that his treatments brought him much gratitude and presents.[57]

Despite gaining the people's trust and gathering affective knowledge, Williams was not able to place any true understanding or meaningful anthropological interpretation on the reasons for the various cultural practices that he observed, especially those related to medical customs. In his opinion, lack of knowledge was not the main reason why the public rejected the services of Burmese doctors; it was because they were not respected by the people. He was unsuccessful in persuading the *nikandan* not to administer various traditional drugs and remedies to his sick son and despite his advice, the child died. Williams exclaimed, 'It would have been a marvel had he lived, considering the amount of drugging he received from his father and his father's advisors. No regular practitioner was called in, or at least none was paid to treat the child'.[58] However, his disdain for the *nikandan*'s attempts to treat his sick son, without recourse to qualified medical help, took no account of the financial and social limitations which prevented indigenous families from seeking professional advice from Burmese or Chinese doctors. He was subsequently unable to make sense of the origins and purpose of the elaborate funeral rites that the *nikandan* and his family arranged for their deceased son,

---

54. Ibid., 118.
55. Ibid., 150.
56. Ibid.
57. It is known that during his long residence in Mandalay, Clement Williams was gifted maps drawn on cloth, which were eventually bequeathed to his nephew, Louis Allan Goss, who joined in his business ventures there. When he returned to England to live in Cambridge in the early twentieth century, Goss gifted some maps to Cambridge University and there are two now held by the British Library.
58. Williams, *Through Burmah to Western China*, 153.

which Williams described as an unnecessary and extravagant expense in view of their reluctance to pay for professional medical advice. He did not consider that, unable to save their sick child in this life, they wished to ensure his safe passage to the next.

As one of the first Europeans to have produced such a comprehensive study of this region of Upper Burma, Williams's book offered a detailed account of his journey, complete with descriptions of the physical and human geography he encountered, providing information about the local population, their customs and trading activities. His ability as a surgeon helped him to gain the trust of the local people and allowed him to introduce hitherto unknown Western medical knowledge to this frontier community. In the first chapter of his book, Williams addressed the various options of telegraph routes to Western China via Burma and dealt with the important issue of trade. He concluded that despite the present unsettled state of the countryside, 'the day is evidently not far distant when Burmah [*sic*] will become the highway for a vast trade with China'.[59] Unfortunately, his prophecy proved to be inaccurate, as although local trade continued to be carried on using various 'historic' routes, no major new routes were ever established by the British, even after their formal annexation of the kingdom in 1886.

Having obeyed the king's command, Williams returned to Mandalay in April 1863. Apart from home leaves to Britain, he resided in the Burmese capital for the remainder of his life, engaging in mercantile activities which, as previously mentioned, occasioned much controversy. These are discussed in the following two sections, beginning with the circumstances surrounding his removal as Political Agent in 1864.

THE CONTROVERSY OVER CLEMENT WILLIAMS'S REPLACEMENT AS POLITICAL AGENT

The army played a key role in the recovery and circulation of knowledge and, as noted earlier, army officers produced some of the earliest exploration narratives whilst engaged on active duties, as well as also holding key positions in the GTS. Although their military connection was seldom mentioned in the accounts they produced, army officers were key players in constructing the myth of imperial expansion as being not based upon military action, but upon the discovery and intellectual and physical acquisition of places and their resources. After returning from his pioneering expedition to Assam in 1835, part of which was dedicated to searching for new trading opportunities,

---

59. Ibid., 43.

Assistant Surgeon George Bayfield was not required to relinquish his army commission.

However, some decades later, the rules had apparently changed, particularly in Clement Williams's case. The authorities at the periphery deemed that medical officers were not to be employed in situations unconnected with their professions, despite the metropole determining that there was nothing in the rules to prevent this. The problem had begun in March 1861, soon after Williams made his first visit to Mandalay, when the then Viceroy, Earl Canning, concluded, 'It is therefore beyond question that Mr. Williams proceeded to Mandalay in 1861 on his private account'.[60] In 1864, his successor, Sir John Lawrence (1811–1879), ratified Canning's ruling and declared that if Williams wished to remain as Political Agent in Mandalay, he would be required to resign his army commission. Lawrence's decision demarcated clear boundaries between officials' public roles and what were considered their private interests, which they followed whilst on furlough.[61] Therefore, Williams would have been obliged to retire from the Army Medical Department on the technicality that he could not hold the appointment of the Chief Commissioner's legitimate correspondent whilst continuing to hold a commission as an assistant army surgeon.[62] Alternatively, he was to return forthwith to his regiment in Rangoon and resume his duties as an Assistant Surgeon.[63]

Whilst place and its objects are key elements in the discovery of knowledge, the nuances surrounding them and their human agents created complexities and tensions within them. The purpose of the Viceroy's intervention was to assert the periphery's claim to be an independent domain for the production of knowledge without the need for authorisation from the centre. However, for this to be effective, the local government and its affiliated organisations had to retain control over any materials produced, especially maps, and for the discoveries to be made under their orders. The GTS were able to repossess Johnson's survey report and his maps, which were redrafted; and in this way, they retained control over dangerous discursive spaces like the frontier regions. Williams had used his medical training, together with his appointment as Political Agent, to develop a close relationship with King Mindon whilst absent from his usual army duties. As the Burmese king had granted him permission to undertake his Irrawaddy expedition, Williams was subject to his orders, as demonstrated by his urgent recall to Mandalay by the king. Therefore, the British Burma Administration was precluded from mediating

60. BL/IOR/L/PS/6/551/Coll. 131/2: Clement Williams to Arthur Phayre, Chief Commissioner British Burmah (25 November 1866), quoting Canning.
61. Ibid.
62. BL/IOR/P/204/67/No. 84/179: Foreign/Political Proceedings (September 1863).
63. BL/IOR/L/PS/6/535 Coll. 1: Secretary of State for India in London to the Governor General of India (India Office, 16 May 1864).

or claiming authority over any knowledge that he acquired, even though it was originally Williams's intention that they should do so.

Following the government's ultimatum, Williams complained to Arthur Phayre, strenuously opposing Earl Canning's comments, which he believed were motivated by personal animosity in order to ruin his career prospects.[64] Obliged to leave public service and denied the career that he professed he had devoted himself to following,[65] Williams alleged that he had suffered pecuniary loss and claimed the sum of 12,000 rupees in recompense from the government.[66] Apart from the financial losses that he incurred in resigning his commission, Williams also lamented the waste of time and effort that he had expended in preparing and securing his present situation, not least the king's consent for his mission to Western China. He told Phayre that he had expressly learnt Burmese, the most difficult language in the East to master, and had studied the country's history, resources, culture and the character of the people, especially to further his relations with the Royal Court.[67] Phayre petitioned the Government of India on Williams's behalf to reconsider its position, pointing out that he had the highest opinion of Dr Williams and citing

> the peculiar circumstances of his appointment at the court of Mandalay, the difficulties which he has had to contend with, the fact of his profession being the means of gaining for him consideration, and, finally the success with which he has established the influence of his appointment, which the king at first showed some reluctance to admit yet which was absolutely necessary in order to carry out the treaty with Burmah, will all plead for consideration.[68]

Phayre also made his views known to the Secretary of State for War, telling him that 'he deprecates the removal of Dr C. Williams from his present post as Agent to the Chief Commissioner, British Burma at Mandalay in consequence of the great difficulty which would be occasioned in supplying his place'.[69]

Williams maintained that although he had ceased officially to practise medicine on behalf of the army, his general scientific qualifications had been most useful in overcoming what he termed 'the rooted objection' of the king

---

64. Secretary of State for India to the Governor General of India (16 May 1864), 3.

65. Williams to Phayre (25 November 1866).

66. BL/IOR/L/PS/6/541, Coll. 22: Letter No. 73 from the Secretary to the Chief Commissioner of British Burma to the Secretary to the Govt. of India (13 March 1865).

67. BL/IOR/L/PS/6/535, Coll. 1: Clement Williams to the Chief Commissioner of British Burmah (Mandalay, 12 August 1864).

68. BL/IOR/L/PS/6/535, Coll. 1: Clement Williams to the Chief Commissioner of British Burmah (7 September 1864).

69. BL/IOR/P/204/68: India Foreign/Political Proceedings (October–December, 1863). Military Department 4, Phayre's note of 15 August 1863. See also IOR/Z/P1347 Index.

and his ministers to allowing an official representative of British authority at court. He stated, 'My very *character* as a medical officer has been, indeed, by conciliating prejudice and disarming suspicion, a most important means to this end'.[70] He also alluded to his role in the successful negotiations of the trade treaty in 1862. After Williams was removed from his position as Political Agent, Arthur Phayre, as Chief Commissioner, strongly recommended to the Government of India that Williams be appointed as Director of Public Instruction on uncovenanted status.[71] However, his intervention was to no avail and consequently, Williams turned his full-time attention to undertaking commercial activities in Upper Burma, which were not always compatible with the interests of the Rangoon government.

After 1867, Clement Williams no longer enjoyed the patronage of Arthur Phayre, who had retired on medical grounds. He soon lost favour with the Rangoon Administration and the new Chief Commissioner, Albert Fytche, and his protégé, Edward Sladen, who replaced him as Political Agent at Mandalay. Fytche was far less empathetic towards the Burmese than Phayre and much tougher in his treaty negotiations with them. He wrote, 'I mistrust the king, always have done and look upon him as an underhand, double dealing and cowardly man'.[72] Fytche was a man much concerned with questions of protocol, not least with what he called the 'intolerable indignity' of being required to remove his shoes when entering into the royal presence. Therefore, from the beginning, Fytche was antagonistic towards Williams and, as previously mentioned, he did not trouble to conceal his dislike of him in his private letters to Sladen. Suspecting him of smuggling arms for the king, Fytche advised Sladen in March 1867, 'I have had my eye on Dr Williams and I will take care that he does not smuggle arms and ammunition – he returns to Mandalay by the next trip of the Nerbudda'.[73] The next section explores the complications that arose when arms and other valuable commodities were trafficked to Upper Burma that exceeded the legal limits permitted by the 1867 Treaty.

DR WILLIAMS'S ARMS TRADE AND HIS DISMISSAL AS AN IFC AGENT

Although the ostensible reason for the rejection of Williams's services as Political Agent at Mandalay was because the role was incompatible with his duties as an assistant army surgeon, it had become apparent to the

---

70. Index for 1 October 1863.
71. BL/IOR/L/PS/6/541, Coll. 22: Memorial by Clement Williams to the Secretary of State for India (July 1865).
72. BL/Mss Eur E290/34: Albert Fytche to Edward Sladen (Rangoon, 11 May 1869).
73. BL/Mss Eur E290/32: Albert Fytche to Edward Sladen (23 March 1867).

Government of India that Williams's extended visits to Mandalay were motivated by self-interest, and that he had become a familiar figure amongst a small group of foreign merchants who had always resided in the Burmese capital. Besides acting as agents or representatives of businesses outside of the kingdom, chiefly in Rangoon, foreign merchants bid for contracts with the king, because without his patronage, it was virtually impossible to penetrate the local business structure.[74] Williams was amongst those who sought to profit from new opportunities following the trade treaties of 1862 and 1867, which permitted both sides free access across the common frontier at Thayetmyo. The Viceroy suspected that in common with other foreigners, Williams intended to enrich himself by bidding for commercial contracts with the king and his *woongyees*,[75] which included supplying them with arms and ammunition.

As commercial traffic between Rangoon and Mandalay increased, Williams developed mutually beneficial business ties with the king and his ministers, becoming one of four of Upper Burma's most prominent merchants: the others being the aforementioned long-term resident, Thomas Spears, as well as Angus Sutherland and Giovanni Andreino.[76] He also became the agent for a number of principals in Rangoon, notably the Irrawaddy Flotilla Company,[77] whose agency he acquired in December 1865, having come to an agreement with the Glasgow firm's Rangoon and Moulmein agents, Messrs Todd, Findlay and Co. In addition to agreeing a salary and commission, they extended a line of credit to him of up to £25,000.[78]

After 1862, the pressure to establish valuable trading arrangements had resulted in an 'open border' policy between the Burmese kingdom and Lower Burma that had enabled questionable and, at times, illegal trading between actors from both countries. The 1867 Treaty especially contributed towards a trade boom in Upper Burma,[79] and one unfortunate outcome was that the British Burma government was unable to control the traffic of arms and other war materials between Rangoon and Upper Burma, even when Preventative Officers travelled on board the IFC's steamers. This situation created conflict across a number of hierarchies that involved both indigenous and European merchants, as well as officials from the British Burma and Burmese governments, including the king himself. Such a volatile situation often led

---

74. Jorg A. Schendel, 'The Mandalay Economy: Upper Burma's External Trade, c. 1850–90', unpublished Ph.D. dissertation (Berlin: October 2002), 340.

75. *Woongyees*: Ministers at the Burmese Court.

76. For further information on long-term trade arrangements, see Emily Erikson, *Between Monopoly and Free Trade: The English East India Company, 1600–1757* (Princeton, NJ: Princeton University Press, 2014).

77. Irrawaddy Flotilla Company; hereafter, IFC.

78. BL/IOR/P/437/69, p. 133: India Foreign Proceedings (Political, October 1866).

79. Schendel, 'The Mandalay Economy', 50.

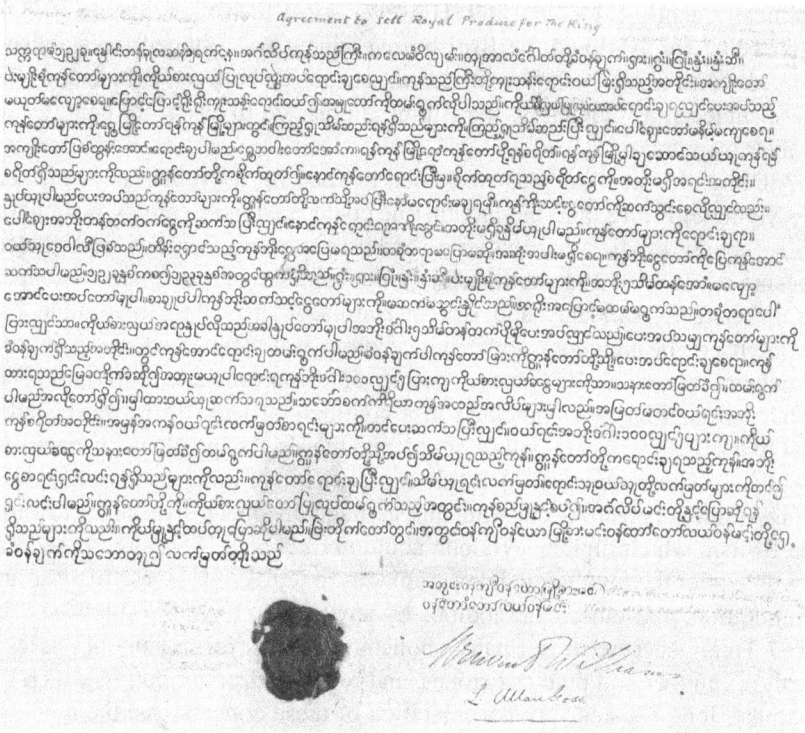

Figure 6.2. Agreement to sell royal produce for King Mindon, signed by Dr Clement Williams and his nephew, Louis Allan Goss, and accompanied by the royal seal, also known as the Lion Seal (1870). *Source:* Courtesy of the Royal Ontario Museum, © ROM (Ref. ROM2018_16380_2).

to disputes between the various parties which could not easily be settled, especially as foreign merchants had no legal redress against local creditors, who were subject to Burmese law. Until the kingdom was finally annexed in 1886, the unstable political situation on both sides of the British-Burma border meant that circumstances were ripe for irregularities and illegal activities to occur, specifically concerning the import of arms beyond the official limit allowed to the king.

Furthermore, with this new commercial traffic, legal disagreements occurred because of a lack of clarity over whether foreign entrepreneurs in Upper Burma should be subject to the jurisdiction of the Burmese or British courts. It became difficult at times to distinguish between private traders and British officials, who were also involved in trade deals with Upper Burma, whether on their own account, or on behalf of the government. It was unclear whether Burmese or British law applied, and consequently, much controversy ensued, despite attempts to clarify the situation with the establishment of the

Political Agent's Court in 1869. However, even then the situation was far from being resolved and the British government was obliged to establish a 'mixed' court to hear cases when disputes occurred between British and Burmese subjects, as inevitably, the Burmese objected to cases not being heard in their own courts.

Although his position was weakened in 1866 by the rebellion of his son, the Myingun Prince, and the fact that he could no longer employ his authority so openly by dictating the terms of business, King Mindon nevertheless became a powerful and subtle actor in the commercial processes now operating between Mandalay and British Burma.[80] The palace revolution had destabilised the kingdom and King Mindon was concerned about reports circulating regarding British aggression, and even probable annexation.[81] In 1867, Arthur Phayre commented in a confidential letter to Edward Sladen that 'the British will be going up soon', and the king's apprehension appeared credible.[82] The possession of a full complement of arms would strengthen King Mindon's position, enabling him to maintain a defensive stance towards the British, which diplomacy alone could not uphold. Therefore, as soon as possible after the revolution, he was anxious to replace his stocks of arms and ammunition, and other commodities by any means, legal or otherwise. The 1867 Treaty succeeded in finally abolishing most royal monopolies, except earth-oil, timber and precious stones, and reducing frontier duties, which the king had long resisted.[83] In consideration of these concessions, the monarch was officially allowed a limited supply of arms and a shipment of 2,000 Enfield rifles had been agreed by the British, on the understanding that this was a special case and that no more arms or ammunition would be permitted. However, the king told Captain Edward Sladen that he considered himself a special case and therefore, he rejected the additional articles in the Treaty because, although they were suitable for ordinary individuals in transacting private affairs, he considered that they were not suitable for kings.[84]

Meanwhile, the regular attendance at Court of foreigners eager to negotiate contracts with the king was resented by Sladen, who observed in his Mandalay diary entry that, the 'foreigner class' danced attendance on the king; and he felt that 'it was unbecoming to himself to be associated with them'.[85] However, the king encouraged the presence of the 'foreigner class' at Court, as

80. Ibid., 252.
81. BL/IOR/P/437/70/104–105: 'Proceedings' entries from the Mandalay diary of Captain Edward Sladen (15 January–13 February 1867).
82. BL/Mss Eur E290/3110–11/3: Letters from Lt. Col. Sir A. P. Phayre (1862–1867, 1866–1867).
83. BL/IOR/P/437/71/No. 112: Reduction of frontier duties and abolition by the King of certain monopolies (May 1867).
84. Ibid.
85. 'Proceedings' entries from the Mandalay diary of Sladen.

although not numerous, they provided a conduit for him to acquire the arms and ammunition needed to help him maintain his fragile hold on his kingdom. But to the Rangoon Administration, the European merchants' involvement in supplying arms and other appurtenances of warlike machinery for iron foundries to the king was politically contentious and certainly contrary to long-term British interests beyond the frontier. With only a Political Agent representing the British Burma government's interests in the kingdom, the traffic of arms was difficult to control. As Sladen's Mandalay diary entry on 2 February 1867 further noted,

> Some of the European residents of Mandalay have lately been trying to induce the Burmese government to enter into contracts with them for the sale and delivery of arms. Amongst them Dr. Williams, formerly the Chief Commissioner's Agent was anxious to conclude a contract for the delivery at Mandalay of 10,000 muskets for which he was paid at the rate of Rupees 35–4 for each musket.[86]

Other firms besides Williams's enterprise were involved in this lucrative trade and there is good reason to believe that the practice was widespread, with many government officials, including those at the highest level, turning a blind eye to it. Even high-ranking officers like Albert Fytche and Edward Sladen appeared complicit in arms trafficking, or at least were prepared to ignore it, if personally advantageous. In his private correspondence, Fytche reported to Sladen that 4,500 muskets had arrived, which the king had ordered, and which had to be paid for before delivery. He told Sladen that the king ought to be much obliged to him for getting him these muskets at such a cheap rate of 30 per cent under the original cost.[87] If, as he claimed, Fytche had negotiated a discount for the king on these weapons, it seems reasonable to suppose that he had received some reward for his efforts.

Since 1865, when the IFC's steamers had been permitted to ply the route between Rangoon and Mandalay, Williams had used his position as the IFC's agent to ship arms and ammunition to the king above the permitted quota.[88] The British Burma government was largely powerless to put a stop to this illicit arms trade, in which the IFC steamer captains also colluded in smuggling rifles, flints and other war materials on the regular routes between Rangoon and Mandalay. However, Williams's tenure as IFC Agent was brief, as in 1867, he was dismissed from his post on the instigation of Sladen, acting jointly with the IFC's lawyer, Mr McColl. Sladen ordered Williams to surrender all the IFC's property, including the Company's premises. Sladen's

---

86. Ibid.
87. BL/Mss Eur E290/33: Albert Fytche to Edward Sladen (23 October 1868).
88. Schendel, 'The Mandalay Economy', 179. In 1868, the IFC's steamer route was extended to Bhamo.

summary action in this matter generated much controversy and acrimony within the business community in Mandalay and Rangoon, once again underlining the instability of political relations between the kingdom and British Burma.

Despite Williams's dismissal from his IFC position, the trade in arms with Upper Burma continued to be an 'open secret' amongst the foreign and indigenous communities of Mandalay and Rangoon.[89] On 25 March 1870, an article appeared in the *Rangoon Gazette* reporting that thousands of arms had been allowed to go through to the King of Burma. Although a Government of India enquiry into the problem of arms smuggling was launched, it proved to be a 'whitewash'. Replying on behalf of the Chief Commissioner, his Secretary stated unequivocally, 'No arms have been forwarded to the King of Burmah excepting those supplied to his majesty by the Government of India and the officiating Chief Commissioner is of the opinion that the editor of the Rangoon Gazette was misled by the dispatch of these arms to comment upon the matter'.[90] Two years later, in 1872, the Chief Commissioner still denied that the trade was being carried on, even after the confiscated cargo of Rangoon traders, Edmund Jones and Company, was found to contain rifles and cartridges, not 'macaroni', as stated on the manifest. It had burst open upon arrival at Mandalay, but the Chief Commissioner resolutely declared that Edmund Jones was not a 'mischievous influence' on the king.[91]

Beyond the jurisdiction of British Burma, merchants like Williams were able to operate with impunity outside the bounds of the law, which at that time was governed under the provisions of the Indian Civil Procedure Code and the Criminal Code. However, the eventual collapse of Clement Williams and his associates' commercial enterprises in Mandalay served as a warning to others about the complications of doing business in Upper Burma, where legal protection of financial interests was not secured against local creditors, despite the establishment of the Political Agent's Court in 1869.[92] Foreign entrepreneurs found themselves subject to Burmese law, where regulations differed markedly from the British, particularly concerning matters of debt, for which defaulters were frequently imprisoned in appalling conditions.[93]

---

89. BL/Mss Eur E290/32: Albert Fytche to Edward Sladen (23 December 1867).

90. BL/IOR/P/438/10, No. 165: Concerning the supply of arms to the King of Burma.

91. Schendel, 'The Mandalay Economy', 350; quoting BL/IOR/L/PS/6, 7: Political Letters from Chief Commissioner to the Foreign Sec. of India (May–July 1873).

92. Ibid., 343.

93. As a special concession on the part of the Burmese government, under the terms of Article V of the Treaty of 1867, the Political Agent at Mandalay was permitted to decide all cases and disputes which arose between registered British subjects in his own court. However, the situation became complicated when cases were brought to the specially established Mixed Court, where the plaintiff or defendant was Burmese, and the opposing party a registered British subject. The cases became

This fate befell Williams's brother, Howard, who spent time in gaol in 1869 for insolvency, before his case was sent for arbitration.[94] Although remedies were sought that might absolve the requirement for British subjects in Upper Burma to submit to Burmese law, political and commercial relations remained fragile, presaging the downfall of a weakened Burmese kingdom within less than two decades.[95]

This occurred in 1885 after reports in the British and Rangoon press regarding the cruel behaviour of King Mindon's successor, Thibaw Min. Vociferous protests at his alleged atrocities and lobbying by merchants in Rangoon for greater trade access to Upper Burma resulted in military action. Although the fall of the last king of the Konbaung Dynasty was swift, it set in motion a gruelling campaign of 'pacification' of rebels in the countryside, which was ravaged by guerrilla warfare and equally cruel measures by the British that lasted until the end of the century. Clement Williams did not live to see this event, as he died of cholera in 1879 during a stay near Florence on his way home to England on leave.

Some years after his death, he became something of a local hero in the West of England after the *Bristol Mercury* published an article which praised his commitment to Burma and its people. The significance of the appearance of the *Bristol Mercury* article in December 1885, a month after the final annexation of the Kingdom of Upper Burma, emphasises the tensions that existed between the centre and the periphery, as well as the many opinions that were expressed, both publicly and privately. The article was intended to posthumously restore Williams's reputation, now somewhat tarnished by his close personal involvement in the political and mercantile affairs of the former Burmese kingdom. The *Mercury*'s article commended Williams for freely entering into the affairs of Upper Burma and for expressing opinions that were always in the best interests of the people. The article also observed

---

almost impossible to resolve as the Burmese claimed immunity, declaring that they were not subject to British law.

94. As previously mentioned, sometime in the late 1860s, Clement Williams was joined in Mandalay by his brother Howard. Thereafter, his commercial activities became a family concern. After Williams died in 1879, his nephew, Louis Allan Goss, joined the firm, before becoming a Government Inspector of Schools following Annexation.

95. Williams's nemesis, Edward Sladen's, reputation was not untarnished by corruption in the heated atmosphere of political affairs between British Burma and Mandalay in the years leading up to Annexation and after. On the morning of 29 November 1885, Sladen was with the king and his queen in the Palace at Mandalay when a large priceless stone of unexampled brilliance set in a ring, part of the crown jewels and regalia since the days of Bodawpaya, was made over to him for safekeeping by the ex-king. Together with other precious jewels, the ruby was listed by the Shwedaik Atwin *woon* and handed to the officer assisting Sladen. Sladen was implicated in its disappearance and subsequently questioned after he returned to Britain in 1886. To this day, the Burmese people mourn the loss of this valuable item in the crown jewels, and although other items were returned to the nation in 1964 by Lord Louis Mountbatten, it has never come to light. Blood red and the size of a pigeon's egg, it was doubtless cut up to avoid detection.

that Williams and his brother had owned large 'godowns'[96] in Upper Burma, which had attracted considerable attention and jealousy. The final section examines Williams's legacy and the diverse ways in which the affective knowledge he attained by his long sojourn in Burma was received both at the centre and on the periphery.

CONCLUDING REMARKS

In order to establish its status as a sphere of knowledge in its own right, the periphery needed to ensure that any new knowledge which entered the public domain should do so in ways that reinforced its claims to authority and certainly did not undermine them. Adherence, wherever possible, to the maintenance of professional standards in various branches like surveying and geography required that amateur accounts should be either suitably transformed or treated merely as useful background information. From the mid-nineteenth century, the Rangoon Administration found itself very much on the periphery, faltering on the edge of not knowing, unable to comprehend the subtle machinations of Upper Burma's polity and excluded from understanding what was really going on. Lacking the benefit of those 'temples of accumulated colonial knowledge', the district officer, whose time was yet to come in Upper Burma,[97] it depended for information upon outsiders and go-betweens, whose pursuit of commercial gain, often motivated by self-interest, meant that their information was not always reliable. The Administration's discrimination towards intelligence received from outsiders inevitably created tensions and ill-feeling between the actors concerned, as well as the loss of potentially valuable information. It hindered progress in many frontier areas for decades to come, nowhere more so than in Burma.

In view of the emerging importance of Yunnan as a buffer state between Britain and France's colonial ambitions, Williams's proposal that the old caravan routes might be adopted for trade between British Burma and Western China was not without merit. The difficulties and expense of building railways and telegraph communications presented an enticing opportunity for commercial expansion, but hostilities and shifting alliances between the various local ethnicities on Burma's north-western frontier, together with Chinese intransigence, proved impossible to overcome. More than thirty years later, there was still no consensus of opinion on the best trade route into Western China. In 1897, R.F.W. Carey, an employee in the service of the Imperial

---

96. Godown: Word commonly use in South and Southeast Asia for a warehouse or storage facility.
97. Bayly, 'Knowing the Country', 3; quoting Leonard Woolf, *An Autobiography, Vol. 1: 1880–1911* (Oxford: Oxford University Press, 1980), 162–165.

Chinese Customs, criticised the misconceived ideas of trade possibilities as being probably derived from 'highly coloured accounts of occasional travellers, who judged what they saw during a few days' stay'.[98] He concluded that although the Chinese carried on a large trade in tea from Yunnan, it was an internal trade unsuited to the tastes of foreigners.[99] Carey's remarks indicate that a wide discrepancy remained between the value placed on official government reports like his own and those by occasional travellers, or go-betweens and informants like Clement Williams.

The controversies that arose over the respective behaviours and activities of Clement Williams and William Johnson accentuate the tensions and complexities that existed in the relationship between the periphery and metropole, and their relative values and objectives as sites of knowledge. Although both actors envisaged their lone missions beyond the frontier as initially 'led by pure zeal to the public service',[100] their findings could not be readily objectified and theorised like those carried out by approved organisations, or sites for the production of knowledge. The activities of these 'amateur' explorer-entrepreneurs failed to gain the recognition and respect that they had hoped for; instead, they were ignored by official sources. As a result, they resorted to pursuing careers directed towards self-interest, for which they attracted considerable enmity.

Nevertheless, their findings are useful to us today, not only for what they tell us about conditions beyond the frontier at that time but also for how the production of knowledge was tendentious. As the preceding chapters have shown, knowledge was often overlooked unless it was obtained by the army or official agencies especially commissioned for the purpose. The next chapter considers the activities of Indian army officer, Frederick Marshman Bailey, whose own journeys of discovery read like chapters from *Boys' Own Adventure Stories* and who, in the early decades of the twentieth century, might be described as one of Britain's first secret agents, operational in the aftermath of the First World War.

---

98. BL/IOR/L/PS/18 B110–B133: Report by R.F.W. Carey, Imperial Customs Service.
99. Ibid.
100. BL/IOR/L/PS/6/551 Coll. 13/1: Asst. Sec. to the Chief Commissioner to Clement Williams (26 December 1866).

Chapter 7

Frederick Marshman Bailey: 'The Right Sort' of Political Officer and Collector

INTRODUCTION

If Francis Whyte Ellis was 'a nearly perfect embodiment of Orientalism as colonial policy',[1] almost a century later, Frederick Marshman Bailey (1882–1967) was colonialism's archetypal dashing hero. With a pedigree that fitted him admirably for a 'career as a soldier, explorer, secret agent, diplomatist and linguist',[2] Bailey's deeds of derring-do appeared to come straight out of the pages of a novel by G.A. Henty.[3] Plucky and steadfast, Henty's heroes were always 'the right sort'. Bailey's persona resembled that of a fictitious hero, conjured up to keep an audience at home committed to the empire's ideals after the carnage of the First World War in Europe had left it bruised and battered.[4] Born in Lahore, the son of an Indian army officer, Bailey spent his early years in the foothills of the Himalayas, where, like William Johnson, he became an accomplished mountaineer.[5] But that is where the similarity between the two men ended, as unlike Johnson, Bailey was not burdened with the classification of 'country-born'. At the age of seven, he was sent home to Britain to be educated at the right establishments: Wellington College, the Edinburgh Academy and the Military Academy at Sandhurst.

1. Trautmann, *Languages and Nations*, 79.
2. BL/Mss Eur F157/886: Obituary of Frederick Marshman Bailey C.I.E. in the *Himalayan Journal* 28, no. 20 (1968).
3. G.A. Henty (1832–1902), a late-nineteenth-century author, enthralled his readers with historical adventure stories. Even today, Henty still has his loyal followers, who formed a society in his name in 1977.
4. BL/Mss Eur F157/810: Notes, messages, newspaper cuttings, map and permits of Frederick Marshman Bailey relating to his mission in Bokara and Turkestan including some notes in invisible ink with photographs of messages when developed (1918–1920).
5. Bailey was a founding member of the Mountain Club of India (1927) and the Himalayan Club (1928).

This chapter will discuss Bailey's activities as a naturalist-collector in the context of a series of rather extraordinary adventures that befell him whilst engaged as a political officer in the Indian army, where he gained a reputation as one of its most intrepid operatives. At a time when national consciousness and anti-imperial sentiments were growing in Britain and throughout the empire, Bailey's exploits were publicised in newspapers and magazines in order to maintain the illusion of the empire's supranatural power. He spent his retirement recounting them to satisfy the public's appetite for true-life tales that glorified the empire. He even entertained the possibility that his book about his mission to Tashkent might be made into a film, as his archive at the British Library contains a synopsis of a film script.[6]

By the first decade of the twentieth century, obtaining up-to-date knowledge about Russian and Chinese threats to India's frontiers became imperative, particularly in view of the weakening central authority in Peking and the clouds of war that were gathering over Europe. In his capacity as a political officer in the Indian army, Bailey was able to use his enthusiasm for trophy-hunting and collecting natural history specimens as a pretext for gathering political and commercial intelligence in the untamed borderlands on India's north-eastern frontier. He hunted and collected many specimens of mammals, birds, butterflies and plants for museums and also for his own personal collection, whilst acquiring political intelligence in regions beyond the jurisdiction of British authority.[7] He undertook many expeditions throughout the Himalayas, Tibet and parts of Central Asia, where he amassed literally thousands of birds, butterflies and large mammals. But unlike his illustrious predecessor, Francis Buchanan-Hamilton, Bailey was an amateur enthusiast, who did not possess the necessary skills in taxonomy to enable him to make scholarly observations about his discoveries. After hunting and preserving his specimens, he dispatched them to the Natural History Museum in London to be classified by experts in the hope that they would be included in scholarly papers, where he might receive recognition for his finds.

Although he is not well-known today and many of the items he collected have been dispersed throughout Britain and abroad, Bailey is still acknowledged as the collector of many museum exhibits, notably at the Horniman Museum in South London and Liverpool's World Museum. As this chapter will explain, Bailey's collecting connected him with a long tradition in natural history that relied on correspondents at the periphery to provide new specimens for specialists in the metropole to identify. It enabled him to establish links with independent scholars, learned societies

---

6. BL/Mss Eur F157/817: Outline account of Frederick Marshman Bailey's adventures in Turkestan 1918–20. See also Frederick M. Bailey, *Mission to Tashkent* (London: Jonathan Cape, 1946).

7. Obituary of Bailey (1968).

and museums that were arguably more meaningful historically than his popular reputation as a spy or secret agent. They allowed him to become part of the history of colonial administrators who crossed frontiers, both literally and figuratively, in search of new scientific knowledge. He was in frequent contact with men like William Ogilvie Grant (1863–1924), Assistant Keeper of the Zoological Department at the Natural History Museum in London, whom he consulted regularly concerning new birds that he had discovered, especially during an overland trip from China to India in 1911. During this expedition, Bailey made a small collection of about sixty bird skins, including several new species that he discovered in Sichuan, a region little-known at the time. He sent them to Ogilvie Grant for identification, asking him to describe them and to ascertain whether any of the eggs were previously unknown.[8]

He also offered some species of birds already identified to the Bombay Natural History Society that had been founded in 1886, with its first journal published in the same year. The Society provided a platform not only for accounts written by scientists in Britain but also for narratives of unexplored terrains contributed by local naturalists and sport-hunters like Bailey. Preservation of specimens from the field was an important aspect of collecting and the Bombay Society taught the necessary skills in order for specimens to reach their destination in the best possible condition. As previously noted in Chapter 2, Bailey arranged for his faithful Tibetan manservant, Putamdu, to travel to Bombay to learn these skills.

Bailey first made his name accompanying the Indian Political Officer, Colonel Francis Younghusband, on his mission to Lhasa in 1903–1904. The mission sought to establish an official British presence in Tibet as a counterweight to possible Russian influence in the region and consequent threats to Britain's Indian frontier. Appointed to his position personally by the Viceroy,[9] Francis Younghusband was a great exponent of Curzon's 'forward policy', which vowed 'to preserve intact and secure, either from internal convulsion, or external inroad, the boundaries of that great and Imperial dominion'.[10] However, the British government was unwilling to establish a permanent British representative in Lhasa for fear of further destabilising the region, which, until 1911, was under the jurisdiction of the Chinese Empire. Instead, the mission succeeded in setting up three trade agencies in the country and Bailey was appointed officer in charge of the post at Gyantse, a city strategically situated in the Nyangchu Valley on the ancient trade and pilgrim routes from India. Staffed by officers selected from the Indian Political Department, the Trade

---

8. NHM/DFZOO/230/22/70–86: F.M. Bailey to W. Ogilvie Grant (14 September 1911).
9. Lord Curzon was Viceroy of India from 1899 to 1905.
10. Henry Caldwell Lipsett, *Lord Curzon in India, 1898–1903* (London: R. A. Everett & Co, 1903).

Figure 7.1. Captain Frederick Marshman Bailey with his manservant, Putamdu, at Sadiya, India (1912). *Source:* **Royal Geographical Society (Ref. PR/050105).**

Agencies served two purposes – not only satisfying the trading lobby but also acting as Britain's 'eyes and ears' in the region.[11] During the First World War, Bailey distinguished himself on the Western Front, serving with the Indian army in Flanders, and in 1915, at Gallipoli. For the latter part of the war, he

---

11. Alex C. McKay, 'Tibet 1924: A Very British Coup Attempt?' *Journal of the Royal Asiatic Society* 7, no. 3 (1997): 412.

was a political officer in Iraq, followed by Persia; and in 1918, he led an under-cover mission to Tashkent, which is described in detail in the next section.[12]

Before the Great War, Bailey's talent as an adventurous explorer and col-lector was recognised when, at the request of the Government of India, he embarked on a mission to solve the mystery of the Tsangpo Gorges. In 1913, he set out with Captain H.T. Morshead on an expedition to establish the route by which the Tsangpo River (Brahmaputra) reached the sea. Their instruc-tions were to survey Tibet's north-eastern frontier with India, as the route from the South through British territory was too difficult to approach because of thick forest and hostile ethnic communities. The pair advanced from the direction of Tibet through treacherous terrains, passing many villages on the way,[13] an experience which Bailey later described in his book *No Passport to Tibet*.[14]

As a result of their exploration, Morshead and Bailey proved conclusively that the Tsangpo-Brahmaputra was a single river and for the first time estab-lished its accurate course and also that its tributary, the Dibang River, flowed around, rather than through, the Himalayan Mountains.[15] Morshead surveyed the entire route and was subsequently awarded the Macgregor Medal by the United Service Institution of India. Bailey was awarded the RGS's Gold Medal for his contribution to collecting valuable information and natural his-tory specimens, particularly his discovery of the Tibetan Blue Poppy, named after him as *Meconopsis baileyi*.[16] On their return, Bailey described the details of their expedition in an article published in *The Scottish Geographical Magazine* in 1914.[17] He concluded his article by noting that in addition to the geographical results, they brought back a small, but interesting collection of mammals, birds and butterflies, which also contained several new species.[18] As a real-life empire hero, unlike those imagined by contemporary authors like G.A. Henty, John Buchan and many others, Bailey's reputation helped to establish the idea of this figure as 'a saviour of the nation from spies, terror-ists and criminals'.[19] The next section looks at the trajectory of his career as a

---

12. Obituary of Bailey (1968).

13. Harish Kapadia, *Into the Untravelled Himalaya: Travels, Treks and Climbs* (New Delhi: Indus Publishing Company, 2005), 53.

14. Frederick M. Bailey, *No Passport to Tibet* (London: Rupert Hart-Davis, 1957).

15. BL/Mss Eur F157/85/2: Map of south-eastern Tibet and the Mishmi Hills by F.M. Bailey and map of north-east frontier (of India) and Tibet showing route of the Tsangpo/Brahmaputra River by F.M. Bailey and H.R. Meade, compiled for Survey of India, published by the RGS (1911–1913).

16. Obituary of Bailey (1968).

17. Frederick M. Bailey, 'Exploration on the Tsangpo or Upper Brahmaputra', *The Scottish Geo-graphical Magazine* 30, no. 11 (1914): 561–582.

18. Ibid., 582.

19. Ted Beardow, 'The Empire Hero', *Studies in Popular Culture* 41, no. 1 (2018): 83.

political officer in the Indian army, particularly in the context of his activities in Central Asia at the conclusion of the First World War.

CONTEXTUALISING BAILEY'S ADVENTURES IN CENTRAL ASIA

Despite the ravages of war in Europe and the collapse of the Russian Empire, the last acts of 'The Great Game' were played out in Central Asia after the end of the Great War and provided the *mise-en-scène* for Bailey's abortive mission to Tashkent between 1918 and 1920. It was a mission predicated upon political outcomes that were perilous and inherently unachievable, and which relied for their success on undercover encounters with anti-Bolshevists and their sympathisers. The empire needed its heroes to reinforce the myth of its power and contemporary newspaper reports in Britain about Bailey's missions appear to have been influenced by the myths surrounding 'The Great Game'.[20] Begun in the mid-nineteenth century, it had arisen through rivalry between the two great powers – Russia and Britain – for control of Central Asian trade routes and mutual fear that their respective empires would confront one another commercially and militarily.

British anxieties about the safety of India were greatly heightened during the First World War after the Bolshevists's seizure of power in November 1917, which resulted in 'the disintegration of civil authority and the disappearance of Russian influence in Persia had reawakened British fears'.[21] Following the collapse of the Eastern Front after the Russian Revolution and the withdrawal of German troops to the West, a large number of German prisoners of war had been released and the collapse of the Russian army raised fears that they might be organised and armed by the agents of the Central Powers. By 1918, the combination of the danger from German and Turkish intrigues in Afghanistan and Persia, created by returning prisoners and disaffected 'native' opinion in India, required that a fact-finding mission should be undertaken in order to judge the mood on the ground in Central Asia. It was under these circumstances that plans for a special mission to Central Asia led by Major Bailey were drawn up.

A life history like Bailey's, so rich in adventures, invites critical comment about whether his exploits offered any meaningful contribution towards building an epistemological framework for understanding journeys of exploration as a means of discovering new knowledge about the empire. The thread becomes entangled when fact becomes confused with uncorroborated

---

20. BL/Mss Eur F157/888: Bailey miscellaneous (1911–1940).
21. L.P. Morris, 'British Secret Missions in Turkestan, 1918–1919', *Journal of Contemporary History* 12 (1977): 364.

accounts by charismatic individuals like Bailey, who found themselves in situations where personality and an appetite for danger encountered *force majeure*. Nowhere is this more evident than in the journey that Bailey undertook in 1918 at the behest of the British government, where he was required to act as Britain's 'eyes and ears' in Tashkent. Conducting himself with stealth, he endeavoured, without success, to act as a broker between the various factions and interests in Central Asia, which was now in tumult after the First World War and the Russian Revolution.

The pressures of war in Europe meant that there were few resources available for the defence of the empire in distant theatres like Turkestan, so the Indian government was obliged to rely upon demi-official stratagems carried out by political officers, who, whatever their shortcomings or misdemeanours, were considered to be 'the right sort' to conduct such covert missions. As Sir William Robertson, the Chief of the Imperial General Staff, argued, in this situation 'what was needed [. . .] was to dispatch to the centres of intrigue and disaffection a few Englishmen of the right type to give our version of the state of affairs'.[22] Acting as an undercover informant, Bailey's mission in Tashkent was intended, where possible, to disseminate anti-Bolshevik propaganda. Although he lacked the means to decisively influence the actions of 'members of a revolutionary group [. . .] threatened on two fronts',[23] it indicates the Imperial government's willingness to authorise clandestine missions by trusted officers before a professionally trained secret service became fully functional.[24]

By the early twentieth century, exploration had become 'a process of physical and material contact and exchange',[25] so that exploration narratives were 'part of a powerful and enduring projection of Western imperial interests onto other parts of the world'.[26] It has been argued that geographic, ethnographic and statistical research formed a vital constituent of colonial empires, not only practically but also as a means of defining their conception of themselves.[27] However, the difficulty occasioned by Bailey's adventurous career lies in sorting out fact from fiction, and myth from reality, in order to make sense of how such an individual came to acquire his reputation as a maverick, ready to pursue intelligence beyond the frontier to protect British

---

22. William Robertson, *Soldiers and Statesmen, 1914–1918* (London: Cassell & Co., 1926), 2, 273.
23. Ibid., 3.
24. First established 1909 as the Secret Service Bureau, it developed into the professional intelligence agencies, MI5 and MI6.
25. James R. Ryan and Simon Naylor, 'Exploration and the Twentieth Century', *New Spaces of Exploration: Geographies of Discovery in the Twentieth Century* (London and New York: I. B. Tauris, 2009), 1–5.
26. Ibid., 1.
27. Ian W. Campbell, 'Settlement Promoted, Settlement Contested: The Shcherbina Expedition of 1896–1903', in *Movement, Power and Place in Central Asia and Beyond: Contested Trajectories*, ed. Madeleine Reeves (London: Routledge, 2012), 65–79.

interests. Tales of his adventures may have been deliberately exaggerated in newspapers to create awe in colonial subjects and inspire fervent support back home for the imperial ideal.

Not unexpectedly, Bailey failed to influence the confused politics in post-revolutionary Tashkent, but his involvement in a risky political venture beyond the frontier, which necessitated adopting a disguise and hiding for long periods, conforms to the format of heroic tales of empire. Bailey's claim to have adopted multiple disguises whilst hiding out in Tashkent[28] suggests that he too may have been influenced by tales he had read about empire heroes during his boyhood. Even Kim,[29] the ragamuffin Irish hero of Rudyard Kipling's book, was adept at disguising himself after being suitably trained at an English school in India. As Ted Beardow has observed, whilst no 'native' is ever portrayed as capable of disguising himself as a European, fictional empire heroes were skilled at disguise.[30] Beardow has also argued that the English gentleman's ability to assume both identities is another symbol of colonisation and an indicator of the belief of belonging to a superior civilisation.[31]

In his book, *Mission to Tashkent*, Bailey described a series of adventures that had befallen him between October 1918 and March 1919, and how he was forced to adopt a variety of disguises as an Albanian deserter, a Romanian prisoner, a teacher of French, and finally, as a Soviet agent.[32] Apparently, this last disguise was so credible that he was able to convince people that he had been hired by Russian Intelligence and sent from Moscow to look for the Anglo-Indian army officer, named Bailey, whom they knew was in the area![33] Although many army officers were talented linguists, it seems rather disingenuous to suggest that the enemy was incapable of discerning a foreign accent or seeing through Bailey's disguises.[34]

After June 1918, the Government of India became responsible for all policies in Turkestan, and Sir George Macartney, the Consul-General in Kashgar, was in overall charge of the mission. Its task was to report on the

---

28. Bailey, *Mission to Tashkent*.

29. Kim is the eponymous hero of Rudyard Kipling's book, *Kim*, first published serially in McClure's Magazine from December 1900 to October 1901, then in book form by Macmillan & Co. Ltd.

30. Beardow, 'The Empire Hero', 80. The explorer, Sir Richard Burton (1821–1890), entered the city of Harar in eastern Ethiopia disguised in Arab dress, which allegedly deceived the Emir of this city, a place forbidden to foreigners.

31. Ibid.

32. McKay, 'Tibet 1924', 416.

33. BL/Mss Eur F157/316: Typescript of *Mission to Tashkent*.

34. Notes, messages, newspaper cuttings of Bailey (1918–1920). See an undated newspaper report quoting that Bailey dressed himself in the uniform of a dead prisoner and 'spent two years as an alleged prisoner of war in an enemy country. He was able to transmit valuable information to our own Government'. The newspaper reported that the ruse of disguising himself as a POW gave him a loophole of escape if he made some small slip in dialect.

situation in those areas of Central Asia where the Bolsheviks had taken control. Macartney was given permission to allow Bailey and his second-in-command, Major Blacker, and their party to enter Turkestan and proceed to Tashkent, which had become the seat of the local Bolshevik government. Because conditions were constantly changing, it was impossible to give explicit instructions; nevertheless, the Indian Foreign Department suggested that this aim might best be achieved by exploiting anti-Bolshevik and pro-autonomous Muslim sentiments.[35] Although officially prohibited from engaging in any active propaganda or entering Russian Turkestan without government orders, Bailey, as leader, was advised that 'should however an emergent opportunity of useful intervention present itself and it be impossible to obtain the order of the Government of India in time', the Consul General in Kashgar could authorise any action.[36] In particular, the mission was tasked with sending regular reports and information on the movements of German and Austrian prisoners of war, who were considered to be one of the main agencies for fomenting aggression in Afghanistan and for successfully intervening in the affairs of Russian Turkestan. Such actions were considered hostile to Britain's imperial interests in India at a time of global turmoil after the First World War, when emerging nationalisms throughout South and Southeast Asia and declining support for imperial objectives threatened their existence.

From the outset, the lack of cohesion and singlemindedness in British policy was strikingly evident. As there had been no specific instructions given to them to proceed to Tashkent, it seemed that the decision was made by Macartney after the mission assembled in Kashgar in June 1918. Of the group, Bailey appeared to be the member who showed the greatest enthusiasm for their visit to Tashkent and he was keen for them to travel in disguise.[37] Although not part of the mission itself, Sir George Macartney accompanied them on his way home to Britain and after their arrival he had to use all his diplomatic skills to justify their presence to the Bolshevik commander in the city.[38] With little accomplished, Macartney and Blacker left Tashkent in mid-September 1918, leaving Bailey there alone, ostensibly to complete the mission, but without any firm objective or plan in mind. It was not known whether Bailey's decision to stay on in Tashkent after the departure of Macartney and Blacker was made against official advice. However, he had already gained something of a name for being a maverick, who ignored orders when he felt the situation demanded it and he later

35. IOR L/P&S/10/722/1 and 2: Bailey's Mission to Kashgar (1918–1921).
36. Ibid.
37. Ibid.
38. Morris, 'British Secret Missions', 371.

admitted on his return to England that he had remained in Tashkent of his own volition.[39]

It was during this period of political instability and chaos in Central Asia, whilst alone in Tashkent, that Bailey acquired a reputation for complicity, after his name was linked with a failed uprising by anti-Bolshevists. Peter Hopkirk's introduction to Bailey's book, *Mission to Tashkent*, has examined in detail Bailey's connections with underground anti-Bolshevist groups, who helped him to escape and with whose aspirations and attitudes Bailey apparently sympathised.[40] Bailey was accused of skulduggery after allegedly acting in league with a white Russian counter-revolutionary organisation led by an ex-Soviet officer called Osipov. Anti-Bolshevist hopes to overthrow the Bolshevist regime were crushed and a wholesale massacre of several thousand of the city's bourgeois population ensued. In one of his reports to the Foreign Department of the Government of India, Bailey described an atrocity committed by the Bolshevists against upper-class men after the failed coup attempt. Around 4,000 'white' Russians in Tashkent were taken to a railway station where they were shot. M. Kelberg, head of the Swedish Red Cross Mission, was amongst the victims.[41]

After this attempted counter-revolution, which the Bolshevists suspected that Bailey had a part in helping to foment, it was impossible for him to reenter Tashkent, as the Bolshevists kept guards on all the entrances.[42] According to unsubstantiated Russian accounts, Bailey's name was linked with the 'British Imperialists' who, it was claimed, were at the bottom of the uprising. However, it was unlikely that 'members of a revolutionary regime in conflict with a rebellious native population and threatened on two fronts would risk their necks by shooting each other at the behest of a British agent'.[43] But labels tend to stick and thereafter, Bailey's reputation for adventures involving espionage and illicit activities beyond the frontier became the basis for claims that he was a secret agent.

Bailey's adventures in the course of escaping from the Bolshevists, who, with some justification, came to regard him not merely as a British Agent, but also as a spy, saw him make use of his linguistic abilities and adopt new identities in order to survive. As he stated in his article in the *Journal of the Central Asian Society*, throughout their time in Tashkent, the group had been kept under surveillance by both the local and the secret police. On 20 October 1918, after Blacker and Macartney had left and unable openly to leave

---

39. Frederick M. Bailey, 'In Russian Turkestan under the Bolsheviks', *Journal of the Central Asian Society* 8, no. 1 (1921): 49–69.

40. Bailey, *Mission to Tashkent.*

41. Bailey's Mission to Kashgar (1918–1921), 1.

42. Ibid.

43. Charles H. Ellis, *The Transcaspian Episode, 1918–1919* (London: Hutchinson, 1963), 148.

the city, Bailey disappeared. By going underground and adopting various disguises, he was able to evade capture by the Bolshevists, who would assuredly have shot him as a spy.[44] In order to do so, he took refuge firstly in Tashkent at the home of a Jewish barrister, named Leter Raizer, where a Miss Houston was the English governess.[45] After Raizer lent him money, Bailey fled to the mountains outside of Tashkent, where he hid out in hills behind the city for some months during 1919 with a Russian General who was also fleeing the Bolshevists. He later fell into the company of an ex-prisoner and disillusioned Communist, who was trying to make his way back home to Serbia. However, having broken his leg, Bailey was obliged to return to the city, where, once again, his contacts hid and nursed him back to health. Bailey eventually escaped from Turkestan and arrived safely in Meshed in January 1920, to the relief of all concerned, although not necessarily to general approbation.[46] He took refuge with the British Military Mission in Meshed, where he stayed with his old friend, the British Consul General, the magnificently named, Sir Trenchard Fowle.[47]

By the time he finally made his way back to India, Bailey was, in his own judgement, an experienced intelligence agent. From 1921–1928, he was appointed to the post of political officer in Sikkim with responsibility for overseeing affairs in Tibet, where he became embroiled in further intrigues.[48] This appointment was followed by periods as the Resident in Baroda, Kashmir, Bhutan and finally, as Envoy Extraordinary in Nepal. He retired from service in India in 1938, having become a personal friend of the Dalai Lama and, whilst in Sikkim, he visited Lhasa on more than one occasion. As mentioned earlier, after his retirement to Norfolk, Bailey began to write his own versions of the adventures that had befallen him in the course of his military service.[49] If the stories that emerged about the period when Bailey was operating alone in Central Asia, hiding from the Bolshevists and adopting many disguises, are credible, then he apparently relied upon the assistance of some rather unusual and dangerous individuals. But if they had been subject to some embellishment by their author, then Bailey's account of his adventures

---

44. BL/Mss Eur F157/810. These miscellaneous papers contain details of Bailey's efforts to evade capture in Tashkent, helped by sympathisers. An unsigned pencil note, perhaps written by Leter Raizer to Bailey, describes how he can hide in the home of an elderly widow, a friend of Mme. Raizer, who has fallen on hard times. Bailey is told where to wait in the street, how to identify the woman, follow her home and then return later. The writer asks if he will pay the widow, or if the writer should take care of it. On occasion, invisible ink was used for communications.

45. IOR/L/PS/10/74, 63: Central Asia, Affairs in Trans-Caspia and Turkestan; miscellaneous correspondence from India, Britain, Kashgar.

46. Morris, 'British Secret Missions', 374.

47. Ibid.

48. McKay, 'Tibet 1924', 416.

49. Frederick M. Bailey, *China–Tibet–Assam: A Journey, 1911* (London: Jonathan Cape, 1945); and also, Bailey, *No Passport to Tibet*.

in Tashkent was rather more useful as inspiration to authors of future spy thrillers than for its historicity.

Following this brief biographical introduction to Bailey's adventures as an Indian-army-political-officer-turned-secret-agent in Central Asia, the next section will focus on his activities as a natural history collector and a sport-hunter for trophies, which acted as subterfuge for obtaining political intelligence and surveying new routes. In 1911, Bailey undertook an unauthorised detour into the Mishmi Hills from Sadiya on his way back to India after home leave. He was not the first army officer to explore the opportunities offered by this frontier region, as expeditions in search of the tea plant and other natural commodities had commenced nearly a century earlier. They will be discussed in the next section in the context of Bailey's expedition, which, although ostensibly for the purpose of sport hunting, also allowed him to acquire up-to-date political intelligence about this increasingly volatile frontier region between India and Chinese Turkestan.

BAILEY'S EXPEDITION INTO THE MISHMI HILLS

As described earlier, throughout his career, Frederick Marshman Bailey took every opportunity, in conjunction with his duties as a political officer, to travel into unexplored regions beyond the frontier; even, on occasion, disobeying official instructions. In 1911, after home leave in Edinburgh, he decided to return to India via the overland route through China, having travelled from Europe to China via the trans-Siberian railway. From Peking he embarked on a route which took him to Batang, in the Chinese province of Sichuan, and then to Sadiya, situated at the junction of the Brahmaputra, Dibong and Lohit Rivers at the foot of the Himalayas. After leaving Sadiya, Bailey ventured into Eastern Tibet and the Mishmi Hills without obtaining official permission from the British or permits from the Chinese in the local area.[50] His unauthorised detour into Mishmi territory, situated in the dangerous frontier zone bordering North-East India and South Tibet, was inhabited by indigenous groups, who did not welcome strangers. His professed reason for departing from the previously agreed route that would take him from Batang to Bhamo, in Upper Burma, was bound up with his interest as a hunter-naturalist in acquiring new specimens for his own personal collection and those created by the expansion of scientific enterprises in the early twentieth century.

---

50. BL/IOR/L/PS/10/183: Secretary to the Govt. of India Foreign Dept., Simla, to F.M. Bailey (6 Nov. 1911).

Bailey's unsanctioned journey was rewarded not only with political intelligence but also by the discovery of rare species of butterflies, including the 'Queen of Spain fritillary'.[51] His quest was also to hunt the Mishmi takin, a wild beast known as *Budorcas taxicolor*, a sub-species found only in North-East India and existing at altitudes of between 1,000 and 4,500 feet. Therefore, he made a detour from Tachienlu,[52] which involved crossing the Beda La Pass, covered at the time in very deep snow, even though it was May.[53] This expedition presented an irresistible challenge to Bailey, as it allowed him to test not only his mountaineering expertise but also his skills at subterfuge as a political officer and to experience the thrill associated with colonial sport hunting, which, since the eighteenth century, had been an activity enjoyed by the 'officer class' of the British empire.

Extreme sport hunting also enjoyed a global appeal, as exemplified by wealthy American, William Louis Abbott (1860–1936), who, in common with Bailey, was one of a number of enthusiastic amateurs interested in exploring and hunting in Central Asia. Abbott was part of a growing body of amateur naturalist collectors who supplied universities and museums and his self-financed expeditions were supported by scholars at the Smithsonian Institution in America. In 1893–1894, he undertook an expedition to Chinese Turkestan, where his quarry was the *Ovis ammon pollii* (Marco Polo sheep). Paul Taylor has suggested that there was a personal code of ethics that developed among Euro-American sport-hunters in Central Asia and the Himalayan regions of British India. Without doubt, their inaccessibility and the danger associated with travelling in these areas, where few Europeans had ventured without incurring mishap and, on occasion, death, engendered a camaraderie borne of shared hardships. The necessity of relying upon local inhabitants as guides and porters, who were familiar with the terrain and the habitats of its flora and fauna, eroded class distinctions between the collector and his supporters.[54]

Bailey's expedition was not novel and throughout the period covered by this book, journeys of exploration for the purpose of observation, natural history and ethnology were often inextricably linked with quests for political intelligence. Their trajectories created complex connections between knowledge, the place of its production and the individuals who produced it. Nowhere is this more so than in frontier regions, where rivalry for control of

---

51. Ibid., 92.
52. Tachienlu, on the western arm of Sichuan; formerly Tibet.
53. Bailey, 'Journey through a Portion of South-Eastern Tibet', 189–190.
54. Paul M. Taylor, 'Smithsonian Naturalist William Louis Abbott's Turkestan Expedition', *Central Asiatic Journal* 59, nos. 1–2 (2016): 262. Taylor is particularly interested in those whom he called sports-hunters, whose quest for rare specimens required them to be personally involved in obtaining the 'trophy', a tradition to which Bailey also adhered when hunting bears in Bhutan.

unchartered territory dominated the political and commercial agenda during British rule in India. Offering the possibility of discovering new trade routes and valuable species of flora and fauna, including the tea plant, borderlands became a space where new connections were made between knowledge and the place of its creation and the individuals who produced it. The region where Bailey and others before him had journeyed today forms part of the Indian frontier State of Arunachal Pradesh. In 1911, the frontier between British India and China had yet to be demarcated and, as was so often the case, when borders were constructed for political purposes, they took no account of indigeneity. In the process, they created tensions by dividing groups who shared racial and ethnic affinities. Even now, these border regions are considered ambiguous, where uncertainties over identities and geographic spaces are viewed as dangerous by security forces on both sides of the divide.[55]

Bailey was not the first European adventurer to travel into Mishmi territory. India's north-eastern frontier and the regions bordering Tibet and Chinese Turkestan had been the focus of attention since the early nineteenth century, and the subject of accounts of earlier missions into this volatile territory. One of the earliest narratives of a journey into the Mishmi Hills and the surrounding region was submitted by the British civilian surgeon, William Griffith (1810–1845). A renowned botanist, Griffith first visited the region in 1835, accompanying Nathaniel Wallich and the geologist, John McCelland, to examine the possibilities for tea cultivation. As discussed in the previous chapter, Griffith made a second visit the following year with George Bayfield under the orders of Francis Jenkins (1793–1866), the Commissioner of Assam. His account of their journey to the Mishmi Hills and the Lohit Valley in 1836 appeared in several publications and was included in a selection of Government Papers in 1873, under the title, 'Journey of a trip to the [*sic*] Meeshmee Mountains'.[56]

On 15 October 1836, Griffith's party left Sadiya, the frontier post of Northern Assam. Following the course of the Karam River, they encountered beautiful scenery and rock formations, which he described alongside other topographical features.[57] After leaving the river, the party followed a path to a village in the jungle, where they found fair-skinned villagers, whom they noted as being very dirty and impoverished. After staying for a few days in the village, they continued their journey down the Karam towards the Mishmi Hills, reaching the Kond Defile on 22 October, where they camped.

55. Ambika Aiyadurai and Claire Seungeun Lee, 'Living on the Sino-Indian Border: The Story of the Mishmis in Arunachal Pradesh, Northeast India', *Asian Ethnology* 76, no. 2 (2017): 379.
56. IOR/V/23/104/110–124: Records of the Government of Bengal (unnumbered, 1873–1874). Selection of papers regarding the tracts between Assam and Burma and on the Upper Brahmaputra.
57. Ibid., 110–112.

During the course of his journey, Griffith made some important botanical discoveries, notably a rare species of flowering plant in the buttercup family, known as *Coptis Teeta*, whose rhizome was used in Chinese medicine as an anti-microbial and anti-inflammatory. Endemic to this small area in the Himalayas, Griffith reported that the plant was without aroma and bitter to the taste and when well-dried over a fire, its colours remained permanent.[58]

In 1868, another English traveller, Thomas Thornville Cooper (1839–1878), also departed from Sadiya, having originally set out on a pioneering journey from Shanghai in an attempt to reach India. His stated objective was 'to determine a practicable trade route between China and India whereby millions of neighbouring empires might enter into commercial intercourse'.[59] Unsuccessful on this occasion, Cooper tried again the following year and subsequently recorded his adventures in a book, published in 1873.[60] He was especially interested in finding new routes through the Mishmi Hills that might be used to supply Tibet with brick tea directly from India, a trade dominated for many years by China. However, Cooper's ambition was thwarted by the jealousy of Chinese officials and the intolerance of the lamas, who had long been involved in this commerce.

On his second attempt, hoping to reach the Tibetan frontier before the lamas could intercept his plans, Cooper's route from Sadiya ran mostly parallel with the Brahmaputra River and took him through Mishmi country.[61] Although the journey through the Mishmi hills severely taxed his strength, he found the people friendly, observing that there was 'no longer any need to fear the enmity of the Mishmi tribes and that there was no reason why a good road should not be made'.[62] Forced by illness to turn back, Cooper nevertheless managed to induce some of the Mishmi chiefs to visit Sadiya, in order to discuss removing the obstacle of getting the tea trade through their territory from Assam to Tibet. Although nothing came of these discussions, the strategic importance of Mishmi country, situated at the junction of India, China and Tibet became well-recognised as a potential trade route, particularly for tea.

As a political officer with access to this earlier information, the commercial and political significance of Mishmi country was not lost on Frederick Bailey, especially in view of recent Chinese activities on the border. Therefore, he decided to embark on his own expedition into their territory, although he had no official orders to do so. But as Cooper had observed some decades

---

58. Ibid.
59. Thomas T. Cooper, *The Mishmee Hills: An Account of a Journey Made in an Attempt to Penetrate Thibet from Assam to Open New Routes for Commerce* (London: Henry S. King & Co., 1873), 1.
60. Ibid.
61. Ibid., 36.
62. Ibid., 247, 253.

previously, 'government expeditions from the nature of their organisation and political responsibility attaching to them, are totally unfit instruments to be used in giving strength to new born trade'.[63] Bailey may have concurred with Cooper, believing that an informal approach on a sport hunting trip might yield greater knowledge about the local situation than an official government deputation.

However, by the early twentieth century, there were compelling reasons politically to prevent solo excursions by adventurers like Bailey in the unexplored frontier regions of the empire, not least because it set a precedent that could be followed by Russian officers. As fears surrounding security between the two empires intensified, the British government had instituted strict rules regarding this activity. In January 1909, a dispatch by Lord Morley, the Secretary of State for India (1905–1910), stated that 'expeditions into these distant regions for the purposes of sport or amusement should be carefully scrutinised and that leave to undertake them should only be given when some special reasons exist for exceptional treatment'.[64]

Previously, in July 1910, Bailey had been refused permission to return to India via Russian and Chinese Turkestan, but no objection was raised to his application a few months later in December.[65] However, a cryptic handwritten note in response to Bailey's request observed, 'When Captain Bailey applied (and was refused) in India he only mentioned shooting. Now it appears that the improvement of his mind is his main object. The question is, "Can H.M.G. recognise that as a special reason for exceptional treatment?"' The respondent commented that it was the Government of India's business to consider that Bailey might find himself for many years in a native state where his frontier knowledge would be of use. Leaving the final decision to the Government of India, the writer nevertheless observed that for every Indian officer who travels in Russian Turkestan, the Russian claim to send their own officers through British frontier states is strengthened.[66] But because he

---

63. Ibid., 36.

64. BL/IOR/L/PS/10/183/3/File 1918/1910/Pt. 7: Minute by Lord Morley (29 January 1909), NE Frontier: travellers; Cpt. Bailey's journey from Batang to Sadiya.

65. Whilst on leave in Edinburgh, after his term as Trade Officer at Gyantse in Tibet had come to an end, Bailey wrote to the Under Secretary of State at the Foreign Office on 9 December 1910, requesting permission to travel to Peking via the Siberian Railway and to take sporting rifles, a shot gun and ammunition with him. He stated, 'I desire to take these weapons for sporting purposes in China only, and do not wish to use them in Russian territory'. On the same day, he also wrote to the India Office asking permission to travel to China, and then to proceed by railway from Peking, via Hanoi and Tali-Fu to Bhamo in British Burma, where presumably he would resume his duties as an Indian army officer upon the expiration of his term of home leave. In this letter, he made no mention of weapons and ammunition, but stated, 'My object in travelling to China is to see the country and the people'; where he hoped that the knowledge gained might be useful should he have dealings with Chinese officials on the Indian frontier.

66. BL/IOR/L/PS/10/183/3/File 1918/1910/Pt. 5–7/Min. 3620: Captain Bailey's Journey from Batang to Sadiya. A series of letters and memoranda from concerned government officials ranging

was 'the right sort' and enjoyed the trust of the imperial establishment, the Government of India was disposed to find a way around this official directive, particularly as they always welcomed up-to-date political intelligence about the situation on the India-Tibet-China frontier.

Even though he was exposing himself and his party to danger, Bailey was especially keen to hunt in the un-surveyed portion of South-East Tibet and the Mishmi Hills, where previously, few European officials had risked entering. In 1909, Captain Noel Williamson, the Assistant Political Officer at Sadiya, had been murdered by the Abor people. In his report, Bailey explained his unauthorised presence in the region as being possibly of inter-est, in consequence of the measures taken after Williamson's murder.[67] This somewhat vague argument allowed him to introduce political intelligence regarding the Chinese presence in these regions into his report, which no doubt helped to temper the government's annoyance that he had ignored official orders. As well as commenting on the extensive and beautiful flora and fauna, Bailey reported the proliferation of new schools in this area, an indication of the considerable extent to which Chinese influence was making itself felt in these borderlands. He also noted that attempts were being made to change Tibetan place names to Chinese.[68] He explained that the reason why no Chinese official attempted to stop his party from entering Tibet was because an American missionary had recently been wrongly arrested. Local officials were in trouble with the American legation and therefore wary of apprehending any more foreigners.[69]

Throughout his journey, Bailey was accompanied by his loyal Tibetan manservant, Putamdu, who had joined him in Peking, courtesy of Thomas Cook, having travelled via Calcutta, where Bailey recorded that he was very pleased to be joined by a friendly face whom he could trust. During this expedition, Putamdu was photographed near the frontier of Chinese Turkestan, wearing Chinese dress, a disguise he may have adopted in order to enable him to gather espionage on Bailey's behalf in a region where a white man would have been conspicuous.[70] As previously mentioned, in order to prepare for this expedition, Bailey had sent Putamdu to the Bom-bay Natural History Society, where he learnt how to skin birds and other specimens.[71] The skins were then dried and sent to England, where the skills

---

from Sir John Jordan, HM's Envoy Extraordinary and Minister Plenipotentiary in Peking, to the Secretary of the Foreign Department of the Government of India and the Viceroy, which testify to the potential international incident that Bailey's 'off-piste' excursion might have caused.

67. Bailey, 'Journey through a Portion of South-Eastern Tibet', 189.

68. Ibid., 191.

69. BL/Mss Eur F157/888/78: Bailey Miscellaneous (c. 1911–1940), including corrected proof copy of his book, *China–Tibet–Assam* (1911).

70. Bailey Collection of photographs, British Library.

71. Ibid., 21.

of taxidermists were applied to them. However, the whole process of collecting specimens in the wet and cold conditions of the Mishmi Hills was
fraught with difficulties. Despite successfully shooting several wild takin,
damp weather conditions made it impossible to dry the skins sufficiently for
dispatch to museums. The problem was compounded by the bundle of skins
accidently falling off a bridge into a stream.[72] Most of Bailey's trophies from
the expedition proved to be of no use and were given to the 'coolies', who
were able to save the meat from the carcasses by throwing them into the
river and covering them with stones, preserving it until they could return to
recover it.[73]

Bailey's unauthorised expedition succeeded in hunting only a few small
mammals, as well as sixty bird skins and eggs, which were also in a poor condition as they had to shoot the birds at close quarters with large shot. These,
as previously noted, were sent to Ogilvie Grant at the British Museum and to
the Bombay Natural History Society. Bailey's expedition had greater success
in collecting around 2,000 butterflies, which comprised between 150 and 170
different species. As they could not all be identified, they too were sent to
experts in London to classify. All in all, the mission was a worthy contribution to lepidopterology, if not to the trophy hunting of rare mammals.[74]

The correspondence that resulted from Bailey's hunting expedition to the
Mishmi Hills contained expressions of official displeasure from the highest level of authority towards his insubordination. But embedded in these
archives is the suggestion that, although officially reprimanded for contraven-
ing the rules, officials were aware that Bailey intended to make an unauthorised hunting trip into the Mishmi Hills. His misdemeanour was overlooked by
senior government officials because his report contained important political
intelligence from potentially hostile and uncharted territory on the imperial
frontier, which, as a political officer, it was his duty to procure. Notwithstanding, Bailey's presence in the Mishmi Hills angered the Chinese, who had
suzerainty in the area and threatened to disrupt the fragile political relations
with British India.

Unlike his predecessors, William Griffith and Thomas Cooper, Bailey
was unable to offer any empathetic comments regarding the condition of
the Mishmi people whom he encountered, nor meaningful interpretations
regarding their social practices and traditions.[75] Although the civilian traveller, Cooper, had found them friendly, Bailey reported that they were difficult

---

72. Bailey to Ogilvie Grant (14 September 1911).
73. Bailey, Proof of *China–Tibet–Assam*, 136.
74. Ibid., 203.
75. In 1911, training in anthropology for colonial officers had yet to be established and it was an
important step in the professionalisation of anthropology.

to manage and so he had resorted to pacifying them with opium, which he reported rendered them always compliant.[76] By supplying the Mishmi with a dangerous drug, Bailey established a precedent that was to have lasting and devastating consequences for the peoples of these border regions, and which still remains an uncontrollable problem. The final section assesses the relative importance of Bailey's roles as an amateur collector and as a political officer, providing intelligence before the formal establishment of fixed borders and a professional secret service.

A LIFETIME OF COLLECTING, INCLUDING
BY ROYAL APPOINTMENT

By submitting specimens that he collected during his expeditions through-out the Himalayas, Bailey was an active participant in the global ambition to extend the boundaries of imperial scientific knowledge about the natural world. This intensified as the Indian Empire's interiors became more acces-sible, resulting in increasing professionalism in the approaches to the study of natural history.[77] From the early nineteenth century, it was led by govern-ment officials like Francis Buchanan-Hamilton, Brian Houghton Hodgson (1800–1894), the Resident in Nepal, and Allan Octavian Hume (1829–1912), Agricultural Secretary to the Government of India and a keen ornithologist.[78] Together with other interested professionals like doctors, military men, cler-ics and missionaries, their ethnographic and biological collecting expeditions were associated with the parallel development of anthropology.[79] Proxy researchers and specimen hunters were much sought-after and like other hunter-naturalists, Bailey presented his specimens to learned societies and museums for study and classification in order to help them determine the evolutionary path that species had taken and the resultant range of life forms. In this respect, Bailey adhered to conventions established in the eighteenth century by the Comte de Buffon and Carl Linnaeus and other naturalists, whose correspondents sent new specimens to them for identification and classification.

76. Bailey, Proof of *China–Tibet–Assam*.
77. By the late nineteenth century, many great museums were eager to receive specimens and the skills of trained taxidermists were much in demand to preserve and stuff animals so that they could be displayed for the public and private viewing in as life-like a form as possible. In London, the leading firm of taxidermists was Rowland Ward Ltd. of 167 Piccadilly. Founded in 1898, it was renowned for its taxidermy work on birds and big-game trophies.
78. Charles Allen, *The Prisoner of Kathmandu: Brian Hodgson in Nepal 1820–43* (London: Haus Publishing Ltd., 2015); and William Wedderburn, *Allan Octavian Hume: Father of the Indian National Congress, 1829–1912* (New Delhi and Oxford: Oxford University Press, 2002).
79. MacGregor, *Curiosity and Enlightenment*, 51.

It has been suggested that in some ways, India was a scientific 'centre' in its own right and rather than merely being part of the centre-periphery axis, 'it was [. . .] a network of science with nodal points of varying degrees of traffic and relevance'.[80] However, it remained the case until well into the twentieth century that it was the intellectual elites in metropolitan centres who analysed the data collected by others; Bailey himself frequently sought advice from experts at the British Museum and other sources.[81] Correspondingly, with the increased requirement for specialised knowledge, amateur sport-hunters and naturalist-collectors throughout the world were encouraged by burgeoning sites of scientific learning, particularly in the new universities, to take advantage of the opportunities presented by their work in remote and inhospitable regions to collect rare and unknown species.[82] These adventurous hunters and collectors were traditionally drawn from the upper classes, who were in a position to finance lengthy expeditions. Their endeavours were matched by a response from learned institutions in providing scientific training, and also a corresponding need for museums[83] to collect and document objects in their collections.[84]

Bailey's passion for naturalist-collecting and sport-hunting legitimated his work as a political officer, especially in border regions, where, when necessary, these pursuits acted as a cloak to conceal his undercover intelligence work. During the first two decades of the twentieth century, he became the 'go-to' political officer for expeditions into undiscovered territories. He made an unauthorised excursion into the Mishmi Hills bordering Eastern Tibet and India in 1911, and surveyed the tributaries of the Brahmaputra River in 1913 with Henry Morshead. Unlike his predecessors, William Johnson and Clement Williams, his excursions, whether sanctioned or not, clearly did not harm his career prospects. In 1918, he became unsuccessfully involved in undercover political intrigues in Central Asia to promote anti-Bolshevist sentiments among the local population. After the First World War, he remained a political officer in the Indian army and was appointed to posts in Sikkim,

---

80. Fa-Ti Fan and John Matthew, 'Negotiating Natural History in Transitional China and British India', *British Journal of the History of Science* 1 (2016): 59.

81. NHM/TR/1/1/27/15: Letter from Bailey's father in Edinburgh to Dr Jordan, on behalf of his son, telling him he does not wish to sell his collection of butterflies (18 October 1906). He asks that Miss E.M. Bowdler Sharpe of the Natural History Museum in London list the most interesting specimens for his son, who was in Tibet.

82. Taylor, 'Smithsonian Naturalist William Louis Abbott's Turkestan Expedition', 257.

83. See Cohn, *Colonialism and Its Forms of Knowledge*; Bayly, *Empire and Information*. See also histories of Charles 'Hindoo' Stuart of the EIC, one of the first collectors of Hindu statuary which now forms the core of the British Museum collection, known today as the Bridge Collection after a subsequent purchaser.

84. The Pitt Rivers Museum in Oxford remains one of the foremost examples of the many anthropological collections founded in Britain from the eighteenth century onwards, becoming even more significant in the nineteenth century.

Bhutan and Nepal, where his involvement in political intrigues continued alongside his collecting. By the time he retired in 1938, his knowledge of the mountainous kingdoms of the Himalayas, on the frontiers of the empire, was without parallel.

Meanwhile, his role as an enthusiastic amateur naturalist was recognised at the highest level when, in 1927, as the Resident in Sikkim, he was approached on behalf of the King and Queen of England to collect specimens of plants and seeds.[85] Unfortunately, some of the later consignments of seeds sent to Their Majesties proved to be defective. Upon investigation, it seemed that indigenous plant-collectors in Nepal, realising the rarity and hence the value of the species, had taken to substituting ordinary garden seeds for the rare varieties.[86] In his letter on behalf of Their Majesties, Sir Clive Wigram regretted that the proliferation of seeds from abroad had taken away their 'exotic' characteristic, which above all is cherished by collectors. He wrote, 'the people in the east are beginning to appreciate the commercial value of good seeds' and that 'this country is now being flooded with seeds from numerous expeditions to the mountains of India'.[87] Plant-hunting was big business, as it had always been, since the days of Francis Buchanan's expeditions on behalf of the EIC.

CONCLUDING REMARKS

Frederick Marshman Bailey was able to combine his enthusiasm for the natural world with his role as a political officer serving with distinction in the Indian army. How then can we evaluate the contribution that he made to colonial knowledge through his collecting and sport hunting? A distinguished soldier and something of an outsider, he was able to use his enthusiasm for these pursuits as a means of concealing his role as a Political Agent, gathering information on behalf of Britain and its government in India. In the course of surveying and reconnaissance work, he produced useful intelligence which was of material interest to the Administration in securing the frontiers of the Empire. He also discovered many fine specimens of flora, birds

---

85. Bailey received a series of letters from a former military colleague, Sir Clive Wigram, Assistant Private Secretary and Equerry to the king (1910–1931), requesting him to send plants and seeds for cultivation in the royal parks and gardens. In his letter, Sir Clive told Bailey that Their Majesties, who were apparently keen gardeners, particularly wished to introduce plants from Bhutan and seeds and bulbs that grew in high mountain areas, such as Gentians, Primulas and Rhododendrons and any showy herbaceous plants. See BL/Mss Eur F157/803.

86. BL/Mss Eur F157/803: Letter from Mrs Bailey to Wigram (5 September 1937), stating that Mr Hay, a Head Gardener at Kew, reported following cultivation of a consignment that only 'a lot of old weeds such as opium poppy had come up'.

87. Ibid., September 1937 and January 1938.

and butterflies for research in order to advance knowledge about the natural world, and in the process, he became part of an enduring network of agents, who have been described in an earlier chapter as *'petits artisans'*.

However, his activities in connection with his role as a sport-hunter for trophies were less laudatory. His description of a bear hunt in Bhutan, where the female was hunted to her death and her cub, who had taken refuge in a tree, was brought down when the *shikari*[88] chopped the trunk, is distasteful today, as sensitivities towards conservation and cruelty to animals have become much greater.[89] In common with many of his class, Bailey hunted with a shotgun all his life and attended many organised shoots throughout the Himalayas. In one day alone on a shoot in Nepal, when he was one of fifty guns who went out, they bagged a total of 1,058 birds in the morning and 296 in the afternoon. This made an overall total of 1,354 shot in one day. Many were common varieties of ducks, shovellers, gadwalls, teals, pochards and mallards and not taken for collecting or study purposes, but merely for sport.[90]

It is difficult to justify such slaughter in the name of sport, which bears little relationship to the ways in which indigenous groups like the Mishmi have always hunted with discrimination in order to conserve their sources of food. Today, Mishmi hunters, who still act as India's eyes and ears on the frontier, 'claim that they are protecting not only the nation's boundary, but also wildlife from Chinese hunters', whom they say 'hunt everything. They come with AK-47s and advanced weapons, they don't spare any animal or bird'.[91] The Mishmi, in common with many people who rely on the natural world to sustain their way of life, assert that they follow taboos, so they do not hunt every animal that comes their way, whereas the Chinese hunt indiscriminately. Sadly, it seems that little has changed in the habits of a new superpower in this region today and those of the British in India in the nineteenth and twentieth centuries.

Having been born and educated into a social upper class allowed Bailey to avoid the undesirable consequences that befell earlier adventurers like William Johnson and Clement Williams. His success was due to being classified as 'the right sort', which entitled him to behave with a degree of impunity during his many adventures, because he was recognised by the British

---

88. *Shikari*: Term derived from Urdu, meaning 'hunter'.

89. BL/Mss Eur F157/812: Bailey's personal journal of their tour of Bhutan, accompanied by his wife and his mother-in-law, Lady Cozens Hardy, who were certainly the first European women to enter Bhutan. It contains many descriptions of his hunting activities, notably details of a bear hunt, which they skinned in Tsalimape.

90. BL/Mss Eur F157/807: Hunting Cards and Licences from shoots attended by Bailey in Britain and India.

91. Aiyadurai and Seungeun, 'Living on the Sino-Indian Border', 380.

establishment as one of their own. But collecting specimens from the natural world also offered him an opportunity to become part of a lineage of scientific knowledge that had commenced in the eighteenth century, which by the early twentieth century connected him with great museums and institutions. The next chapter will investigate how these fragile networks of knowledge have survived, in part through the global agency of many men like Bailey, whose individual contribution towards mapping its vast ecology by amassing naturalistic collections is of greater lasting importance than his heroic deeds as an undercover agent. His connection as a collector with leading museums and scholars was continued by the subject of the next chapter, ICS officer, Philip Mills. Like Bailey, Mills was an amateur enthusiast, but with considerably greater intellectual abilities, which he applied to the study of the peoples of the Naga Hills on the border between India and Burma. Throughout many years spent as an ICS officer, Mills amassed an impressive historical archive of non-written sources about a society that previously had very limited, or non-existent, contact with Europeans. His research contributed towards the advancement of anthropology during the 1920s–1930s.

Chapter 8

J.P. Mills ICS: Collecting and Photographing the Naga Peoples of North-East Burma

INTRODUCTION

The prime business of an anthropologist is to record the varieties of social life. The main point of theory accordingly, to permit the ethnographer to make more exact and comparable observations, and it is the factual reports which really constitute anthropological advance.[1]

The early case histories in this study are set in the period before the formal limits of British rule in India were fixed and when European cultural difference was at its most varied and complex.[2] It was a time when major collections like those of Major General Charles 'Hindoo' Stuart 'offered a hallucinatory glimpse into a world which, if it threatened, never quite overwhelmed the poetics of imperial perspective'.[3] Collections by cosmopolitan gentlemen-connoisseurs like Claude Martin and Charles Stuart[4] reflected a fascination with all that was rare and unknowable about the 'other'. By the mid-nineteenth century, private collecting had made way for displays in museums, zoos and world exhibitions, where the Eurocentric vision could be 'secured against the politics of disorder and the "ethnographic chaos", encountered on the frontiers of the empire'.[5] These public spaces allowed

---

1. SOAS/PPMS 19/Box 42/4: Quote by Rodney Needham (1923–2006), British social anthropologist, in a rough draft of Verrier Elwin's Obituary by Christoph von Fürer-Haimendorf.
2. Maya Jasanoff, *Edge of Empire: Conquest and Collecting in the East, 1750–1850* (London: Fourth Estate, 2005), 6.
3. Gregory, 'Power, Knowledge and Geography', 80.
4. See Chapter 1.
5. Julian Jacobs, Alan MacFarlane, Sarah Harrison, and Anita Herle, *The Nagas: Hill Peoples of Northeast India – Society, Culture and the Colonial Encounter* (London: Thames & Hudson, 1990), 17.

the imperial perspective or 'ideal' to be permanently fixed in the public consciousness, the exotic tamed by Western reason, and claims to new knowledge negotiated and made legitimate.[6]

As we have seen throughout this book, even though it had no reason to negate the authority of the metropole, the periphery wished to establish itself as a sphere of knowledge in its own right. For more than a century, seekers of knowledge had produced a diverse range of responses directed towards defining its importance and relevance to the interests of the metropole. Their quests ranged from intellectual pursuits to more practical material matters, involving the acquisition of political, commercial, topographical and botanical information, gained during private and officially sponsored expeditions. Tensions were created by competing claims to authority and status from individuals and institutions, for which scholarly journals were important sources of influence and validation.[7] Sites of publication at the periphery like *Asiatic Researches*, the *Asiatic Society of Bengal* and the *Madras Literary Society* vied with publications at the centre to introduce new geographies of knowledge. They endeavoured to rival those of the RGS and the Royal Asiatic Society for their intellectual content, as explorers, eager to establish their credentials, submitted accounts of their discoveries to these newly authoritative forums. Although anthropological, political and geographical information was supported as a necessity, the periphery's response to journeys of discovery by self-promoters like William Johnson and Clement Williams was frequently one of ambivalence or even disdain, as their activities were considered to be questionable.[8]

As we have seen in the case of Charles 'Hindoo' Stuart, since the eighteenth century, in situations of unequal power relations, the collection of diffuse material objects had made knowable that which was rare and strange to European audiences. By the end of the nineteenth century, interest was focused on colonial anthropology; that is, the scientific study of humans, their behaviour and the societies in which they lived. This gave rise to a corresponding need by museums to acquire and document ethnographic objects from these societies for their collections. Founded in 1884, the Pitt Rivers Museum in Oxford remains the foremost repository of the many ethnographic collections in Britain, to which James Philip Mills and John Henry Hutton were leading contributors in the first decades of the twentieth century. They spent much of their careers as ICS officers collecting many objects of material culture, and photographing and studying the peoples of the Naga Hills on the border of North-East India and Burma.

---

6. Gregory, 'Power, Knowledge and Geography', 81.
7. Sadan, 'The Texts and Their Authors', 9.
8. Wendy James, 'The Anthropologist as Reluctant Imperialist', in Talal Asad (ed.), *Anthropology and the Colonial Encounter* (Ithaca, NY: Cornell University Press, 1973), 42–43.

This chapter focuses on Mills's use of photography to document the lives and traditions of the Nagas, as well as his extensive collection of material objects. On occasion, he was joined by the Austrian anthropologist, Baron Christoph von Fürer-Haimendorf. Their most famous expedition occurred in 1936 against the Kayo-Kengyu, headhunters in the hilltop *khels*[9] of Pangsha, a region situated outside the areas administered by the British. During this punitive raid against headhunters, Mills and Haimendorf were presented with a unique opportunity to photograph beyond the jurisdiction of British control, an episode which will be discussed in detail in a later section.

As in many cultures throughout the world, the use of the term 'tribe' when describing the Naga population is problematical, because in common with many culture groups, they displayed diverse linguistic, cultural, kinship and political patterns, which from the earliest days of contact in the 1830s presented the British with seemingly ethnographic chaos which they needed to categorise and understand.[10] Composed of numerous small villages, known as *khels*, which straddled the hilltops, each Naga community possessed its own unique customs, political systems and language, which challenged colonial classification.[11] Photography and the collection of items of material culture assisted ethnographer-administrators like Mills in his attempts to comprehend the totality of Naga society in order to exert control over such diverse communities on behalf of the colonial government.[12] As a new technology created for the purpose of interpreting culture, photography was increasingly used to understand and interpret cultural differentness.[13] However, Mills and 'the Baron's' (as he called his friend, Haimendorf) use of photography to represent and emphasise cultural difference created something of a paradox, as the objects the Nagas employed in their everyday lives, that Mills and his ICS colleague, Hutton, avidly collected for public display, were themselves material examples of the Nagas' own unique 'technologies'.

As previously discussed, photography as a medium for documenting historical sites and monuments had come to public attention through the early photographs of Linnaeus Tripe (1822–1902), especially those he took during Arthur Phayre's 1855 Mission to Ava in Upper Burma.[14] Tripe's proficiency with the camera prefigured its increasing popularity, in capturing images of not only the colonial landscape and its exotic built environment, but also of its people in the course of their daily lives. The apparent wonderment evinced by

---

9. *Khels*: Local name for clusters of villages along the tops of the Naga Hills.
10. Jacobs et al., *The Nagas*, 17, 21.
11. Ibid., 17.
12. Ibid., 25.
13. Elizabeth Edwards (ed.), *Anthropology and Photography, 1860–1920* (New Haven and London: Yale University Press, 1992), 6.
14. See Chapter 6.

the Burmese Court at Tripe's 'sun pictures', produced by this new apparatus from Europe, manifested cultural diversity between early developments in Western technology and lack of awareness of them by the Burmese, as they did not yet have the technological knowledge to operate the photographic equipment given to them by the British.[15] Although Henry Yule used very few of Tripe's photographs to illustrate his official narrative, preferring instead the traditional paintings of the missions' artist, Colesworthey Grant (1813–1880), they offered a fascinating insight into its potential use as an authoritative tool in the search for new sources of colonial knowledge.

By the early twentieth century, there had been impressive technological advances in photographic equipment, as the camera became more portable and easier to manage in the field. The design and manufacture of smaller cameras with lenses that allowed perspective to be altered and photographs taken from a distance made it possible for anthropologists and colonial administrator-ethnographers to practise participant observation less conspicuously from 'inside' of a community like that of the Naga people.[16] Despite providing a seemingly less obtrusive means of gathering information, the camera still carried the potential to intrude and disrupt the lives of indigenous people, as it sought to capture the imperial perspective of societies in the throes of exposure to the West and its modern ideas. The use of photography in colonial settings affected indigenous cultures, as it visually transformed previously unknowable perceptions of their histories for many minorities, especially those without longstanding literary traditions.[17] Therefore, historical images of semi-nakedness and poverty could be read by contemporary indigenous communities as visualisations that reflected upon their modern identity in a manner that was discriminatory.[18] Although the many photographic portraits taken of the Nagas by Mills and Haimendorf testify to their subjects' patience in posing for the camera, there is no contemporary record of what the Nagas thought of the ICS officer and the anthropologist's intrusion into their world.[19] Indeed, some of the photographs that they apparently posed for willingly, especially studies of bare-breasted, attractive females, might be viewed as sexually provocative images that the subject was unaware of projecting and which do not sit comfortably with the viewer of today.

15. Yule, *Narrative of the Mission*, 52.
16. Alan Macfarlane, 'An Introduction to Professor Christoph von Fürer-Haimendorf's Naga Photographs', in Richard Kunz and Vibha Joshi (eds.), *A Forgotten Mountain Region Rediscovered* (Basel: Christoph Merian Verlag, 2008), 28.
17. Mandy Sadan, 'Historical Photography in Kachin State: An Update on the Impact of the James Henry Green Collection of Photographs', *South Asia: Journal of South Asian Studies* 30, no. 3 (2007): 466.
18. Ibid., 464.
19. Jacobs et al., *The Nagas*, 21.

Meanwhile, anthropology advanced slowly during the nineteenth century from early findings by missionaries, independent academics, explorers and colonial administrators, whose ethnographic accounts were reported in scholarly journals, government reports and memoranda. Eventually, it evolved as a separate field of academic inquiry from museum-based comparative studies of objects from diffuse areas, to studies which emphasised social, cultural and structural characteristics and, increasingly, involved field work. Nevertheless, the development in training as an academic discipline taught by university departments and its emergence as a profession took many years to accomplish.[20] Before the advent of formal anthropological training for frontier officers and the establishment of a dedicated Frontier Service in 1922, as we have seen, information was gathered by a rather diverse assortment of interested individuals, including administrator-ethnographers, amongst whom Philip Mills was an exceptional example.

Although without formal training in anthropology, Mills's achievements deserve to be recognised as pioneering the advancement of anthropology, as it became of increasing importance politically to colonial governments in the management of frontier minorities in the early twentieth century. Always referring to himself as an amateur, his scholarly observations concerning the Naga peoples demonstrated great insight into their customs and cultural practices, due principally to his fluency in their language and many years spent living amongst them.[21] These attributes enabled him not only to meticulously gather objects of material culture and take numerous photographs documenting their lifeways but also to observe and study their traditions related to the practice of headhunting. Even though his role as a government official meant that he was involved in punitive expeditions against headhunting villages outside of the areas administered by the British, Mills wrote many perceptive articles on its implications for the collective wellbeing of the village and its contribution to its soul force. However, prior to further discussions about Mills's career, the importance of his museum collections and photographic archive, as well as his famous Pangsha expedition, the next section looks briefly at the impact created by the political arrangements that had separated the frontier areas from the rest of Ministerial Burma.

---

20. Until the 1920s, philological, evolutionist, racialist and historical anthropology formed the basis of studies undertaken by the Royal Anthropological Institute of Great Britain (founded in 1870) and its affiliates. In 1914, Sir Richard Temple, as Fellow of the Institute, recommended to the Royal Commission on Higher Education that colonial officials should be trained in anthropology, particularly in languages and racial characteristics. Although the First World War put a halt to progress, in 1921, Temple, under the auspices of the RAI, set up a committee representing all anthropologists in British education to collect and publish anthropological information 'for the use of Imperial services, teachers, missionaries and others'.
21. SOAS/PPMS 58/Box 1: James Philip Mills, 'Anthropology as a Hobby', Presidential Address to the Royal College of Anthropology (1953).

THE ESTABLISHMENT OF THE BURMA
FRONTIER SERVICE

In Burma, due to lack of financial and military resources, areas which comprised vast unexplored territories of well over a third of the total land area set apart from the rest of Burma were largely occupied by 'hill peoples'. Groups like the Nagas were left to live according to their own laws and customs under the rule of their hereditary chiefs, whose allegiance the British hoped to secure. The British Burma Administration showed little concern for their advancement or education, leaving this responsibility largely to the missionaries who colonised them with Christianity. This, in turn, brought them some limited access to Western education and a small range of social welfare projects often run in conjunction with the mission stations.[22] It was into this haphazard arrangement of administered and un-administered territory on Burma's north-eastern frontier with Assam that the young ICS officer, J.P. Mills arrived to begin his career in the Naga Hills, which was to last for over three decades until his retirement in 1948.

The colonial government required 'a pragmatic knowledge of its subjects', so that they would continue to administer themselves without disrupting established rule in areas where the British exerted very little direct control.[23] Therefore, part of the official duties of ICS officers posted to the frontier regions was to acquire ethnographic information on the so-called primitive races, in order to satisfy the government's need to know what was happening. But as the need grew to integrate the knowledge spheres generated in the periphery with those of the metropole, the requirement for specialised knowledge increased, which was matched by a response from the universities in providing training for anthropologists.[24] This also converged with the requirement for men with specialised knowledge to administer the hill peoples of Burma; a matter that had been of concern to its administration since 1905, when discussions with the Government of India had called for the inauguration of a dedicated Burma Frontier Service. This idea was

---

22. For a fuller discussion on these issues, see Ashley South, *Ethnic Politics in Burma: States of Conflict* (London and New York: Routledge, 2008); Robert H. Taylor, *The State in Myanmar* (Honolulu: University of Hawai'i Press, 2009); and Martin Smith, *State of Strife: The Dynamics of Ethnic Conflict in Burma* (Singapore: Institute of Southeast Asian Studies; Washington, D.C.: East–West Center Washington, 2007).

23. BL/IOR/L/PS/20/D174/31: Archibald Rose, Report on the Chinese Frontiers of India (Calcutta, Govt. of India Foreign Department, 1911).

24. In 1885, a new department of anthropology in the University Museum at Cambridge was formed under the guidance of Baron Anatole von Hügel (1854–1928), and encouraged by Wynfrid Duckworth (1870–1956) and Sir William Ridgeway (1858–1926). Cambridge University also established a separate lectureship in anthropology in 1900, a post first filled by Alfred Cort Haddon (1855–1940), with a diploma course following in 1908.

rejected at that time on the grounds that the cadre would be too small, but it was considered that there would be no difficulty in obtaining the right class of officer if some latitude were allowed in recruitment.[25] Unfortunately, the relaxation of the more stringent rules of entry to the ICS, including admitting non-Europeans, did not solve the problem, and young recruits to the Burma Provincial Service could not be won over by the prospect of an active outdoor life and sole responsibility for large unspoilt areas of the frontier.

The main reason why suitable officers could not be found to fill appointments on the frontier was because, unlike India, the Burma Provincial Service was not considered a *'sahibs' service'*.[26] The problem arose because it accepted mixed-race recruits, many of whom were Indian or of other Asian descent; consequently, as a service, it was regarded as socially inferior. New ICS recruits from Britain found themselves at a disadvantage from the outset, as anyone joining the Burma Provincial Service had first to prove that he was a 'gentleman',[27] a dilemma succinctly summed up by Mr F. Lewisjohn, the Chief Secretary to the Government of Burma, quoting the opinion of a very experienced frontier officer,

> Human nature and especially female human nature in the lump is snobbish and officers who belong to a service with inferior pay and inferior prospects of which the greater part is not pure European and which under the rules is treated as an Indian service will continually knock up against people who treat them differently from the way in which they treat members of recognized European services.[28]

As Lewisjohn concluded, 'If we want *sahibs*, and we are all agreed on that, we must have a *sahibs' service*, then the main difficulty of recruitment will have been removed'.[29] Lewisjohn's use of the phrase *'sahibs' service'* was a 'not-so-subtle' way of proposing that if the new Burma Frontier Service was staffed by 'pure Europeans', the present difficulty would be removed and the 'right sort' of officer would be appointed from the outset.

Lewisjohn deemed that urgent action was required, as he noted in his letter in 1920, 'We are only at the beginning of our responsibilities on the northeastern frontier and it is imperative that there should be no further delay in putting the recruitment of the officers who will have charge of that hardly

25. BL/IOR/L/PS/18/B375/2: Announcement of the creation of the Burma Frontier Service, *Burma Gazette Extraordinary* (Rangoon, 20 December 1922).

26. BL/IOR/L/PS/10/1073/File 3722/1922, Letter No. 256P–2M–9: Mr F. Lewisjohn, Chief Secretary to the Government of Burma, to the Political Secretary, Government of India (20 August 1920).

27. Ibid., para 5.

28. Ibid.

29. Ibid.

explored country, on a satisfactory footing'.[30] By 1920, the first indications of militant nationalism had begun to stir throughout the Burmese countryside, whipped up by militant monks, known as 'political *pongyis*'[31] who preached a message which mixed traditional Buddhist values and folk beliefs with political opposition to the colonial government. The Burma government was anxious that their influence should not reach the so-called backward tracts of the frontier districts. It was therefore imperative that the right sort of officer should be recruited, who could be trusted to maintain order over vast territories, where local infrastructure like roads, schools and hospitals was poor or non-existent.

Therefore, one of the last acts of the Governor, Sir Reginald Craddock's (1864–1937), official career was to establish the Burma Frontier Service. On 20 December 1922, *The Burma Gazette*, Rangoon, published details of 'a new service called the Burma Frontier Service to provide officers for the service in the Shan States, the Kachin Hills and the Chin Hills'.[32] The new cadres would number thirty-five for the Frontier Service and 193 for the Burma Civil Service respectively. The *Gazette* went on to say that this new service only formalised what has been the actual state of affairs,

> Conditions in the Shan States and in the Chin and Kachin Hills are utterly different from those in Burma proper and demand a totally different type of officer. The Assistant Superintendents acquired a specialised knowledge and experience which fits them for further service in the hills and unfits them for the ordinary administrative posts in the plains.[33]

The Burma Gazette also noted that it had been very difficult to find suitable recruits and it had been with the utmost difficulty that local government had found enough men to fill the posts, because the Burma Civil Service had narrowed the field from which officers could be selected to fill frontier posts and receive adequate training. As Stephen Feuchtwang has argued, 'there are grounds for considering the turning point of the late 1920s as a move toward an anthropology more suited to colonial administrative need or else as a change which met with new colonial administrative needs more than the previous anthropology could'.[34] What he has called 'the fit' between

---

30. Ibid.

31. 'Political *pongyi*' is the name given to itinerant militant monks in the 1920s who took advantage of the separation between the *Sangha* (priesthood) and the state to preach a political message combining demands for independence with folkloric memories of the mediaeval Burmese state. For further information, see Emanuel Sarkisyanz, *Buddhist Backgrounds of the Burmese Revolution* (The Hague: Martinus Nijhoff, 1965).

32. Announcement of the creation of the Burma Frontier Service, 1.

33. Ibid., 2.

34. Stephen Feuchtwang, 'The Colonial Formation of British Social Anthropology', in Asad (ed.), *Anthropology and the Colonial Encounter*, 84.

the academic discipline of social anthropology taught in the universities and other sponsoring institutions had an impact upon the British imperial state,[35] so that 'during the period of the twenties and thirties there was undoubtedly tension between officialdom and the expanding subject of anthropology'.[36] It was not until the 1930s that Colonel James Green of the Frontier Service received the formal qualification of a diploma in anthropology from Cambridge that would assist him in the conduct of his professional duties.

The period between the two World Wars was the time when social anthropology really came into being as a profession and when it began to produce the knowledge necessary to colonial governments. The 1920s–1940s saw the formation of functionalist and social anthropology under the leadership of Bronisław Malinowski (1884–1942) and Alfred Radcliffe-Brown (1881–1955), where investigation into how social groups behaved, analysing customs, social organisation, laws and traditions was undertaken with a view to supporting more complex interactions with 'native' peoples and to improving their education 'on modern lines' in a situation of contact with colonial rule.[37] Before the inauguration of the Frontier Service, it was a particular case of happenstance that, after joining the ICS in 1913, James Philip Mills (always known as Philip) decided to devote his career to the study and uplift of the Nagas of the Burma frontier. In 1916, he was appointed to serve at Mokokchung in the heart of the Naga Hills, and details of his career are discussed in the next section.

THE CAREER OF J.P. MILLS

As Mr Lewisjohn acknowledged in his letter to the Political Secretary of the Government of India in August 1920, service on the frontier 'necessitated the possession of a facility for acquiring languages, of a temperament naturally sympathetic with the ways of savage tribes and of a capacity for leading a solitary life in distant spots cut off from the companionship of one's fellows for long periods'.[38]

Scarcely a job description to attract the fainthearted and one that might only be of interest to the most adventurous young officer or local recruits eager to gain employment in the service of the colonial government. But as we have seen throughout this book, life on the frontier attracted resourceful

---

35. Ibid., 97.
36. James, *The Anthropologist as Reluctant Imperialist*, 42.
37. Rev. E.W. Smith of the International Institute of African Languages and Cultures (IAI) and RAI in Memorandum XII of the IAI (1932), in Feuchtwang, 'The Colonial Formation of British Social Anthropology', 83.
38. Lewisjohn to the Political Secretary (20 August 1920).

individualists and lone adventurers, men like Philip Mills, whose resolve to live and work in frontier districts, isolated from other European company and the usual attractions of the Club, overcame the challenges that Lewisjohn envisaged. A scholar with considerable linguistic ability and an interest in anthropology, Mills dedicated his ICS career of more than thirty years to researching the ethnography of the Naga Hills, as well as overseeing the welfare of its people. In order to do so, he immersed himself in the task of becoming proficient in Assamese and local dialects. As an administrator-cum-ethnographer, he made it one of his main objectives to understand how colonial power would affect original cultures, including headhunting, which would inevitably vanish.[39] He therefore placed on record his understanding of the reasons for headhunting and the cultural practices associated with it as a fundamental part of Naga tradition. However, as described, headhunting was outlawed in territory that was administered by the British and it was part of Mills's official responsibilities to take punitive action against the practice of it where possible. It was for this reason that he undertook a punitive expedition of considerable force to Pangsha in 1936, in the expectation that it would intimidate Naga warriors from making headhunting raids into British-controlled territory.

Mills was born in 1890 and educated at Winchester College and Corpus Christi College, Oxford. Having joined the ICS in 1913, he was posted to Mokokchung in 1916 as a sub-divisional officer, where he spent his spare time fishing, cultivating his garden, and also studying birds and plants. The Naga Hills were protected inside a so-called inner line, allegedly to prevent the people being exploited as many of their villages had never been visited by a white man.[40] When Mills took charge of the Mokokchung district, he was aged only twenty-six, and at that time, he lived alone in a bungalow, where his nearest neighbours were missionaries and also the ICS officer, William Archer (1907–1979), whose wife, Mildred, was an art historian.[41] Soon after he arrived in the district Mills became interested in learning about the Nagas' culture and was encouraged by his older colleague, the anthropologist, J.H. Hutton, who was his Deputy Commissioner. Between them they wrote five monographs on the Nagas[42] and collected over 2,000 objects for the Pitt Rivers Museum in Oxford. Some artefacts were also donated to Cambridge, where Hutton became an academic after he retired from colonial service.

---

39. Alban von Stockhausen, *Imagining the Nagas: The Pictorial Ethnography of Hans-Eberhard Kauffmann and Christoph von Fürer-Haimendorf* (Stuttgart: Arnoldsche Art Publishers, 2014), 228–9.

40. BL/Mss Eur C847: Geraldine Hobson, 'My Father in the Naga Hills: The Indian Civil Service Survivors Remember the Raj', Part 1, *Indo-British Review* 12, no. 2 (1998): 63.

41. Mildred Archer is mentioned in the section concerning indigenous painters in Chapters 2 and 9 of this book.

42. Hobson, 'My Father in the Naga Hills', 62.

Figure 8.1.   J.P. Mills with one of the slave children rescued during the Pangsha Expedition. J.P. Mills Photographic Collection (Ref. PP MS 58/Y.29, SOAS Library). *Source:* 1936, The Estate of Christoph von Fürer-Haimendorf. The Estate is currently (2015) represented by Nicholas Haimendorf, son of Christoph von Fürer-Haimendorf.

By 1933, Mills had attained the rank of Deputy Commissioner, when, like his predecessor Hutton, he was placed in charge of a district of over 4,300 square miles and around 178,000 people. For the next ten years, he became deeply involved in the problems and welfare of the area under his care, which included inadequate health care, lack of vaccination and land shortages arising from occupation by tribesmen from neighbouring areas, which inevitably caused much friction.[43] In 1943, Mills was appointed Advisor to

43. Ibid., 69.

the Governor for Tribal Areas, with overall responsibility for tribal matters in North-East India, meaning that his expertise was available to all those working in the many and varied areas of Assam and the North-East Frontier Agency, now known as Arunachal Pradesh. One of his prime tasks was to make good the McMahon Line, which was negotiated in 1910 by Sir Henry McMahon (1862–1949) in a convention between India, China and Tibet. For the first time this fixed the international boundary between India and Tibet to run along the Great Himalayan Range, but although accepted by Tibet, China refused to sign.[44] In 1948, Mills and his family left Assam for the last time, but not before they had experienced personal tragedy. In 1946, while accompanying her father on one of his regular tours throughout the Hills, Mills's daughter, aged fifteen, died from malaria several days' march from medical help. Soon afterwards, the family returned to London, where Mills took up a post as a Reader in anthropology at SOAS, before ill-health forced him to retire in 1955. He died of heart disease in 1960.[45] The next section describes his famous expedition to Pangsha in 1936 in the company of Christoph von Fürer-Haimendorf.

THE PANGSHA EXPEDITION

Ordinarily, Philip Mills made many tours of duty throughout the Naga villages in the course of his day-to-day work, one of whose purposes was to count taxable households – a procedure which many villagers tried to evade for obvious reasons. But for those whom he found were at home to him, Mills liked nothing better than to be invited into their houses, where he bartered for domestic objects with red wool, as money was not used at that time in Naga communities. However, exceptionally in 1936, he was called upon by the Government of India to lead an expedition to Pangsha to punish its tribesmen, who had been crossing over into the administered areas in order to take heads from villages protected by the British. As the tribesmen of Pangsha had also captured several slaves in the course of their raids, including at least one child, the expedition's intention was also to rescue the captives and to teach the headhunters a lesson by plundering and burning their *khels*, situated along the ridges. The operation was carried out between November and December and involved a detachment of 150 soldiers of the Assam Rifles under the command of Major Williams and numerous indigenous labourers.[46] Although military pacification was a tried and tested method of

---

44. Ibid., 70.
45. Ibid.
46. Termed in the Mills report as 'coolies'.

colonial control, its effect was limited; as one villager explained to another ICS officer, simply burning a village and going away was of no use and the people just laughed and re-built their houses.[47]

Recounting their experiences at Pangsha in his tour diary and also in letters to his wife, Mills explained how the tribesmen had attempted to cut the party off as they made their escape after burning their villages and they were obliged to run for their lives. As he wrote, 'We knew the supreme moment had come and that the Pangsha were going to try and overwhelm us and annihilate us by sheer weight of numbers'.[48] As the attackers chased Mills and his party of soldiers and 'coolies'[49] down the hills towards the river, the Pangsha men's spears rained down upon them. In response, the Pangsha were met with a hail of bullets from the Assam Rifles, which succeeded in keeping the angry tribesmen at bay until they had crossed the river to the safety of their camp. Despite being heavily outnumbered, Mills's party were able to make their escape, as shields and spears were no match against the soldiers' bullets, which doubtless cost the Pangsha warriors many lives, a statistic that Mills does not record in his tour diary. Soon afterwards their chief came to Mills to sue for peace

Ever alert to new opportunities to add to his collection for the Pitt Rivers Museum, Mills even found time after the previous day's raid and their lucky escape to visit the hilltop village of Panso. However, he took the precaution of taking a strong escort of the Assam Rifles with him. He was keen to acquire what he called a real 'crash helmet', headgear used for fighting made of cane, and also a very fine drum and some ladies' combs.[50] Mock-fights were a common way of resolving conflicts, particularly amongst the Eastern Naga groups, and they used special helmets like the one described by Mills, as well as wooden swords, in order to avoid serious injury.[51] Continuing his quest for collectible items for the Pitt Rivers Museum, Mills recorded that the following day he and the Baron had visited Longtang, the village of craftsmen, 'as no collector can resist seeing things made', where once again he bartered for objects with red wool.[52] Upon his return to his base at Imphal, Mills received a telegram from the Government of India on 13 December confirming the abdication of King Edward VIII. Having received regular updates throughout their expedition via the *dak*[53] on the growing crisis in London that they

47. Jacobs et al., *The Nagas*, 25; quoting W.G. Archer's notes in his Tour Diary of 1946.
48. SOAS/PP MS 58/Box 1/58/9/144764/6, 16: J.P. Mills to his wife (27 November 1936).
49. Coolies: Local labourers hired on a daily or weekly basis, today considered as a racialist term.
50. Mills to his wife (27 November 1936).
51. Alban von Stockhausen, 'Christoph von Fürer-Haimendorf's Naga Expedition of 1936/7 and its Photographs', *Archiv für Völkerkunde 61/62 3–30. World Museum Vienna* (2013): https://www.academia.edu/8863041/.
52. Mills to his wife (27 November 1936).
53. *Dak*: A system of mail delivery or passenger transport by a relay of bearers or horses stationed along the route.

feared would wreck the empire, Mills felt that, all things considered, it was the best way out.[54] The news from London of Edward VIII's abdication must have seemed surreal to them given that they had recently fled for their lives, retreating from an attack by over 500 Pangsha warriors in reprisal for burning their villages.

Meanwhile, Haimendorf had persuaded Mills to let him accompany their expedition against the Pangsha, as he wished to research further into the anthropology of the north-eastern frontier areas of Assam and Burma, after residing with the Konyak group of the Nagas since the beginning of the year. Haimendorf had promised the people of Wakching (the village where he spent most of his time during his stay in the Naga Hills), that he would try to bring some heads back for them from Pangsha, so that the villagers also might attain certain privileges associated with the taking of heads. Naturally, no heads were taken during the punitive raid by the British, but Haimendorf managed to retrieve some ancient animal and human heads from houses that were plundered by the expedition. This allowed the villagers of Wakching to hold Feasts of Merit, wear special clothes and ornaments and build a house of a particular shape and set up a carved post, thereby gaining social eminence and assurance of immortality in the songs sung by the clan.[55]

In many ways, as a professional anthropologist, Haimendorf was the true cultural representative on the Pangsha expedition, as he had received training in anthropology at the University of Vienna during the 1920s, when the presiding influence was that of the theoretical framework of the Kulturkreislehre. It was first presented in 1898 by the German anthropologist, Leo Frobenius (1873–1938), who introduced the idea of cultural diffusion.[56] The diffusionist school of thought, to which Mills and Hutton also adhered, believed in the transmission of cultural characteristics or traits from the common society to all other societies. Cultural diffusion looked for references within different geographical regions by comparing different elements of material culture, religion and social structure.[57] In 1932, Hutton reviewed N.E. Parry's (b. 1884) monograph on the Lakhers, in which he defined diffusionism as extremely important and 'likely to throw light on the stratification of cultures in the Assam-Burma Hills since the features described are some of them typically Naga and some typically Kuki, while others appear to belong to neither of

---

54. SOAS/PP MS 58/File 11/MS 380571: Typescript of thirty-one letters from J.P. Mills to his wife whilst on a tour of duty on the North Eastern frontier of India, edited by her.

55. SOAS/PP MS 19/Box 50, 2871–2882, 2879: Article by J.P. Mills, 'The Effect on the Naga Tribes of Assam of their Contact with Western Civilization', written when Mills was Director of Ethnography for Assam Kohima, Naga Hills Assam.

56. Stockhausen, 'Christoph von Fürer-Haimendorf's Naga Expedition', 21.

57. Ibid.

these cultures'.[58] On his return to Europe, Haimendorf produced his magnum opus, *The Naked Nagas*, a book first published in 1939 and translated into English by the publishers Methuen and Company of London. His narrative and photographs brought the experience of an unknown people into many European homes for the first time. Affectionately dedicated to his friend, Philip Mills, he asserted that his book was not intended as a scientific work, but an attempt to bring the life of a little-known people to public attention.[59]

As detailed previously, unlike Haimendorf, Mills was without professional training as an anthropologist, but his many years living amongst the Nagas, his ability to speak the local languages and, not least, his own erudition had enabled him to make close study of the conceptual reasons associated with the traditions of headhunting. These attributes provided him with affective knowledge about frontier communities, who had been ignored and neglected by the colonial government for so long. They allowed him to give many insightful lectures after he took up an academic post at SOAS on his return to London in 1948, and also to write many articles about the reasons for headhunting. Through participant observation, he came to the understanding that it was bound up with the concept of *Aren*, which the Nagas considered to be the soul force of the village – it makes the crops flourish and the children and the cattle increase.[60] *Aren*, Mills explained, is contained in the soul and the soul is contained in the head. As he made clear, the only way to increase a village's supply of *Aren* was to take a head, and with it, the soul of someone from another village.

It is the intense need for *Aren* that causes Nagas to take the great risks involved in headhunting, as in these areas the defence is highly organised. As Mills wrote,

> Not only does the headhunter take his life in his hands, he also takes his soul, because if he is killed and his head taken away by the defenders, his body, if recovered, is buried without ceremony, his name is not uttered, he can never be sung about and no children can be named after him. He has no place in the World of the Dead and is 'extinguished'.[61]

After their Pangsha expedition, Mills noted that Haimendorf sat up half the night writing their anthropological diary, which they hoped to publish,

---

58. BL/Mss Eur F185/144, ix: Forward by Dr J.H. Hutton ICS of N.E. Parry ICS, *The Lakhers* (London: Macmillan & Co., 1932).

59. Christoph von Fürer-Haimendorf, *The Naked Nagas* (London: Methuen & Co., 1939), vii.

60. SOAS/Ms 144764/6/PPMS 58/Box 1, 1924–1958: Typescript of abstract for a lecture on 'The Naga Headhunters of Assam', presented to the Royal Central Asian Society (file 9); and Typescript of a lecture, 'The Effect of Ritual upon Industries and Arts in the Naga Hills', presented to the Congrès International des Sciences Anthropologiques et Ethnologiques, Londres (file 6).

61. Ibid., file 9.

together with photographs that they had taken. Mills took numerous photographs with his camera, although it 'was very old and not as good as the Baron's', as he admitted to a rare fit of jealousy at the superiority of his friend's photographic equipment.[62] It was of exceptional quality, chiefly due to the new technology of the Zeiss lenses of his German Contax II camera, which meant that Haimendorf was able to take photographs more unobtrusively than conventional cameras of the time.[63] In particular, its small design, with a telescopic lens, made it easily portable, so that he was able to document dance performances in sequences and at different angles. They included some impressive images of various 'head-receiving' dances that were performed after they returned from the Pangsha expedition.[64]

Photographs carry complex messages about the political and social relations that existed in the context in which they were taken, and contextualisation of the photographer and the subject's cultural background is an important indication of their social and political differences that defined the ways in which they interpreted their subject. As non-written sources of historical information, Mills and Haimendorf's numerous photographs visually categorised the ways in which Naga cultures differed or resembled one another; similarly with the artefacts that Mills and Hutton collected. The next section looks at the ways in which Mills's photography provided a new source of visual knowledge, which portrayed a so-called primitive society as one that was more advanced and with greater social and cultural structure than previous sensationalist written descriptions had acknowledged. It compares Haimendorf's more sophisticated photography with Mills's photographic output, as superior technology and interchangeable lenses had allowed him to place a more visually dramatic and exciting interpretation upon the unfamiliar, sensual and strange.[65]

CONTRASTING MILLS AND HAIMENDORF'S APPROACH TO COLONIAL PHOTOGRAPHY

During the early decades of the twentieth century, when relations with the 'primitive other' were still characterised by expressions of fear, revulsion and fascination, Philip Mills and Christoph von Fürer-Haimendorf's photographs represented a unique departure from established ways of

---

62. SOAS/PPMS 58/9 Ms 144764/6, 26: Mills's diary entry for 10 December 1936.
63. Stockhausen, 'Christoph von Fürer-Haimendorf's Naga Expedition', 22.
64. See SOAS/PP MS 58/02/A & B: Cristoph von Fürer-Haimendorf's archive of photographs.
65. David Green, 'Classified Subjects: Photography and Anthropology', *Ten.8: Photographic Journal* 14 (1984): 35.

understanding headhunting communities. The mimetic technology of photography allowed them to capture many of the Naga peoples' rituals and cultural practices in ways that had never before been attempted, thereby raising awareness of their function and meaning within a pre-modern society. A combination of photography with participant observation allowed them to gather compelling evidence of a dynamic and organised society, still considered by the West as barbaric, and where nudity was regarded as a sign of a primordial and uncivilised state.

Earlier theories of race and anthropometric studies were founded upon an innate belief in the superiority of the white man and the notion of primitivity, for which nakedness was a symbol. These theories, which were associated with wildness or savagery, still prevailed until well into the twentieth century, even though anthropometric evaluations of naked subjects by using photography to measure and compare their bodies were discredited by later anthropological discourse. As mentioned earlier, the political impact of colonial photography later created concerns about the ways in which historical images reflected an impoverished and uncivilised society that threatened to compromise identities and perceptions of self in the modern world.[66] Willem van Schendel, meanwhile, has suggested that de-colonisation marked an important moment when a shift in political relations resulted in a resurgence of ways of understanding nudity in ethnic groups, when it was regarded as evidence of underdevelopment.[67]

In marked contrast to their intimate photographic studies and Mills's insightful articles, Colonel G.E.R. Grant Brown, a keen ethnographer and one of Mills's ICS contemporaries, sought to emphasise the civilising influence of colonial rule upon those whom he termed the 'savage native'. In 1911, he contributed an article to the *Journal of the Burma Research Society* entitled, 'Human Sacrifices near the Upper Chindwin',[68] which the very first review of the Society's new journal described as 'a rather gruesome account which illustrates the wide range from barbarism to civilisation which is so eminently a characteristic of the province of Burma'.[69] Grant Brown made no attempt to offer an explanation of the meaning behind the rituals that his article described in harrowing detail about the sacrifice of children as young as six or seven years of age. Nor did he have any direct contact with its subjects, admitting that he had obtained his information from a third

---

66. Sadan, 'Historical Photography', 464.

67. Willem van Schendel, 'The Politics of Nudity: Photographs of the Naked Mru of Bangladesh', *Modern Asian Studies* 36, no. 2 (2002): 346–349.

68. G.E.R. Grant Brown, 'Human Sacrifices Near the Upper Chindwin', *Journal of the Burma Research Society* 1, no. 1 (1911): 35–40.

69. Otto Blagden, 'Review of *The Journal of the Burma Research Society*, Vol. I, Parts I and II; Vol. II, Part I; Rangoon, 1911–1912', *Journal of the Royal Asiatic Society of Great Britain and Ireland* 45, no. 1 (1913): 209–211.

party – a Shan – whom he had met on one of his tours of duty. However, Grant Brown was careful to note that the child victims were brought from 'villages in un-administered territory, never from the territory administered by the British'.[70]

Although always referring to himself as an amateur, Philip Mills used photography in order to help fulfil the requirements of functionalist and social anthropology by producing a continuous record of the daily lives of the Nagas. He built up his archive over the course of thirty years of living and working amongst the Naga people. Haimendorf's contribution was more transitory, covering a sojourn of just over a year between 1936 and 1937, when, as noted, he worked as a professional anthropologist amongst the Konyak Nagas, based mainly in the village of Wakching. Despite possessing superior photographic equipment, allowing him to work with different perspectives and giving him the facility to operate on a more professional level, Haimendorf was limited by a much briefer acquaintance with his subjects.[71] Mills's photographs, although taken with an older camera, without interchangeable lenses, brought a degree of empathy to his studies that could only have been acquired by virtue of many years spent in the field, allowing him to truly know the Nagas in the context of their natural environment. His close relationship with his subject's cultural background is reflected in his photographs, which are devoid of showiness or elaborate poses, and point to the social and political differences that defined the ways in which he and Haimendorf approached and interpreted their subjects.

A study of the historical and cultural environment in which photographs are produced requires an understanding of both the photographer and his subject's cultural background, as contextualisation of the image is critical to the creation of hypothesis and analysis.[72] Mills's photographs did not display fascination with a strange people who followed an archaic, not to say barbaric, way of life. Nor did they aim to create the impression of an exotic society, recently discovered by adventure travellers, but as sources of visual information, they enhanced his academic studies and supported his work with the colonial government as an advisor in ethnology. Context is particularly important when images are produced under colonial conditions, as in Mills's case, where his subject was 'captured' both figuratively by the camera and through his authority as a colonial officer. Despite his close connection with the Nagas, his photographic work inevitably formed

70. Grant Brown, 'Human Sacrifices', 35.
71. Stockhausen, 'Christoph von Fürer-Haimendorf's Naga Expedition', 20.
72. Elizabeth Edwards (ed.), *Anthropology and Photography, 1860–1920* (New Haven and London: Yale University Press, 1992), 5, 36.

a part of the colonial effort 'to categorise, define, dominate and sometimes invent, an "other" and that representation became a form of cultural and legal power'.[73]

Meanwhile, much of Haimendorf's work found its way into the public domain, especially after the publication of his book, *The Naked Nagas* – copies appeared in many European households, including Britain, after it was translated into English in 1939. His book was influential between the wars and afterwards in shaping the image that the European public, especially Germans, had of the Nagas. Working between the wars, when developments in anthropological research were on the increase, both men's photographs offered the possibility of 'fulfilling the Malinowskian dream of seeing the world through native eyes'.[74] Haimendorf was influenced more directly than Mills by Bronisław Malinowski and others due to his anthropological studies in Vienna, and later London, where he attended Malinowski's famous seminars.

Their work among the Nagas occurred when visiting outsiders, including anthropologists, still considered nudity as an indication of 'primitivity, closeness to nature, indecency and sexual titillation'.[75] These traits are evident in many of Haimendorf's photographs, especially those reproduced in his book, *The Naked Nagas* – its provocative title was intended to attract a popular readership. According to one of his reviewers, Haimendorf had selected the more sensational parts of his material on half a dozen tribes located on the crests dividing the drainage systems of the Irrawaddy and Brahmaputra rivers.[76] His intention was to present the Nagas as 'an exotic society', unlike other groups, such as those in the Chittagong Hill Tracts,[77] who were not extensively photographed and studied by anthropologists.[78] However, the book was credited with being more than merely entertaining, providing 'details not usually given in more formal cultural descriptions'.[79] Nevertheless, Haimendorf later admitted that, although useful to professional ethnographers, his book was not an academic study, but 'reflected the impression of

73. Edwards, *Anthropology and Photography*, 33.
74. Macfarlane, 'Introduction', 27.
75. Schendel, 'The Politics of Nudity', 346.
76. Sarah du Bois, 'Review of *The Naked Nagas*', *American Anthropologist* 43, no. 4, Part 1 (1941): 663.
77. During British rule from 1860 to 1947, the Chittagong Hill Tracts were designated 'an Excluded Area' and were largely off-limits to all but a few such as missionaries and government officials, like Reginald A. Lorrain who, in 1907, founded the Lakher Pioneer Mission in an area near the Lushai Hills that bordered Assam on the east and Arakan on the south. Being the first mission in the area, government officials wasted little time in co-opting Lorrain's missionaries to offer the people some rudimentary education in exchange for a schoolhouse and supplying some labourers to build it.
78. Schendel, 'The Politics of Nudity', 345.
79. Ibid.

a Western observer exposed for the first time to close contact with an Indian tribal people persisting in an archaic way of life'.[80]

Some of Haimendorf's most famous photographs relate to the rituals and the dances that accompanied the 'head-receiving' ceremonies, when the victorious warriors returned to their village. As noted, in order to photograph this spectacle, Haimendorf had promised the men of Wakching that he would endeavour to obtain some previously captured heads from plundered villages on the Pangsha expedition. In his book, in a chapter entitled, 'The White Headhunter', Haimendorf described how he distributed fragments from heads he took from a 'head tree' to his friends in Wakching, and also to 'coolies' who accompanied the expedition, allowing them to perform the rituals, hold feasts of merit and wear the customary body ornaments associated with someone who has taken a head.[81] Although ethically questionable, Haimendorf's plundered heads gave Nagas living in a British administered area, where headhunting was forbidden, the opportunity to participate in its customs without fear of reprisals and punitive raids, as had occurred to the Pangsha men. Haimendorf also benefited from the distribution of head fragments, as he was able to capture on his camera the important and increasingly rare ceremonies that resulted from his plunder, which he carried back himself in a basket to avoid the risk of *genna* (taboo) to the labourers on the Pangsha expedition. He therefore spared his friends in Wakching the great risks involved in headhunting. After deciding that the heads could be legitimately received by their villages, the elders treated Haimendorf to a series of 'head-receiving' dances and ceremonies that were performed when the fragments reached the various villages, allowing him a unique opportunity to capture rituals that were outlawed by the British.[82]

As discussed, understanding the context in which a photograph was taken is all-important, as is the status of the photographer in relation to his subject and whether the photograph was intended for private or official consumption. Alban von Stockhausen has described Haimendorf as an 'opportunist', who appeared happy to be working under the Vienna Institute's leadership, although he does not seem to have been an active supporter of National Socialist ideas. Like many who were educated in Germany and Austria in the early twentieth century, Haimendorf was not immune to the political and cultural influences associated with the rise of extreme right-wing political ideologies during the 1930s. They must have had some influence on the aesthetics associated with

---

80. Stockhausen, 'Christoph von Fürer-Haimendorf's Naga Expedition', 26.
81. Ibid., 14.
82. Ibid., 15.

his photography.[83] The spectacle of 'physical power and the purity of instinctive actions' presented by the dances of the returning warriors, where force is vital and overwhelming, may have had unconscious influences upon him as a gifted young anthropologist who escaped Europe during the 1930s to work in South Asia and later, in Britain, with his English wife.[84]

It is possible to trace a correlation between Haimendorf's photographs of the spectacular ceremonies and dances involved in receiving heads that he witnessed in Naga villages in 1936 with the influence of the political ideology of fascism and its fusion with aesthetic forms centred upon the body and the exhibition of physical prowess.[85] These theories found their purest photographic expression in Europe during the 1930s, notably in the propagandist films of Leni Riefenstahl (1902–2003), where 'the spectacle is the dramaturgical form of fascism uniting the political rally with the art of theatre'.[86] Later, it found expression in Riefenstahl's celebration of the vigorous displays of masculine power in her two books of photographs of the Nuba tribes of Southern Sudan in the mid-1970s.[87]

For the scholar of the present, perhaps one of the more troubling aspects of Haimendorf's photographs, and to a lesser extent those of Mills, was the seemingly endless images of attractive, bare-breasted young women, artfully posed to display to advantage their charms in a way that may be characterised as sensual and, in some cases, sexually exploitative. It is difficult to determine how their provocative poses served to elucidate Naga culture and traditions, unless for the purpose of showing off their jewellery and body ornaments. As Stockhausen admitted, the technical facility of Haimendorf's equipment allowed him to indulge his personal fascination and excitement, particularly when a beautiful woman crossed his path.[88] This raises questions about the impact of these photographs on European society as perpetuating the myth of primitivity among 'naked savages' that had become entangled with a

83. von Stockhausen, *Imagining the Nagas*, 228–229. Stockhausen writes, 'Haimendorf's affiliation with the Nationalist Socialist policies of the Nazis expressed in one article only in 1940, "Die Stellung de Naturvolker in Indien und Sudostasien", was packed full of National Socialist terminology'. Stockhausen concludes, 'Haimendorf does not seem to have been an active supporter of National Socialist ideas, but at least for some time he did not mind being in favour of the regime when he had the possibility to work for the Vienna Institute under the leadership of the National Socialist and to publish a clearly ideological volume. He was clearly an opportunist who wanted to keep several options open for himself without questioning the consequences in much depth'.
84. Ibid.
85. Green, 'Classified Subjects', 36.
86. Ibid.
87. Ibid., 35.
88. Stockhausen, 'Christoph von Fürer-Haimendorf's Naga Expedition', 20.

Figure 8.2. Ao Girl called Pangchonglila laughing. J.P. Mills Photographic Collection (Ref. PP MS 58/W.32, SOAS Library). *Source:* 1926, The Estate of J.P. Mills.

professional anthropologist's attempts to raise awareness of the meaning of ritual and tradition within a pre-modern society.

CONCLUDING REMARKS

Philip Mills spent one of the longest sojourns of any anthropologist as a participant-observer among the Nagas. During thirty years of living and working amongst them, he built up a photographic archive that stands as a priceless historical record of a complex society that had evolved over many generations. His photographs carry intricate messages about the political and social relations that existed between himself, as a representative of the colonising authority and as an independent scholar committed to the visual representation of historicity in Naga society, as well as being a guardian of their welfare. His work amongst the Nagas for almost three decades straddled two worlds, one being his status as senior ICS officer, whose images would be used to categorise, define and inevitably dominate the colonial subject; the other as an insightful observer, whose photographs and collections of cultural objects were intended to advance academic understanding of indigenous peoples. His frequent tours visiting hilltop *khels* gave him the opportunity to enter their homes and in the course of participating in their day-to-day activities, he was enabled to acquire many items for the Pitt Rivers Museum, paying only with red wool. In a non-monetised economy like the Nagas', where barter in goods or services was the medium of exchange, this raises questions about how fair the trade of wool was for such intrinsically valuable items which could not be replicated elsewhere.

Although of poorer quality because of inferior camera equipment, Mills's photographs contain less evidence of characteristics which emphasise primitivity and the apparently uncivilised environment in which their subjects lived. Unlike Haimendorf's, their intention was to appear less visually dramatic or sensual, traits that have been criticised for reducing 'the historical complexity of the social process to the presence of mere spectacle'.[89] By contrast, Mills's photographs endeavoured to dispel the notion of primitivity and of naked savages who required civilising, as he fixed his lens on the clusters of *khels*, where the enormous roofs of the houses displayed craftsmanship that had been handed down through many generations.[90]

Mills's regular presence among the Nagas enabled him to witness the cultural evolution of Naga society at a time of great political change. He recorded their customs and traditions in the environment where they took place and despite his official position, he too became familiar with the symbolism of head-receiving ceremonies that followed the warriors' return to the village, that were intended to utilise the 'soul force' of the captured head for the benefit of the community. His photographs of young warriors taken whilst touring the Konyak country with Hutton depicted the elaborate hairstyles worn by the warriors, their tight belts with *doas*[91] thrust into them, and the tattoos and brass chest ornaments that denoted their status as headhunters.

---

89. Green, 'Classified Subjects', 35.
90. See SOAS/PP MS 58/02/C/24 & 58/02/B31: Photograph entitled 'Angs House' in Mills's photographic collection.
91. *Doas*: Machete.

In 1943, Mills was appointed Advisor to the Governor for Tribal Areas, with overall responsibility for tribal matters in North-East India, meaning that his expertise was available to all those working in the many and varied areas of Assam and the North-East Frontier Agency, where his prime task was to make good the McMahon Line.[92] He faced many challenges, not least among them land shortages – occasioned where neighbouring ethnic groups occupied land, – lack of health care due to insufficient medical resources and vaccinations, as well as adjudicating marital disputes. Faced with the trappings of encroaching modernisation, Mills's concern was always for the welfare of the peoples of the Naga Hills. After he became Director of Ethnography for Assam in 1945, he witnessed the detrimental effects that contact with Western civilisation had on their communities when he identified the introduction of money as one of the critical changes.[93] He observed that increasing use of coin to pay bride price and wages for work done on roads had led to a fall in the birth rate and diverse ethnic groups dying out. Marriage payments used to be made in cattle and rice, but now it was far easier to make a prompt payment in cash. Mature men had cash that enabled them to buy immature young brides – brides whose children were often sickly. Increasingly, the use of coin in centres like Kohima and Mokokchung had also allowed the possessor of money to gratify his taste for 'foreign clothes and other rubbish' in the foreign-owned shops. Meanwhile, the presence of government and other officials, as well as the Assam Rifles, increased the risk of prostitution by girls who, having quarrelled with their families, had run away to Kohima to become sex workers.[94]

Throughout a long ICS career that had begun in 1913, Mills discovered his own true 'soul force' in 1916, when he was appointed to a position as a junior officer at Mokokchung. He successfully combined his official mandate to rule over the peoples of the Naga Hills with a genuine desire to know them in their own environment and oversee their wellbeing. He documented his experiences in a photographic archive and built up a large collection of material objects. Above all, his long stay among the Nagas gave him a unique insight into a way of life that by the time he retired in 1948 was on the point of vanishing.

---

92. Hobson, 'My Father in the Naga Hills', 69.
93. Mills, 'The Effect on the Naga Tribes', 2873.
94. Ibid., 2879.

Chapter 9

The Last Word from the Women of the Empire

INTRODUCTION

East India Company Wives,
The children left behind,
The flowered cups and saucers broken on the voyage,
The fragile sense of self that cracked in transit,
And lies beneath a slowly turning fan, past salvaging.[1]

The lacuna in this book about the numerous ways that human agents inter-acted with diverse individuals and objects to produce knowledge under many different circumstances has been the absence of the contribution of women. This appears to endorse the all too readily accepted truism that women played only a minor role in the making of empire and in generating knowledge about it. Yet, despite the scarcity of female voices in the colonial archive, might not some women have managed to escape the confines of the feminine colonial space to make connections with different people and objects in new places? This chapter seeks to examine the lives of selected women, mainly those who have been mentioned in this book, to investigate how they too may have influenced the circulation of knowledge in the sphere of colonial social and political control.[2] Even though they represented only approximately one-third of the non-indigenous population of India, British and European women did travel to the subcontinent and some lived there for considerable periods of

---

1. Barbara Rendall, 'East India Company Wives (Extract)', in 'Ethnicity, Nationalism: 21st–Century Time Bombs', *Queen's Quarterly* 102, no. 1 (1995): 253.
2. See critical reviews of Ashley L. Cohen (ed.), *Lady Nugent's East India Journal: A Critical Edition* (Delhi: Oxford University Press, 2014) by Vibha S. Chauhan, *Indian Literature* 59, no. 4 (2015): 206–209; and Priyasha Mukhopadhyay, *Journal of Colonialism and Colonial History* 17, no. 2 (2016): Project Muse.

time.[3] Those who did so belonged predominantly to the upper classes of British society and the majority made the long sea voyage to India accompanying a spouse or other male relative who had been appointed to a position in the EIC, or after 1858, the Government of India. Women seldom travelled alone, and those rare females who did risked public criticism and the loss of their reputation.

The part played by women in knowing India arose principally through their experiences of travel writing and collecting, which implicated them in the circulation of new ideas and information. From the early nineteenth century, these activities allowed mainly elite, educated women to 'self-fashion' and speak as men could with the authoritative voice of one who knew the country.[4] Letters home and journals were the primary instruments through which colonial women could express themselves and it is when referring predominantly to these objects that we recollect Pascal Schillings and Alexander van Wickeren's theory that the interchange between human actors, different objects and spatial contexts created new knowledge.[5] It is by interrogating the part played by women in these interactions, and the views they expressed thereof, that we may learn more about how women have influenced the ways in which colonial political and social life was represented, both at the centre and on the periphery of empire.[6]

Therefore, this chapter examines the interactions of a small number of women whose histories may go some way towards offsetting the disparity between the knowledge produced by female colonisers in comparison with men. Although their stories denote only a fraction of the experiences of the non-indigenous females who visited India, those selected represent a cross-section of colonial society, from upper-class females, to those in the lower strata, who were often obliged to fend for themselves in harsh circumstances.[7] Some were widowed and left without financial means of support; while any lone European female who attempted to earn her own living in India was considered very unusual and not respectable.

We begin by recalling Chapter 2 of this book, which described the arrival in Bengal in 1811 of Lady Maria Nugent when she accompanied her husband Sir George Nugent, who had been appointed as the new Commander-in-Chief

---

3. Herbert Hope Risley and Edward Albert Gait, *Report on the Census of India, 1901* (Calcutta: Office of the Superintendent of Govt. Print., India, 1901).

4. Jasanoff, *Edge of Empire*, 7. See also Joanna Goldsworthy, 'Fanny Parkes (1794–1875): Female Collecting and Curiosity in India and Britain', in *The East India Company at Home, 1757–1857*, eds. Margot Finn and Kate Smith (London: UCL Press, 2018), 131–52.

5. Schillings and van Wickeren, 'Towards a Material and Spatial History', 206: 'It is through the practices of human actors that different objects and spatial contexts are brought into interplay in the processes of knowledge production'.

6. See John Plotz, *Portable Property: Victorian Culture on the Move* (Princeton, NJ: Princeton University Press, 2008), 45–46.

7. Risley and Gait, *Report on the Census of India*.

for India. As an upper-class woman, with the leisure to combine travel and writing, Lady Nugent was at liberty to express her opinions about Indian life and society in a domain that was free from the social codes and conflicts that characterised the private domestic sphere for most women in Britain at that time. We recollect also that Lady Nugent was an 'old hand' at life in the colonies, having previously seen service in Jamaica, where she had made it her mission to bring Christian salvation to the souls of those whom she called 'the blackies'.[8] This time she travelled eastwards, rather than westwards across the Atlantic Ocean, and by the end of her stay in India, she viewed the British Empire from a global perspective. We will investigate whether, as a well-travelled woman (unusual for her time), Maria Nugent's opinions on colonial life had mellowed since her return from Jamaica in 1805.

During the intervening years, before she left England for Bengal, she had given birth to four children, whom she decided to leave in the safe custody of their friends, Lord and Lady Buckingham, in order to spare them the rigours of the tropical climate. Freed from domestic responsibilities and the social obligations incumbent upon her in England, Nugent now had the leisure and affluence to travel with her husband, Sir George. She recorded her impressions in her *Journal of East India*,[9] which reveal her opinions about this new and intensely fascinating country. Despite the pain of missing 'her dear children', a circumstance that befell most upper- and middle-class women who accompanied their husbands on their postings to India, Nugent was captivated by the sights and architecture she encountered, from the bustle of the bazaar to the majesty of the Taj Mahal. Nevertheless, she did not fail to record in her *Journal* anything that displeased her or which offended her critical eye.

There were of course other less elite women who also accompanied their spouses or other male relatives to India, as indicated by the case of Hannah Johnson, mentioned in Chapter 5, who emigrated from England with her husband, Thomas Johnson, when he took up employment as a sub-conductor in the Ordnance Department of the EIC's army. Although the Company did not specifically encourage its employees to take their spouses to India, being a covenanted officer who had attained the rank of Sergeant Overseer, Thomas Johnson's wife was permitted to accompany him. By the time their son, William Henry, was born in 1832, Hannah Johnson was resident in Mussoorie, a recently settled town in the foothills of the Himalayas, where life was primitive in the extreme. Thomas and Hannah Johnson were attracted by the colder climate of the Himalayan foothills, away from the heat of the plains, and after

8. McCullough, 'Lady Maria Nugent', 24. See also Frank Cundall (ed.), *Lady Nugent's Journal: Jamaica One Hundred Years Ago. Reprinted from a Journal Kept by Maria, Lady Nugent, from 1801 to 1815* (London: Adam & Charles Black, 1907), 53.

9. Maria Nugent, *A Journal from the Year 1811 till the Year 1815, Including a Voyage to and Residence in India, with a Tour to the North-Western Parts of the British Possessions in that Country, under the Bengal Government*, vol. 1. (London: T. and W. Boone, 1839).

Johnson Senior's retirement, they decided to settle there, living on his modest Company pension. By this time, their son William had obtained a position with the GTS of India at nearby Dehradun.[10]

Although women like Hannah Johnson accounted for the majority of the non-indigenous 'white' female population of India, they did not enjoy the privileges that accompanied Lady Nugent's elite status, as the wife of the Commander-in-Chief. Often lumped together under the classification of 'poor whites', they seldom possessed sufficient leisure or education to write a journal. Although to a great extent this has prevented the voices of ordinary women from being heard, secondary sources drawn from newspapers and court reports provide a picture of how difficult life in India could be for a woman without the legal protection and financial support of a husband or male relative. Lone females were looked upon with suspicion and their morals questioned, being regarded as little better than prostitutes, even though there was often no evidence to suggest that they were living off immoral earnings, as a case discussed later in this chapter will demonstrate.

Despite the lack of primary sources in the form of diaries or letters written by lower-class women about their experiences in India, in the early 1840s, one male resident of Mussoorie left a series of letters that provide an illuminating account of the hardships of life, especially for women, at this frontier station in the foothills of the Himalayas.[11] Mauger Fitzhugh Monk (1815–1849), from the Channel Island of Guernsey, came out to India originally to serve in the EIC's army. However, after being accused of misconduct with a fellow officer's wife, he was obliged to buy himself out of his army commission with money supplied by his father. He then decided to try his luck in Mussoorie, where many men like him lived by their wits on the boundaries of the empire and endured conditions that were little better than those of the indigenous population. The prospect of making their fortunes, or paying off debts accumulated elsewhere, was sufficient incentive to draw such opportunists to towns like Mussoorie, which had only been settled fifteen years earlier in 1820.[12] Monk's account in his letters to his family of his own precarious existence amply illustrate how 'chancers' like him flocked to these border towns seeking ways of making money by becoming associated with the various new infrastructures required by newcomers. Monk tried his luck firstly by becoming a schoolmaster at an establishment run by a Scotsman named Mackinnon,[13] then as a hotelkeeper. Other commercial ventures

---

10. See Chapter 5.
11. Monk, *Letters of a Mussoorie Merchant*.
12. Ibid., 10.
13. His first appointment was as head assistant at a newly-established school, owned by a Scotsman named Mackinnon. Monk boasted that he had been appointed to the role and was preferred over

followed, including opening a school of his own and even gelding horses, all of which failed, leaving him even deeper in debt.[14] Monk's letters home, especially those addressed to his father, veered between complaints about his life, which he described as monotonous, to elation when he announced a new venture – his marriage and the birth of a child – to despair when they died, or his business ventures failed.

Monk's experiences were not uncommon and even the cooler climate of the foothills of the Himalayas could not mitigate the hardships of life for Europeans on this colonial frontier, especially for women. They were dependent upon the support of a man in order to survive and the uncertainties inherent in this way of life impacted upon them, not least from the dangers they faced in childbirth. Whatever their social status, all women faced risks in bearing and raising children, but giving birth in England, although hazardous, meant that at least they were in familiar surroundings and near to family. Living far from adequate medical attention, both men and women faced the prospect of early widowhood and the burdens associated with being lone parents. These were just two of the many dangers that faced ordinary people, as Monk's letters revealed through his accounts of the deaths of his own infant children and his first wife. Should a European woman be widowed after her husband had succumbed to disease – a frequent occurrence – she was even more vulnerable. As a lone female left without adequate financial means to provide for herself and any children, and unable to work, the only remedy was to return to Britain – if she could afford the passage – or remarry as quickly as possible.

Despite all his prejudices and racist comments in his letters home, after a couple of years' residence in Mussoorie, Monk decided to marry a woman of mixed race, declaring himself 'not infected by the prejudices of Europeans'.[15] In November 1842, he married Elizabeth Lewin, aged twenty, whose father was a retired officer in the service of the late Begum Samru (c. 1753–1836), whom coincidentally Lady Maria Nugent had visited during her travels around Northern India, which will be described in the next section. In his letters home, Monk described his new wife as 'the loveliest and most amiable girl of colour I have seen in the country. Her descent by her father's side is Jewish, evident enough in the contour of her beautiful face and in her eye'.[16] However, mindful of her mixed race, Monk requested that friends and family at home should refrain from 'all allusion to the warmer blood which runs in her veins'.[17] In a subsequent letter, he was obliged to explain that local

---

'country-born scholars'. He later quarrelled with Mackinnon and decided to go into business on his own account.

14. Monk, *Letters of a Mussoorie Merchant*, 145.
15. Ibid., 86.
16. Ibid.
17. Ibid., 110.

prejudice decreed that his new wife would not be received socially by a 'high-caste covenanted servant's lady', to whom his sister-in-law had recommended she be introduced.[18]

Early marital bliss was soon marked by tragedy when, the following year, Monk's daughter died three days after her birth. His misfortunes continued throughout the 1840s, as various business ventures failed. Although 1844 saw the birth of a healthy son, his wife's health deteriorated, and she died after giving birth to another daughter in September 1846. Left a widower with two small children, Monk struggled on for a while, until overwhelmed by ill-health, debts and business failures, he decided suddenly to return home to England, leaving his new wife behind – she was a sixteen-year-old widow, named Ann Weller, whom Monk had married some months earlier, in August 1849. Having started his own school and once again failed, Monk resolved to try his hand at opening an insurance office agency after he returned from his visit to England. This was never to be, and Monk died at Meerut on 9 December 1849. His journey was primarily motivated by his wish to escape his creditors, who, in his absence, would seize his property and make what they could from its sale. His only son, Hugh, was left under the guardianship of the Revd Isaac Lewin, the brother of his first wife, who described his new spouse as a girl of no family or education and considerably younger than Monk.[19] The bulk of Monk's property in Europe was left to his son Hugh until he became of age. Meanwhile, Isaac Lewin, who was settling Monk's affairs in India, declared that his second wife, Ann Weller, wanted to remarry as soon as possible – and 'with a pretty face and a few thousands', Lewin was of the opinion that she would certainly succeed.

A frontier town like Mussoorie attracted its share of lone women and widows, and many, like Ann Monk (née Weller), were young and of mixed race. They came in search of a new husband, after the first one had been carried off by a sudden illness or other misfortune. There was no suggestion that Ann Monk was a prostitute, but, like all low-status women, with little or no education and only a pretty face to recommend her, she needed to survive in the harsh moral climate of nineteenth-century India. As detailed in Chapter 5, in June 1851, she married William Henry Johnson at the nearby town of Landour.[20] They had five children together and it appears that she outlived him because, as previously discussed, Johnson died in Kashmir in unusual circumstances in 1883. It is little wonder therefore that only a few exceptional women found themselves in a position to contribute towards the production of knowledge in any significant form, or to produce new ideas concerning the

18. Ibid., 118.
19. Ibid., 237.
20. See p. 136.

meaning of the objects they encountered. Those females who could consider doing so were invariably well-educated for their time and living in secure domestic circumstances. But as always, there were exceptions, as the case of Emma Roberts (1794–1840) demonstrates.

Although women were not permitted to work, when unexpectedly presented with changed circumstances that left them impoverished, some lone females were able to overcome the stigma of their unmarried status and find respectable employment. In rare cases, the women who were able to use their talent to earn their own living were middle-class and well-educated. Roberts became a professional writer in India at a time when public opinion viewed such women with suspicion and as oddities. As an example of travel writing by a female author who, unlike Maria Nugent, was obliged by circumstances to make her writing pay, Roberts contributed towards furthering knowledge about the social consequences of living in India. As will be described, she became well-known for her advice to both men and women in her book, *The East India Voyager*,[21] as well as for her other written output.

In 1828, after her sister's marriage to an army officer, Captain R.A. McNaughton, Roberts accompanied the newly married couple to India. Although a spinster untroubled by the dangers of childbirth, she nevertheless faced her own challenges when her sister died in 1830, only two years after they had arrived in India. As an unmarried woman, she had become a financial burden to her widowed brother-in-law. Without the financial means to pay for her passage home to England, she made use of her skills as a writer – honed whilst living in Bath with her friend, the 'bluestocking', Letitia Landon (1802–1838) – to write for periodicals, becoming the first woman and one of the very few English journalists in India.[22] Journalism allowed Roberts a critical voice with which to comment publicly on the social life of India and the behaviour and customs of both its indigenous and European population. She made her trenchant views known on the conduct of the British (especially the men) towards the 'native' population, and her work earned her a reputation as an authority on Anglo-Indian life. She became known during her lifetime as the 'domestic historian of India'.[23]

Meanwhile, Mildred Archer might be considered the 'lodestar' of this chapter concerning women in India who contributed towards the production of knowledge. Her unpublished research in the British Library, entitled 'Women in India', explores the lives of several of the women discussed in this study and it has guided the author's attempts to bring their achievements to greater

---

21. Emma Roberts, *The East India Voyager, or Ten Minutes' Advice to the Outward Bound* (London: J. Madden & Co., 1839).
22. Letitia Landon: Feminist writer and poet.
23. Priya Shah, ' "Barbaric Pearl and Gold": Gendered Desires and Colonial Governance in Emma Roberts's *Scenes and Characteristics of Hindostan*', *Studies in Travel Writing* 16, no. 1 (2012): 32.

Figure 9.1. Mildred Archer with a Chang elder in Helipong, Nagaland, taken by her husband William (1947). *Source:* **Reproduced by permission of University of Cambridge Museum of Archaeology & Anthropology (Ref. P.113014.WARC).**

attention. As mentioned in Chapter 2, Archer's scholarship on the social history contained in Company paintings, together with her important research concerning the histories of the lives of the Indian artists who made them, produced knowledge in a previously neglected field.[24] Through her understanding of these objects, she illuminated little-known aspects of Indian life and the traditions that had been maintained by generations of indigenous artists. As the wife of an ICS officer, W.G. Archer (1907–1979), she accompanied her husband on his postings in Northern India from 1934 to 1947. The Archers began their life together in Bihar, later moving to Patna in 1940, where Mildred Archer encountered the descendants of painters' families. Here, she discovered the vestiges of a cultural environment that allowed her to become a pioneer in a field which had previously received little attention from scholars. After their return to England, William Archer was appointed Keeper of the Indian section of the Victoria and Albert Museum in 1954; while Mildred Archer became the Keeper in charge of prints and drawings at the India Office Library.

---

24. An art historian and a graduate of Oxford University, Mildred Archer was one of the first people to recognise the genre of Company Painting. This was the name given to work made by Indian artists in the eighteenth and nineteenth centuries, when they adapted their traditional techniques to reproduce drawings of natural history specimens and other works of art for consumption by European collectors. She also employed her considerable talents during her husband's postings in India to become an expert on paintings made by European artists under Indian patronage.

However, we begin our consideration of the role that women played in producing knowledge by examining in more detail the experiences of Lady Maria Nugent, as recounted in her *East India Journal*, from 1811 to 1815. Originally, Nugent wrote her journals for her family and friends, but they were first published for private circulation in 1839. Although neglected for many years, her writings have been taken up by contemporary scholars, most notably by Ashley L. Cohen. Her publication in 2014 offers an in-depth critical introduction of Maria Nugent's life, as well as an up-to-date edition of her *Journal* describing her sojourn in India, including the lengthy tour of the Upper Provinces that she undertook with her husband, Sir George Nugent, between 1812 and 1813.

LADY MARIA NUGENT: WIFE, MOTHER AND JOURNAL-WRITER

We previously encountered Lady Maria Nugent in Chapter 2, as she made her way up the Hooghly River towards Calcutta in January 1811 on the three-decker East Indiaman, *Baring*, in the company of her husband, General Sir George Nugent, who was on his way to take up his appointment as the new Commander-in-Chief of the army. Lady Nugent was particularly excited by the prospect of becoming acquainted with all the sights and experiences that this new land had to offer and she had the firm intention of devoting her time to accumulating mementoes to take back to England. Having had to bear the pain of leaving her four 'dear children' at home under the guardianship of Lord and Lady Buckingham, she resolved to make a collection of curiosities, drawings and paintings with which to delight them on her return. She was in good company in her enthusiastic pursuit of 'Indian treasures', as fellow members of the British community in Bengal, like Sir Elijah Impey, the Supreme Court Justice, and his wife Mary, were already established as patrons of the arts. They were soon to be joined by another avid collector. Francis Rawdon Hastings, Lord Moira, was appointed as the new Governor General in 1813 and, as we know from Chapter 3, he purloined the natural history drawings commissioned by Francis Buchanan-Hamilton for the EIC.[25] Aside from potential rivalry over the acquisition of paintings and drawings, the Nugents soon had another reason to dislike Lord Moira. Shortly after his arrival in Bengal, Lord Moira assumed the role of Commander-in-Chief of the army for himself, thus making Sir George's position redundant. Despite interventions on his behalf in England by his

---

25. See Chapter 3.

friend and patron, Lord Buckingham, who had the ear of the Prince Regent, George Nugent was unable to retain his post and he resigned. He chose to remain in India another year, until relieved of his command, but was obliged to live in considerably reduced circumstances.[26]

In her *East India Journal*, Maria Nugent recorded details of the people she met, their customs and culture, and the many different places she visited, including descriptions of architecture and manufacture. Her most vivid accounts were generated during a tour that she made with the General of the Upper Provinces between July 1812 and August 1813, travelling by boat along the River Ganges. Although her elite position in Indian colonial society entitled her to every available comfort, Maria Nugent was not immune to loneliness and the physical and mental hardships of life in the subcontinent, thousands of miles away from home. Her letters describe how she spent the first eighteen months of her residence in Calcutta coping with depression, caused by separation from her children, and physical illness that was at times life-threatening. She wrote to her friend Lady Temple, 'Ever since I left England, I have at times given myself up to a sort of Despair and my health has suffered severely from it. The last three days I have been in it still and unable to leave my room'.[27] Doubtless, the opportunity to get out of the fetid heat of Calcutta and see something of the countryside in the company of her husband was an occasion that lifted her spirits. Misfortunes awaited them on their return to Calcutta, however, as Lady Nugent was pregnant but miscarried soon afterwards and, as mentioned, they were greeted with the news that Sir George had lost his position to Lord Moira and that the last ship home before the monsoon had already departed.

However, as a loyal wife, Lady Nugent wrote to Lady Temple that she was glad that she had not gone home early, as her husband now needed her support.[28] During their tour of the Upper Provinces, she noted in her *Journal* that she and Sir George had often sat together on deck to watch the dawn breaking. Her comment offers a rare glimpse of domestic intimacy and an indication that, despite the pain of leaving her children behind, her decision to accompany her husband to India was motivated by genuine affection for him, even though at times, it had caused her much distress. Regardless of these difficulties, Maria Nugent's entries in her *East India Journal* demonstrate that she was a woman of spirit, unafraid to express her own critical opinions concerning the customs and sights that she encountered, particularly during her tour of the Upper Provinces. During their voyage up-river, she expressed

---

26. Cohen, *Lady Nugent's East India Journal*, xxviii.
27. Ibid., 359, xxviii.
28. Ibid., xxviii.

Figure 9.2. Watercolour of Maria, Lady Nugent in her tonjon with a retinue of twenty-four attendants. This painting records an evening outing in Calcutta on 24 April 1812, as described in the *East India Journal* of Lady Nugent. *Source:* Image courtesy of Simon Ray, London.

disgust on witnessing the way that the sick and the dying were abandoned on the riverbank. She approved of cremation as a hygienic method of disposing of the dead in view of the climate, but not the residue of half-burnt bodies and skulls being thrown into the river.[29]

Throughout both her tours in the East and West of the British Empire, Maria Nugent's writing proclaimed that she was staunchly Christian and, as described earlier and in Chapter 2, she had made it her mission whilst in Jamaica to convert 'the blackies', as she called them. She recorded that after successfully converting twenty-four members of her household in Jamaica, she treated all of them to celebratory cake and wine.[30] Childless at that time (two of her children were later born in Jamaica), Nugent appeared to use her 'whiteness' to armour herself against the racial hierarchy that she encountered. Its reification allowed elite women like her to claim personhood and critically, it also gave them the right to exclude 'the other'.[31] Anne Shea has interpreted Nugent's religious proselytising as a means of exercising her personal power over labouring black women. She cultivated a maternal relationship with them that externalised her own 'whiteness' as a 'thing' or an

29. Ibid., 75.
30. Anne Shea, 'Property in the White Self: Assessing Lady Nugent's Jamaican Journal', *Women's Studies* 30, no. 2 (2001): 179.
31. Ibid. See also Cheryl I. Harris, 'Whiteness as Property', *Harvard Law Review* 106, no. 8 (1993): 1707–1791.

object that could be owned, used and even lost.[32] It also provided her with a pathway for criticising male behaviour and misconduct in Jamaica, and she was particularly exercised by abuses towards women by 'white' males, citing in her *Journal* the case of a clergyman who beat his wife.[33] Her attempts to introduce critical knowledge about imperial misconduct, especially as a solitary white woman from the ruling class, were doubtless unwelcome in a domain free from the normative social codes of life in Britain. Nevertheless, she proved that she was not without a critical voice and was prepared to put on written record her disapproval of such abuses, rather than turn a blind eye to them.

Having returned to England from Jamaica in 1805, when Nugent arrived in Bengal nearly a decade later, we discover her still in critical voice; this time, however, she was prepared to view India much more tolerantly, as an immersive experience in which she actively engaged as a fascinated traveller. This was due partly to her growing maturity and experience of travel and also because until 1814, the EIC prohibited the proselytising of the indigenous population; although whilst in Bengal she did try to convert her servants, but only succeeded with her personal maid. Unlike her experience in Jamaica, throughout her time in India, Maria Nugent came into contact with a greater number of elite indigenous women, many of whom were of royal descent. During her tour of the Upper Provinces, she described a memorable meeting with the elderly Begum Samru,[34] who had begun her career as a nautch girl,[35] and eventually rose to rule over the eighteenth-century Kingdom of Sardhana, near Meerut. Begum Samru became a high-profile ally of the British in their fight against the Marathas and during the early nineteenth century, Europeans were accustomed to call on the famous Begum to pay their respects whilst on tour in Northern India.

Accompanied by two British gentlemen, who acted as translators from behind a curtain in the zenana, Nugent sat beside the elderly Begum, whose glory days as an alluring dancing girl were now long past, as was evident from her account of the Begum's clothes, which she described being more like a man's than a woman's. Nugent wrote, 'She wore trousers of cloth of gold, with shawl stockings, and a Hindoostanee – a dark turban but no hair to be seen; and an abundance of shawls wrapped around her in different ways'.[36] Nugent described the accoutrements of the zenana and its occupants as shabby; however, they made sufficient impression for her later to make a sketch from memory of the elderly Begum. As was customary during the

---

32. Shea, 'Property in the White Self', 175.
33. Ibid., 181. See also Cundall (ed.), *Lady Nugent's Journal*, 226.
34. Begum Samru: Also written 'Samroo'.
35. Nautch girl: Female dancer at the former Mughal Court.
36. Nugent, *East India Journal*, vol. 2, 51.

days of Mughal rule, the Begum offered gifts of jewels to her foreign visitors that Nugent dismissed disdainfully as fakes and quite unlike those previously lavished on British *'nabobs'*. Her acerbic remarks about the poor quality of the gifts and the shabbiness of the zenana allowed Nugent the opportunity to underline the Mughals' subjugation by the British and the reduced circumstances in which the Begum and her entourage now found themselves.

Maria Nugent also visited the Munni Begum (1720–1813) and other high-ranking members of the former Mughal Court, including the emperor. Now residing in Delhi and dispossessed of his political power, she once again observed their impoverished circumstances, particularly those of the women in the zenana. Nugent commented disparagingly in her *Journal* that the customary gifts of jewels were of glass, or mock stones, that appeared to her to be a sham and a means of keeping up appearances. In her opinion, this was an indication that now that they were subject to colonial rule, Mughal authority had waned.[37] Even though her *Journal* was initially intended for private consumption by her family and friends, such observations were clearly political in their intent to establish a narrative of British authority and political power over a vanquished enemy. Her *Journal* allowed her to stamp her own opinion on the current political situation in India and to demonstrate that she too could speak with the authoritative voice of British supremacy, usually reserved for men. Her journal-writing enabled her to express personal opinions as a woman, and also her superiority as a visitor who had condescended to meet these ladies, now divested of their power, but who yet remained 'curiosities' to imperial eyes, not least because of their seclusion.

By focusing on these women's garments, outward appearance and the details of the dilapidated conditions in the zenana, Nugent sought to deprive them of their status as formerly influential females in Mughal politics. Isolated now from contemporary sources of power and influence, they lived in dark, shabby quarters.[38] Although she represented the zenana as a space full of intrigue, Nugent was unable to comprehend that just because these women lived in seclusion, it did not detach them from any substantive political function of their own.[39] As Ashley Cohen has pointed out in her introduction, Lady Nugent proved incapable of understanding the political machinations afoot during her visit to the zenana of the Mughal Court at Delhi, when the emperor's mother, Qudsia Begum, tried to engage her in negotiations on the subject of the king's allowance.[40] Meanwhile, in contrast to these sequestered women, Nugent had the freedom to move at will through their country,

---

37. Cohen, *Lady Nugent's East India Journal*, xxxi.
38. Chauhan, 'Critical Review of *Lady Nugent's East India Journal*', 209.
39. Cohen, *Lady Nugent's East India Journal*, xli.
40. Ibid.

enjoying mornings on deck in the sunshine with her husband, as their boat slowly moved up-river. These once-powerful women of the Mughal Empire were guarded by eunuchs, whom Nugent described as 'great, fat disgusting looking creatures, who seemed to have the whole government of the zenana in their power'.[41] Her description of the Begum Samru, a once-beautiful dancing girl, as looking more like a man in old age deprived her of femininity; whilst the eunuchs, already emasculated, were now mere disgusting creatures and passive bystanders to the rule of the all-powerful British EIC.

A woman's private journal, with its reflections on the colonised individual and the colony, offers its own way of analysing and appropriating the occupied land; and as Lisa Nevarez has observed, 'Military conquest alone does not determine the colonial space'.[42] Nugent's description of the passing landscape and its buildings, especially important historical sites like the Taj Mahal, allowed her to objectify India through travel writing. But she also took possession of the objects that she saw, which she demonstrated by an act of vandalism when she carved her name at the top of one of the minarets in the Taj Mahal. By her symbolic act of defacing one of India's most beautiful and revered monuments, Nugent was appropriating this mausoleum to a beloved wife and recreating it as a now-colonised space. As an elite female of the colonial ruling class, Nugent's disfigurement of the minaret was an attempt to usurp the mystique and power with which Mumtaz Mahal (1593–1631) had so beguiled the Emperor Shah Jahan (1592–1666).

Whilst in Bengal, Maria Nugent also made her views on miscegenation and 'improper' marriages with 'native' or Eurasian women known through the medium of her *Journal*.[43] One entry referred to the distasteful sight of mixed-race couples dancing together at a ball given for the purpose of allowing them to meet one another. Although her reforming zeal was less evident in India than it had been in Jamaica, she remained intensely religious. During her stay in India, she took steps to actively prevent mixed-race marriages by reforming the Bengal Orphan Society, an organisation that 'groomed half caste or mixed-race women for marriages with European men'. Lady Nugent was not alone in her strict moral stance over unattached 'white' men consorting with mixed-race local females and inappropriate social practices. Some decades later, another woman also made her trenchant views known to the general public about inappropriate behaviour on the part of the colonisers who came out to live and work in India from Britain. Obliged to earn her

---

41. Ibid., 81.

42. Lisa Nevarez, 'Inscribing the "Taaje" Gender and Colonization in Lady Maria Nugent's India Journal', in *The Male Empire under the Female Gaze: The British Raj and the Memsahib*, eds. Susmita Roye and Rajeshwar Mittapalli (Amherst, NY: Cambria Press, 2013), 39.

43. Mukhopadhyay, 'Review of *Lady Nugent's East India Journal*'.

own living, Emma Roberts worked as the first female European journalist in India, and through her employment became a well-known arbiter of the correct way for men and women to conduct themselves in both the domestic and public spheres. Her many publications as a journalist included travel writing, although it is doubtful whether she was able to experience first-hand all of the objects and places that she wrote about, therefore her reportage was reliant upon secondary accounts.

EMMA ROBERTS: THE FIRST FEMALE
JOURNALIST IN INDIA

As a spinster, Emma Roberts's decision to remain in India after the death of her married sister in 1832 was made possible by her ability to support herself financially. For a couple of years, Roberts earned her living as a journalist, writing for various British and Indian publications, until ill-health forced her to return to England. This experience gave her a unique insight into the ways colonial society functioned that she used when writing her books. Her work as a journalist in India allowed her to voice critical opinions regarding the conduct of the British community, particularly concerning the way that they treated the indigenous population. She deplored the shabby treatment and insolence that so often marked social relations between colonised and coloniser. One of her most famous books was *The East India Voyager*, published in 1839, in which she dispensed advice to young men and women who were about to embark on their first posting to India. As well as practical recommendations about items to take with them, she schooled them in the 'dos and don'ts' of colonial etiquette and the correct way to behave.

Roberts paid particular attention to the domestic circumstances of the wives, whose presence she viewed as an important antidote to banishing irregular domestic arrangements, where a British man lived with a mixed-race mistress or *bibi*, who presided over his household according to her own customs. In her writing she spoke directly to those *memsahibs* who would be responsible for overseeing the correct management of the household and its servants, seeing their mission as one of 'fostering a sense of restraint in her spouse and instilling in him a sense of satisfaction with the "calm delights of wedded life"'.[44] From henceforth, the *memsahib* would be responsible for promoting Christian values, proper habits of economy and a sense of moral rectitude in the domestic sphere over which she now ruled and which ultimately would bring its influence to bear upon the governance of the empire.

---

44. Shah, '"Barbaric Pearl and Gold"', 39. See also Emma Roberts, *Scenes and Characteristics of Hindostan, with Sketches of Anglo-Indian Society* (London: W. H. Allen & Co., 1835), vol. 1, 27.

Roberts advised newcomers to India to maintain their distance, as over-familiarity with the colonised subject would set them on the slippery slope towards undermining British prestige.[45] However, she believed that knowing how to speak the local language was key to avoiding many of the disagreements and misunderstandings that occurred between colonised and coloniser. Therefore, she urged the young Griffin, as the EIC cadets were known, to make it a priority to study the local language of the district where he had been posted and to speedily engage the services of a '*moonshee* [*sic*]'.[46] Roberts opined, 'Without a competent knowledge of Hindostanee, he can never hope to succeed in any public department or emerge from a state of *Griffinhood*'.[47] Despite referring to them in racist terms as 'black fellows', her advice regarding the necessity of learning the local language was founded on the view that Anglo-Indians[48] had alienated the local population with their haughty and imperious manners, treating them little better than rough brutes.

Furthermore, Roberts considered that the British inherently despised Indian customs and their outlook upon life, however elevated the Indian's intellectual and social level.[49] As a journalist, she had the opportunity to confirm this view as she was familiar with the comments expressed in Indian periodicals about British intolerance towards them. Indian periodicals expressed the view that the British maintained a strong prejudice towards the indigenous community and claimed that a 'native' would never do anything for them except for money.[50] She asserted that Anglo-Indians treated their servants shabbily by engaging their services and taking their product, but not paying them adequately. For their part, servants tried to exact their revenge by refusing to perform certain duties that they said were contrary to their religion.[51] Roberts may have been mistaken in criticising servants' excuses of religion for refusing to perform certain tasks, as it was of course contrary to Muslim and Hindu beliefs to handle any animal products related to the pig or the cow.[52]

On the subject of food, she warned Europeans who refrained from eating pork and beef in order not to offend the 'natives' that this could lead to a situation where showing too great a respect for idolatry implied 'a mistaken

---

45. Roberts, *The East India Voyager*, vol. 1, 117.

46. *Munshi*: In the Mughal Empire and British India, *munshis* were teachers of the native language and other subjects, as well as secretaries and translators employed by Europeans.

47. Roberts, *The East India Voyager*, vol. 1, 105.

48. In this context, Anglo-Indians mean those 'white' British residents who came out to India to work for the EIC.

49. Roberts, *The East India Voyager*, vol. 1, 106.

50. Ibid., 107.

51. Ibid., 109.

52. As is well-known, in 1857, a rumour began to spread through the ranks of the sepoys of the EIC's Bengal army that new gun cartridges issued for the Enfield rifle were smeared with cow and pig fat, and disaster ensued for all concerned in the Great Revolution.

compliance with the superstitious notions of people whose religious belief has assumed the lowest and most degraded forms'.[53] While deploring the shabby treatment of the indigenous population by her fellow Anglo-Indians, Roberts firmly maintained her own Christian moral values, condemning anyone who showed tolerance towards 'native' religion and culture as 'degrading' to British standards. In today's parlance, her attitude might be regarded as 'virtue signalling' by someone who was as prejudiced against Indians and their way of life as any of her compatriots and convinced, like them, of her own racial and social superiority. Little appears to have changed in the decades since Maria Nugent had made it her mission to civilise 'the blackies' and save their souls.

Roberts was on surer ground when she offered practical guidance to the traveller on what personal items to take out to India. Her recommendations to would-be *memsahibs* stimulated a two-way flow of ideas and cultural exchange. As returnees they became responsible for the diffusion of Indian culture in Britain through the introduction of objects such as shawls and other garments, as well as culinary skills. Her advice ranged from advising women to leave all jewellery behind, except a watch, as the 'natives' were very clever at interpreting any ornaments, to supplying a reading list of suitable books for the Griffin to read on the voyage out, so that he might usefully employ the idle hours at sea. Her suggestion that newcomers to India take portfolios of books, prints and drawings of fashionable objects that could be easily copied facilitated the circulation and exchange of new ideas between the metropole and the periphery. As Nupur Chaudhuri has contended, from the mid-nineteenth century, it was through these innovations and imports that a segment of middle-class Victorian women in Britain came to know the Indian Empire.[54] Conversely, as the century progressed, women setting up home in India became agents, who were responsible for importing British possessions, customs and culinary practices into the colonial domestic sphere, which, in turn, were adapted by their servants and the merchants who supplied their needs.

However imbalanced, imperial collecting became a form of cultural exchange, as many items of interest, souvenirs and other collectibles were sent back to Britain. As Maya Jasanoff has intimated, the foreign objects and curiosities that men and women brought back with them played an important part in shaping British images of empire at home.[55] The introduction of objects such as Indian cuisine, clothing and other artefacts into the homes

53. Roberts, *The East India Voyager*, vol. 1, 117.
54. Nupur Chaudhuri, 'Shawls, Jewelry, Curry and Rice in Victorian Britain', in *Western Women and Imperialism: Complicity and Resistance*, eds. Nupur Chaudhuri and Margaret Strobel (Bloomington and Indianapolis: Indiana University Press, 1992), 232.
55. Jasanoff, 'Collectors of Empire', 112.

of the dominant coloniser was not only mutually beneficial to the economic systems of the respective countries, it also introduced a complex new dimension into the politics of colonial cultural interchange.[56] For example, in the hands of an inventive Indian chef, the spicy South Indian sauce became mulligatawny soup, derived from the Tamil words *miḷagāy/miḷagu* (chilli/pepper) and *taṇṇi* (water). This resulted in a reciprocal exchange of culinary ideas, as curries, rice and kedgeree became staples of the middle-class table in Britain, after returning 'old India hands' introduced these dishes and which in time were adopted by other households.[57]

Despite her inherent prejudices as a member of the colonising community, Roberts was a rare female who managed to support herself by working for a living in India – a unique achievement. She overcame the misfortune of her sister's early death, which left her stranded in India without adequate financial means, to escape the confines of the colonial feminine space. Roberts held radical opinions and views on the shortcomings of the British in India, encouraged by her apprenticeship in Bath at the home of Letitia Landon. But like Maria Nugent, she was unable to set aside her innate prejudice against what she considered were the idolatrous religious beliefs and the degrading lifeways of the 'natives', and she cautioned newcomers to India against succumbing to them, as earlier colonisers had done.

For a time during the eighteenth century, British men had lived harmoniously with Indian women, who raised their mixed-race children, even sending some home to Britain to be educated. They wore Indian clothes, ate Indian food and embraced Indian culture and its ways of living.[58] But by the time that Emma Roberts was reporting as the first British female journalist in India, outlooks had narrowed and despite her talent, she saw it as a duty to uplift and instruct the indigenous population. Although being remarkable for forging her own way as a professional woman in India at a time when public opinion considered such women odd or even suspect, the objects produced by Emma Roberts, notably her writing, cannot really be viewed as uncomplicated contributions towards the production of knowledge. The didactic tone which permeated most of her writing was founded upon the stern belief in the superiority of a Victorian Christian ethos that prevented her from showing true empathy towards India and its people, thereby gaining affective knowledge about them. Her views might best be understood in light of her own less than felicitous domestic situation, as she wrote, 'there cannot be a more

---

56. Chaudhuri, *Shawls*, 232.
57. In 1833, a year after her sister's death, Emma Roberts went home to England due to ill-health. She returned to India in 1839, where she died a year later. During the 1830s, she edited the sixty-fourth edition of Maria Rundell's book, *A New System of Domestic Cookery*, first published in 1806.
58. Jasanoff, 'Collectors of Empire', 106.

wretched situation than that of a young woman who has been induced to follow the fortunes of a married sister, under the delusive expectations that she will exchange the privations attached to limited means in England, for the far-famed luxuries of the East'.[59] While her circumstances and didactic attitude restricted Roberts's ability to cross boundaries and foster a genuinely sympathetic outlook towards India, the subject of the next section, Fanny Parkes, provides a more encouraging example of a woman who truly attempted to engage with India and its people.

FANNY PARKES: INDEPENDENT TRAVELLER

Emma Roberts was not alone in pursuing an independent life, as another redoubtable woman, Fanny Parkes (1794–1875), became well-known for her lone tours of Upper India; although of course, she was always accompanied by a retinue of servants. Like Roberts, Parkes also wrote about her experiences, famously publishing her memoirs, *Wanderings of a Pilgrim in Search of the Picturesque*, in 1850.[60] They were the result of twenty-four years of keeping a journal, starting in 1822, about her life in India with her husband, whom she had accompanied on his postings, notably to Allahabad. Unlike Emma Roberts, Parkes had more freedom and security to get to know India. She did not have to earn her living from writing about her travels, as she enjoyed the financial support of her husband. She had the leisure and the resources to travel independently wherever she wished during the cold weather, while her husband remained at his post.

In her draft notes on 'Indian Women',[61] Mildred Archer has compared Emma Roberts rather unfavourably to her contemporary, Fanny Parkes. Archer declared that Roberts did not have Parkes's enquiring mind and insatiable appetite for information, nor did she comment on Indian painting, which was, of course, Archer's personal passion. However, like Roberts, Fanny Parkes held equally strong opinions about Indian society and its customs, condemning, for instance, the practice of *suttee*.[62] Despite her robust criticisms of aspects of India, Parkes's writing projected an altogether more relaxed attitude towards the people and places that she encountered in her wanderings throughout the North of the country, describing them as 'vagabonding'.

---

59. Roberts, *Scenes and Characteristics*, vol. 1, 33.
60. Fanny Parkes Parlby, *Wanderings of a Pilgrim in Search of the Picturesque, During Four-and-Twenty Years in the East: With Revelations of Life in the Zenāna* (London: Pelham Richardson, 1850).
61. BL/Mss Eur F236/488: Mildred Archer, 'On Indian Women'.
62. Parkes, *Wanderings of a Pilgrim*, vol. 1, 91–95.

Parkes was as curious as Emma Roberts and Maria Nugent were to learn about the life of women in purdah and she went to great lengths to obtain permission to visit a zenana. She eventually received an invitation in 1835 from her friend, Colonel Gardner (1770–1835),[63] who had married an elite member of the Cambay family and resided at his country estate at Khasgunge in Uttar Pradesh. Accompanied by her husband, Fanny arrived there on 27 February 1835 in order to witness marriage ceremonies. She stayed several days and visited the Colonel's zenana, although her husband was obliged to return to his work. She spent time with the Begum, whom Fanny described as 'a very lively little old woman [. . .] magnificently dressed in pearls diamonds and emeralds [. . .] so that she looked more like a lump of glittering gold and crimson and pearls than a living woman'.[64] Even though, as Fanny observed, the women's days in the zenana were monotonous, much of them filled by eating opium and sleeping, she refrained from critical comments. Unlike Maria Nugent, she concentrated on learning the family history and minutely describing the details of their living quarters and apparel. It appeared that Colonel Gardner was an amateur botanist, named 'William Linnaeus' after the great man, who was his godfather. A gentleman of true cosmopolitan tastes, Gardner had laid out an extensive and beautiful garden at Khasgunge, where he had spared no expense in cultivating many flowers, shrubs, fine trees and rare plants. At its centre, he had built a delightful shady pavilion and it was one of the pleasures of the Begum and her attendants to spend the day in this garden. According to Parkes, the Begum herself, although not a botanist, was very knowledgeable about the medicinal qualities of the Indian plants and the dyes that could be produced from them, that were in daily use in the zenana and about which Parkes was fascinated to learn.[65]

In contrast to the moralising tone of Emma Roberts's writing, Fanny Parkes's observations offered a rare glimpse into a world appreciated by the few British men who were privileged to cross this divide and experience life in the domestic sphere of Indian elites. Her appreciation of India and the lives of the people whom she encountered offered first-hand knowledge untainted by political or religious opinions that were biased in favour of the British. Therefore, her journals have proved to be of lasting worth for the affective knowledge they provided, gathered from authentic sources about the ways in which some British men and their families had formerly lived very congenial and contented lives with Indians, adopting their customs, costumes and cuisine. But as we have seen throughout this study, by the mid-nineteenth

---

63. For further information about William Linnaeus Gardner, see Narindar Saroop, *Gardner of Gardner's Horse: 2nd Lancers, Indian Army* (New Delhi: Palit & Palit, 1983).

64. Parkes, *Wanderings of a Pilgrim*, 394–395.

65. Ibid., 397.

century, the conversation had changed, as knowledge production became much more formalised and intimacy with the indigenous population was proscribed. The rhetoric had hardened against men of an earlier generation, like Colonel Gardner, who were willing to cross boundaries to appreciate the opportunities for such mutually beneficial co-existence.

By the middle of the century, the number of 'white' females who came out to India to enjoy the security and respectability of marriage to an elite British officer was still small compared to the number of males. Respectfully addressed as *memsahibs,* they remained primarily confined to the colonial domestic sphere, where they were charged with managing the household and servants; meanwhile, socialising was usually restricted to activities at the 'whites-only' club. On occasion, they ventured out to perform philanthropic duties; or the more intrepid might accompany their husbands on their tours up-country during the cold weather. Their predecessors, women like Maria Nugent, the redoubtable Miss Roberts and Fanny Parkes, were privileged to enjoy comparatively more freedom in exploring and writing about the wonders they encountered in the subcontinent, which also allowed them to visit Indians in their homes, including the zenana. The next section considers the situation of women of a lower socio-economic class, who did not enjoy the advantages of financial security and education that gave these women the self-confidence to know India on their own terms and later write about it. Obliged to fend for themselves in a male-dominated society, their impecunious and lone status was regarded with suspicion and they were often branded as prostitutes, even though their behaviour exhibited no evidence of such activity.

LONE WOMEN: OR, PROSTITUTES BY ANY OTHER NAME

By the mid-nineteenth century in India, the term 'prostitute' had become a catch-all word that stigmatised non-elite, lower-class women living without appropriate male protection. The moral climate in British India had become much more censorious towards women, both European and of mixed race, who endeavoured to live within 'white' colonial society without the support of a husband or other reputable male relative. The lack of a spouse placed such women in a vulnerable position and laid them open to accusations of being prostitutes, even though they were often without foundation. Furthermore, it tainted the reputation of any man who associated with them, whatever his intentions, as we shall see in the example described below.

In March 1848, a rather curious court case was widely reported in the Bombay newspapers of an army officer, Lieutenant William Hervey Walton, and a woman, named variously as Ellen Julia Veronica Anglahm, or Barnwell, and now known as Mrs De Souza. On the evening of 23 February, the couple gave false testimony to the Archdeacon of Bombay when applying for a marriage licence, with the intention of being wed the following day. Apparently, the reason for the haste was because Walton had been posted elsewhere; and after both swore to the Archdeacon that there was no lawful impediment to prevent their marriage, he duly issued them with the licence. But it soon transpired that they were both still married to other people and had the marriage taken place, they would have been bigamists. It was halted by the intervention of Lieutenant Walton's fellow officers, who had got wind of the affair and quickly appraised his commanding officer of the situation. Enquiries revealed that since 1840, the prospective bride had been the lawful wife of Monoel Edward De Souza, a Goan of Portuguese descent, from whom she had been separated for some years. Furthermore, according to an announcement in the *Bombay Times* on 7 March 1846, Walton had also contracted a marriage two years previously with a woman named Mary Jane Dobson, who originally came from Lancashire in the North of England.[66]

As a result, Lieutenant William Hervey Walton, a commissioned officer of the 29th Regiment Native Infantry, was summoned to appear before a court martial on 1 March 1848 on charges of perjury and of having falsely denied the report of his intended marriage to his superior officer.[67] At his court martial, Walton denied the charge of perjury and, somewhat disingenuously, stated that he believed that Mrs De Souza's (formerly Anglahm/ Barnwell) first marriage was null and void, having been assured of this by 'all the Roman Catholic authorities and the family of Mr De Souza'.[68] All parties believed that Mrs De Souza's marriage had been dissolved by a Catholic priest, although in fact he had no power to do any such thing.[69] Walton was able to defend himself successfully and to deny the charge of perjuring himself to the Archdeacon because an oath in a private matter, such as obtaining a marriage licence, could not be deemed perjury. No mention of his own marital status was made at his court martial and although Walton was acquitted of all charges, he was disgraced. His claim to the Court that he believed Mrs De Souza's earlier marriage had been dissolved implied that he knew it had taken place, but he had taken no steps to verify this directly with her husband, Monoel Edward De Souza, who was still alive and currently living in Bombay. Although he was acquitted of the charges by the court martial, colonial society did not exonerate his behaviour and Walton was accused of

---

66. Announcement in the *Bombay Times* (7 March 1846).
67. Report of Court Martial of Lieutenant William Hervey Walton in the *Bombay Times* and *Journal of Commerce* (29 March 1848).
68. Ibid.
69. Ibid.

disgraceful conduct unbecoming the character of an officer and a gentleman and forced to resign his commission in June 1848.

As stated, although some women were obliged to resort to prostitution, colonial society suspected any woman of being a prostitute, who, for whatever reason, did not live with a legal spouse or a respectable male relative, unless there were attenuating circumstances, as in the case of Emma Roberts, who had benefited from a middle-class education in England and possessed talent as a writer. Even so, Roberts's situation was still considered highly unusual. Meanwhile, when the aforesaid Mrs De Souza was summoned to appear before the court martial for purposes of identification, she described her occupation as a milliner. She claimed to have returned to Bombay after leaving her husband, in order to set up in business as a milliner, a service that was much in demand at that time and considered a respectable occupation for lower-class women. Notwithstanding, colonial society adopted a harsh and unforgiving attitude towards any woman who appeared to deviate from its strict moral codes, condemning as a prostitute lone females who endeavoured to support themselves, even when following a reputable trade like millinery.

Not only were the couple accused of being potential bigamists, Mrs De Souza's married name and also her maiden name, Anglahm, indicated that the would-be bride was of mixed race – that of Goan-Portuguese descent – and therefore unacceptable to mix socially within colonial society. Public opinions expressed in the newspapers about Walton's misconduct ranged from those who accused him of committing adultery with a married woman, even though she had been living independently from her husband for some years; to those who said that if it was the case that Walton truly believed she was not married, then he was guilty of proposing marriage to a woman who had lived for years as another man's mistress. Whatever shades of opinions were expressed, Anglahm/De Souza was unanimously categorised as a prostitute.[70] Outraged correspondents continued to write to the press throughout April and one of them even wondered that as this woman was a prostitute, would she be entitled to benefits from the Military Fund in the same way as 'ladies'. Furthermore, what about any offspring with which she might be encumbered, irrespective of who the father was. The Editor replied, rather dolefully, that he was afraid that under the law, she would indeed be entitled to benefits from the Military Fund. He concluded that 'the only remedy was that no person with one atom of manhood, or feeling of self-respect would marry a common prostitute'.[71] And anyone who did was beneath contempt and should not be allowed to continue in military service.

---

70. From the *Telegraph and Courier*, reprinted in the *Bombay Times* (29 March 1848).
71. Letter to the Editor in the *Bombay Times* (1 April 1848; printed 15 April).

Walton's army service record left the matter in no doubt by stating bluntly that he had 'married a common prostitute', even though the marriage had not actually taken place. 'By leaving a card at their mess superscribed 'Mr and Mrs Walton', he had 'wilfully offered a gross insult to his commanding officer and fellow officers', as they would now be obliged to recognise the marriage and receive the bride socially, something that was unthinkable if indeed she was a prostitute and, even worse, one of mixed race.[72] Lest there be any doubt of the military authorities' opinion of Walton's suitability to continue to hold the king's commission, his service record also referred to two false drafts made out to a 'native' drawn on funds that he did not possess, thus condemning him as a fraudster.[73] The final charge flung at Walton was that he had acquired a colloquial proficiency in the Hindustani language and let the side down by associating too closely with the indigenous population; therefore, his disgrace was absolute.

Although the circumstances of Walton's proposed marriage were highly irregular and it is likely that both parties were intending to commit bigamy, the malicious manner in which it was reported, both in the proceedings of the court martial and subsequently in newspapers and letters, indicates a deeply divided and racially prejudiced society. It was assumed that unattached women must be prostitutes, who were seeking any means possible of entrapping the unwary male. As one newspaper rather cynically commented, 'Mr Walton's tastes are about the most singular that can be imagined, in wishing to marry a female whom anyone could have had without the bother of a marriage ceremony'.[74] His reasoning being that as members of the military and other European men had access to prostitutes, why would any man go to the bother of marrying one of them? But this begs the question of the true nature of the relationship between Walton and Mrs De Souza. Until the Matrimonial Causes Act of 1857, it was impossible to obtain a divorce and even then, it had to be procured by a private Act of Parliament, which was available only to the very wealthy few. It would appear that many ordinary people were obliged to commit bigamy unless they lived openly out of wedlock, as many undoubtedly did; but if discovered, they were roundly condemned.

Although the case described above became something of a *cause célèbre* throughout the Bombay Presidency, it was extremely difficult for a woman at any level of society to exist independently in India, far from home, without the prerequisite protection of a respectable male. Based on comments made by Mauger Fitzhugh Monk in his letters home from Mussoorie, it would seem Walton's misdemeanours, although sensationalised in the Bombay

---

72. Report of Court Martial of Lieutenant William Hervey Walton (29 March 1848).
73. BL/IOR/L/MIL/12/73, 211: Lieutenant William Hervey Walton's record of military service.
74. Editorial article, *Bombay Times* (1 April 1848), *Times of India*, 263.

press chiefly because of his position as an army officer, were not uncommon. The more distant the location from the great cities of the Presidencies, the greater the likelihood of sexual misconduct. Monk's letters described a colonial society that was riven by petty jealousies and calumnies, and Mussoorie as a community where everyone looked out for themselves. As discussed, Monk had bought himself out of his commission in the army with financial assistance from his father after he had been accused of living in open adultery with a European woman, whom he had allegedly purchased from her husband, something which he denied.[75] Whatever the truth of these allegations, Monk admitted that adultery was rife and that after coveting another man's wife, it was enough to walk off with her. He claimed that he had been offered his comrade's wife, 'a fresh pretty importation from Limerick for thirty-five rupees and a case-bottle of Grog!'[76] It is therefore little wonder that in such a degenerate moral climate, lone women were held in contempt by men, especially by the soldiery, and frequently labelled as prostitutes, whatever their true circumstances.

Thus, without adequate education and the support of a well-to-do spouse, the outlook for women in colonial India throughout the nineteenth century until the end of empire was bleak. The prospect of any achievement by them in producing knowledge, except in very limited circumstances, like the reciprocal exchange of domestic commodities and luxury items between the periphery and the metropole, was virtually non-existent. Only the few highly motivated and educated women like Emma Roberts, Fanny Parkes and the wealthy, privileged Lady Nugent were successful. There is one scholar, however, whose interest in women in India united most of those described in this chapter – Mildred Archer, the wife of an ICS officer. She used her time in the country to become an expert in Indian paintings and even though her interest did not extend, as far as we know, to helping socially excluded and poorer women, she is a worthy exponent of the capabilities and achievements of women in contributing towards knowledge about India.

CONCLUDING REMARKS: MILDRED ARCHER AND WOMEN IN INDIA

As explained in Chapter 2 and also earlier in the text, Mildred Archer's contribution to producing knowledge about India is not in doubt. She was able to apply her Oxford University education and knowledge of art history to undertake pioneering research into the ways in which Indian artists adjusted

75. Monk, *Letters of a Mussoorie Merchant*, 73.
76. Ibid., 58.

their styles to suit the requirements of the British, who became avid collectors during their occupation of India. In her capacity as an art historian, Mildred Archer's many publications also included those about British artists like Thomas Daniell (1749–1840), and his nephew William (1769–1837), who, with many others, had taken up residence in Bengal in search of commissions from their fellow countrymen. As Archer noted, the wealth and the generosity of *nabobs,* both Indian and English varieties, attracted many portrait painters to India. As many British wanted souvenirs to take home with them on completion of their tours of duty, views of landscapes and architectural wonders were popular subjects that could be rendered in the style understood by European visitors. There was also a brisk trade in miniature paintings, required by those who wished to send likenesses home to their families, and which continued well into the nineteenth century until overtaken by photography.

Soon, Indian artists were painting subjects that would appeal to British tastes in subtle colours, to which Archer gave the broad definition of 'Company Painting'. Building upon her scholarship, contemporary scholars have gone much further in their research, understanding how these artists came from a range of backgrounds. Possessing a variety of artisanal skills, Indian painters adapted them to produce exquisite work, not only for decorative but also for scientific purposes. Following her return to England after the end of the Second World War, Archer continued her work at the India Office Library, where she took up a post as the Keeper in charge of prints and drawings. Whilst her services to the study of Indian painting and its related social history are indisputable, it is to a consideration of her own evaluation of the women in India who had proceeded her sojourn there that these final paragraphs are directed.

Mildred Archer considered Fanny Parkes's *The Wanderings of a Pilgrim in Search of the Picturesque* as 'one of the most sprightly and vivid of the journals written by women in India in the nineteenth century'.[77] She understood Parkes as someone who was never bored, who never reviled India, and even though at times depressed during her twenty-four years in the country, soon recovered her good spirits and found something to interest her and study. Presented with gifts on her departure after visiting an Indian household, Parkes was often the subject of gossip and insinuations, namely that she had gone for the sake of the presents. Angry at being called avaricious, Parkes rejected these criticisms from people who had no curiosity respecting 'native' life and manners and regarded them with contempt.[78] Archer recorded in her notes that she first encountered Fanny Parkes in Mussoorie, while she was staying at the house of her relative, a Miss Swetenham, where she discovered

---

77. BL/Mss Eur F236/488: Un-edited notes of Mildred Archer. See section on Fanny Parkes.
78. Parkes, *The Wanderings of a Pilgrim,* vol. 2, 216.

two volumes of *The Wanderings*. She delighted in walking the same paths that Fanny had galloped along over a century earlier in 1838 and like Fanny, she too marvelled at the snows on the surrounding mountains. In her notes, Archer described how Fanny had spent the years after arriving back in England at St. Leonards-on-Sea, a provincial seaside town, nostalgically editing her journals surrounded by many of the Indian curiosities that she had collected during her years of wanderings. Archer perhaps empathised with the ennui felt by the returned traveller for those days of colour and excitement that had marked her own years spent in India.

In contrast to her empathy with Fanny Parkes, Mildred Archer's judgement of Emma Roberts was less generous. Although admiring of Roberts and judging her to be tough, having much in common with Parkes, Mildred Archer thought she lacked the latter's sensitivity. She accused her of not writing with such a vivid style, nor, unlike Fanny, reacting with such freshness to the Indian scene. She did not possess Fanny's light-hearted and carefree attitude to her travels. This may have been because Roberts was a professional writer who had to make her living as a journalist and was therefore emotionally detached from what she wrote. Plagued as Roberts was by the Victorian desire to uplift and improve, Archer judged her as solemn and serious. Furthermore, according to Archer, she had no feeling for the arts and never referred to Indian painting. Nevertheless, she remarked that although Roberts had 'no great love of India', ever the professional writer, she was anxious to return there in 1839 in order to compare the changes that had occurred after the abolition of the EIC's commercial privileges and the introduction of steam navigation and overland communications. In this ambition, Roberts appeared to be a professional and dispassionate journalist, and an unbiased observer, keen to report the facts without sentimentality.

In her unedited notes, Archer described a journey allegedly made by Roberts in the company of three gentlemen who, setting out from Mussoorie, had trekked across the Himalayas to Simla. According to Archer, quoting from *Scenes and Characteristics of Hindostan*, Roberts and her companions experienced very rugged conditions on their trek, camping in and scrambling through snow that was frequently knee-deep, sometimes up to their waists.[79] Although Roberts addressed every aspect of life in India in her book, it appears that she omitted to include details of her Himalayan trek.[80] When drawing up her notes, Archer might have been using an edition of Roberts's book that is no longer in print when she described how Roberts maintained

---

79. BL/Mss Eur F236/488: Mildred Archer quoting Roberts's book, *Scenes and Characteristics of Hindostan*, vol. 2, 10, 46.
80. As an acute observer of Anglo-Indian society, Roberts reported on every detail from the 'slovenliness of shops' and 'boarding houses', to 'funerals' and 'Bengal brides'.

that she was prepared beforehand for all the perils that this trek would entail, namely that they would encounter cold and hunger and the rebellion of their servants. However, Archer's notes cast some doubt on whether Roberts actually experienced the trek. Roberts maintained that despite the hardship, she valiantly pushed on, stating, 'Our ardour in the pursuit of the picturesque led us to think lightly of such things'.[81] Roberts also reported that she was launched with considerable celerity across these fast-rushing streams, from the higher to the lower bank perched on a wooden slide.[82] In her notes, Archer wondered what Emma Roberts wore on this very demanding expedition and enquired 'did she clamber in her voluminous petticoats and skirts and if so, did they not deter her from crossing roaring Himalayan streams on rope bridges and tree trunks over the river?'[83] If conditions crossing the mountain ranges were as treacherous as Roberts described, it would have been virtually impossible for even the toughest female traveller to undertake such a journey, especially in unsuitable clothing, a fact which did not escape Archer's attention.

As a journalist, Emma Roberts's stated mission was to represent her impressions of India to her readers and above all, to invite them to share her perspective of the ups and downs of Anglo-Indian life, all conveyed against a background of the picturesque. Her reporting was based on encounters, hearsay and what she read in newspapers and other sources, and not always from first-hand knowledge that she herself had discovered or experienced. Therefore, it is possible that Roberts's description of her trek was not written entirely from personal experience and that she reported what others had told her about the conditions during such a journey across the Himalayas, gathering information during her stay in Mussoorie. Her descriptions were intended to thrill a home audience with tales of exotic adventures in picturesque locations. Therefore, her writing might better be considered as reportage, based on others' experiences, which may explain Archer's comment that Roberts's prose lacked the freshness of Fanny Parkes's first-hand accounts of her adventures.

The ability of women to produce first-hand knowledge about India was constrained by many factors. Chief amongst them was their inability to roam at will and enjoy the freedom to react to their surroundings and the objects that they found in them, in the same way as men were able to do. Even an independent and intrepid reporter like Emma Roberts was unlikely to have experienced all the events that she wrote about. Maria Nugent and Fanny Parkes's more privileged social position accorded them greater scope, but

---

81. Archer quoting *Scenes and Characteristics of Hindostan*, vol. 1, 6–7.
82. Ibid., vol. 2, 46.
83. Ibid.

they too lacked the depth of scholarship and experience to produce original knowledge on the same terms as men. Female contributions, like their lives, were confined primarily to the colonial domestic sphere, where, as agents for the cultural exchange of objects, they shaped traditions, use of language, and culinary practices. Their main achievement as women who had experienced life in India was that they transported their knowledge of the domestic sphere back with them to Britain, where the practices and objects that they had encountered became ingrained in aspects of British life. Mildred Archer's scholarship concerning Indian art and the indigenous artists who adjusted their styles to suit British requirements has made an enduring contribution to the collaborative ways in which colonial knowledge was accrued. In these achievements, she was the equal of any man.

Afterword

Only those who have never really experienced life across and between cul-
tures can afford the illusion, after all, that it is a simple affair. Nor is it a
question of blithely apportioning blame, or claiming that this or that group
deliberately set out to distort what should have been limpid and obvious.[1]

The germ of an idea for this book began more than fifteen years ago when, browsing in a bookshop at Yangon's Mingaladon Airport, I discovered that an assistant army surgeon named Clement Williams was born and brought up in the parish of Saint Decuman, Watchet, not far from my home in Somerset. The idea that a local man, a doctor no less, should leave his home in this small port on the Bristol Channel to travel as far as Madras and Upper Burma in the mid-nineteenth century, somehow made the concept of the colonial encounter more personal. This is not to suggest that historians can ever presume to 'know' their subjects; they can only interpret their ideas, opinions and actions from what has been left behind. In Williams's case, this turned out to be quite a lot, as I learnt after reading his book about his journey along the Irrawaddy River and studying the India Office Records in the British Library. As Tony Ballantyne has suggested, 'thinking through life histories is a powerful way of reconstructing imperial webs or networks and recovering the role of these connections in the making and remaking of imperial culture'.[2]

---

1. Sanjay Subrahmanyam, 'By Way of a Conclusion: On India's Europe', in *Europe's India: Words, People, Empires, 1500–1800* (Cambridge, MA, and London: Harvard University Press, 2017), 325.

2. Tony Ballantyne, 'The Changing Shape of the Modern British Empire and Its Historiography', *The Historical Journal* 53, no. 2 (2010): 445. See also David Lambert and Alan Lester (eds.), *Colonial Lives across the British Empire: Imperial Careering in the Long Nineteenth Century* (Cambridge: Cambridge University Press, 2006).

The periphery was the place where agents united with objects to produce the knowledge necessary to govern the empire. But its subaltern status meant that the information and ideas produced there required mediation and validation by the centre, which inevitably resulted in tensions, as it strived continuously to prove that it was of equal worth. This book has trespassed beyond official sources in the archives to discover how a rather motley collection of individuals on the periphery played their part in producing knowledge that did not conform to traditional patterns. Their discoveries broke new ground by forging pathways of knowledge that offer a more discursive historical construct upon which to base our understanding about the people who helped us to know India.

'One way to disturb essentialised views of India that had been colonialism's legacy is to unravel the internal fragments'.[3] The fragments of knowledge accumulated by outsiders have revealed that colonial knowledge was produced through a 'set of shifting, uneven, and often unstable, inter-regional and global connections'.[4] It has been this study's objective to explore a range of heterogeneous outsider voices who interacted with indigenous people throughout the period of British rule. However, finding other case histories to accompany Dr Williams's story took several years to accomplish, as the project's intention was to explore those who dared to trespass across rigidly drawn imperial boundaries. As further histories of lesser-known actors on the imperial margins were uncovered, they suggested themes that coalesced around the idea that their discoveries and explorations were as effective in the formation of colonial knowledge as those sanctioned by official sources.

From the late eighteenth century, the growing importance of the written word in British commercial life led to the production of manifold written documents between the EIC's Court of Directors and its covenanted servants, where stories about unknown or long-forgotten pioneers of knowledge might be found.[5] They included men like Francis Whyte Ellis and Francis Buchanan-Hamilton, upon whom the Company depended for scientific, cultural and linguistic expertise and whose scholarship was the hallmark of Orientalist government. Their surveys and journeys throughout India put them in contact with a wide range of indigenous informants away from the main civil and military sources, offering them the opportunity as scholars to contribute towards a richer understanding of the country and to establish networks beyond its shores.

---

3. See Sugata Bose, *A Hundred Horizons: The Indian Ocean in the Age of Global Empire* (Cambridge, MA: Harvard University Press, 2006); Sugata Bose, 'The Indian Ocean Rim: An Inter-Regional Arena in the Age of Global Empire', in *Modernity and Culture from the Mediterranean to the Indian Ocean*, ed. Leila Fawaz (New York: Columbia University Press, 2002).

4. Ballantyne, 'The Changing Shape of the Modern British Empire', 451.

5. Huw V. Bowen, *The Business of Empire: The East India Company and Imperial Britain, 1756–1833* (Cambridge: Cambridge University Press, 2006).

After India was placed under the direct control of the Crown in 1858, the government relied progressively on official organisations like the army and the GTS of India as sources of knowledge. Inevitably, these official bodies became distanced from maintaining close, informal relations with the local population, unlike those that Ellis and Buchanan formed during the course of their many surveys and tours of India. Contact declined with important centres of calculation like Raja Serfoji II's Court at Tanjore, where hybrid knowledge was produced by the European and indigenous intelligentsia who frequented it. Long gone were the days of Colonel Gardner's mixed-race ménage at Khasgunge in Uttar Pradesh, where he and the ladies of his zenana lived in affluence surrounded by beautiful gardens. Institutionalised knowledge production gradually displaced the informal personal networks that had existed under the rule of the EIC. New, officially sanctioned knowledge, empowered by statistics, began to produce a regularised, abstract and coherent vision of the empire that was much less dependent on the production of affective knowledge.[6]

In the mid-nineteenth century, independent and adventurous entrepreneurs like Clement Williams and his contemporary, William Johnson, still succeeded in establishing and maintaining affective relationships with colonised subjects at a time when there was a shift in the culture of India's governance to more impersonal bureaucratic processes. But rather than being welcomed as providers of hard-to-obtain intelligence from beyond the frontier, Williams and Johnson found themselves outcasts. Government officials were more concerned about social status and imperial prestige than making optimum use of the diverse talents available to them, as the GTS's treatment of William Johnson has demonstrated. Their reaction to Johnson's journey to Khotan and rejection of his maps and reports contradicted the opinions of the RGS's members in London, who praised him for his courage in daring to conduct such a dangerous expedition. Likewise, chambers of commerce throughout England, eager to learn about a new trade route into Western China, acclaimed Clement Williams's Irrawaddy mission; meanwhile, it was derided by the Rangoon Administration and he was excluded from participating in future expeditions to that area.

Despite the establishment of the Indian army's Intelligence Branch in 1878, whose purpose was to collect and collate information from all over the empire, no apparent consensus regarding expected outcomes or information management appeared to exist between periphery and centre. The process of acquiring information was conducted without adequate coordination or planning between the two hubs. Nor was it scrutinised for its relatedness to

---

6. Ballantyne, 'The Changing Shape of the Modern British Empire', 433.

wider issues, especially when covert intelligence was obtained from beyond the Indian frontier. Considered alone, such information could have lacked meaning, but when linked with other sources, it might have formed valuable intelligence.[7] As Frederick Marshman Bailey's case history has shown, until the establishment of formal institutions in the early twentieth century, espionage was largely conducted on an ad hoc basis.[8] When Bailey ventured into unknown territory in the Mishmi Hills or decided to remain alone for more than a year in Tashkent, hiding out from the Bolshevists, he was not ostracised by the authorities after he returned. Armed with his commission in the Indian army, his education in Britain and a social pedigree which marked him out as a *sahib*, he was a trusted member of the British establishment and his adventures were lionised in the British press.

Preoccupation with engaging the 'right sort' of individuals to manage imperial affairs and gather information took precedence over ability and affinity with local communities. Metropolitan attitudes towards the conduct of frontier affairs showed little understanding of the needs of minorities. When concerns about the management of the Burma frontier were raised in 1905, correspondents like Mr F. Lewisjohn, Chief Secretary to the Government of Burma, were more preoccupied with ensuring that they should establish a '*sahibs*' service' by recruiting gentlemen, rather than men with specialised knowledge, who had an empathy with those whom Lewisjohn termed 'savage tribes'. After policies were eventually drawn up in 1922 for the inauguration of a dedicated Frontier Service, there was no attempt to manage existing information, nor incorporate the knowledge gained from the pioneering work amongst the Naga people of dedicated ICS officers like Philip Mills and J.H. Hutton.

Critical to the analysis of how colonial knowledge about India evolved is a consideration of the part played by women and indigenous actors, which, in both cases, presented problems. Little or no direct testimonies

7. Addressing a conference in New York in 2013 about the CIA's appetite for collecting and keeping all personal data in light of debates about genomic privacy, the Agency's Chief Technology Officer, Ira 'Gus' Hunt, stated: 'The value of any piece of information is only known when you can connect it with something else that arrives at a future point in time'. As he explained, 'Since you can't connect dots you don't have, it drives us into a mode of, we fundamentally try to collect everything and hang on to it forever'. Hunt's remarks also raise ontological issues about that lack of coordination and 'joined-up thinking' between the metropole and the periphery in the production and collection of knowledge throughout the period of empire, in whatever form it took. Quotation from M. Sledge, reporting Hunt's remarks at GigaOM's Structure Data Conference, New York City, in the *Huffington Post* (30 March 2013). For information on genomic privacy, see David R. Dowell, *NextGen Genealogy: The DNA Connection* (Santa Barbara, CA: Libraries Unlimited, 2015).

8. Established in 1909 as the Secret Service Bureau, MI5 and MI6 soon grew from modest beginnings to become professional and effective intelligence agencies. MI5, founded by Captain (later Major General) Vernon Kell, played a central role in the capture of most of Imperial Germany's intelligence agents in the UK at the start of the First World War: https://www.mi5.gov.uk/history.

existed by indigenous informants, whilst evidence of female contributions was limited to writing by educated women in travel journals and other publications. Women's voices provided a muted but nonetheless cogent view of their experiences of living in India. But only in one exceptional circumstance, namely that of Emma Roberts, was evidence found of a woman who had earnt her own living in India. Elite women like Lady Maria Nugent and Fanny Parkes did enjoy one advantage over men, in that they were able to visit the zenana, but their experiences provoked different responses. Parkes manifested a much more sympathetic reaction towards Mughal royal ladies, now impoverished by British rule, than Nugent, who viewed them with disdain. Although she did not produce any knowledge through her writing, mention was made about the case of Mrs De Souza, in order to highlight the plight of women left without a respectable male to support them. Mrs De Souza's attempts to contract a potentially bigamous marriage with Lieutenant William Hervey Walton were widely reported by newspapers in the Bombay Presidency and other parts of India, illustrating how lone women of mixed race or white lower-class women were frequently stigmatised as prostitutes by the colonial authorities and public opinion.

Uncovering the voices of colonised people was fraught with difficulties, as few sources by colonisers made reference to their indispensable participation in any enterprise. Although this demanded investigation in a separate chapter, lack of ability in local languages prevented the author from acquiring more substantive knowledge about the part they played. Undoubtedly, there is evidence to be found in Indian archives, pointing the way to the possibility of future research in this important area. However, fragments of indigenous voices were recovered from letters found in the 'Translations of the Mackenzie Collection', that were sent by Brahmins and other high-caste 'native' scholars like Narrain Row.[9] They travelled tirelessly from village to village on behalf of Mackenzie's great survey, searching local archives (*keyfeyeats*) for information about agricultural revenues, cultural history and lineages of local families, revealing in the process early practices of history writing in India's regional traditions. Trudging throughout the countryside, in sickness and health, these learned foot soldiers brought the complexity of the colonial experience sharply into focus by acting as collaborators with British Orientalists during the early colonial period.

One of the rare cases where a servant's role was acknowledged concerned Putamdu, the Tibetan manservant of Colonel Bailey, who accompanied his master on many of his expeditions, having previously gone to Bombay to

---

9. Mantana, *The Origins of Modern Historiography*, 4. See also Wagoner, 'Precolonial Intellectuals', 783–814.

learn the art of skinning and preserving birds.[10] During Bailey's expedition to the Mishmi Hills, Putamdu was photographed near the frontier of Chinese Turkestan wearing Chinese dress, which he may have adopted as a disguise to enable him to gather espionage in a region where Bailey, a white man, would have been conspicuous.[11] Half a century earlier, pundits disguised as pilgrims and mendicants, with instruments hidden in their robes, had undertaken covert surveying missions in hostile territory on behalf of the GTS. Clement Williams's manservant, Raj Singh, undertook a similar role (though without disguise), when he visited local communities near Bhamo in Upper Burma, seeking information which he hoped would assist Williams in continuing his journey towards Western China.

Although the conduct of the EIC created much scandal because of its unregulated mercantile activities, paradoxically in terms of how knowledge about India was obtained, it permitted a much more flexible approach to its creation during the early decades of its occupation of India. Company servants enjoyed a closer association with indigenous people that was largely unconstrained by concerns about class and race, nor was there yet a need for firm social boundaries to be put in place between colonised and coloniser in order to enforce a civilising mission. One of the most lasting contributions to creating new scientific knowledge was made by Francis Buchanan-Hamilton, whose modest invention of a system of paper index slips produced significant advances in methodologies of classification. Unfortunately, Francis Whyte Ellis's early death left little opportunity for his great erudition in understanding India's languages and culture to be appreciated. As covenanted servants of the EIC, both men left a legacy of scholarship that was seldom emulated by their successors.

The key transformations in the ways that information was acquired occurred after the embodied knowledge of the pre-colonial era was replaced by institutionalised forms, which did not become deeply embedded within imperial governance until the early twentieth century. Throughout the long nineteenth century, there was a gradual loss of patrimonial and affective knowledge, as the networks created by the Mughals' system could never be maintained, nor could close contact with those whom Christopher Bayly called the 'knowing people'. Whilst it may be regarded as rather fanciful, ordinary people in the pre-colonial period – midwives, barbers, *harkaras*, *kasids*, *dak* runners, women in zenanas, mendicants and bazaar hawkers – might be imagined retrospectively as a rudimentary form of 'Mughal internet'. They gleaned, digested and re-circulated information on a daily basis, constantly

---

10. Bailey, Proof of *China–Tibet–Assam*, 21.
11. BL/Photo 1083/33(56): Putamdu in Chinese dress at Tachienlu, Bailey Collection of photographs.

distributing it to appropriate sources which, in time, reached the ears of officials. The British failure to retain and adequately manage the Mughal legacy of knowledge networks available from both European and indigenous sources at all levels of society and, where possible, to make appropriate connections eventually cost them the empire.

Collectively, their status as colonisers precluded the British from accessing trusted networks within the local population; therefore, as the case histories have described, they compensated for this deficiency by obtaining information on an ad hoc basis from outsiders, either European or members of the local population. They were obliged to fall back on an assortment of collaborators, assistants and agents, whom they never entirely trusted and whose contribution was always deemed ancillary. Although knowledge from beyond the Indian frontier was required by the government, people who crossed borders, or who transgressed racial and social boundaries, were characterised as untrustworthy and potentially treacherous.[12] As a result, private and public conflicts, disagreements between metropole and periphery about the management of information acquired, accusations of financial self-interest, or questionable dealings with foreign governments created ruptures and tensions throughout the period of empire in India; factors which all played a part in preventing knowledge from being employed in ways that might have benefited colonised subjects as well as their rulers. From the earliest days of empire, the guiding principle of those who governed India was to exploit the country's resources and its people. Their interests were focused upon commodifying India's raw materials and commissioning land and revenue surveys that would allow them to impose taxation on the local population. Little concern was shown for the welfare of the subjects whom they governed; it was left to the missionaries and, on rare occasions, enlightened ICS officers like Philip Mills, to fill this gap.

The ways in which knowledge was used to legitimate British imperialism in India involved multiple strategies and policies by government, implemented in many ways by diverse actors. As we have seen, its production was never a straightforward affair. It was complicated by politics, lack of funds and patronage, bitter rivalry, venality, illness and even death; difficulties which confronted not only the colonisers but also their indigenous collaborators and assistants. Nevertheless, the obstacles encountered were overcome by the courage and ingenuity of actors, who were willing to surmount mental and physical barriers in the quest for new knowledge. Bound together by a diverse range of connections – economic, political, scientific and cultural – the

---

12. Anna Winterbottom, 'Hybrid Knowledge: Review of Simon Schaffer et al. (eds.), *The Brokered World: Go-Betweens and Global Intelligence, 1770–1820* (Sagamore Beach, MA: Science History Publications, 2009)', *History Workshop Journal* 71 (2011): 267.

knowledge they produced extended beyond the limits prescribed by the term 'colonial' to reach networks throughout the world.

The purpose of this study has been to investigate those who, for one reason or another, were considered to be outsiders on the margins of the imperial enterprise. Although it might appear that, scattered across a time span of more than a century, they lacked any common bond or connection, they created webs of knowledge that bound them to one another by elusive threads. Francis Buchanan-Hamilton's private passion for botanising evolved into collecting habits by adventurers like Frederick Marshman Bailey, who supplied metropolitan museums with knowledge and exhibits that informed the public. Previously, such knowledge was the preserve of private individuals like the eighteenth-century collector, Major Charles 'Hindoo' Stuart. In one of the few examples that we have of Francis Ellis's scholarship, he endorsed his commitment to traditional forms of land tenure in a treatise on Mirasi Right, which obliged landholders to respect local customs, as well as endowing them with privileges. Mirasi Right preserved a way of life that had endured for generations, but it was abolished by the Ryotwari system introduced by Thomas Munro. Whereas Ellis used scholarly disquisition to leave fragments of historical knowledge about Southern India, a century later, Philip Mills used the technology of the camera to record the vanishing way of life of the Naga people, employing photography to preserve their culture and history for posterity.

Meanwhile, lone adventurers, Williams and Johnson, aspired to open up new channels of communication and trade routes beyond the imperial boundaries. They left accounts of their perilous journeys across unexplored mountain ranges and rivers in a book and in maps and reports, which evinced a pioneering spirit that might inspire future explorers. Enmeshed within the production of these webs of knowledge has been the participation of indigenous assistants, whose courage in searching treacherous terrains for new botanical specimens, travelling long distances seeking ancient manuscripts, tracking wild animals or entering unknown villages has received scant acknowledgement. Until the early twentieth century, lack of opportunity prevented the majority of women from actively engaging in the pursuit of knowledge, but those who did were recognised in the unpublished work of Mildred Archer, herself a pioneer of India's cultural history. Through her contribution to the history of Indian painting, Archer provided inspiration for future researchers in her field of study.

The histories in this book account for only a few of the numerous unrecorded contributions and conversations buried in the archives. They demonstrate that like many other unknowns who embarked on the long journey towards knowing India, they made different choices which took them along unconventional pathways that did not always lead to success. But all, in their own way, contributed towards the production of enduring and yet ever-changing networks of understanding. However minor or incidental their contribution, they added to the collective store of knowledge about India by helping to supply the intellectual building blocks required to construct an empire, acquiring information about its languages, topography, natural history, artefacts and ancient culture and traditions, and many other areas of interest. Like birds building a nest with twigs, leaves and other detritus, their scraps of knowledge provided a framework which allowed cultural authority to become the strategy through which power over imperial subjects might be justified and maintained.

Bibliography

MONOGRAPHS

Ali, Daud, ed. *Invoking the Past: The Uses of History in South Asia*. Oxford: Oxford University Press, 1999.

Allan, David. *Commonplace Books and Reading in Georgian England*. Cambridge: Cambridge University Press, 2010.

Allen, Charles. *The Prisoner of Kathmandu: Brian Hodgson in Nepal 1820–43*. London: Haus Publishing Ltd., 2015.

Archer, Mildred. *Company Drawings in the India Office Library*. London: Her Majesty's Stationary Office, 1972.

———. *Natural History Drawings in the British Library*. London: Her Majesty's Stationary Office, 1962.

Archer, Mildred, and Graham Parlett. *Company Drawings: Indian Paintings of the British Period*. London: Victoria & Albert Museum, 1992.

Arnold, David. *Colonizing the Body: State Medicine and Epidemic Disease in Nineteenth-Century India*. Berkeley, CA: University of California Press, 1993.

Asad, Talal, ed. *Anthropology and the Colonial Encounter*. Ithaca, NY: Cornell University Press, 1973.

Atwill, David G. *The Chinese Sultanate: Islam, Ethnicity, and the Panthay Rebellion in Southwest China, 1856–1873*. Stanford, CA: Stanford University Press, 2005.

Bailey, Frederick M. *China–Tibet–Assam: A Journey, 1911*. London: Jonathan Cape, 1945.

———. *Mission to Tashkent*. London: Jonathan Cape, 1946.

———. *No Passport to Tibet*. London: Rupert Hart-Davis, 1957.

Baker, Christopher J., and David A. Washbrook, eds. *South India: Political Institutions and Political Change, 1880–1940*. Delhi: Macmillan Company of India, 1975.

Bayley, William H., and William Hudleston, eds. *Papers on Mirasi Right Selected from the Records of Government and Published by Permission.* Madras: Pharoah & Co, 1862.

Bayly, Christopher A. *The Birth of the Modern World, 1780–1914.* Oxford: Blackwell, 2004.

———. *Empire and Information: Intelligence Gathering and Social Communication in India, 1780–1870.* Cambridge: Cambridge University Press, 1996.

Bayly, Martin J. *Taming the Imperial Imagination: Colonial Knowledge, International Relations, and the Anglo-Afghan Encounter, 1808–1878.* Cambridge: Cambridge University Press, 2016.

Bernez, Marie-Odile, ed. *L'héritage de Buffon.* Dijon: Éditions Universitaires de Dijon, 2009.

Blackburn, Stuart H. *Print, Folklore and Nationalism in Colonial Southern India.* Delhi: Permanent Black, 2003.

Bose, Sugata. *A Hundred Horizons: The Indian Ocean in the Age of Global Empire.* Cambridge, MA: Harvard University Press, 2006.

Bowen, Huw V. *The Business of Empire: The East India Company and Imperial Britain, 1756–1833.* Cambridge: Cambridge University Press, 2006.

Breckenridge, Carol A., and Peter van der Veer, eds. *Orientalism and the Postcolonial Predicament: Perspectives on South Asia.* Philadelphia: University of Pennsylvania Press, 1993.

Broc, Numa. *La Géographie des philosophes. Géographes et voyageurs français au XVIIIe siècle.* Paris: Ophrys Editions, 1974.

Buchanan, Francis. *A Journey from Madras through the Countries of Mysore, Canara and Malabar,* 3 vols. London: T. Cadell & W. Davies and Black, Parry & Kingsbury, 1807.

Caldwell Lipsett, Henry. *Lord Curzon in India, 1898–1903.* London: R. A. Everett & Co., 1903.

Campbell, Alexander D. *A Grammar of the Teloogoo Language, Commonly Termed the Gentoo, Peculiar to the Hindoos Inhabiting the North Eastern Provinces of the Indian Peninsula.* Madras: College Press, 1816.

Cederlöf, Gunnel. *Founding an Empire on India's North-Eastern Frontiers, 1790–1840: Climate, Commerce, Polity.* Oxford: Oxford University Press, 2014.

Chakrabarti, Pratik. *Materials and Medicine: Trade, Conquest and Therapeutics in the Eighteenth Century.* Manchester and New York: Manchester University Press, 2010.

Chatterjee, Partha. *The Nation and Its Fragments.* Princeton, NJ: Princeton University Press, 1993.

Chaudhuri, Nupur, and Margaret Strobel, eds. *Western Women and Imperialism: Complicity and Resistance.* Bloomington and Indianapolis: Indiana University Press, 1992.

Chopra, R.C., and I.C. Chopra. *Notes from Drug Addiction with Special Reference to India.* New Delhi: The Council for Scientific and Industrial Research, 1965.

Cohn, Bernard S. *Colonialism and Its Forms of Knowledge.* Princeton, NJ: Princeton University Press, 1996.

Cooper, Thomas T. *The Mishmee Hills: An Account of a Journey Made in an Attempt to Penetrate Thibet from Assam to Open New Routes for Commerce*. London: Henry S. King & Co., 1873.

Cundall, Frank, ed. *Lady Nugent's Journal: Jamaica One Hundred Years Ago. Reprinted from a Journal Kept by Maria, Lady Nugent, from 1801 to 1815*. London: Adam & Charles Black, 1907.

Das, Satyajit. *Selections from the Indian Journals, 1933*, vol. 1. Calcutta: Firma K. L. Mukhopadhyay, 1963.

Dowell, David R. *NextGen Genealogy: The DNA Connection*. Santa Barbara, CA: Libraries Unlimited, 2015.

Driver, Felix. *Geography Militant: Cultures of Exploration and Empire*. Oxford: Blackwell, 2001.

Driver, Felix, and Lowri Jones. *Hidden Histories of Exploration: Researching the RGS–IBG Collections*. Egham: Royal Holloway, University of London, in association with the Royal Geographical Society with IBG, 2009.

Edney, Matthew. *Mapping an Empire: The Geographical Construction of British India, 1765–1843*. London and Chicago: University of Chicago Press, 1997.

Edwards, Elizabeth, ed. *Anthropology and Photography, 1860–1920*. New Haven and London: Yale University Press, 1992.

Ellis, Charles H. *The Transcaspian Episode, 1918–1919*. London: Hutchinson, 1963.

Erikson, Emily. *Between Monopoly and Free Trade: The English East India Company, 1600–1757*. Princeton, NJ: Princeton University Press, 2014.

Fawaz, Leila, ed. *Modernity and Culture from the Mediterranean to the Indian Ocean*. New York: Columbia University Press, 2002.

Finn, Margot, and Kate Smith, eds. *The East India Company at Home, 1757–1857*. London: UCL Press, 2018.

Fischer-Tine, Harald. *Low and Licentious Europeans: Race, Class and 'White Subalternity' in Colonial India*. New Delhi: Orient Swan, 2009.

Fitzhugh Monk, Mauger. *Letters of a Mussoorie Merchant: Mauger Fitzhugh Monk, 1828–1849*, edited by Sailli, Ganesh. New Delhi: Niyogi Books, 2006.

Foucault, Michel. *The Order of Things: An Archaeology of the Human Sciences*. London and New York: Routledge, 1989.

Geertz, Clifford. *Local Knowledge: Further Essays in Interpretive Anthropology*. London: Fontana Press, 1993.

Hales, Stephan. *Vegetable Staticks: Or, an Account of Some Statical Experiments on the Sap in Vegetables . . . Also, a Specimen of an Attempt to Analyse the Air*. London: W. & J. Innys, 1727.

Hevia, James. *The Imperial Security State: British Colonial Knowledge and Empire-Building in Asia*. Cambridge: Cambridge University Press, 2015.

Hope Risley, Herbert, and Edward Albert Gait. *Report on the Census of India, 1901*. Calcutta: Office of the Superintendent of Government Printing, 1901.

Jacobs, Julian, Alan MacFarlane, Sarah Harrison, and Anita Herle. *The Nagas: Hill Peoples of Northeast India – Society, Culture and the Colonial Encounter*. London: Thames & Hudson, 1990.

Jasanoff, Maya. *Edge of Empire: Conquest and Collecting in the East, 1750–1850.* London: Fourth Estate, 2005.

Kapadia, Harish. *Into the Untravelled Himalaya: Travels, Treks and Climbs.* New Delhi: Indus Publishing Company, 2005.

Kaye, George R., and Edward H. Johnston. *Catalogue of Manuscripts in European Languages. Vol. II, Part II: Minor Collections and Miscellaneous Manuscripts.* London: His Majesty's Stationary Office, 1937.

Keck, Stephen L. *British Burma in the New Century, 1895–1918.* London: Palgrave Macmillan, 2015.

Konishi, Shino, Maria Nugent, and Tiffany Shellam, eds. *Indigenous Intermediaries: New Perspectives on Exploration Archives.* Canberra: ANU Press, 2015.

Kopf, David. *The Brahmo Samaj and the Shaping of the Modern Indian Mind.* Princeton, NJ: Princeton University Press, 1979.

———. *British Orientalism and the Bengal Renaissance: The Dynamics of Indian Modernization, 1773–1835.* Berkeley and Los Angeles: University of California Press, 1969.

Kunz, Richard, and Vibha Joshi, eds. *Naga: A Forgotten Mountain Region Rediscovered.* Basel: Christoph Merian Verlag, 2008.

Lambert, David, and Alan Lester, eds. *Colonial Lives across the British Empire: Imperial Careering in the Long Nineteenth Century.* Cambridge: Cambridge University Press, 2006.

Latour, Bruno. *Science in Action.* Cambridge, MA: Harvard University Press, 1987.

Leclerc, Georges Louis. *La statique des végétaux, et L'analyse de l'air: expériences nouvelles lûes à la Société royale de Londres.* Paris: Jacques Vincent, 1735.

Macgregor, Arthur. *Company Curiosities: Nature, Culture and the East India Company, 1600–1874.* London: Reaktion Books, 2018.

———. *Curiosity and Enlightenment: Collectors and Collections from the Sixteenth to the Nineteenth Century.* New Haven and London: Yale University Press, 2007.

Malinowski, Bronisław. *A Diary in the Strict Sense of the Term.* London: Routledge & Kegan Paul, 1967.

Matthew, Henry C. G., and Brian Harrison, eds. *Oxford Dictionary of National Biography.* Oxford: Oxford University Press, 2004.

Mizutani, Satoshi. *The Meaning of White: Race, Class and the 'Domiciled Community' in British India, 1858–1930.* Oxford: Oxford University Press, 2012.

Nair, Savithri Preetha. *Raja Serfoji II: Science, Medicine and Enlightenment in Tanjore.* New Delhi: Routledge, 2014.

Nilakanta Sastri, Kallidaikurichi A. *Development of Religion in South India.* Bombay: Orient Longmans, 1963.

Noltie, Henry. *The Cleghorn Collection: South Indian Botanical Drawings, 1845–1860.* Edinburgh: Royal Botanic Garden, 2016.

Nugent, Maria. *A Journal from the Year 1811 till the Year 1815, Including a Voyage to and Residence in India, with a Tour to the North-Western Parts of the British Possessions in that Country, under the Bengal Government*, vol. 1. London: T. and W. Boone, 1839.

Orsini, Francesca. *The Hindi Public Sphere, 1920–1940: Language and Literature in the Age of Nationalism.* Oxford: Oxford University Press, 2002.

Parkes Parlby, Fanny. *Wanderings of a Pilgrim in Search of the Picturesque, during Four-and-Twenty Years in the East: With Revelations of Life in the Zenāna.* London: Pelham Richardson, 1850.

Peers, Douglas M., and Nandini Gooptu, eds. *India and the British Empire.* Oxford: Oxford University Press, 2012.

Plotz, John. *Portable Property: Victorian Culture on the Move.* Princeton, NJ: Princeton University Press, 2008.

Pratt, Mary Louise. *Imperial Eyes: Travel Writing and Transculturation.* London and New York: Routledge, 1992.

Raj, Kapil. *Relocating Modern Science: Circulation and Construction of Knowledge in South Asia and Europe, 1650–1900.* Basingstoke: Palgrave Macmillan, 2007.

Ramaswami, Nallathagudi S. *Tanjore Paintings: A Chapter in Indian Art History.* Madras: Kora's Indigenous Arts and Crafts Centre, 1976.

Reeves, Madeleine. *Movement, Power and Place in Central Asia and Beyond: Contested Trajectories.* London: Routledge, 2012.

Roberts, Emma. *The East India Voyager, or Ten Minutes' Advice to the Outward Bound.* London: J. Madden & Co., 1839.

———. *Scenes and Characteristics of Hindostan, with Sketches of Anglo-Indian Society,* vol. 1. London: W. H. Allen & Co., 1835.

Robertson, William. *Soldiers and Statesmen, 1914–1918.* London: Cassell & Co., 1926.

Roger, Jacques. *Buffon: A Life in Natural History.* Ithaca, NY and London: Cornell University Press, 1997.

Roy, Tirthankar. *India in the World Economy: From Antiquity to the Present.* Cambridge: Cambridge University Press, 2012.

Roye, Susmita, and Rajeshwar Mittapalli, eds. *The Male Empire under the Female Gaze: The British Raj and the Memsahib.* Amherst, NY: Cambria Press, 2013.

Ryan, James R., and Simon Naylor, eds. *New Spaces of Exploration: Geographies of Discovery in the Twentieth Century.* London and New York: I. B. Tauris, 2009.

Sadan, Mandy. *Being and Becoming Kachin: Histories beyond the State in the Borderworlds of Burma.* Oxford: Oxford University Press, 2013.

Said, Edward. *Culture and Imperialism.* London: Chatto & Windus, 1993.

Sarkisyanz, Emanuel. *Buddhist Backgrounds of the Burmese Revolution.* The Hague: Martinus Nijhoff, 1965.

Saroop, Narindar. *Gardner of Gardner's Horse: 2nd Lancers, Indian Army.* New Delhi: Palit & Palit, 1983.

Schaffer, Simon, Lissa Roberts, Kapil Raj, and James Delbourgo, eds. *The Brokered World: Go-Betweens and Global Intelligence, 1770–1820.* London: Science History Publications, 2009.

Schiebinger, Londa, and Claudia Swan, eds. *Colonial Botany: Science, Commerce and Politics in the Early Modern World.* Philadelphia, PA: University of Pennsylvania Press, 2005.

Singaravélou, Pierre. *L'École française d'Extrême-Orient ou l'institution des marges (1898–1956): Essai d'histoire sociale et politique de la science colonial.* Paris: Harmattan, 1999.

Smith, Martin. *State of Strife: The Dynamics of Ethnic Conflict in Burma*. Singapore: Institute of Southeast Asian Studies and Washington, DC: East-West Center Washington, 2007.

Smyer Yu, Dan, and Jean Michaud, eds. *Trans-Himalayan Borderlands*. Amsterdam: Amsterdam University Press, 2017.

South, Ashley. *Ethnic Politics in Burma: States of Conflict*. London and New York: Routledge, 2008.

Srinivasa Ramaswami, Nallathagudi. *Madras Literary Society: A History, 1812–1984*. Madras: Madras Literary Society, 1985.

Stoddart, David. *On Geography and Its History*. Oxford: Blackwell, 1986.

Stoker, Valerie. *Polemics and Patronage in the City of Victory: Vyasatirtha, Hindu Sectarianism, and the Sixteenth-Century Vijayanagara*. Berkeley, CA: University of California Press, 2016.

Stoler, Ann Laura. *Along the Archival Grain: Epistemic Anxieties and Colonial Common Sense*. Princeton, NJ: Princeton University Press, 2010.

Streich, Anne M., and Kim A. Todd. *Classification and Naming of Plants*. Lincoln: University of Nebraska-Lincoln Extension, 2014.

Subrahmanyam, Sanjay. *Europe's India: Words, People, Empires, 1500–1800*. Cambridge, MA and London: Harvard University Press, 2017.

Sundari Mantena, Rama. *The Origins of Modern Historiography in India: Antiquarianism and Philology, 1780–1880*. New York: Palgrave Macmillan, 2012.

Swarup Misra, Anand. *Nana Saheb Peshwa and the Fight for Freedom*. Lucknow: Information Department, Uttar Pradesh, 1961.

Taylor, Robert H. *The State in Myanmar*. Honolulu: University of Hawai'i Press, 2009.

Taylor, Roger, and Crispin Branfoot, eds. *Captain Linnaeus Tripe: Photographer of India and Burma, 1852–1860*. Munich: DelMonico, 2014.

Thompson, Peter R. *The East India Company and Its Coins*. Honiton: Token Publishing, 2010.

Thunberg, Carl Peter. *Flora Japonica: Sistens Plantas Insularum Japonicarum*. Leipzig: I. G. Mulleriano, 1784.

Trautmann, Thomas R. *Aryans and British India*. Berkeley, CA: University of California Press, 1997.

———. *Languages and Nations: The Dravidian Proof in Colonial Madras*. Berkeley, CA: University of California Press, 2006.

———, ed. *The Madras School of Orientalism: Producing Knowledge in Colonial South India*. New Delhi: Oxford University Press, 2009.

van Rheede, Hendrik. *Hortus Indicus Malabaricus*, 12 vols. Amsterdam: Johannis van Somersen & Joannis van Dyck, 1678–1703.

von Fürer-Haimendorf, Christoph. *The Naked Nagas*. London: Methuen & Co., 1939.

von Stockhausen, Alban. *Imagining the Nagas: The Pictorial Ethnography of Hans-Eberhard Kauffmann and Christoph von Fürer-Haimendorf*. Stuttgart: Arnoldsche Art Publishers, 2014.

Waller, Derek J. *The Pundits: British Exploration of Tibet and Central Asia*. Lexington: University Press of Kentucky, 1988.

Wedderburn, William. *Allan Octavian Hume: Father of the Indian National Congress, 1829–1912*. New Delhi and Oxford: Oxford University Press, 2002.

Williams, Clement. *Through Burmah to Western China, Being Notes of a Journey in 1863 to Establish the Practicability of a Trade-Route between the Irawaddi and the Yang-Tse-Kiang*. Edinburgh and London: William Blackwood & Sons, 1868.

Withers, Charles W.J., *Geography, Natural History and the Eighteenth-Century Enlightenment*. Oxford: Oxford University Press, 1995.

———. *Placing the Enlightenment: Thinking Geographically about the Age of Reason*. Chicago: University of Chicago Press, 2007.

Withers, Charles W.J., and David Livingstone, eds. *Geography and Enlightenment*. Chicago: University of Chicago Press, 1999.

Woolf, Leonard. *An Autobiography, Vol. 1: 1880–1911*. Oxford: Oxford University Press, 1980.

Yule, Henry. *Narrative of the Mission Sent by the Governor General of India to the Court at Ava in 1855*. London: Smith, Elder & Co., 1858.

JOURNAL ARTICLES

Aiyadurai, Ambika, and Claire Seungeun Lee. 'Living on the Sino-Indian Border: The Story of the Mishmis in Arunachal Pradesh, Northeast India'. *Asian Ethnology* 76, no. 2 (2017): 367–95.

Arens, Esther H. 'Flowerbeds and Hothouses: Botany, Gardens and the Circulation of Knowledge in Things'. *Historical Social Research / Historische Sozialforschung* 40, no. 1, Special Issue: Law and Conventions from a Historical Perspective (2015): 265–83.

Arnold, David. 'Plant Capitalism and Company Science: The Indian Career of Nathaniel Wallich'. *Modern Asian Studies* 42, no. 5 (September 2008): 899–928.

Athanasiou, Athena, Pothiti Hantzaroula, and Kostas Yannakopoulos. 'Towards a New Epistemology: The "Affective Turn"'. *Historein* 8 (2008): 5–16.

Axelby, Richard. 'Calcutta Botanic Garden and the Colonial Re-ordering of the Indian Environment'. *Archives of Natural History* 35, no. 1 (April 2008): 150–63.

Bailey, Frederick M. 'Exploration on the Tsangpo or Upper Brahmaputra'. *The Scottish Geographical Magazine* 30, no. 11 (1914): 561–82.

———. 'In Russian Turkestan under the Bolsheviks'. *Journal of the Central Asian Society* 8, no. 1 (1921): 49–69.

———. 'Tibet and the Mishmi Hills: Journey through a Portion of South-Eastern Tibet and the Mishmi Hills'. *The Geographical Journal* 39, no. 4 (1912): 334–47.

Ballantyne, Tony. 'The Changing Shape of the Modern British Empire and Its Historiography'. *The Historical Journal* 53, no. 2 (June 2010): 429–52.

Bayly, Christopher A. 'Knowing the Country: Empire and Information in India'. *Modern Asian Studies* 27, no. 1 (February 1993): 3–43.

Beardow, Ted. 'The Empire Hero'. *Studies in Popular Culture* 41, no. 1 (Fall 2018): 66–93.

Bewell, Alan. 'Romanticism and Colonial Natural History'. *Studies in Romanticism* 43, no. 1, Romanticism and the Sciences of Life (Spring 2004): 5–34.

Blagden, Otto. 'Review of *The Journal of the Burma Research Society*, Vol. I, Parts I and II; Vol. II, Part I; Rangoon, 1911–1912'. *Journal of the Royal Asiatic Society of Great Britain and Ireland* 45, no. 1 (1913): 209–11.

————. 'Review of *The Journal of the Burma Research Society*'. *The Journal of the Royal Asiatic Society of Great Britain and Ireland* (January 1913): 209–11.

Blake, David M. 'Colin Mackenzie: Collector Extraordinary'. *British Library Journal* 17, no. 2 (1991): 128–50.

Bourne, John M. 'The East India Company's Military Seminary at Addiscombe, 1809–1858'. *Journal of the Society for Army Historical Research* 57, no. 232 (Winter 1979): 206–22.

Buchanan, Francis. 'Commentary on the *Herbarium Amboinense*'. *Memoirs of the Wernerian Natural Society* 5, no. 2 (1824–5): 307–84.

————. 'On the Religion and Literature of the Burmas'. *Journal of Asiatic Researches* 6 (London reprint, 1807): 163–308.

Callaway, Helen. 'Review of *Tensions of Empire: Colonial Cultures in a Bourgeois World*, edited by Frederick Cooper and Ann Laura Stoler'. *Journal of the Royal Anthropological Institute* 4, no. 2 (June 1998): 368.

Charmantier, Isabelle, and Staffan Müller-Wille. 'Carl Linnaeus's Botanical Paper Slips (1767–1773)'. *Intellectual History Review* 24, no. 2 (2014): 215–38.

Chauhan, Vibha S. 'Review of *Lady Nugent's East India Journal: A Critical Edition*, edited by Ashley L. Cohen'. *Indian Literature* 59, no. 4 (July–August 2015): 206–9.

Colquhoun, J.A.S. 'Essay on the Formation of an Intelligence Dept. for India by Captain J.A.S. Colquhoun, Royal Artillery'. *Journal of the United Service Institution India*, Proceedings 4, no. 18 (1874): 1–75.

Day, Tony, and Craig J. Reynolds. 'Cosmologies, Truth Regimes, and the State in Southeast Asia'. *Modern Asian Studies* 34, no. 1 (January 2000): 1–55.

Derksen, Maaike. 'Local Intermediaries? The Missionising and Governing of Colonial Subjects in South Dutch New Guinea, 1920–42'. *The Journal of Pacific History* 51, no. 2 (2016): 111–42.

Desousa, Valerian. 'Modernizing the Colonial Labor Subject in India'. *Comparative Literature and Culture* 12, no. 2 (2010): 1–11.

Driver, Felix. 'Hidden Histories Made Visible? Reflections on a Geographical Exhibition'. *Transactions of the Institute of British Geographers* 38, no. 3 (2013): 420–35.

du Bois, Cora. 'Review of *The Naked Nagas*, by Christoph von Fürer-Haimendorf'. *American Anthropologist* 43, no. 4, pt. 1 (1941): 663.

Elliot, Walter. 'Mr. F. W. Ellis'. *Journal of the Indian Antiquary* 4 (1875): 219–21.

Englehart, Neil A. 'Liberal Leviathan or Imperial Outpost? J. S. Furnivall on Colonial Rule in Burma'. *Modern Asian Studies* 45, no. 4 (July 2011): 759–90.

Fan, Fa-Ti, and John Matthew. 'Negotiating Natural History in Transitional China and British India'. *British Journal of the History of Science* 1 (2016): 43–59.

Fold, Niels, and Philip Hirsch. 'Re-thinking Frontiers in Southeast Asia'. *The Geographical Journal* 175, no. 2 (June 2009): 95–7.

Frost, Mark. 'Pandora's Post Box: Empire and Information in India, 1854–1914'. *English Historical Review* 131, no. 552 (2016): 1043–73.

Grant Brown, George E.R. 'Human Sacrifices near the Upper Chindwin'. *Journal of the Burma Research Society* 1, no. 1 (1911): 35–40.

Green, David. 'Classified Subjects: Photography and Anthropology'. *Ten.8: Photographic Journal* 14 (1984): 30–7.

Gregory, Derek. 'Power, Knowledge and Geography. The Hettner Lecture in Human Geography'. *Geographische Zeitschrift* 86, no. 2 (1998): 70–93.

Grieco, Allen J. 'The Social Politics of Pre-Linnaean Botanical Classification'. *I Tatti Studies in the Italian Renaissance* 4 (1991): 131–49.

Harris, Cheryl I. 'Whiteness as Property'. *Harvard Law Review* 106, no. 8 (June 1993): 1707–91.

Heins, O.K. 'Rising of the Dungens or Mussulman Population in Western China'. Translated from the *Russian Military Journal* for August 1866. *The Edinburgh Review* 127 (1868): 357–96.

Hobson, Geraldine. 'My Father in the Naga Hills'. The Indian Civil Service Survivors Remember the Raj: Part 1. *Indo-British Review* 12, no. 2 (1998): 61–70.

Irschick, Eugene F. 'Order and Disorder in Colonial South India'. *Modern Asian Studies* 23, no. 3 (July 1989): 459–92.

Jasanoff, Maya. 'Collectors of Empire: Objects, Conquests and Imperial Self-Fashioning'. *Past and Present* 184 (August 2004): 109–35.

Johnson, William H. 'Report on His Journey to Ilchí, the Capital of Khotan, in Chinese Tartary'. *Journal of the Royal Geographical Society* 37 (1867): 1–47.

Koditschek, Theodore. 'Review of *The Origins of Modern Historiography in India: Antiquarianism and Philology*, by Rama Sundari Mantena'. *Victorian Studies* 57, no. 2 (Winter 2015): 296–98.

Kolsky, Elizabeth. 'Codification and the Rule of Colonial Difference: Criminal Procedure in British India'. *Law and History Review* 23, no. 3 (Fall 2005): 631–83.

Kumar, Deepak. 'Science and Society in Colonial India: Exploring an Agenda'. *Social Scientist* 28, nos. 5–6 (May–June 2000): 24–46.

Lees, James. 'Administrator-Scholars and the Writing of History in Early British India'. *Modern Asian Studies* 48, no. 3 (May 2014): 826–43.

Mason, Kenneth. 'Johnson's Suppressed Ascent of E 61'. *Alpine Journal* 34 (1921): 54–62.

McKay, Alex C. 'Tibet 1924: A Very British Coup Attempt?' *Journal of the Royal Asiatic Society* 7, no. 3 (November 1997): 411–24.

Mizutani, Satoshi. 'Constitutions of the Colonising Self in Late British India: Race, Class and Environment'. *Zinbun* 38 (2005): 21–75.

Morris, L.P. 'British Secret Missions in Turkestan, 1918–1919'. *Journal of Contemporary History* 12, no. 2 (April 1977): 363–79.

Mukhopadhyay, Priyasha. 'Review of *Lady Nugent's East India Journal: A Critical Edition*, edited by Ashley L. Cohen'. *Journal of Colonialism and Colonial History* 17, no. 2 (Summer 2016): Project Muse.

Nair, Savithri Preetha. 'Diseases of the Eye: Medical Pluralism at the Tanjore Court in the Early Nineteenth Century'. *Social History of Medicine* 25, no. 3 (August 2012): 573–88.

———. 'Illustrating Plants at the Tanjore Court'. *Marg* 70, no. 2 (2018–2019): 44–51.

———. 'Native Collecting and Natural Knowledge (1798–1832): Raja Serfoji II of Tanjore as a "Centre of Calculation"'. *Journal of the Royal Asiatic Society* 15, no. 3 (November 2005): 279–302.

————. ' ". . . Of Real Use to the People": The Tanjore Printing Press and the Spread of Useful Knowledge'. *The Indian Economic and Social History Review* 48, no. 4 (October/December 2011): 497–529.

Noltie, Henry J. 'John Bradby Blake and James Kerr: Hybrid Botanical Art, Canton and Bengal, c. 1770'. *Curtis's Botanical Magazine* 34, no. 4 (December 2017): 427–51.

Peers, Douglas M. 'Between Mars and Mammon: The East India Company and Efforts to Reform Its Army, 1796–1832'. *The Historical Journal* 33, no. 2 (June 1990): 385–401.

Peterson, Indira V. 'The Cabinet of King Serfoji of Tanjore: A European Collection in Early Nineteenth-Century India'. *Journal of the History of Collections* 11, no. 1 (1999): 71–93.

Prain, David. 'A Sketch of the Life of Francis Hamilton (Once Buchanan): Sometime Superintendent of the Honourable Company's Botanic Garden, Calcutta'. *Annals of the Royal Botanic Garden, Calcutta* 10, pt. 3 (1905): 1–75.

Raj, Kapil. 'Beyond Postcolonialism . . . and Postpositivism: Circulation and the Global History of Science'. *Isis* 104, no. 2 (June 2013): 337–47.

————. 'Colonial Encounters and the Forging of New Knowledge and National Identities: Great Britain and India, 1760–1850'. *Osiris* 15, Nature and Empire: Science and the Colonial Enterprise (2000): 119–34.

————. 'Jardin de Lorixa'. *Marg* 70, no. 2 (2018–2019): 52–3.

Rawlinson, Henry C. 'On the Recent Journey of Mr W. H. Johnson from Leh, in Ladakh, to Ilchí in Chinese Turkistan'. *Proceedings of the Royal Geographical Society of London* 11, no. 1 (1866–7): 6–15.

Reddy, Sita. 'Ars Botanica: Refiguring the Botanical Art Archive'. *Marg* 70, no. 2 (2018–2019): 14–23.

Rendall, Barbara. ' "East India Company Wives (Extract)". In "Ethnicity, Nationalism: 21st-Century Time Bombs"'. *Queen's Quarterly* 102, no. 1 (1995): 253.

Risoe, V.S. 'Obituary: Col. F. M. Bailey, C.I.E.'. *The Himalayan Journal* 28 (1968): BL/Mss Eur F157/886.

Sadan, Mandy. 'Historical Photography in Kachin State: An Update on the Impact of the James Henry Green Collection of Photographs'. *South Asia: Journal of South Asian Studies* 30, no. 3, The Northeast and Beyond: Region and Culture (2007): 457–77.

Schillings, Pascal, Alexander van Wickeren. 'Towards a Material and Spatial History of Knowledge Production. An Introduction'. *Historical Social Research / Historische Sozialforschung* 40, no. 1, Special Issue: Law and Conventions from a Historical Perspective (2015): 203–18.

Searle, Geoffrey R. 'Review of *Public and Private Doctrine: Essays in British History Presented to Maurice Cowling*, edited by Michael Bentley'. *The Historical Journal* 38, no. 3 (September 1995): 729–31.

Shah, Priya. ' "Barbaric Pearl and Gold": Gendered Desires and Colonial Governance in Emma Roberts's *Scenes and Characteristics of Hindostan*. *Studies in Travel Writing* 16, no. 1 (2012): 31–46.

Shea, Anne. 'Property in the White Self: Assessing Lady Nugent's Jamaican Journal'. *Women's Studies* 30, no. 2 (2001): 175–97.

Sloan, Phillip R. 'John Locke, John Ray and the Problem of the Natural System'. *Journal of the History of Biology* 5, no. 1 (Spring 1972): 1–53.

Srivastava, Mukesh. 'Mosaic of Narrative Manipulations: Power and Production of Subjectivity in (Post) Colonial India'. *Economic and Political Weekly* 27, no. 4 (January 1992): 47–57.

Stein, Aurel. 'Johnson's Map and the Topography of the K'un-Lun, South of Khotan'. *Alpine Journal* 34 (1921): 62–68.

Tappe, Oliver. 'A Frontier in the Frontier: Sociopolitical Dynamics and Colonial Administration in the Lao–Vietnamese Borderlands'. *The Asia Pacific Journal of Anthropology* 16, no. 4, Frictions and Fictions – Intercultural Encounters and Frontier Imaginaries in Upland Southeast Asia (2015): 368–87.

Taylor, Paul M. 'Smithsonian Naturalist William Louis Abbott's Turkestan Expedition'. *Central Asiatic Journal* 59, nos. 1–2, Migration and Nation-Building in Central and Western Asia: Turkic Peoples and Their Neighbours (2016): 255–74.

Taylor, William C. 'On the Present State and Future Prospects of Oriental Literature, Viewed in Connexion with the Royal Asiatic Society'. *Journal of the Royal Asiatic Society of Bengal* 2, no. 3 (1835): 1–12.

Trautmann, Thomas R. 'Does India Have History? Does History Have India?' *Comparative Studies in Society and History* 54, no. 1 (January 2012): 174–205.

Tsing, Yuan. 'Yakub Beg (1820–1877) and the Moslem Rebellion in Chinese Turkestan'. *Central Asiatic Journal* 6, no. 2 (June 1961): 134–67.

Turnbull, David. 'Local Knowledge and Comparative Scientific Traditions'. *Knowledge and Policy* 6, nos. 3–4 (1993): 29–54.

Unknown. 'Obituary: Mr. W. H. Johnson'. *Proceedings of the Royal Geographical Society and Monthly Record of Geography* 5, no. 5 (1883): 291–3.

van Schendel, Willem. 'The Politics of Nudity: Photographs of the "Naked Mru" of Bangladesh'. *Modern Asian Studies* 36, no. 2 (May 2002): 341–74.

Venkatasubramanian, Rajesh. 'Patrons and Networks of Patronage in the Publication of Tamil Classics, c. 1800–1920'. *Social Scientist* 39, nos. 3–4 (March–April 2011): 64–91.

Vicziany, Marika. 'Imperialism, Botany and Statistics in Early Nineteenth-Century India: The Surveys of Francis Buchanan (1762–1829)'. *Modern Asian Studies* 20, no. 4 (October 1986): 625–60.

von Stockhausen, Alban. 'Christoph von Fürer-Haimendorf and His Work among the Nagas'. *Archiv Weltmuseum Wien* 61–62 (2013): 3–30.

Wade Chambers, David, and Richard Gillespie. 'Locality in the History of Science: Colonial Science, Technoscience and Indigenous Knowledge'. *Osiris* 15, Nature and Empire: Science and the Colonial Enterprise (2000): 221–40.

Wagoner, Phillip B. 'Precolonial Intellectuals and the Production of Colonial Knowledge'. *Comparative Studies in Society and History* 45, no. 4 (October 2003): 783–814.

Walker, John. 'A Memorandum Given by Dr Walker, Professor of Natural History, Edinburgh, to a Young Gentleman Going to India, with Some Additions'. *The Bee, or Literary Weekly Intelligencer* 17 (1793): 330–33.

Watson, Mark F., and Henry J. Noltie. 'Career, Collections, Reports and Publications of Dr Francis Buchanan (Later Hamilton), 1762–1829: Natural History Studies in

Nepal, Burma (Myanmar), Bangladesh and India. Part 1'. *Annals of Science* 73, no. 4 (October 2016): 392–424.

Weiss, Richard W. 'Print, Religion and Canon in Colonial India: The Publication of Ramalinga Adigal's *Tiruvarutpa*'. *Modern Asian Studies* 49, no. 3 (May 2015): 650–77.

Wiegand, Wayne A. 'The Politics of Cultural Authority'. *American Libraries* 29, no. 1 (1998): 80–2.

Winterbottom, Anna. 'Hybrid Knowledge. Review of *The Brokered World: Go-Betweens and Global Intelligence, 1770–1820*, edited by Simon Schaffer, Lissa Roberts, Kapil Raj, and James Delbourgo'. *History Workshop Journal* 71 (2011): 267–73.

Withers, Charles W.J. 'Geography, Natural History and the Eighteenth-Century Enlightenment: Putting the World in Place'. *History Workshop Journal* 39, no. 1 (Spring 1995): 137–64.

———. 'Place and the Spatial Turn in Geography and in History'. *Journal of the History of Ideas* 70, no. 4 (2009): 637–58.

NEWSPAPERS

Bombay Times (7 March 1846).
Bombay Times (29 March 1848).
Journal of Commerce (29 March 1848).
Bombay Times (1 April 1848).
Bombay Times (15 April 1848).
Times of India (10 February 1883).
Huffington Post (30 March 2013).

DISSERTATIONS

Emmett, Robert C. 'The Gazetteers of India: Their Origins and Development during the Nineteenth Century'. M.A. diss., University of Chicago, 1976.

McCullough, Kayli. 'Lady Maria Nugent: A Woman's Approach to the British Empire'. M.A. diss., Miami University, 2012.

Schendel, Jörg A. 'The Mandalay Economy: Upper Burma's External Trade, c. 1850–90'. Ph.D. diss., University of Heidelberg, 2002–3.

UNPUBLISHED MANUSCRIPTS

Fisher, Elaine. 'Translating Vīraśaivism: The Early Modern Monastery as Transregional Religious Network'. Draft submitted to Oxford University Press in June 2016 for publication in an edited volume on the South Indian Maṭha.

MANUSCRIPT COLLECTIONS

Additional Francis Buchanan-Hamilton Papers. 1800–1802. Mss Eur D639. British Library, London.

Archer Collection. 1929–1986. Mss Eur F236. British Library, London.

Archives of the British Association for Cemeteries in South Asia (BACSA). Mss Eur F370. British Library, London.

Banks Papers. Series 72.160–169. State Library of New South Wales, Sydney.

Bailey Collection. Photo 1083. British Library, London.

The Buchanan-Hamilton Collection of Paintings. Linnean Collections, London.

Colin Mackenzie Papers: Translations (1821). Mss Eur Mack Trans. British Library, London.

The Correspondence of Sir James Edward Smith. Linnean Collections, London.

East India Company's Bonds Bill. 16 July 1807. HC Deb, vol. 9, cols. 833–836. House of Commons, London.

East India Company General Correspondence. 1602–1859. IOR/E. British Library, London.

Erskine Collection. 1773–1852. Mss Eur C9–10, D26–32. British Library, London.

Four Letters to Karl Jordan from Frederick Bailey. 18 Oct.–13 Nov. 1906. TR/1/1/27/15. Natural History Museum Archives, London.

Henry Thomas Colebrooke papers (1811–1814). Mss Eur B149. British Library, London.

Home Miscellaneous. 1600–1918. IOR/H. British Library, London.

Indexes to the Proceedings. 1702–1945. IOR/Z/P. British Library, London.

India Office Records: Public & Judicial Department. 1792–1955. IOR/L/PJ. British Library, London.

L'Empereur, Nicolas. Ellémans botanique des plante du Jardin de Lorixa, leur vertu et quallité, tans conus que celle qui ne le sont pas, avec leur fleur, fruis et grainne, traduit de louria an francés, contenans sept thome. Ms 1916 bis. Muséum national d'Histoire naturelle, Paris.

Letters to William Ogilvie-Grant and others, mostly concerning the collection of birds. 1900–1914. DF ZOO/230/22. Natural History Museum Archives, London.

Map of the Maingnyaung Region, Located between the Chindwin and Mu Rivers in Upper Burma, in the Present-day Sagaing Region. Maps.Ms.Plans.R.c.1. University of Cambridge, Cambridge.

Official Publications. 1768–1957. IOR/V. British Library, London.

Papers of Col Sir Edward Sladen. 1845–1891. Mss Eur E290. British Library, London.

Records of the East India Company Library. 1801–1994. Mss Eur F303. British Library, London.

Papers of Francis Buchanan-Hamilton (1762–1829). 1795–1823. Mss Eur Buchanan. British Library, London.

Papers of James Philip Mills. 1924–1958. PP MS 58. SOAS Archives & Special Collections, London.

Papers of Lt-Col Frederick Marshman Bailey. 1827–1976. Mss Eur F157. British Library, London.

Papers of the Lakher Pioneer Mission to the Lakher (or Mara) people of the South Lushai Hills. 1905–1978. Mss Eur F185. British Library, London.

Papers of Professor Christoph von Fürer-Haimendorf. 1917–1990. PP MS 19. SOAS Archives & Special Collections, London.

Political and Secret Department Records. 1756–1951. IOR/L/PS. British Library, London.

Proceedings and Consultations of the Government of India and of its Presidencies and Provinces. 1702–1945. IOR/P. British Library, London.

Raja Serfojee of Tanjore Collection. 1801–1803. IOR/NHD7/1001–1116. British Library, London.

Records of the Board of Commissioners for the Affairs of India. 1620–1859. IOR/F. British Library, London.

Records of the Military Department. 1708–1957. IOR/L/MIL. British Library, London.

Sutton Court Collection. 1756–1832. Mss Eur F128. British Library, London.

Zain al-Din, Shaikh. A pangolin or scaly anteater, from Lady Impey's collection. 1779. Add Or 4667. British Library, London.

Index

www.ingramcontent.com/pod-product-compliance
Lightning Source LLC
Chambersburg PA
CBHW060148280326
41932CB00012B/1675